Praise for
DACHAU SONG

"Don't forget, Zipper, this whole civilization of man has been built by very few people, and I'm talking to one."
—JOHN D. ROCKEFELLER III to HERBERT ZIPPER

"I read the book with growing suspense. It is written with crystal clarity and with a knowledge of European dimensions rarely found among Americans!"
—SEBASTIAN FELDMAN, Writer for
the Rheinische Post, Dusseldorf, Germany

"In Dachau, Herbert Zipper secretly led an orchestra. He survived the Nazis to champion his beloved art."
—PATRICIA WARD BIEDERMAN, Los Angeles Times

Dachau Song

PETER LANG
New York • San Francisco • Bern
Frankfurt am Main • Paris • London

Paul F. Cummins

Dachau Song

PETER LANG
New York • San Francisco • Bern
Frankfurt am Main • Paris • London

Library of Congress Cataloging-in-Publication Data
Cummins, Paul F.
Dachau song / Paul F. Cummins.
p. cm.
Includes bibliographical references.
1. Zipper, Herbert. 2. Conductors (Music)—
United States—Biography. 3. Holocaust survivors—
United States—Biography. I. Title.
ML422.Z56C8   [B]   784.2'092—dc20   91-28480
ISBN 978-0-8204-1729-5 (hardcover)
ISBN 978-1-4331-2575-1 (paperback)

Bibliographic information published by **Die Deutsche Nationalbibliothek.**
Die Deutsche Nationalbibliothek lists this publication in the "Deutsche
Nationalbibliografie"; detailed bibliographic data is available
on the Internet at http://dnb.d-nb.de/.

Cover design by James F. Brisson

The painting of Herbert Zipper on the front cover is by the artist, Paul Bochner.

© 1992, 2001, 2010, 2013, 2014 Peter Lang Publishing, Inc., New York
29 Broadway, 18th floor, New York, NY 10006
www.peterlang.com

All rights reserved.
Reprint or reproduction, even partially, in all forms such as microfilm,
xerography, microfiche, microcard, offset strictly prohibited.

Contents

Acknowledgments ix

PRELUDE: xi
Preface to the Third Edition xv

FIRST MOVEMENT: 1
    I   Train to Dachau 3
    II   "Fin de Siècle" to "Fin de Millennium" 13
    III War to the Academy 29

SECOND MOVEMENT: 49
    IV   A Young Conductor in the Gathering Storm 51
    V   Dachau: Arbeit Macht Frei 75
    VI   Buchenwald 93

THIRD MOVEMENT: 111
    VII Manila: Reunion and a New War 113
    VIII Liberation: Dr. Zipper Gives A Concert 133

INTERLUDE: 153
    Patriot of the Globe 155

FOURTH MOVEMENT: 159
    IX   America: The New World Symphony to the
           New World 161
    X   Chicago 179
    XI   Manila Revisited 193

FIFTH MOVEMENT: 213
    XII California 215
    XIII China 229

CODA: 251
    Vienna: Return 253

Endnotes 265

References 273

Index 303

Drawings: Between Chapters are by Herbert Zipper.

Dedication

To the memory of Walter and Otto Zipper, Hedy Zipper Holt and Trudl Dubsky Zipper.

To Henry Holt and Lucy Horwitz.

To the memory of Jura Soyfer and those others of the six million whom Herbert left behind in Dachau and Buchenwald and to those who suffered and died in Manila.

To Ruthie and Lee, Mimi and Ken, Anna and Emily, Liesl and Richard, and Julie and Paul.

To the Richard D. Colburn family.

To Maryann.

And, of course, to my dear friend Herbert.

"In the prison of his days
teach the free man how to praise."

    - W. H. Auden

"Stay humane Dachau mate
"Be a man Dachau mate."

    - Herbert Zipper and Jura Soyfer

Acknowledgments

I would like to thank many people for their help in preparing *Dachau Song*: Dale Pontius, William Lowman, Benito Legarda, Jack Pepper, Karen Melamed, James Halsema, Pamela Wade, Nancee Cortes, Grant Beglarian, Toby Mayman, Grace Nash, and Dr. Eric Simon for their observations and information; the late Hedy Zipper Holt and her son Henry Holt and daughter Lucy Horwitz for hours of enjoyable and invaluable reminiscing; Helli Andis for her memories of Vienna & Jura Soyfer; Richard D. Colburn for sharing his recollections of the Chicago and Los Angeles years; Fini Rudiger Littlejohn and Leon Askin for sharing their memories of Vienna in the 1930's; Barbara Polikoff for her charming and informative chronicle of the early years of the Music Center of North Shore; the late Bruno Bettelheim for sharing his reminiscences and thoughts about Freud's Vienna and the Holocaust; Keith Colburn for his interest, encouragement and support; Dina Wigmore, Paul Bochner, David Colloff, Liesl Erman, Anna and Emily Cummins for proofreading and offering suggestions for several drafts; Mr. William Butts, who challenged me to make major revisions which resulted in a far better book; Patricia Ward Biederman for her insights and encouragement; Jean Campbell and Susan Cloke for their careful and helpful editing; Warren Spaeth for his devoted proof reading and his insights and ideas for improvement; Peter Levitt for helping me find my own voice in the biography; Megan Asher and Linda Kamberg de Martinez for typing several drafts; Adrienne McCandless for her assistance; Paul Bochner for his superb portrait of Herbert; Peter Mandell and The Simon Wiesenthal Center for information about the Holocaust; Barbara Distel at the Dachau Museum for her kind help. And, for first introducing me to Herbert, for her ideas and her close and critical editing, and for her love and encouragement, my wife, Mary Ann.

PRELUDE

Prelude

> Defenceless under the night
> Our world in stupor lies;
> Yet, dotted everywhere,
> Ironic points of light
> Flash out wherever the Just
> Exchange their messages:
> May I, composed like them
> Of Eros and of dust,
> Beleaguered by the same
> Negation and despair,
> Show an affirming flame.
>
> - W. H. Auden, "Sept. 1, 1939"

The project of writing the story of Herbert Zipper presents interesting problems for a biographer. Zipper's life has been one of little inner conflict. His frustrations have not been with himself but with the mess men have made of this planet. His marriage was loving and happy and he cannot recall any periods of serious depression or neurosis. Rather his conflicts have been with the outside world. Zipper and I have speculated that our own compatability is probably due in part to our concern with "what could be." We find ourselves fantasizing about new programs to change this school, that social institution, that political problem. The biographical problem, however, is clear: how to make engaging the story of a sane, rational man seeking to promote intelligent projects. Zipper's life does not offer fertile ground for deep psychological excavations and discoveries of hidden secrets. As a friend once said to him, "Herbert, you are boringly sane."

I first learned of Herbert Zipper in 1972 from my wife, Mary Ann, who had just heard him speak at a music educator's conference. She came home inspired by this 72 year old man's passionate defense of the Arts in education and in life. Since then I have gradually come to know "Dr. Zipper" and, as I learned more and more about his life, I became convinced that his story must be told. Lives such as his are all too rare and must be recorded to serve as a beacon in the growing gloom and darkness. How has this man survived and emerged so affirmative about life and its possibilities? What resources was he able to draw upon? What lessons did he learn in the horrors of Dachau and Buchenwald and during the fall of Manila? How was it that he came to see that the Arts are not an ornament in our lives but are the very essence of life itself? The questions haunted me and when, in 1986, my Board of Trustees granted me a half-year sabbatical, I asked Zipper if he would like to work together and to be the subject of a biography. Although he has never been much of a self-promoter, he agreed to the project and we began. With cassette recorder and notebook in hand, I came to his home several mornings each week and began to take down his story. Then, each afternoon, I would write. When the sabbatical ended, I had compiled a crude rough draft. I then spent the next three years meeting Zipper every Sunday morning at 8:00 a.m. sharp, revising several drafts, adding stories as he recalled more and more events, adding incidents from his current experiences, and coming to know more about him. Also, in 1988 and again in 1990, my wife and I accompanied Zipper to Austria and spent many days visiting his old haunts in Vienna and in the countryside. These trips uncovered both events and feelings and added a valuable dimension to the book. My biographical problem has been to present a critical, evaluative account of a life I have come to admire. I also found it difficult to verify stories since so many of his contemporaries are dead. Nevertheless, each draft has gained a little more objectivity and I have managed to verify many accounts so that the final draft, I believe, tells an accurate story.

I believe his story is also instructive because of its remarkable span: From his birth in "fin de siècle" Vienna, in the twilight of the Hapsburg Empire, to the depression of the 1930's, the rise of Hitler, imprisonment in Dachau and Buchenwald, escape to Manila and then incarceration by the Japanese, to the new world of America and a life of music education, and now in the twilight of his own amazing life, to a new venture traveling to China as an honored consultant and conductor. Europe, America, Asia - he has served on three continents. His life has also spanned three centuries: from the 19th Century Hapsburg world to the 20th Century with its horrors and glories, and now in his educational work preparing American and Asian young people for the approaching 21st Century. There are too few leaders today who have any real concept of posterity. Whether the cause be despair or greed or simply ignorance, we live in a century wherein exploitation of human and natural resources has become epidemic.

Herbert Zipper has often said, "I want to be a good ancestor!" Perhaps we all share this wish. But the challenge is not just to dream but to make dreams come true; to actively bring wishes into concrete reality. All of his life, Herbert Zipper has found ways to do just this. From organizing concerts in the latrines of Dachau to helping found community schools in America to showing Chinese youth how to play a Beethoven string quartet, Zipper has been a builder. Whatever the practical obstacles, he has found ways to overcome and to "only connect" people with each other, with ideas, with the Arts, with their better selves. His own integrity is contagious - being with him makes one want to be less trivial, more involved in the real stuff of life.

Men such as Herbert Zipper often go to their grave with their stories relatively unknown. Even many of Zipper's friends and associates do not know the full richness and drama of his life. Such people are usually overlooked by the media because their stories are not glamourous or flamboyant. Often society is not sensitive to nuance and subtlety of character; quiet, humble courage is often overlooked in favor of sensationalism and self-advertisement. One unusual feature of Herbert Zipper is his disinterest in publicizing or even acknowledging his own achievements. Bringing joy to others through his projects has pleased him most and he has rarely sought credit for himself. I offer this story of a different kind of hero in hopes that I may add a touch to our understanding of heroism and human worth. Herbert Zipper once told me that he learned in prison camp the joy of giving; it is my joy to give to the readers of this book the story of this courageous man.

Preface to the Third Edition

When the first and second editions of *Dachau Song* were published, Herbert Zipper was still alive. The book was a source of pleasure for him, and I am grateful and proud that he believed the book accurately captured some of the drama and pain, as well as the triumphs and deep concerns of his life.

Herbert Zipper died on April 21, 1997, just six days short of his 93rd birthday. We had a standing appointment (Sundays, 8:00 A.M.) for over ten years, and the day before he died, I was three minutes late; he was annoyed at my lack of punctuality. Clearly, he was Viennese to the very end.

Herbert is gone now and my wife and family and I miss him dearly. Nevertheless, his legacy remains and continues to inspire people across the globe. His presence in many peoples' lives is also evidenced by a series of factors. For one, the concert hall at the Colburn School, named after his friend Richard Colburn, is itself named Zipper Hall. In addition, at my school, Crossroads School, our library has a special collections room—The Herbert Zipper Room—which contains his music and books, letters, photographs, memorabilia, and a large collection of books about the Hapsburg Empire, Vienna in the 19th and 20th centuries, the Holocaust (particularly books about Dachau and Buchenwald), and other events relating to his life and times. Thirdly, there is a new and expanded version of his *Dachau Lied*, orchestrated by composer Lucas Richman, which has had several performances in the United States and is available though the Herbert Zipper Library at Crossroads School. Finally, there is a wonderful video of his life, *Never Give Up*, which was created by Terry Sanders and Frieda Lee Mock, friends of Herbert's and academy award winners. *Never Give Up* (available though Crossroads) was itself nominated for an academy award and has been shown in theaters and on television all across the country.

I should mention also that this third edition corrects a rather embarrising omission from the previous ones: it includes the actual score of the *Dachau Lied*.

I am grateful that Peter Lang Publishing Company has vowed to keep *Dachau Song* in print. While Herbert Zipper was not a celebrity, his life was simply too inspiring and too instructive to be lost. He was truly an extraordinary man.

April 25, 2001

FIRST MOVEMENT

I   Train to Dachau

II   From Fin de Siècle to Fin de Millenium

III   War to the Academy

Chapter I

Train to Dachau

Believe me, who for thousands of years
has chewed this toughest of food, Know
That from the cradle to the bier
No man can digest the ancient bitter dough.
Trust one of my kind, this show
Is made only for a God's delight
He dwells in an ageless aureole,
Us he has thrust in darkness out of sight
And you are fit for only day and night.

—Mephistopheles from [1]
Goethe's *Faust-Part One*

A 1938 article in the Parisian newspaper, *Le Soir* (*The Evening*), written by the French correspondent in Vienna, M. Pertinax, was headlined: "J'ai Vu Mourir L'Autriche" (I saw Austria die). He was not the first. Over the centuries from the plains to the east along the Danube the invaders have marched, Huns, Avars, Magyars, Turks. And on March 12, 1938 once again the Barbarians, this time from the north, invaded yet were welcomed into the ancient city of Vienna. This invasion would trample under foot the final flowers of Viennese culture and grace. The Hapsburg Empire had crumbled in 1918, and the post World War period, culminating in the Great Depression of 1929, had brought ruin to many more lives. Yet somehow the arts, literature, science, philosophy all remained vital. When the Nazi gangsters of Adolph Hitler marched into Vienna, overnight this center of European culture dwindled into a provincial German burg.

Herbert Zipper and his family were a well-to-do middle class Jewish family living in the first years of this century in a large home within sight of St. Stephen's Cathedral in the first district of town. They were, however, not a religious family and paid little attention to Jewish ritual or custom. Like many Viennese Jews they considered themselves primarily Viennese and, until March 12, 1938, were proud of this allegiance. On this day their blindness to the essential and deep-rooted anti-semitic nature of their city hit them full force. Their comfortable illusions were shattered and their pride in being Viennese was destroyed.

By the time Hitler invaded Austria to reclaim it for Germany, many Viennese Jews saw what was coming and left the city and the country. Having heard Hitler speak several times and having read of atrocities at Dachau, Herbert Zipper knew that Jews were in for terrible times, though neither he nor anyone else could foresee just how devastating these times would be. But, in retrospect, it should have been clear to them. They didn't perceive what they should have been able to perceive. Hitler's speeches were anything but ambiguous and the history of anti-semitism in both Germany and Austria was immense. The Zipper family, like many other middle-class Jewish families had reached such a level of comfort and psychic satisfaction with "being accepted" into acceptable society that they had become blind to their own status. They would never be fully acceptable to gentile society. They were living in a dream which turned into the inevitable nightmare which Adolf Hitler had promised. Finally, after the troops arrived on March 12, Zippper and his family began making plans to escape from their beloved city. It took time, however, to pack and sort out the accumulation of several generations of books, antiques, clothes, memorabilia and the like. But even more time consuming was the process of acquiring legal papers to leave. The 34-year-old Zipper, who five years earlier had experienced Hitler's rise to power in Düsseldorf, urged his family - mother, sister, and two brothers - to leave immediately. He was voted down in a family council.

Why could not the Zipper family and thousands of other Jewish families have seen the extreme peril they faced and made every effort to escape, to leave Vienna before or immediately after the Anschluss on March 12th? The answer is both complicated and simple. Quite simply, many Viennese Jews did not consider themselves Jews as much as they did Viennese. They had helped build Vienna; its golden age was due largely to their contributions. This Golden Era of Vienna we remember today in terms of its leading artists and intellectuals. The list of famous Jewish-Austrian figures is staggering: in psychology, Sigmund Freud; in philosophy, Edmund Husserl, Martin Buber, Ludwig Wittgenstein; in music, Gustave Mahler, Karl Goldmark, Arnold Schoenberg, Oskar Strauss, Erich Korngold, Eugen Zador, Hans Gal, Karl Weigel, Eric Zeisl, Ernst Toch; in letters, Theodore Herzl, Edward Hanslick, Karl Kraus, Egon Friedell; in literature, Arthur Schnitzler, Peter Altenberg, Stefan and Arnold Zweig, Herman Bahr, Richard Beer-Hofmann, Franz Werfel, Hermann Broch; conductors such as Otto Klemperer, George Szell, and Bruno Walter; in film, Erich von Stroheim, Otto Preminger, Josef von Sternberg, Fred

Zinneman and Billy Wilder and the list goes on and on. Given this massive array of talent and contributions and given the status which they had largely helped to bestow upon Vienna, how could the Jews of Vienna have expected anything other than decency? How could they have anticipated revilement, rejection and, ultimately, an attempt at total extermination? It was, then quite literally, unthinkable. Nevertheless, given the history of anti-Semitism in Austria, they should have thought the unthinkable. As George Berkley writes, "The story of the Jews in Vienna is the story of what may be the most tragically unrequited love in world history." [2]

The story begins in medieval times when Vienna, as a central trading center of Europe, attracted Jewish traders and money-lenders. As early as 966 A.D. the phrase "Jews and other legitimate merchants" appears in the city's records. Over the next four centuries the Jewish community grew in numbers and in successful ventures and their success aroused hostility. Perhaps because of their strange ways and customs, the Viennese Gentiles in 1421 launched the first attack. As George Berkley relates, in a 1988 study *Vienna and Its Jews*, the 1421 pogrom was officially sanctioned: "All Jews who refused to become Christians (the vast majority) were either executed or expelled. Their goods were expropriated and their children were forcibly baptized. For the first but not the last time in modern history Vienna destroyed its Jewish community." [3]

During the next few centuries Jews gradually returned to Vienna and "by the mid-1600's a Jewish community of some five hundred families was living along the banks of the Danube in a small ghetto called Leopoldstadt, named after the reigning sovereign, Leopold I."[4] Despite numerous restrictions placed upon them, these Jews too became successful. And, as in 1421, it happened again. This time, in 1670, Leopold expelled all of Vienna's Jews, converted their synagogue into a church, and eliminated all signs of their culture. However, their removal was a financial disaster for the city and, once again, Jews were allowed to return. They were not missed for their cultural contributions or for their religious customs; they were permitted to return because their absence hurt the economic well-being of the comfortable Viennese who threw them out in the first place. The hypocrisy and nastiness of the Viennese to their Jewish fellows defies comprehension. Yet, despite the hostility of rulers such as Maria Theresa, gradually the returnees regained rights and privileges. One is staggered by the realization that "by 1848 Austria was the only major power in the Western World that was still imposing medieval restrictions on its Jews."[5] They were subjected to "restrictions on residence, land ownership, trade, and even on religious organizations... They had to pay special taxes and crippled or invalided Jewish veterans received no exemptions from these burdens while those who stayed in the army in peacetime encountered frequent discrimination."[6]

Finally, in 1849 Emperor Franz Joseph I granted full constitutional rights to Jewish immigrants. Vienna's Jewish population increased from about 6,000 in 1860 to 147,000 in 1900. And with this influx came the talent and creativity that was to make Vienna the cultural center of Europe. As Stefan Zweig wrote "Nine-tenths of what the world celebrated as Viennese culture in the Nineteenth Century was promoted, nourished, and even created by Viennese Jewery." And these contributions continued and grew in the first 38 years of the 20th Century. So one returns to the question: How could Austria and Vienna treat their Jews as they did on and after March 12, 1938? And, how could the Jews have been so blind to their history and their tenuous status?

Until March 12, 1938 the Jews of Vienna considered themselves as loyal and proud Viennese citizens first and Austrians or Jews second, much as many French consider themselves Parisians above all else. This explanation while probably accurate is still, nevertheless, difficult to accept fully. Given the history of how the Viennese treated Jews and given the clear disgust with which the Jews of Leopoldstadt were blatantly regarded, it is difficult to see why the Viennese Jewish middle class was in fact so proud of being Viennese. Why were they so eager to be members in this club? Had they unconsciously accepted notions of inferiority which assimilation would assuage? In any event, to be treated as anything but equal Viennese was simply inconceivable. In fact, large numbers of Jews sought acceptance in the social mainstream by converting to Christianity and "by 1900 Viennese Jews had the highest conversion rate of any Jewish Community in the world."[7] Berkley argues that "the appeal of assimilation resulted less from a need to overcome anti-Semitism's economic and professional effects than from a desire to counter its social and psychological impact. Most of Vienna's Jews wanted to integrate as much as possible into the city they so passionately loved."[8] To abandon Vienna did not seem a serious option, at the same time. The Zipper family was no exception to the prevailing sense that while Hitler was a menace he was not as dangerous as some believed. They did realize then, however, that they were no longer Viennese; now they were Jews. But still operating out of a false sense of security they decided not to leave immediately, as Herbert Zipper implored. Instead, in good middle class fashion the family set about to pack and to make their plans. On March 12, 1938, Zipper's father, Emil, by a stroke of good fortune, was in England on business. He immediately traveled to Paris and set about securing papers to rescue his family from their beloved Vienna.

During the next two months, while Jews were being reviled, humiliated and arrested in Vienna, Herbert Zipper frequently slept away from home, calling first by telephone before coming home to see if it was safe. His precautions were not sufficient and on the evening of May 27, 1938, a plain clothesman came to the Zipper home at 120 Hietzinger Hauptstrasse and said that the three young brothers, Herbert, Otto, and Walter, must come with him. When the plainclothesman knocked at the Zipper residence, he asked Herbert Zipper to bring along his typewriter. This confused the three brothers who thought the typewriter was perhaps going to be used as evidence in some way. Actually, there were so many citizens being arrested the police simply needed more typewriters. The policeman took the three men down to the local precinct station by streetcar and, as it turned out, none of the four of them knew what was coming next. Quite remarkably, and perhaps indicative or symptomatic of the overall fog which enveloped Vienna, not even the Austrian police really knew what was happening and what process they were helping along. To illustrate, the policeman returned to the Zipper home a few days later to apologize to Hedy Zipper, the sister of the three "criminals," saying if he had known they were to be sent to a concentration camp he would have warned them and urged them to escape.

The three Zippers and some twenty others were detained at the police station filling out identification papers and then were taken downtown to a public school on Karajangasse which had been converted into a makeshift detention center. The street had been named after a doctor who was the personal physician of the Habsburg Emperor Franz Joseph I and who was also the father of the late conductor Herbert Von Karajan. At this point no one knew what was going on. Zipper, however, was not expecting anything favorable and began to create a rumpus. His brother Otto, suffering from a lung ailment for which he received Pneumothorax treatments, must be allowed to go to the hospital, Zipper insisted. He admonished the Austrian guards that they would be held personally responsible if anything were to happen to Otto. Here, perhaps, was one of the last acts of a middle class Jew asserting his authority over a Viennese working class gentile. Zipper still believed he had the social power and status and rights to issue warnings and to assert himself. Finally, the police relented and Otto was driven to the hospital, an act which probably saved his life. Given his physical condition there is little chance that he would have survived the days and months to come.

For two full days Walter and Herbert Zipper and approximately 500-700 others were locked up in the school with nothing to do but wonder what was going to happen. Occasionally a Nazi official would appear and scream irrational nonsense designed, as best Zipper could determine, merely to intimidate. In fact, the Austrian police did seem intimidated by it all. For a brief moment the Austrian police and authorities were caught in a dilemma: did they recognize their allegiances and responsibilities to their fellow citizens or were they to transfer their allegiances to the new bully on the block? It did not take them much time to wrestle with this dilemma. If any of the prisoners had known where they were going to be sent, they might have tried to break out and escape.

On the evening of the second day, Zipper, his brother Walter and about 20 others were loaded into a paddy wagon and told they were to be taken to Elizabeth Promenade - synonymous with police headquarters. The wagon, however, began moving in a different direction - toward the Westbahnhof, a train station. The driver soon admitted that they were to be carted off to Dachau and Zipper's fears dropped to a deeper level.

As early as 1934 Zipper and other Austrian and German Jews knew what kind of place it was. Dachau had been established in 1933 and the word had spread quickly. An Austrian newspaper, *Die Stunde* ("The Hour"), for which a friend of Walter Zipper named Robert "Bobby" Kahan was a writer, had published a series in 1934-35 describing the conditions at Dachau. Already the name Dachau had become synonymous with terror and brutality.

When the many paddy wagons arrived at the Westbahnhof, they did not go to the passenger loading area but instead to the Gueterbahnhof, the freight loading area. The Nazis did not want anyone to see what they were doing. Perhaps at some deeper level even the pigs are aware of the nature of the mud they are wallowing within. Also, at the freight area the wagons could drive right up to the train doors and deposit their "freight" - the Jews of Vienna. Here at the train station the SS men began screaming at them, shouting obscenities and beating the slow moving and bewildered prisoners. Zipper was grabbed by the hair, smashed with a rifle butt in the chest breaking two of his ribs, and slugged in the face closing his left eye. Some men in their confusion went in the wrong direction. They were shot and killed. Zipper and the others were then pushed and slammed into 3rd class passenger trains and ordered to sit on benches, with heads raised staring at the light, five to a bench facing each other. In this manner they were transported from Vienna to Munich. During this trip Zipper believed that this was the end: that he would probably be killed. At Munich they were pushed into freight cars and packed like herrings in a tin. The events of the subsequent train trip have been preserved in a letter Zipper wrote to a friend, Eric Simon, a year later in June 1939:

During this day of May 30th we did not get anything to eat; we were standing for seven hours in the gymnasium in the Karajan Gasse, but at that moment, traveling to the railway station, we seventeen men forgot hunger and fatigue. Not a word was spoken. We all knew that something terrible was in store for us.

As the wagon turned into the freight terminal our guard said, "Get out fast and into the railway car even faster, otherwise you are out of luck."

The wagon stopped, the door was flung open. We jumped out, Walter ahead of me, I was one of the last ones. There was earsplitting, vociferous shouting.

What followed is rather difficult to describe. I will try, although I know that it is impossible to fully communicate the horror of this nightmare. What I can describe objectively are the actual happenings, but what they did to us as they were done to us, the extreme physical and verbal injuries, are not describable at all. This is too bad, because it would be important for all who want to know and feel the full truth to get valid and vivid information of our state of mind at that time.

As I jumped out of the wagon I saw Walter lying on the floor of the railway car's entrance in front of me. Immediately I received the blow of a fist on my left eye and a number of heavy blows against my chest from the butt of a rifle. The entrance to the car I did not reach through my own power because I was lifted up by my hair and propelled by kicks from behind. How I got to my place in the car's compartment I don't remember exactly. What I remember is the ear-splitting screaming of the SS men and being pushed by rifle butts and bayonets and being dragged by my hair. When I finally arrived at the seat assigned to me, the place appeared to me as being occupied by lunatics. We were ten men in the compartment; opposite me was Walter; all sat at the very edge of the bench with heads uplifted high. Staring as if hypnotized into the light at the ceiling. This was the position we had to assume, ordered by command of the SS guards, for the duration of the thirteen-hour trip, interrupted only by furious exercising and brutal beatings. An SS man in gray uniform, steel helmet and armed to the teeth, shouting commands, was with us throughout the first few minutes.

My first clear thought was: These then are the genuine "neo-barbarians." This is what they really are. Everything that had been written and told about them did not come near to the essence. Here are the facts: The various tortures and excrutiating torments of a physical and psychological nature are not left to the initiative of the individual SS guard, who incidentially were replaced every half hour, but are being inflicted on us, as became evident beyond the shadow of a doubt, according to the prescribed rules, drilled in by the Nazi authorities. Nazi ideology does not permit free reign of the raw instincts of brutalized monsters. That would be a mistake, because eventually the worst brute after a while will have spent his sadistic impulses and for at least a short time may become tame. This cannot be permitted and, consequently, brutality, inhuman behavior to the extreme and unmitigated pitilessness are being trained to perfection. The SS man, as long as he is on duty such as in this instance, has to follow the instructions he has received to the letter. If he does not, it will be judged refusal of duty and as such severely punished. Subsequently, in Dachau, I found this confirmed by former SS men who became inmates because of supposed insubordination.

The first instruction we received was "calling attention." This had to be done whenever an SS man passed by which happened every so often. The person seated at the outside corner and facing the oncoming guard had to shout, "Attention," whereupon all of us had to jump up, eyes into the light. The person opposite the attention shouter had to yell, "Reporting obediently, ten Jewish swine in the compartment." The railway car had eight compartments. You can figure out how often and in what rapid succession this "report" was heard during the thirteen hours of our trip.

There were other Nazi utterances worth mentioning, for instance, "Who does not like it here? The best thing for you would be to let yourself be shot at once, or hang yourself immediately when you arrive in Dachau. This now is a joy ride. The real seriousness of life begins in Dachau. If anyone wants to die just say so. Nobody comes out alive from Dachau," etc.

What the SS guards called "sport" started after a while: "Kneel down, get up, kneel down, get up," twenty times, thirty times, forty times, etc. You have to imagine that this happened in the compartment packed with ten people, kneeling every other second in the narrow space between the two benches, eyes looking into the light. Closed windows, curtains drawn; it was summer, the air was hot and sticky; we did not have anything to eat or to drink for twenty-four hours during which we could not use a toilet. If one could not fully kneel or was not fast enough up or supported oneself with one's hands on the opposite person, one received heavy blows with the rifle butt or bayonet.

Two men over sixty were among us. One of them, after about ten minutes of this "sport" fainted. The treatment for fainting was administered according to the following procedures: First, the patient's head receives heavy blows from a clenched fist, and at the same time is kicked with a foot. If this does not have the desired result, a bucket full of water is emptied over the patient's head. If the patient still does not wake up and remains lying on the floor he is lifted up brutally by his testicles. All these procedures are accompanied by a set of curses they obviously had to memorize. For instance, "Croak you old Jewish swine, all your life you have swindled the people," or "You lecherous Jew sow all your life you have seduced Aryan girls," and more of the same.

All of us, naturally, received more or less heavy injuries during the trip. Comparatively speaking I got off modestly, only two or three broken ribs and the closed left eye. Of course, some died during the trip, some were beaten to death, some shot. I don't know how many perished. I only saw four corpses that were carried past our compartment. There were some who lost one eye, many who lost some of their teeth. Those who made defensive motions were shot on the spot and quite a few lost their minds. Many became mentally disoriented at the very beginning of the trip. The man who sat next to me once whispered, "Are we in the movies?"

We were not allowed to move, to speak or to step out. These thirteen hours never ended. Many never recuperated fully from the nightmare of this trip.

Somehow this introductory journey into German concentration camp life did not affect my mind adversely. I still remember the thoughts that went through my mind during that night. I soon convinced myself that I would never regain freedom alive except if there was revolution in Germany for which, however, there was no prerequisite. I remember that during this journey we brothers bid farewell to each other by means of the language of the eyes. I also remember that after a while I broke through that mental layer called fear for one's life, fear of pain, fear of death. It might have been curiosity and the resolve to hold out to the last at all cost in order not to give in to these barbarians that kept me going. It is possible that I owe it to this resolve that throughout the following nine months I remained untouched. It is a basic characteristic of fascism to attack with ferocity when detecting fear and weakness and to avoid confrontation with the opposite. I am not at all claiming to be strong and fearless but I have learned during the course of my imprisonment how to fake it. I soon realized that this was the only defense left at one's disposal.

Shortly before we arrived at our first destination we had to sing, together and individually. When my turn came the "Ode to Joy" came to my mind and I started singing,

"Joy, the god descended Daughter of Elysium." At the passage, "all mankind are brothers" the SS guard furiously interrupted me shouting, "What are you singing, you bolshevistic Jew swine?" Upon which I jumped up and in military and Germanic attitude shouted, "Reporting obediently, poem by Schiller, music by Beethoven." After that for a while we remained unmolested.

At 11:30 a.m. on May 31st we arrived at a train station and were loaded into cattle wagons. One hundred fifty men in each, tightly packed like sardines. When the doors were locked we were without guards. But it was pitch-dark and the atmosphere became suffocating. We did not know what was in store for us; nobody dared to speak. The horror of the situation defies verbal description.

Whatever he might have become in the old Vienna, leading a life of genteel music making, of pleasant intellectual discussions in fashionable coffee houses, of living in a relatively homogeneous culture, all of this was shattered, forever, in March and the months following in 1938. And by the time Herbert Zipper returned to Vienna in February of 1939, all was changed. As the poet W. B. Yeats wrote: "All changed, changed utterly." The story of Herbert Zipper's life has two distinct phases: B.D. and A.D. -

Before Dachau and After Dachau. The train trip to Dachau was for Herbert Zipper the most terrifying and shocking event in his life: "I began to learn who I really was; I grew up that night."

Chapter II

From Fin de Siècle to Fin de Millennium

> Give me those days with heart in riot,
> The depths of bliss that touched on pain,
> The force of hate, and love's disquiet—
> Ah, give me back my youth again!
> —Goethe

The streets of the old section of Vienna were surfaced with what looked like cobblestone but were actually hard wooden tiles which had been soaked with tar. As a child, Herbert Zipper would fall asleep to a unique sound: not iron horse hooves or stone but a warm, inviting sound, like the musical sound of a wooden, bass xylophone. This wooden pavement ("Stoeckel Pflaster") was almost an extension of the home, like wooden halls. The echo of the horses' hooves was a mellow clippity-clop that is in Zipper's memory, the essence of old Vienna. To lie in bed as a child and hear this fairy tale sound was utterly beautiful.

Herbert Zipper's father, Emil, was the youngest of eleven children. Born on September 24, 1875, in the 27th year of Franz Joseph I's reign, he grew up in Vienna and, following his induction into engineering, attended technical college also in Vienna. Zipper's mother, Regina Westreich ("Rosie"), the oldest of three sisters was born on October 19, 1877, completing only high school as was customary for girls at the time. Emil and Rosie met in Vienna and were married in 1901. In 1902 their first son, Walter, was born, followed by Herbert in 1904, Hedy in 1907, and Otto in 1914.

The Zipper home was located just a few houses from the Stephansplatz, the heart of the city. Here was the central station for the Stellwagen (horse-drawn buses) which reached out to twenty-one different districts. From the Stephensplatz it is just around the corner to the Graben. A contemporary (1902) account of the Graben described it as a place:

> "Whose broadside of shops arouses every dormant sense of covetousness, appeals to every taste, and can satisfy the caprices of the most fastidious; the Graben, with its Cafes Dores, provided with red velvet couches, but whose

patrons swarm over the sidewalks in summer time, protected by quantities of coquettish little awnings; the Graben, always crowded with promenaders, both men and women - the Boulevard des Italiens of Vienna. There the fashionable world and all strangers assemble in the morning and again in the evening... Here - on the Graben - from ten a.m. to mid-day, and from six to nine p.m., there is a constant coming and going - a rush and palpitation of life, the 'demi monde' especially turning out in force."[9]

Emil and Rosie moved into this elegant business district, just a couple houses away from the landmark St. Stephen's Church called Stephansdom, and began their married life in a rental apartment at "31 AM Graben."

Around the corner from their home was the square and St. Stephen's Church. The tower is a restoration of one begun by Duke Randolph IV in about the middle of the 14th Century, the original tower being declared unsafe in 1860. From this tower in 1683 Count Starhemberg could watch the movements of the invading Turks and here, in 1805, the Viennese watched the approach of Napoleon's invading forces, there one can see the plains of Hungary, then Galicia, the Carpathian mountains, the Black Forest, and the beloved Danube. It stands high above the surrounding buildings, a gorgeous monument to human creativity and determination. Here the young Herbert Zipper could look out over the city and over history and dream his boyish dreams.

One of Zipper's earliest memories is looking out the front living room window and seeing regal processions. It was particularly thrilling to see the man who then had held the Austro-Hungarian Empire together for almost sixty years (1848-1907) and who would continue on until 1916, Emperor Franz Joseph I. Each year at the feast of Corpus Christi - a Catholic celebration of the Eucharist - the Emperor joined in a splendid procession of all the nobility, in elegant carriages, marching slowly down the street in front of the Zipper home. The whole street was laid out with gorgeous carpets and bleachers for people to witness the procession of the entire Habsburg family in full regalia. Zipper watched them in awe, the Esterhazys, the Kinskys, the families who over the years had been the powers of Austria, the patrons of Haydn and Beethoven. Historian Z.A.B. Zeman describes the scene:

"The Corpus Christi procession outshone all others. The restraint of Lent and the grave pomp of Easter had been left behind: this was a dazzling occasion. The soldiers and gendarmes lining the streets had ivy leaves in their helmets; the archdukes arrived separately, in crystal caleches drawn by six greys' then the Emperor, accompanied by Archduke Franz Ferdinand, came in a carriage of gold and crystal, drawn by eight horses."[10]

Zipper could not only watch history pass by his home but he could see everywhere in town monuments of the past. For just in front of his home, on the Graben, stood a huge statue of "Trinity Column" popularly called "Pest Säule," the Plague Column, a historic reminder of the European plague epidemic of the 17th Century which struck Vienna most severely in 1679 when it wiped out one third of its population. "The Trinity Column was built by Emperor Leopold I as a thanksgiving for the plague having spared at least a portion of Vienna's population. Leopold can be seen kneeling at the foot of the column, an ugly, bizarre creature with a superb Hapsburg lip and a great deal of humanity. The column put up in 1687, which was designed by the leading artists and craftsmen of the day, including the young J.B. Fischer von Erlach, was something entirely new and startling: a mixture of theatrical hyperbole, fervent faith and joyous rapture."[11] In another part of town, the young Zipper often saw the statue of a survivor of the Plague and heard his legendary story, "Der liebe Augustin."

The story has it that during the height of the plague epidemic, a famous street musician, Augustin, one night when he had drunk a bit too much wine, went to sleep in the middle of the street. In the Vienna of that year there always were corpses of plague victims lying on the streets and undertakers were roaming through the city at night collecting the corpses and throwing them into open plague pits. The fast asleep, motionless Augustin was mistaken for a corpse by the under-takers, lifted onto their wagon and then thrown into the next plague pit. The following morning, Augustin cold and shivering, woke up to his precarious predicament. Unable to get out of the deep pit by himself he took his bag pipe, that still was fastened to his belt, and began playing lustily. Pedestrians passing by, hearing music rising from the dead were frightened out of their wits and making the sign of the cross, ran away from that spooky experience. Eventually, however, some recognized the very much alive Augustin and helped him out of his predicament. It is the event that Augustin immortalized with a ditty that is known all over the world, albeit with different words.

> O beloved Augustin all has been lost;
> Cane is gone, coat is gone
> Augustin lies in filth;
> O beloved Augustin all has been lost!

As the legend has it, from the event of this day on, Augustin continued to go around the city singing, playing and cheering up people without contracting the dread disease. It was believed that he had a charmed life. He was a Zipper childhood hero and, perhaps, unconsciously, a model for Zipper at Dachau. In any event, the parallels, as we will see, are striking.

Like many young children of his day, Zipper took an early delight in reading fairy tales of the Brothers Grimm and Hans Christian Andersen and, in his eighties, he still remembers reading "The Golden Pot" by E.T.A. Hoffman. As a child, he committed a great deal of poetry to memory which he would recite to his delighted family and their friends. One early memory, along with the Corpus Christi Procession, is reciting poetry at his grand aunt's house before he was three years old. These experiences may well have been the beginning of the development of an exceptional memory - a memory which would play a key role in his later prison camp experiences. As early as six years old he also began to read the works of Wilhelm Busch, a satirical cartoonist whose woodcut drawings were superb works of art accompanied by short lines of distinctive, rhymed verse. Busch really has no counterpart in the last half of the 20th Century. His drawings and verse were critical of all aspects of the German speaking world and were enjoyed by adults and children alike. Some of them were anti-semitic but, secure in their Viennese identity, even these the Zipper family read and laughed at. In addition to the poetry of Busch, Emil (Papa) Zipper was always reading substantial and philosophical works. For example, on Saturday afternoons, usually after lunch, he would read to his children librettos of operas as well as Heine, Goethe, Schiller, and other classic German writers. He had little time for trivia, and young Herbert quickly internalized this quality. For all his life Zipper has had little traffic with the inconsequential or the frivolous.

In addition to books, music was an integral part of the Zipper home. Like most good Viennese families of the time, the Zippers provided music lessons for their children. One could walk up and down the streets of old Vienna and from every window hear children practicing their instruments or singing. In the Zipper family, Walter studied piano and cello, and Herbert and Hedy studied piano. Otto, who was born in 1914 when the First World War was already in progress, had no formal instruction although he was very musical. The world of Vienna changed radically in 1914 and Otto, his brothers believed, did not grow up with either the same advantages or sense of security and confidence in the future.

Because at an early age he demonstrated an unusual musical talent Zipper's parents sought a piano teacher when he was only 5 years old. His first piano teacher was an Italian, Herr Radovani. The young Zipper disliked his clumsy way of walking and even more his clumsy way of teaching. He was almost a caricature of the old-fashioned, knuckle-thwacking tyrant and he would rap Zipper's fingers with his pencil when the child made a mistake. His exercises for a 5 year-old were exceedingly boring. The next teacher, Madame Vukovic, played the piano well and amused her pupil with her huge concert accordion. After her, he studied for the longest time with Ernst Pilzer, a student of Emil Sauer (Chair of the Piano Department at the Vienna Academy). With Pilzer he developed a life-long love of Bach, Mozart and Beethoven, also his mother's favorites. Rosie Zipper never had to tell her son to practice; he just did it - usually 2 hours a day from age ten on.

From his earliest days the Vienna of Mozart, Beethoven, Schubert was implanted deep in his soul. He and Walter would listen and talk about music for hours upon hours. At a very early age, Zipper and his brother Walter would go alone to concerts, to the Vienna Opera, to the standing room area in the Fourth Floor Gallery. "Once," Zipper recounts, "we stood for five hours to get standing room tickets and then stood another five hours listening to Wagner's *Tristan*. What we forget today is that to enjoy music one had to either go to the concert hall or opera or to make music oneself." Young Zipper did both. His mother was also a fine musician; an excellent sight reader, with a good ear. "I remember often playing, with delight, four-handed music with her." He also heard Pablo Casals for the first time when he was 9 years old (1913). The concert was memorable because Casals revolutionized cello playing. He would, for example, move his thumb out from the neck of the cello to play on the string in first position thus allowing a longer reach for the little finger and he would play melodies across strings to avoid sliding on only one string. Young cellists of the day, such as Emmanuel Feuermann, could not have played the way they did without Casals, and Zipper himself learned Casals' new techniques, techniques he would come to teach members of his own orchestras in years to come. Zipper also heard, during these years, a variety of young pianists: the young Walter Gieseking, wild Ignaz Friedman, pianists-composers such as Eugen D'Albert, Ferruccio Busoni, Liszt student Emil von Sauer, and, after World War I, virtuoso pianist and composer Sergei Rachmaninoff.

By 1908 the Zipper family had outgrown their little apartment on AM Graben and so they made the first of several moves. First they moved to the westernmost province of Austria, Voralberg, to the Hotel Europe in Bregenz with a view of Lake Constance. There the family engaged their first governess, an elderly French-speaking lady. In the spring of 1909, they moved to a home with a garden in Dornbirn, a 30-minute train ride from Bregenz. Soon a new governess was hired, Emma Kaspar. Emma was to remain with the family for many years and had a profound influence on Zipper and his sister.

Emma was raised in Alsace, then a German province next to France, and educated in a Catholic convent. Her father, an officer in the German Army, answered an advertisement placed by Emil Zipper. So she arrived at the garden gate in Dornbirn, looked into the garden and, as Zipper recounts, "Saw my bearded father in his bathrobe carrying a huge water spray gun. My brother and friends, my mother, Ernst Stefan, and I also had water guns and water bottles and we were having a water fight. We were giggling and laughing and here came this woman from a convent to teach us French. She wasn't sure she should stay with these crazy people."

But stay she did. Zipper was five when Emma was hired and she was his main teacher during most of his and Hedy Zipper's childhood. She was hired to teach them French, reading, writing but she taught them much more. Zipper and his sister loved their lessons with her so much that, by comparison, school was a bore. Schools then were rigid and didactic given over to enormous amounts of memorization and rote learning. But Emma, an intuitive radical, involved them in the process of learning. She introduced them, at an early age to magical children's literature, to E.T.A. Hoffman and others. She considered Grimm's Fairy Tales to be too gruesome so she invented her own stories, charming and delightful. By contrast, as they grew older she introduced them to the dark and turbulent world of Dostoyevsky and passed on to them her own brand of humanism. As she grew intellectually, in her own reaction against the Catholic Church, she passed her curiosity and learning on to Herbert and Hedy Zipper. Moving from a convent to the cultural and intellectual freedom of the Zipper family was for Emma an exciting revelation and she shared her excitement with her young tutees. The combination of Emil Zipper's agnosticism and Emma's evolving humanism were, no doubt, a major factor in Zipper's own agnosticism and humanism.

She was also fascinated by art and passed her fascination on to her young charges. At this time there were a series of monographs, known as "Blue Books," on painters available in the book stores and Emma began giving these to Zipper when he was only 6 years old. There were "blue books" on Michelangelo, Da Vinci, Raphael, Rembrandt, Durer, and so on. From this early age Zipper began a life long love affair with the visual arts and Emma was a prime motivator. Emma herself, of course, was a major beneficiary of this household dedicated to culture and, often to the humor of Papa Zipper.

Life in the Zipper household was not only a surprise to Emma but to many who visited. Visitors were astounded by the dinner conversations, the play of wit, rapid fire ideas which jumped from jokes to politics to philosophy in aphoristic humor about every subject imaginable. Lunch conversations with Emil Zipper were sprinkled with jokes. Usually the humor was typically Viennese but modified by the middle-class Jewish experience. A typical Papa Zipper joke would be:

> A man comes to the Rabbi and says: "Rabbi, I can't stand it. I live in a one-room apartment with my wife, three infants, my father and mother-in-law and two cousins. I have no privacy, no quiet. Everyone argues. It's awful.
> The Rabbi says: "Do you have a goat?" "Sure," he responds. "Well," says the Rabbi, "put the goat in your apartment room."
> Next week: Rabbi, "so how is it?" "Awful, awful" says the man. I can't stand it. The goat butts everyone. I have no privacy, no quiet." Rabbi: "Take the goat out and get rid of it."
> Next week: The Rabbi asks him how is everything. The man responds, "very comfortable."

And then there were the steady stream of Hungarian jokes, about the fictional Count Mikos:

> When asked by his friend "Is it true you had an affair with Countess Esterhazy?", Mikos replied, "What kind of a question is that?: a gentleman always enjoys and keeps quiet." Or who answered the same question with: "Do I say yes, then I'm a swine; do I say no, then I'm a liar."

In addition to the Hungarian Count Mikos there was a steady stream of jokes about the mythical Viennese Count Bobby and his friend Rudy. For example, Rudy says to Bobby, "You know what happened to me yesterday? I hit a roofer with my car." Bobby: "You don't say! How did you get up there with your car?"

Emil's sense of humor, passed on to his son, was to enable Zipper to endure many a dark moment in the years to come.

Hedy Zipper's reminiscences of childhood parallel those of her brother as a time of being happy and undisturbed, their home echoing with her mother's laughter, laughter often provoked by Emil Zipper's leaps from seriousness to humor, and the laughter of a house always filled with young people and always, always with music. She too remembers that their father spent a great deal of time with them, often showing the children the mysterious delights of his photographic darkroom. And, equally important in her early years was her brother.

"When I was 10, Herbert was the one who introduced me to music, taking me to concerts, recitals, operas, rehearsals." These years were for Hedy Zipper, and for other young women, times of security, protection, and comfort. Women in the middle class didn't work: it simply wasn't done and, furthermore, to do so would have been to deprive someone else of a job who desperately needed the work. Of all the young girls Hedy knew during those years not one went to college. She herself went to high school only until she was fourteen. Girls like Hedy Zipper were raised to grow up at home and then get married and preside over their new home. They didn't go out alone. Hedy didn't have an unchaperoned date until she was 21. Whenever she went anywhere with a young man, her brother was there to accompany her.

After living in Bregenz and Dornbirn for one year the Zipper family moved back to Vienna in 1910. At this time there were two residential areas where the middle class resided, the 13th District (Hietzing) and the 19th (Döbling). The Zippers first moved to Vega Gasse in the 19th District. Then in 1913 they moved and rented a large apartment in Hietzinger Hauptstrasse. As the young Herbert Zipper walked from his home to the local public school, he may have passed any number of historical figures. For Vienna in January of 1913 saw a remarkable confluence of men and women who were, in their time, destined to play leading roles on the world stage. Leon Trotsky sat at the Cafe Central working on his latest issue of Pravda while sipping steaming mocha. Joseph Dzhugashvili, who would later be known as Stalin, visited Vienna for five weeks doing research and writing essays on socialism. Josep Broz, later to be known as Marshall Tito, was working in Vienna as a car mechanic and enjoying the night life. And in February, 1913, as the young Zipper was walking to his music lesson, Arnold Schoenberg was preparing his new Chamber Symphony for a concert at which his new 12-tone music would be resoundingly rejected by confused and angry audiences. During 1913 Sigmund Freud was at work on his essay, Totem and Taboo, while "about nine tramway stops northeast of Freud's study, a twenty-three year old artist subsisted at Meldemannstrasse 25."[12] His name was Adolph Hitler.

Until the Hapsburg Empire approched its doom, Emil Zipper supported his family as an inventor. Before the First World War he designed a variety of devices. One invention was a pair of dancing figures for department store windows. Another was a device to automatically measure pieces of fabric to be cut. It was an almost robotic contraption which could, in a few seconds, measure, determine price per inch, cut, and roll up the fabric. He would then contract out these inventions for production. In the early years of electro-magnetics, Emil Zipper had a vision of widespread future applications. Most of the time he employed a draftsman to make blueprints of his ideas and a patent attorney, Dr. Laufer, a handsome, diminutive man with a great mane of hair, who like many others of the day, did his work in a coffee house - in his case, the Cafe Central.

In 1914, Emil Zipper invented a different kind of a machine for weaving. In the older weaving machines at one point in the process workers had to suck out thread, a practice which led to widespread lung disease. Emil's machine eliminated this dangerous stage. Because of such inventions he was hired by a combine of textile companies as a technical director and was, because of his work, exempted from service in the army.

He was not, however, a nine-to-five worker and, in addition to his industrial inventions and factory administration, he was an avid photographer and devoted father. On weekends he spent many long hours in his darkroom developing the photos he took during the week. For Walter, Hedy, and Herbert, being with their father in the darkroom (where he often sang operatic arias to them) were among their most cherished hours. For Herbert Zipper the example of this innovative, radical thinker may have shaped his own sense that the world was a place to be changed, to improve, beliefs that became part of his fiber early in his life. Emil Zipper passed on to his son the Enlightenment world view that by the exercise of reason man could control his environment and lead the good life. In addition, by 1914, as historian Gerhard Masur wrote, "Europe stood in a relation to the rest of mankind never before achieved by any other civilization. She was the hub of the world."[13] Reason and its new honored partner science was ushering in a veritable El Dorado. And to top it off, the young Zipper was living in a city which was at the center of the Universe, living at a time when war was seemingly a thing of the past. In retrospect, it is easy to see how the Zipper family, like everyone else, was completely unprepared for the collapse of the Empire and the destruction of European self-confidence.

By contrast to his education at home, school played a mixed role in his life. Zipper entered elementary public school at the 2nd grade. he had done all the first grade work, and then some, at home with Emma Kaspar. The school was about 15 minutes walking distance from home in a building erected in the 1800's. The classrooms were lit by gas lights and heated by large coal ovens serviced from the hallways. Sometimes, especially on cold, snowy days, the classrooms were filled with coal smoke which necessitated opening the windows through the first period. There were over 50 children in the class and they sat upon wooden benches, two seats to each, and attached were little tables to each seat. The tables were fitted with carved grooves for pen and pencil and an ink pot. School hours were from 8:00 a.m. to 1:00 p.m. and 8:00 to 12:00 noon on Saturdays.

Later, in 1914, Zipper skipped 5th grade because he passed an exam to which all children were entitled if they maintained top grades on all subjects throughout the first four years. For his elementary school years Zipper's main teacher was Lehrer Fischer, a delightful man who made every day of school enjoyable. He played the violin well and when the class had regular monthly written tests (Schularbeit), he would play solo sonatas by J.S. Bach. Every morning he first went from bench to bench inspecting each child's ears and neck to see if they were truly clean. This peculiar procedure was done in a friendly way with little jokes and a smiling face. Each period was begun with a song and it was during these elementary years that the emerging young musician experienced for the first time the thrill of singing in parts.

Middle school was a drudgery compared to life with Lehrer Fischer. It was for Zipper a pressure-filled waste of time. When he entered middle school in the fall of 1914, the war had already started and soon the younger teachers were conscripted. For the next five-six years, Zipper and his classmates suffered through a procession of tired, older, second-raters who seemed to have little interest in their subject and little awareness of the conflagration taking place in Europe. In some instances they appeared downright ignorant. There were, fortunately, a few exceptions. One was Dr. Adler who taught Natural Sciences and was able to spellbind the large, rowdy group of teenagers assigned to him. Another exception was Dr. Krebs who taught history and geography. He had actually traveled many times to Africa and brought back not only artifacts but first-hand knowledge. Both were retired university professors who left Zipper's school just before the end of the war. A third bright light was Zipper's Visual Arts teacher, Prof. Roller, (the brother of Mahler's stage designer, Alfred Roller) who tried to steer Zipper from music into art. He encouraged Zipper to work from live models. And though Zipper stayed with music, he gained from Roller an open-minded attitude toward contemporary art.

Religion, however, played a distinctly minor role in Herbert Zipper's upbringing. Emil Zipper's father had been a cantor, and his mother was the daughter of a rabbi, but Emil did not participate in religious activities and became a free thinker who later, in America, became a militant Democrat. His wife was more conscious of her Jewish background. Nevertheless, the Zipper family did not observe religious days such as Passover or Yom Kippur or Rosh Hoshanna. Zipper did grow up with a sense of his Jewish cultural heritage but without extensive religious instruction and no participation in services. He and his brothers were never bar mitzvahed. Consequently, in the dark moments of his life Zipper has not turned to God or any such sense of a divine power but instead has relied on his own inner resources and his personal, Existential code.

These childhood years were happy ones. Vienna was a city bustling with activity. Middle class families like the Zippers enjoyed the benefits of material success and found it easy to ignore or accommodate the steady under-current of anti-semitism which permeated Viennese society. And along with success came a deep devotion to the arts. Aristocrats and middle class citizens alike, including large numbers of Jews, served as patrons of the arts, while the artists, the young intellectuals, found inspiration in rebelling against the sterility of materialism and petty bourgeois values. Although Zipper was only a child during this ante-bellum period from 1904 to 1914, children always sat with the elders and were exposed to adult conversation at meals. The debates and issues of the day were as common at dinner as potatoes and boiled beef.

For example, one night at dinner a guest, young composer Ernst Stefan, volunteered that Friedrich Schiller represented an obsolete point of view. Zipper's uncle hit the ceiling: "How dare you say this about one of the great minds of Europe!" A long discussion followed. This was a typical dinner - discussions of the impending war, what would happen afterwards. Other discussions would focus on events of the day: the Colonel Redl scandal in June of 1913; the Second Balkan War between Serbia and Bulgaria with Turkey, Greece and Rumania joining the Serbians; in October of 1913, the hundreth anniversary of the Battle of Leipzig; visits to Vienna of Enrico Caruso and a twelve year-old child prodigy named Jascha Heifetz. For Zipper it was a shock to come to America after World War II and to discover the degree to which children are left to themselves to form a separate children's culture with their own commercial music, trivial topics, and materialistic values. The absence of family unity with adults to provide intellectual and cultural models for the young he found sad, if not tragic. In his own childhood, not only was his family a major source of his education but so too in a curious and paradoxical way was the very city of Vienna.

For a young student the visual experience of Vienna was edifying. For in the quarter century before Zipper's birth Vienna had been transformed into a virtual architectural museum. The old inner city had been notable for its palais of the aristocracy, its residence of the emperor, its Baroque Hofburg, and its Gothic Cathedral of St. Stephen's. Now a whole new main street and set of accompanying buildings and new styles was added. The inner city for both protection and as an expression of social exclusion had been surrounded by a wide belt of space. Originally designed for defense, this glacis separated the inner city from the suburbs and provinces. But with the liberals taking control in the 1860's a new plan for the city emerged - the Ringstrasse. This street was designed not only to maintain a certain military function but to erect a series of public buildings and one surmises, to allow the upper middle class a place to promenade and to feel superior to those outside the circle. According to Carl Schorske: "In the new Ringstrasse development, the third estate celebrated in architecture the triumph of constitutional Recht over imperial Macht, of secular culture over religious faith. Not palaces, garrisons, and churches, but centers of constitutional government and higher culture dominated the Ring. The art of building, used in the old city to express aristocratic grandeur and ecclesiastical pomp, soon became the communal property of the citizenry, expressing the various aspects of the bourgeois cultural ideal in a series of Prachbauten (buildings of splendor)."[14] What Schorske does not mention is that this "communal property" of the citizenry was really property of the Viennese gentile elite and was only on loan to the Jews whose tenancy could be revoked in a moment's notice. But for a young man growing up in this city, the traditions, the strength of the buildings, the deep sense of history communicated a sense of solidarity which had a lasting impact. Seeing oneself as a part of the tradition which produced Goethe, Beethoven, Schubert, looking at their larger than life statues on the corners of everyday streets fired the imagination of the young musician who began to see himself as one who, too, someday would be a great leader, an inventor like his father, a musician, an artist, a leading figure in society. The very air he breathed gave him the expectation that he would someday fit neatly into this solid tradition. How could he realize that Jews would not be allowed to penetrate the inner ring, that the gorgeous baroque or Renaissance facades concealed dark faces which frowned upon Jews? How could he know that this rich culture contained class distinction so deep and so wide that despite all his learning, his yearning and his achievements, he would never be allowed in. So in a curious way the buildings he loved begat a false sense of reciprocity, a sense which later would almost cost him his life.

Nevertheless, at the time he did enjoy walking around the Ringstrasse. The Ringstrasse was a major boulevard, totally surrounding the inner city, polyhedral in shape, accentuated by a set of buildings which, according to the Sixteenth Century principle selected the historical architectural style associated with the building's purpose: The Gothic Rathaus, the Baroque Burg Theater, the Renaissance-style University, the Classical-Greek Parliament Building. These buildings inspired the young Zipper who found in many of them an aesthetic pleasure that was sensuous. To wander around the Ringstrasse as well as other places such as Die Freyung or the Herrengasse was an education in style and form, history and contemporary aesthetics. Architects such as Heinrich Festal (1828-

1883), Theophil Hansen (1813-1891), Fisher Von Erlach (1656-1723), Comillo Sitte (1843-1903), Otto Wagner (1841-1918) and Alfred Loos (1870-1933) were visual instructors from whom Zipper learned by observing.

Frequently in those days, and whenever he has returned to Vienna, Zipper would go to the Josefsplatz which houses the National Library Building, with the monument of Joseph II in the square. Erlach was Italian inspired and his style borrowed from its classical antecedents replete with urns, heroic portals, statuary, and fountains alive with dolphins and tritons. It is true Baroque. This building Zipper regards as Fisher Von Erlach's finest achievement and he would often just commune with the building gaining, in his words, "a sense of elevated living." He was aware, even before publication of the spate of books about Vienna's golden age, that he was living in a city that would some day take its place in history with Athens, Rome and Florence. It was an inspiring place to be. Zipper himself describes the effect of growing up in Vienna:

> It was through my first teaching experience in America that I became aware of the difference between knowledge acquired through institutional learning, through books, lectures, the modern information media etc., and "knowing" as derived from actual live experiences; the difference between knowledge that merely employs our intellectual faculties and knowing that adds to it in equal measure emotional responses to our experiences. I began to understand why native born Americans had problems with grasping fully the history of their European roots. They simply are deprived of the physical encounter, the "living with" the monuments of their past.
>
> When I grew up in Vienna, from early childhood on, the history of the city into which I was born, was all around me. From the initial Roman settlement in the 1st Century at Carnuntum, not far from what today is the center of Vienna, to our time, an unbroken chain of architectual landmarks have been preserved, giving an indisputable testimony to the history of our roots. When we began to learn facts, these landmarks provided for us the feelings.

The only building Herbert Zipper really disliked was the Votivkirche which was built as thanks to Francis Josef who was saved from an assassination attempt. It was a Gothic structure which to Zipper seemed somehow like 'Ersatz Gothic': not a modern interpretation of Gothic, like the City Hall, but in a cheap copy of an old style. He was drawn into the contemporary debates of modern functionalism versus historicism. The benefits and beauties of both sides of the new style versus the ring style were apparent to Zipper who in a curious way embodies both impulses in his own being. He is on the one hand a graceful, elegant Viennese gentleman and on the other hand, a radical futurist. The duality of the architecture of Vienna, it would seem, was in his very bones.

In addition to walking through the city, Emil Zipper took his sons and daughter to museums and art exhibits and to the places where he worked, his office peopled by draftsmen, to factories and experimental workshops. For example, he built a paper factory in 1916-1917 in Upper Styria and there Zipper was initiated into the craft of making paper, how to use the lathe, what strength paper to use and other exotic processes. The two brothers and their sister also gained from their mother and father an enormous respect for great achievers. "Our heroes were men like Marconi, the inventor of the wireless (Walter and I would telegraph each other through the walls with a wireless gift from our father), Edison, Zeppelin, Michelangelo, Rembrandt, Breughel, Amundsen, Helmholtz, and Humbolt." Probably his own notions of heroism, his own ambitions and goals of what a hero does and how he prepares for his life's trade were being formed. And while other Europeans turned to notions of the superman, the Neitzschean man of action, Zipper's heroes were men of the mind, rationalists whose dreams of a better world came not through conquest but through creation, through order, and through enlightened community harmony. Unaware of how being Jewish would make him an outsider, he was, of course, equally unaware of how his 18th Century rationalism would place him outside of the prevailing forces in the 20th Century. So while Hitler, Lenin, Stalin, Mussolini, and others read and designed strategies of social conquest, Zipper devoured books about painting and drawing. He was especially fond of Gobineau's, *The Renaissance*, a book which he and Walter read over and over, delighting in the accounts of the personalities such as Michelangelo and Da Vinci who came to life as speaking actors in the book. He also was deeply influenced by Victor Hugo's *J 'Accuse* and by the works of Romain Rolland. In the fifth year of high school each student was required to give a formal lecture. Zipper gave his on "Impressionism and Expressionism," a talk which focused on painters such as Kokoschka, Schiele, and Klimt. To his great surprise many faculty attended his one-hour lecture including Professor Roller.

This first decade of Herbert Zipper's life was, on the surface, an ideal childhood: a secure, comfortable middle-class home, two intelligent and caring parents, a city the center of European culture, a time of international peace. Zipper himself looks back upon it with fondness and pride. And, in fact, in this agnostic, humanistic household the young Zipper absorbed and developed a personal faith which came to govern his life and to enable him to survive the concentration camp experience. Yet it was a faith for which he has paid a certain price. The combination of self-confidence growing out of the security of his home and the ostensible security of his city and culture along with the committment to scientific inquiry, and the 18th Century rationalism which permeated his home and his education — all these forces combined to produce a faith in civilized rationalism. It was a faith which at times seems almost freakish given the radical irrationalism which has characterized the 20th Century. As the century has unfolded with one nightmare following another, Zipper has doggedly held to his faith with an almost clinical objectivism. His faith is the primary source of his sense of self-definition and it has enabled him to weather any number of storms. Yet it often seems an impenetrable wall which keeps his emotional life under control. Later in his life his objective, rational controlling inner self enabled him to detach himself from the hideous events going on around him. He himself would come to see this characteristic as peculiar and quite different from all those around him. But it is a peculiarity he does not dwell on and when he speaks of his first ten years of life what he remembers most "was the utter security of the home. My father kept pressing problems away from us. We grew up in the complete confidence that tomorrow would be as secure as today, that society had solved all economic and cultural problems, that the millennium of peace and prosperity had arrived. Was this harmful to us? I think not." It may be that this security enabled him, Walter, and Hedy to experience the vicissitudes of the Twentieth Century with unusual emotional strength and confidence; it may be that it had other effects. This security, warmth, and fairy tale world however, was jarred in the summer of 1914.

As Stefan Zweig wrote: "Then, on June 28, 1914, in Sarajevo, the shot was fired which in a single second shattered the world of security and creative reason in which we had been educated, grown up and been at home — shattered it like a hollow vessel of clay."[15] Before Sarajevo, in the spring of 1914, Franz Werfel reported an encounter with Franz Kafka on a beautiful day Am Graben, where people enjoying the warming sun strolled obviously carefree, elegantly and in large numbers at noon. Kafka, very excited, whispered to Werfel: "Franz, don't you notice too that all this soon will be gone? There are not human beings any more, only ghosts, they only don't know it!"[16]

Chapter III

From War to the Academy

"We are living in a great time; I remember when it was still small."

—Karl Kraus

"Death folded his hands above the goblets from which we drank. We did not see him, did not see his hands."

—Joseph Roth, *The Emperor's Tomb*

In early June, 1914, Herbert Zipper, age ten, passed his entrance examination to high school. Later that month, on Sunday, June 28, Archduke Franz Ferdinand and his wife the Countess Hohenberg were assassinated at Sarajevo by South Slav nationalists. On July 28, Austria declared war on Serbia and during the months from July to November further declarations of war were issued and the comfortable world of the Austro-Hungarian Empire came crashing down. On August 3, Lord Grey issued his prophetic and now famous observation: "The lamps are going out all over Europe; we shall not see them lit again in our lifetime." It was but the first of two world-wide conflagrations that Zipper would experience. Steeped in the secure life of family, music, and material well-being, the young Zipper suddenly found himself surrounded by issues of war, survival, political conflict, and economic crisis. People gave their gold rings and jewelry to the government to finance the war and got back steel in return - with the inscription *Gold gab ich für Eisen* - "Gold I gave for iron." The irony of this "reverse alchemy" is rather striking. For in alchemy the objective is to refine metals into gold; to move from lesser to greater value. But in war we find the reverse: turning gold into metal as human life and creativity are transformed into death and destruction. In like fashion, Zipper had grown up reading Grimm's and Anderson's fairy tales and Amundsen's Explorations; but now he was reading poems by a radical he met one day in Schoenbrunn Park, a huge park attached to a gorgeous palace designed in the 17th Century by Fisher von Erlach. The park contained a little zoo, a beautiful aboretum, and a little theatre, but mostly it was a place where the Viennese would gather to promenade and to talk.

In 1914, when war broke out, the Zipper family was preparing to go on a summer vacation. The trip was, of course, canceled. Instead Zipper,

Walter, Hedy, with Emma and Aunt Nelly would go to the park at Schoenbrunn practically every day. It was there that he met a tall, handsome young poet in his twenties named Thorn. The poet had first been attracted to Nelly and also appreciated the younger boy's curiosity and began explaining to him what was happening in the world. Thorn was a passionate radical who began Zipper's political education. The two engaged in long conversations in which Thorn challenged Zipper's middle-class values and attacked the reverence for the imperial establishment which he regarded as "bourgeois bilge." That Austria had ushered in the millennium with its comfortable, sterile, middle-class notions was, said Thorn, absurd. Furthermore, he argued, slipping into war was a disaster. It was good only for the manufacturers of weapons, the merchants of death, the capitalist profiteers who feed off the death of innocent young men. Zipper and the young poet met for several weeks and the young boy came to see that this was a war without issues. Young and impressionable, Zipper came home and repeated these ideas to his entrepreneurial father. Generally a moderate humanist, Emil Zipper was furious to have his values challenged and forbade his son to see Thorn any more. Nevertheless, the seeds were planted. In these formative years during the war, Zipper began to gain an increasing sense of political complexities and a sense of intellectual independence. Because of Thorn, Zipper - even at this early age - came to distrust the headlines and the wartime journalistic propaganda. The Austrian newspapers reported victories but one morning when Zipper read the headline: "Lemberg Still In Our Possession," he wondered if it's *still* in our possession how can we call this a victory? Questions like this began to bother him.

In 1916 an event occurred the import of which the twelve-year-old Zipper could not fully understand but which he observed had a profound impact on all around him. Emperor Franz Joseph died. The man who for 68 years had presided over the strange consortium of nations, language groups, cultures, ethnic groups, and religious backgrounds which was known as the Hapsburg Empire and as the Austro-Hungarian Empire passed to his final rest at five minutes past 9:00 in the evening on November 21, 1916. As historian A.J.P. Taylor writes, "With Francis Joseph there went the last fragment of the Hapsburg core, long dead, but still hard; there remained at the centre echoes, ghosts, emptiness."[17] Over the emptiness the Archduke Carl was to preside for two years but somehow everyone knew that with the death of Franz Joseph the Hapsburg reign was finished. For three days the people of Vienna lined up to have a final walk past the corpse of their Emperor as it lay in state at Schonbrunn. "On November 25, 1916, the funeral procession, escorted by a hundred mounted soldiers and by workers bearing torches, made its way down the Ringstrasse, the street which Franz Joseph had built. Only a few of Europe's rulers took part in the procession... The people of Vienna who followed the procession stood in silence around the church. If they felt grief, the grief was numbed. They were hungry."[18] When the corpse was brought downtown from Schonbrunn, the 12-year-old Zipper stood with his class-mates from the Goethe Gymnasium. It was a gray, drizzling November day; (Rent was paid four times a year then in Vienna and there was a saying which applied to this day — "it was a day as ugly as November rent"). The hearse was drawn by black horses and everyone took off their hats as the hearse passed by. Somehow everyone knew that not only had a man died but a historical epoch had ended. The war dragged on for two more years and Vienna became more and more drab. For the first of two times in his life Herbert Zipper saw his country dying. This time it was an empire coming to an end; the next time it would be merely a nation.

While the carnage took place on battlefields all over Europe, Zipper was attending school. There were no battles in or near Vienna; total war did not yet exist; it was fought at the fronts by the conscription armies. At home it was difficult to learn the truth about the war. Viennese writer and diplomat Berta Szeps writes in a letter of January, 1917, of a trip to Switzerland: "What a pleasure to get the first Swiss newspapers. I breathed this air of freedom as if I had come out into the open after having been imprisoned for weeks in a stuffy room. One thing has really shocked me, though. Until I saw the Swiss newspapers I had not realized with what a dreadful and monstrous tissue of lies we are surrounded in Vienna. I understood immediately that if it goes on like this, Austria and Germany are lost..."[19] The censorship of the Austrian press was such that the Viennese citizens were led to believe for a long time that they were winning the war. (There was a joke circulating in Vienna about the war in 1917: "The situation in Germany is serious but not hopeless; the situation in Austria is hopeless but not serious.") Zipper's father was exempted from serving in the Army because he was the technical director of an industrial combine of some sixty to seventy plants deemed vital to the war effort. In spite of the propaganda and press censorship, the Zipper family were not blind patriots. In 1914, Zipper's maternal grandparents came to live with the family. Grandfather Emanuel Westreich possessed a fine inquiring mind and was outspoken in his criticism of the war and its generals. And, although Grandfather Westreich died in 1917, his criticism and attitude toward the Austrian administration and press fertilized the seeds planted by Thorn and gave further impetus to a budding political radicalism in the young Viennese high-school student.

On October 24, 1918, the Austrian-Hungarian Army surrendered. And on November 11, Germany signed an armistice. World War I was over. Zipper and two of his classmates, Hess and Ascherman, stood on the steps of the Parliament Building and, on this cold, drizzily day, they heard Karl Seitz read the Declaration of the Republic of Austria. The three young students who were genuine Republicans shouted hurrah, and Zipper felt imbued with the spirit of Beethoven, another ardent Republican. Szeps provides a different response to the transformation of Austria: "The horror was indescribable. Not only had we lost a war, but the whole empire had fallen to pieces. Nothing but a crippled torso, unable to move by itself, remained of the Austria that had ruled and united other countries for centuries."[20] While Vienna had escaped the ravages of bombing and fighting, compared to the days before 1914, it was a dismal place. Food had become very scarce and of poor quality. In the winter of 1918-19, there was widespread hunger accompanied by a flu epidemic in which thousands died, including the Zipper's former next-door neighbor, the famous artist, Egon Schiele. Nineteen Eighteen was, as one art historian writes, "That 'annus terribilis' which at last saw an end to the war, but also death for hundreds of thousands of victims of starvation and disease, reaping a terrible harvest among the leading artists of the modern Viennese movement. At the beginning of the year, Klimt died from the after-effects of a stroke. Wagner died in April... Moser in October... Schiele died in the same month from Spanish influenza. It was the end of an era."[21] In addition, inflation became an overriding force. A pre-war twenty-cent opera program now sold for 10,000 times as much. Zipper had to ride his bicycle with leather tires (there was no rubber until 1921) all over the city to buy some rotten potatoes here, some beets there. Inflation was so bad that every village issued its own *Notgeld* ("emergency money").

In 1918, Zipper had reached his full height of 6'1" and had outgrown all his clothes. One consequence of the war was that all overcoats were sent to the soldiers and, consequently, adequate clothing was unavailable to civilians. Zipper's winter coat was made of paper. For two years there was an invalid with one wooden leg selling bootlaces on the Kärntnerstrasse (the Fifth Avenue of old Vienna) bragging that his laces were the real thing: "Schuhriemen, Schuhbänder, kein Papier, kein Stroh, sondern nur rein garantiert echte Ware." ("No paper, no straw but real genuine goods.") Although Vienna in the post war period was economically shaky and though it gradually moved from progressive socialism to increasing levels of authoritarianism and fascism, culturally the city remained alive and vital until the Nazi invasion. Berta Szeps writes: "In other directions also Vienna proved itself strong enough to withstand the storms of fate that had ravaged over it. A new wave of artistic creation and thought developed in the midst of the first post-war years... Now belief and faith in human progress was needed, and it was found in the strong will to save Austria, not as a political empire, but as an empire of culture, art, and civilization for the whole world."[22] Zipper likens the city to a person whose legs have been amputated but who still feels the sensation of pain. Even though Vienna was no longer the capital of an Empire, it was still the cultural center of Europe. The monarchy was lost but the cultural vitality remained.

And in the 1920's Vienna was still an exciting place for a young musician to receive his education. It was also exciting in other ways.

As a rule, Zipper does not discuss his romantic experiences with anybody; not even with his closest friends. Sometimes he and his brother Walter exchanged amusing anecdotes about incidents that appealed to their sense of humor; but serious involvements were never discussed. When I asked Zipper to relate some escapades of his early manhood, he was willing to tell a few stories.

During the four years of World War I, Austria lost many millions of men. Within the successor states of what once was the Austrian-Hungarian monarchy an entire generation was decimated. Legions of single women, among them many young widows converged on the Austrian summer resorts in the early 1920's. They came from Budapest and Prague, Brno and Zagreb, Hamburg and Berlin. Single men were in a distinct minority and soon Zipper was involved in numerous, short-lived affairs.

In the Vienna of Zipper's youth erotic experiences between the sexes were vastly different from what they are today, especially in the U.S. Young people, who were attracted to each other, met for a considerable time in hour-long conversations at coffee houses, took long walks through the Vienna woods, strolled through the beautiful parks, sat on the park benches. Consciously or subconsciously they hesitated to break the delicious fragility of romantic courtships with the ultimate intimacy. Instant sex was never sought and rarely happened. Nevertheless, there was one unusual occasion when it did happen.

Zipper was an avid rock climber and was travelling on a train from Innsbruck to Zell am See, from where he planned to climb the "Wiesbachhorn," one of the main peaks of the "Hohen Tauern." When the train stopped in Kitzbuhel, a beautiful girl entered the compartment which until then Zipper occupied alone. She was tall and slim, had shiny black hair, large, dark eyes, high cheek bones and a very light complexion.

The girl obviously seemed to be upset, and taking her seat opposite of Zipper, immediately began to talk to him.

This was her story: She was taking her vacation in Kitzbuhel, enjoying a daily swim in the "Schwarzsee" until today when it became known that more than 20 people had been infected with polio whereupon the lake was declared off limits. Certain that she likewise would become a victim of the dreaded disease, she was in a state of near panic. She was, she said, going to be married in two months.

Arriving in Zell am See she left the train with Zipper who tried in vain to console her. She took a room in the same inn and Zipper invited her to dine with him. What little she managed to eat was consumed between intermittent outbursts of tears.

It was about one hour after they had retired to their respective rooms when the distraught girl knocked on Zipper's door. She was afraid to be alone. She could not possibly sleep and seemed to be even more agitated than before. She begged to be forgiven for intruding and asked whether he was not afraid of catching the polio bug, being with her after all in the same, confining room. Jokingly, Zipper reassured her that in fact it was the bugs who were afraid of him.

After a while the girl asked whether he would allow her to sleep in the same bed with him. He obliged but with no intention of taking advantage of the situation. She, however, had other intentions. As she told him later, she needed to bury her fears in love making. What began as a quiet night became unexpectedly one of the wildest. And it continued for three nights and days. Early in the morning of the fourth day she was gone. They never knew each other's name; they never saw each other nor heard from each other again. The event disappeared like a mirage. His vacation ended without the conquest of the Wiesbachhorn.

Parenthetically, to return to the omnipresent Count Bobby, Zipper recalls Bobby on the subject of sex: His friend Rudy meets him after Bobby's wedding. Rudy: "Say, how was your wedding night?" Bobby: "In all honesty I was disappointed." Rudy: "No! Why?" Bobby: "You see, my bride turned out to be a virgin. Obviously nobody else wanted her."

Throughout his young manhood, Zipper did enjoy a few affairs of the heart which inspired his loyalty for a least a few months. But none were so compelling that he even considered marriage. Besides, he was single-mindedly focused on becoming a musician and music was a demanding mistress.

During his middle school and high school years Zipper was convinced that he was going to make music his career. He received formal training from his piano teachers but most of his education was self-acquired. He read and studied theory books on his own; he attended every concert and opera he could; and, he played music at every opportunity. He played four-hand piano with Rosie, violin and piano sonatas with uncle Arthur Paunzen — a good amateur violinist; and he sight read everything he could lay his hands on. Each day was a new musical adventure.

Zipper completed his high school education in 1921. Now began a period of intense music study for a year and half under the tutelage of Felix Rosenthal. Rosenthal was a pianist, a composer, and primarily a theoretician who embraced the theories of Heinrich Schenker. Schenker, a contemporary of Rosenthal, had an enormous influence on many musicians of the time. He developed a unique approach to listening and anlalyzing compositions from Bach to Brahms in terms of their architecture. Great music, Schenker explained, was not just a string of beautiful melodies but a total plan which the composer often conceived in a flash of inspiration and which dictated to the entire process an organic unity. With Rosenthal, Zipper learned about Schenker and the so-called "Schenker method." But Rosenthal was not just an acolyte of Schenker who disapproved of music since Brahms considering it a disintegration of musical thought. On this point Rosenthal parted company with Schenker and supported new composers. He even performed (in the Urania - a public lecture building next to the Aspern Bridge) Zipper's first public composition - a piano piece in the style of early Schoenberg. Two times a week they would meet for the entire morning with huge homework assignments between meetings. Mostly they studied strict counterpoint. As a result of this intensive study, Zipper entered the State Academy of Music and the Performing Arts as a second year student and attended the Academy from 1923 to 1928. His principal teacher was the celebrated composer of Lieder, Joseph Marx.

Joseph Marx was born in Graz on May 11, 1882 and studied musicology with the German composer Erich Wolf Degner, Director of the Styrian Music Society of Graz. Marx's first composition was published in 1911 and by the time Zipper began his studies with him in 1923, Marx had published a number of choral compositions as well as chamber music and symphonies. As a composer he described himself as a "Romantic Realist." Marx came to Vienna in 1914 where he taught at the State Academy, becoming Director of the Academy from 1922-24. Then from 1924 to 1927 he became rector of the Hochschule (college) fur Musik.

Marx was thus in his early 40's when Zipper studied with him. He had a Ph.D. and the titles Hofrat, Director and Professor. Students addressed him as: "Herr Hofrat." He was a large and heavy set man with a huge head and a thick mane of greyish hair. He spoke with a very slight lisp and expressed himself in well-rounded phrases. He dressed rather carelessly; his necktie was never in the center of his chest, his trousers were baggy and his shoes always looked unshined. However, all this belied his larger-than-life personality. Whenever he entered a large gathering, a concert hall or theater he was noticed immediately.

Marx could be rather inconsistent to his students. To some he took a real interest; others he often ignored. He was never married, but there was always a young woman in his home who opened the door of his apartment whenever Zipper visited him. Zipper remembers quite a few of them. However, female composition students had a difficult time with him and never lasted beyond one semester. During Zipper's first semester in Marx's class there were two girls enrolled. Whatever work they brought he tore apart mercilessly. Toward the end of this semester he once remarked in the presence of these girls: "Women at best can sing and play the piano, but they should better stay at home, cook and mend socks." That kind of "male chauvinist" prejudice against women seeking a professional career was very much in evidence in the Vienna of those days and to some extent is there still today. (There are, for example, no women employed today in the Vienna Philharmonic.) The two girls, incidentally, were never seen after the first semester.

Marx did not pay much attention to Zipper during the period of strict counterpoint. But when he started to write fugues and other polyphonic music, Marx began to take an interest in young Zipper. After class he sometimes took him to his home near the Academy in the Traungasse to continue to work with him on the music that Zipper had written. Marx always gave specific, demanding, and meticulous assignments: for example, "Zipper, you write a double fugue in the style of Bach as Busoni would have transcribed him." Almost always Marx gave composition assignments in which a model was to be emulated.

Genuine praise Marx never bestowed upon the students. Zipper remembers only two instances when he received a personal verbal pat on the back. Once, in class when he played a new overture that he had written, Marx remarked: "Mmm, quite an appetizing piece." (When praise came from Marx, a man with a huge appetite, it was often in the form of food images.) And the other time toward the end of Zipper's last year with Marx, when he had to improvise at the blackboard on a given motif Marx suddenly exclaimed: "Zipper you are a very musical guy." This rather amused Zipper after five years of grueling examinations and tests with him.

In referring to the masters of composition, Marx never failed to mention Debussy. In fact there hardly was ever a class session when he did not refer to this French composer in one context or another. To his students of the early 1920's Debussy was a new experience. His music as well as that of all contemporary French composers was not performed in Vienna during World War I and for a couple of years after the war. Zipper remembers, for instance, that it was years after 1918 before the Vienna State Opera revived Saint Saens' opera *Samson et Dalila*. Whether Marx's intimate knowledge of Debussy's music was gained in pre (World War I) or postwar years, Zipper was not certain. But he remembers that Debussy was held up as a model in the pursuit for the expansion of the tonal world, its structure and expressiveness and as a challenge to his students toward explorations.

During these years Marx was also advisor to the Turkish government on music education and traveled to Ankara in that capacity. He also helped establish a music conservatory in Istanbul. During his absences Zipper and his classmates were presented with several guest teachers One such guest was the composer Maurice Ravel.

Ravel came to the "Academy" with the reputation of a renowned and accomplished French composer and a fine teacher. Later it was learned that his teaching experience was limited to private instruction of few students. He obviously was uncomfortable facing comparatively large classes. Zipper's class even exceeded its regular size by students from other composition and theory classes who, out of curiosity attended as auditors. Regarding Ravel's teaching Zipper writes:

"I do not recall having learned a great deal from Ravel as an instructor. However, he acquainted us with a large body of contemporary French music of which we had little or no knowledge. This widened considerably our musical horizon. Much of the work of composers such as Faure, Chabrier, Satie, etc. we only learned through Ravel's presence. Yet, he rarely analyzed this music for us but rather drew our attention to the individual characteristics of each author's musical idiom.

Ravel was exceedingly charming, well dressed and always created a pleasant, relaxed atmosphere when he was in our midst. He listened with obvious interest to our compositions, sometimes offered polite suggestions but never heavy criticisms. We students who were brought up by the very severe teaching methods prevalent at that time, especially in the German speaking world, did not feel that we sufficiently profited; we definitely missed the penetrating critic. We admired his music but not his teaching.

As a performer he was also disappointing. During his first days with us he gave a recital of his music in the Academy theater, packed with the students. The first piece on the program was his own Sonatina. When he appeared on stage and after he had acknowledged our ovation, he turned to the piano, hesitated for a moment and disappeared in the wings. He returned with a score under his arm and was followed by a member of the faculty who turned out to be his page turner. Then, with his eyes glued to the pages, Ravel proceeded with a performance the quality of which I should like to describe with a remark whispered to us by Marx who sat among his students: 'Anyone of you who would play this beautiful piece like that in public, would be expelled from this institution.' Yet, we all were charmed by the faint smiles that came over Ravel's face with every mistake he made, and there were many."

In addition to the guest lecturers there were also workshops from time to time offered by Richard Strauss. Strauss was a tall, slender and elegant man. He always was well and conservatively dressed, more like a bank director than an artist. He spoke with a slight Bavarian accent under normal conditions, but on occasions, when he unleashed his sarcastic humor, his accent resembled that of a Munich cab driver. His remarks in regard to the students' work were usually short, very much to the point and exceedingly helpful. His way of expressing himself could be compared to one feature of his music. There, passages of supreme beauty often are interrupted by violent turbulence; likewise in verbal communication Strauss could be the perfect gentleman, speaking with a fastidious selection of words interrupted by a sudden outbreak of choice vulgarities. One day when a student excused himself for not bringing a composition because of lack of inspiration, Strauss argued that one must be able to write every day: "You are not a composer," he said, "if you have to wait until the muse shits on your head." For Strauss discipline was essential. He once told Zipper's class, "Don't try to be original; if you have something to say, you can't prevent it."

As Joseph Marx always found a reason to mention Debussy, Strauss never missed an opportunity to refer to Mozart whom he called his model and his master. In his critical assessment of students' work he always recommended examining how Mozart solved similar problems in specific passages of an aria, a string quartet, a symphony, etc. Strauss never drew attention to his own works.

However, the most important lessons that Zipper and his classmates learned from Richard Strauss were during his rehearsals at the Vienna State Opera which Zipper frequented as part of his curriculum. Strauss was a man of few words, but his advice to the singers and the orchestra often included unforgettable pearls of musical wisdom. Equally unforgettable were Strauss conducting performances of various Mozart operas, and according to Zipper, Strauss' *Cosi Fan Tutti* in the 1920's made all performances of this opera that he has heard since seem pale.

From the remarkable teachers — Marx, Ravel, Strauss — the fortunate young Zipper gained a wide knowledge of both traditional and contemporary music, even some music "hot off the press." He learned how composers set about their work and he learned how to study a piece of music measure by measure, passage by passage. And most of all he gained a deep respect, a life-long respect, for discipline, for painstaking craftsmanship. And, conversely, he developed an almost visceral intolerance for sloppiness of any kind. His natural bent toward order was sculpted into a passion for careful, organic, elegant quality.

During these rigorous academic years at the Academy, Zipper began to learn the skills of conducting. Every Thursday evening, forty to fifty students at the Academy would come to the Zipper home and Zipper would conduct as he and his fellow students would play through the main works of the symphonic literature. The Zippers had rented a huge apartment in 1913 - it was, in fact, a double apartment (120 and 120A Hietzinger Hauptstrasse) with two separate entrances. In the center of the two units was a huge entry hall - two stories high - approximately 28 feet high - which could accommodate all the students. It even had a billiard table which was pushed aside during the Thursday evening concerts. (As an aside, Emil Zipper was a superb billiard player who passed his skills on to his sons. Consequently, the young conductor-composer regularly trounced such luminaries as George Szell and conductor Fritz Stiedry.) The entry hall had two adjoining rooms at either end which could be opened up creating a room over 100 feet long from the back garden windows to the front wall. At the back of the hall was the kitchen where Rosie and Hedy would prepare open-faced sandwiches and small pastries, beer and lemonade.

At 7:00 p.m. the musicians would begin arriving and the music would begin rather promptly at 7:30. Zipper picked the music almost every week. He would go to the archives of the Gesellschaft der Musikfreunde, the oldest and most famous music society in Austria which possessed a magnificent collection of all classical music. The Director of the archives, Prof. Eusebius Mandyczewski, was a teacher of Zipper's at the Academy. He was also a friend of and one of the chief editors of the collected works of Brahms. Mandyczewski kindly allowed Zipper the use of music unavailable to others. Always upon entering the Gesellschaft one would see the librarian, Doubrava, sitting on a high stool writing symphonies of his own. He was also organist at the Karls Kirche and was a character. On one occasion, when Zipper was looking for a piece of music, a woman came in and asked for Il Trovatore. Doubrava, sitting at his stool, mumbled, "yes, yes." Then she said, "Actually I want mostly the overture." "Yes, yes," he muttered, and climbed up a long ladder to the topmost shelf mumbling as he climbed, upon reaching the top he turned to her and said, "besides, Il Trovatore doesn't have an overture."

Zipper would enter the top floor of the building and there would sit Doubrava: "Ah, Zipper. Good to see you," he would say without looking up, and at the same time shoving the huge catalog over to Zipper. Each week Zipper would come for a Haydn or Mozart symphony or the Bach Brandenburgs or Beethoven, Brahms, or Dvorak symphonies which were then fairly recent compositions. One must remember that Emil and Rosie Zipper had often seen Brahms strolling through the streets of Vienna.

The Thursday evening rehearsals were not light-hearted affairs but were serious rehearsals and lasted until 10:00. Often professional musicians joined this student pick-up orchestra and sometimes soloists of the day joined to play concertos. Erna Gal, sister of composer Hans Gal, for example, once joined them along with a well-known cellist of the day, Wilhelm Winkler. Also, Eric Simon, Zipper's lifelong friend, played second clarinet. For the students, these Thursday evening concerts were a rare opportunity to learn the symphonic repertoire. For Zipper it was a unique time to learn the craft of conducting. And for Emil and Rosie and Hedy Zipper these were evenings to cherish.

Conducting can be learned only by doing it and Zipper learned his craft not only at these Thursday evenings but by conducting a Jewish Community Orchestra and a union orchestra. He also began his professional career by conducting the Vienna Madrigal Society upon recommendation of its founder, the composer Hans Gal upon his leaving Vienna to assume the directorship of the conservatory in Mainz, Germany.

Zipper was immersed not only in music during the nineteen-twenties, he was also acquiring a love of the visual arts. On one evening in 1923 he was coming home from the theatre at 10:00 and noticed some drawings exhibited in the front window of the Richard Lanyi Bookstore. The store on the Karntnerstrasse, just west of the Ring, regularly exhibited contemporary works of art — including etchings of Zipper's well-known artist-uncle, Arthur Paunzen. Zipper paused to look at a series of nude, expressionist drawings of a noted Viennese artist, Oskar Kokoschka. The nineteen-year-old Zipper stood at the window, entranced by the drawings, when a man approached him and inquired: "Do you like them?" Zipper responded that, yes, he liked them but that he didn't fully understand the artist's intentions. The man introduced himself as Oskar Kokoschka and proceeded to explain his ideas to the young student. In good Viennese fashion they then continued their discussion walking up and down the street. Kokoschka invited Zipper to look at his work soon and Zipper visited his studio a half dozen or so times. He was fascinated by the distortion of forms in service of a deeper psychological reality; he was also intrigued by the layered use of the color which seemed to expose hidden levels of the human spirit. Discussions with Kokoschka opened up new vistas for Zipper and the artist's statements about the nature of art had a profound impact: "The consciousness of visions is not a state in which one perceives or understands an object but a position in and of itself which must be experienced for itself."[23] Kokoschka also expressed the view that there is a fourth dimension to art: "the other three dimensions are based on the vision of both eyes... the fourth dimension is based on the essential nature of vision, which is creative."[24] Kokoschka had returned from Dresden to Vienna for just the year of 1923 and he departed again in 1924 but he and Zipper continued to correspond until Kokoschka's death in 1980.

Bumping into Kokoschka reminded Zipper of Count Bobby bumping into Rudy one day on the Kärntnerstrasse. Rudy inquired: "Say, where did you get that beautiful walking stick? Bobby: "Well, it's nice but it's too long for me." Rudy: "No problem, just cut it." Bobby: "Nonsense. I would not dream of cutting off that beautiful ivory handle." Rudy: "Of course not, cut it on the bottom, at the end." Bobby: "But on the bottom it is not too long."

In addition to this friendship with Kokoschka, Zipper frequented several other art-book stores and attended almost every exhibition in town. The most famous bookstore in town was Hugo Heller's, a store which Zipper first visited in 1921. Hugo Heller's was a bookstore, a gallery and a ticket agency all in one. It was a large store with a number of rooms and a stock of books from all over the world: Upton Sinclair and Sinclair Lewis from the United States as well as German translations from French, Russian, Italian, and Spanish literature. The huge front window featured displays of books and contemporary art. Inside the front door on the right was a table where an agent sold tickets and made reservations to cultural events all over town. One young agent during Zipper's visits was named Rudolf Bing. Hugo Heller held the first exhibition of Arnold Schoenberg's paintings in October of 1910, an exhibit which included forty-one portraits and at the opening of which the Rose Quartet played the first and second Schoenberg Quartets. Hugo Heller, a leading intellectual of the time, held a salon for artists and intellectuals and also was a member of Sigmund Freud's psycho-analytic society, delivering a paper in October of 1912 on "Lou Andreas-Salome as a writer." Heller was also the publisher of Freud who spoke often in Heller's salon. As an impressario Heller managed Bruno Walter and Gerhart Hauptman among others. Heller's bookstore, located in the inner city District I, was a gathering place for the intellectuals and always, upon entering, one would hear loud and long discussions and debates taking place. Here one would come to buy the latest edition of Freud or prints of Kokoschka or Schiele or Klimt or books about twelve-tone music. Zipper would often go to Heller's to meet friends or purchase a book. Heller died in 1923 but Zipper continued, off and on, to visit the store until 1938.

Zipper was enthralled by the Secessionist Movement and by the leading contemporary architects and artists. His favorites included Adolph Loos and his disciples, Schiele who in the Twenties was now beginning to inspire respect as well as controversy, and the French Impressionists who were now becoming known in Vienna. He was continually stimulated as well as bewildered by the conflicting claims of the academy and the traditionalists such as his uncle and the radical claims of a Schoenberg, Klimt or Kokoschka.

During this period Zipper and other artists and intellectuals would gather with great frequency in what has become almost synonymous with Vienna, the coffee house or cafe. As one critic writes:

> "The cafe was, arguably, the city's finest social and cultural achievement. It provided an extension of one's own living-room with the addition of service, a full range of national and foreign newspapers and magazines and frequently billiards as well. One could have post addressed to one's cafe and eat and drink there for weeks on end on credit. Each cafe was known for and proud of a particular kind of clientele which gave the cafe its character, and most of the cafes in the city centre could boast at least one regular guest especially eminent in his field. If you wished to move in literary circles, for example, and meet Kraus or the leader of the *Jung Wein* group of writers, Hermann Bahr, then you only had to visit the appropriate cafe and wait for the appropriate moment to introduce yourself. If you wished to meet Klimt or any of the artists associated with him, then you went to the Cafe Museum, close to the Secession building itself.
>
> The Cafe Museum was a remarkable place, not least because it had been designed in and out by Loos. In keeping with his radical ideas about decoration it was suitably plain, even spartan in appearance, a fact which had earned it the nickname 'Cafe Nihilism'." [25]

Vienna in the 1920's was not only a center of musical ferment and artistic experimentation, it was also the home of Karl Kraus whose monthly publication of his magazine, *Die Fackel* ("The Torch") was an event as welcome as a new composition by Schoenberg, Hindemith or Kurt Weill. It is difficult to find an English counterpart for Kraus. He was a quintessential Viennese Jewish intellectual who possessed a scathing wit and a virtuoso use of language. Kraus was truly unique and somehow captured or embodied the spirit of the times. A brilliant, iconoclastic writer whose puns and allusions were so wedded to the German language as to all but rule out translation, Kraus inspired young intellectuals like Zipper to go beyond conventional thought, to question easy assumptions, and to deliberately puncture bourgeois complacency. *Die Fackel* ran from 1899 to 1936 when Kraus, age 62, died of heart failure. With its 922 issues over 24,000 pages, *Die Fackel* ranks as one of the more amazing journalistic achievements in literary history. Kraus was a moralist, satirist, pacifist, prophet, social critic, iconoclast, and self-appointed guardian of truth. Wherever he encountered hypocrisy, half-truths, sentimentality, mediocrity of thought, or just plain stupidity, he attacked. And he attacked with a biting, rapier-like pen unparalleled perhaps since Swift. The targets of his wrath ranged from egg substitute ("made of diluvial chalk and baking powder" and which tastes like "ersatz toothpaste") to the vulgar insensitivity of vacation pleasure excursions to Verdun (where "1-1/2 million men had bled to death"). Besides *Die Fackel*, Kraus's masterpiece was *Die Letzten Tage Der Menschheit* (*The Last Days of Mankind*) a satirical, biting philosophical study of World War I.

In addition to Karl Kraus' controversial articles, a controversial novel appeared in 1922 which not only incited strong feelings but led to the first Nazi murder of a Jew. Zipper, like many Viennese purchased his copy of Hugo Bettauer's satirical novel *The City Without Jews* (a book ultimately translated into English and made into a silent film). It became a best seller and, in retrospect, was rather prophetic. The novel, not without historical precedent (as in 1421 and 1670) describes a Vienna which has decided, once again, to expel all its Jews. As a result the financial stability of the city disintegrates and massive social problems occur. Zipper feared the book was frighteningly possible although not terribly well written. The book did, however, fan the flames of Vienna's latent anti-semitism and in 1925 a young man named Otto Rothstock walked into the office of Bettauer (a middle-aged journalist who had converted to Protestantism) and shot and killed him. Rothstock had resigned from the Nazi party only a month before the murder and most assumed he resigned only to avoid direct implication for the party. He was tried in court, acquitted as mentally insane, sent to a mental institution and released 20 months later when the doctors could find no evidence of mental illness. Not only was Bettauer's book prophetic, his own subsequent fate was but a preview of coming attractions for those who could see.

During the 1920's Zipper developed a passion for the writings of Goethe and committed long passages to memory. As some men can recite chapter and verse from the Bible, Zipper cites lines and scenes from Faust. His impromptu recitations even in the 1990's are delivered with a reverence and awe for the language which is inspiring. He recalls, however, Count Bobby saying to a friend, "I don't see what's so great about *Faust*; it's just a bunch of familiar quotes."

Besides the intellectual attractions of politics, music, literature and philosophy, and the allurements of women, Zipper acquired another passion during his student years - the mountains. He spent most of his weekends there - in the winter skiing and in the summer rock-climbing. Sport trains left from Vienna for the mountains on Saturday afternoons and Sunday mornings. Nearly a quarter of a million people would leave Vienna on weekends, most of them as members of Alpine clubs enjoying nominal fares on these special trains. A typical fare for a round trip was the equivalent of one dollar, i.e., five shillings. Ski lifts did not then exist. There were a few cable car lines and a couple of cog-wheel railways frequented mainly by tourists. Zipper hardly ever used them. He reminisces about these times with a deep feeling:

"Going up a mountain by one's own power through the winter landscape with the snow covered trees of its forests and the blue shades contrasting with the sunlit white of the slopes was one of the great experiences of our life. Working one's way up on sealskin covered skis through deep virgin snow to the high peaks could take the better part of a day. The exhilarating down hill skiing then became the bonus of the hard uphill work.

In summer, scaling the celebrated walls of the Austrian Alps was an experience very different in kind and purpose from skiing. Here one was less concerned with the outer world but rather with concentration on one's own inner resources.

Frequently, I was asked by nonclimbing nature lovers why we, the climbers, again and again risked our lives by laboring our way up treacherous walls to summits that one could reach with relative ease by walking up from other sides. 'What kind of victory do you try to win by fighting a mountain?' was the recurring question. We do not fight for victory with mountains! In climbing an Alpine wall we learn how to conquer our fears; we learn how to act at all times with concentrated deliberation; we learn what it takes never to give up and we become aware of the depth of our mental and physical capacities in action. We learn many lasting lessons about ourselves. Mountain climbing has values that no other activity can provide."

And so, by 1927, Zipper was becoming a dedicated musician, a mountain climber, a political socialist, and somewhat of a worldly wise young man. One evening in February was to radically change his life. His sister Hedy had come down with the flu and she asked her brother if he would please accompany her two friends without her, otherwise they too would have to miss a masked ball. Reluctantly Zipper agreed to be a good sport. He arrived at the ball as the chaperone of the two girls and he told them to go off and have fun, to behave themselves and to come check in with him every 30 minutes. He then retired to a corner and sat down to enjoy reading a couple of books he brought along.

While he was sitting there a very young girl, her sister, and her sister's date entered. The two girls went to the dressing room and through the door Zipper could see the young one began to comb and smooth her long blond hair. Zipper describes the moment as "being struck by lightning." Though he had no way of knowing what would transpire, the quickening of his pulse, his visceral reaction to seeing this young girl told him his life was about to change. He walked up behind her and said, "Will you dance with me?" The tiny 4'10" girl, age 14, looked up at his 6'1" and said, "Sure." Zipper was a poor dancer and his partner, Trudl Dubsky - already a professional dancer - laughed. "Well then," he said, "teach me." They danced. They also exchanged phone numbers and addresses and the next day he sent her a bunch of roses.

He then began seeing her two or three times a week and phoning her every day. At first he was partially attracted by her obvious talent and grace. She had a way of gesturing with her hands that to him was pure poetry. Without realizing it, her every movement suggested artistic sensuousness. He was fascinated by this tiny sylph who was unlike any Viennese girl he had ever known. And she, in turn, was interested in him - his passions, his thoughts, his musicality, his values. They talked and talked, occasionally after a movie but often in coffee houses. In particular, they would meet at the Cafe Schottenthor on the Ringstrasse opposite the University. In this cafe with its wooden floors and marble top tables, filled with the aroma of rich coffee and stale cigarette smoke, they would meet, amidst people of all ages, and discuss Dostoyevsky, expressionist art, dance, music, and politics. One day, when Trudl was on tour with the Bodenwieser Ballet Co., Zipper came to the cafe with her sister Minnie, who was then studying at the University. The head waiter, who had observed Trudl and this same man together for months, looked upon Zipper with scorn. He would not even bring them their bill. It was only when Zipper introduced Minnie to him as Trudl's sister that he became courteous again. In addition to becoming absorbed in his affection for Trudl,

Zipper being a savvy diplomat courted Trudl's mother who was a singer. He would accompany her and before coming to the Dubsky home studied the repertoire Madame Dubsky enjoyed singing.

When they began their relationship in 1927, Zipper was a 23 year-old university student. Trudl was only fourteen but she had become an independent young woman. She was already a member of a well-known dance group, The Bodenwieser Ensemble. Madame Bodenwieser, a professor at the State Academy of Music and Performing Arts, thought of Trudl as her most gifted student. Trudl secretly joined the academy at age 9 deceiving her parents who thought she was attending regular academy. By the time they found out it was too late: Trudl was a committed dancer and refused to leave the school - much to the consternation of her father, an insurance company executive. At first he tried opposing her but her will to dance was indomitable. Even at age 10 he could not control her. By 14 she was financially independent, dancing with the company, and by age 17 she was a teacher there. Sometimes Zipper would come by the studio and when the dance-piano accompanist would step out for a smoke, Zipper would improvise at the piano for the dancers. He also delighted in the antics of Madame Bodenwieser, a character and master of the mixed metaphor.

At first they dated in the fashion of the times, taking long walks, exchanging glances, talking for long hours. There were weeks upon weeks of meaningful looks. A long period of getting to know each other. The prolonging itself was a delicious and tantalizing time. For this was not the age of instant gratification but an age of leisurely courtship. Zipper knew immediately upon meeting Trudl that he was deeply in love. Love for the fourteen year-old girl came more slowly but she too came to the realization. Often she kept him waiting - punctuality for her was not a working concept. She became absorbed in whatever she was doing and lost all sense of time. One day after keeping him waiting for over an hour, he said to her, "Trudl, I can't waste my life waiting for you. Perhaps we should call it quits." She grabbed his hand and said, "Don't ever say that again." Later she told him that at that instant, she knew.

A short time later, when Trudl was about fifteen and a half years old, Zipper rented an apartment room and they became lovers. It was not wholly unusual to have such a place for romantic trysts but for a girl of Trudl's age it was certainly bold and unconventional. Trudl, however, was an exceptionally mature and independent young lady and both were convinced this was the love of their lives.

Sixty-three years after this event, Zipper would recall this time in his life in poignant, perhaps idealized, but nonetheless adoring words:

In order to describe my early, and, at that time for me, unique relationship to Trudl, it is necessary to understand one aspect of my affairs with women before I met Trudl. Until then, practically without exception, it was the women who took the initiative. From the time when I was still a teenager until 1927, whether amorous affairs took place in bed, in rowboats, on meadows or benches, in forests or on mountain tops it was the women who made the advances. A mixture of courtesy, pride and vanity often forces one to become a lover without volition. It was only from women with whom I worked professionally and from my students that I distanced myself decisively and without exception. My dentist's good-looking daughter whom I taught music theory, many years later when she was married and had children told me that she thought I was a cold fish for not noticing her expectations beyond music theory lessons.

My love life A.T. (Ante Trudl) had also its rather unpleasant aspects in that it necessitated frequent breaking-up procedures that I usually had to initiate. Though I had numerous affairs during those years I really did not know the nature of love.

It struck me for the very first time like lighting when I met Trudl who then, for all practical purposes was still a child.

I learned then that true love was not caused by sexual desire but by a mysterious affinity of electro-magnetic power. For a long time sexuality did not enter our relationship. It begun to build up slowly late in 1927 like one of those long Beethoven crescendos with the climax reached only late in 1928 on that afternoon in the Little Mahler Strasse apartment. It was not like one of those tumultuous Wagnerian climaxes but like one reached in the third movement of Beethoven's quartet, opus 132.

When I was waiting for Trudl to ring the bell for the first time, I was waiting for a very young woman who was as precious to me as nothing else in the world. For that moment I gathered all the gentleness that I was capable of. It was not an act of lust but an act of inspired mutual love. We both never forgot it.

It was, however, not simply a period of falling in love and idyllic music making, but one of political tension. This tension erupted on July 15, 1927 with riots in the city and the burning of the Palace of Justice. This occurred on the same day that Herbert Zipper and Trudl Dubsky had a crisis of their own.

SECOND MOVEMENT

IV   A Young Conductor In The
      Gathering Storm

V   Dachau

VI   Buchenwald

Chapter IV

A Young Conductor in the Gathering Storm

"Even then time was moving faster than a cavalry camel but in those days no one knew what it was moving towards."

Robert Musil, *The Man Without Qualities*

On November 11, 1918, Emperor Charles, the grand-nephew of Franz Joseph, issued a statement which included the words, "I renounce all participation in state affairs." The Hapsburg Empire died "not with a bang but a whimper." The provisional National Assembly had created the independent state of German-Austria. However, the Treaty of St. Germain and the Treaty of Versailles forbade the joining of the two German states and compelled the change of the name from German-Austria to Austria.

Once Europe's second largest state with a population of over fifty million, this new state now comprised only 32,000 square miles with a population of less than seven million. A joke of the times had one Austrian asking another, "What do you want to do today?" The second one replies, "Take a walk around Austria." The first one says, "Fine, but what shall we do in the afternoon?"

Thus a small, new, and inexperienced state was created which from the beginning was beset with political and social complexities and contradictions. To a degree there was a "revolution" carried out in Austria after the war. A new democratic system of government emerged and propertyless classes acquired more political and social power than they had prior to the war. This "revolution" was promulgated by the left wing Social Democrats who emerged after the War and throughout the nineteen twenties as the majority party in Vienna, a city that housed one third of the entire population of Austria. The Social Democrats were opposed on the right by the Christian Socials and the nationalists—the Pan German Peoples Party and the Agrarian League. During the twenties the Christian

Socialists held an equally strong majority in the rest of the country owing to the Catholic peasantry and the conservative classes.

The Social Democratic rule of Vienna, unbroken in the entire decade of the 1920's under the leadership of Karl Seitz, Hugo Breitner and Julius Tandler carried out an ambitious program of working class housing ("Wohnhausbauten"), health plans, adult education and other educational reforms that gave the city throughout Europe the unique reputation as the "Red Vienna."

However, there was a deep suspicion and animosity aroused on the part of those who stood to lose power and prestige as the Social Democrats made gains. The aristocracy, military, and bureaucracy, along with the Church (resenting the anti-clericalism of the socialists) all feared a greater degree of socialism or even Russian influence than was remotely likely. Furthermore, ideas of liberalism had never deeply penetrated the small townsmen and peasants who comprised over half the population. These provincial groups were generally taught by the church and school to defer to authority. After the defeat in the war, the economic upheaval, the political insecurity, many people were susceptible to demagogues and to absolutist arguments. Paramilitary groups were formed, one such group being the *Heimwehr*, ("Home Defense"). This was a private army of the nobleman Starhemberg - a fascist leader.

Tensions between left-wing social democrats and right-wing Christian Socialists and the Heimwehr grew. In January of 1927, in Schattendorf in the province of Burgenland, a worker and a boy were killed by gunfire during a clash among various political groups. The left wing saw the deaths as the responsibility of the right. Three ex-soldiers were accused of the murders and brought to trial. The trial took place in July and the three were acquitted. Riots followed and on July 15, the Palace of Justice was burned. The police, with the consent of Chancellor Seipel, fired on the crowd and in the ensuing bloodshed eighty-nine people were killed and many more wounded.

Zipper recalls the day vividly. On the evening of July 14 Trudl had wanted to see a movie. They went to the theatre early and sat down in the lounge to wait. Trudl suddenly felt terribly ill. Zipper took her to the Zipper family doctor, Dr. Steiner, who diagnosed the problem, acute appendicitis, requiring an immediate operation. Zipper took her home and her parents brought her to a small private sanitorium in Pötzleinsdorf (XVIII District) the next morning. The next day Zipper came early to the sanitorium just after the operation was over. It was performed by Prof. Moscovic - since in those days, the top surgeons were often university professors. Because he couldn't talk to Trudl who was still under anesthesia,

Zipper took a taxi to his father's office at #3 Volksgarten Strasse, to meet Walter. On the way to his father's office which was adjacent to the burning Palace of Justice, he encountered a mob who overturned his taxi. Scrambling out of the taxi, he shouted to the mob that he was one of them, a Social Democrat. He then hurried into his father's office on Volksgarten Strasse. Later he and Walter walked six miles home and, seeing a flower shop open, Zipper bought a dozen red roses.

Only a block away from where his taxi was overturned, the Social Democrat leader, Otto Bauer, standing beside the monument of Austrian writer Ferdinand Raimund, made a speech trying to calm down the people. A spontaneous demonstration had erupted, a two-day general strike was enacted, but the leadership had virtually abandoned the people by misjudging their mood. As a result, the fascists emerged from the crisis stronger. In retrospect, it would seem that the people's violent reaction to the acquittal only confirmed the anxieties of many and added fuel to the fascists' claim that they and they alone could maintain order. The next day, July 16th, Zipper set out at 6:00 a.m. to walk an hour and a half to the sanitorium and delivered the red roses to a weak but smiling Trudl. Mama Dubsky was there and was moved to tears by the gesture.

Meanwhile as the political scene was becoming more complex and threatening not only in Austria but throughout Europe, Zipper was completing his studies at the Academy and ready to begin his professional career. The year was 1929. He was 25 years old, tall, handsome, and an accomplished musician seeking to make his way as a conductor. He secured his first job as the Conductor of the Vienna Madrigal Society. Almost simultaneously, the world-wide depression began with the fall of the stock market in October of 1929. A banking crisis hit Europe first in Vienna in 1929. Austria was particularly susceptible to the economic crisis because it had not yet adjusted the economy of an empire, to the needs of a small state. Before the Depression Austria had from ten to twenty percent unemployment. In February, 1933, more than two thirds were idle. By 1937 unemployment was still 33 percent above that of 1929. Zipper recalls two popular jokes of the day. One was that "There are only 100 schillings in Vienna; everyday some one else has them." The other was the statement that there are three different ethnic groups in Austria: "Die Schnorrmannen (the hustlers), Die Pleitonen (the bankrupt), and Die Prolongobarden (the stallers)." Economic conditions were, however, no joke and as historians have comprehensively explained, the tensions, anxieties, fears were to affect every Jew in Europe.

Meanwhile one had to make a living and, in spite of the Depression in Austria beginning with the failure of the Österreichische Boden Credit

Anstalt (the Tiffany of Central European banks), Zipper managed to find work. Although money was in short supply, for the resourceful Zipper work was not. He had secured his first official engagement in 1929 as Director of the Vienna Madrigal Society. It had been founded and directed by Hans Gal who left in 1929 to become the Director of a music Hochschule (conservatory) in Mainz and told Zipper that he knew no one better suited to replace himself. The Society was a group of 20 singers who would meet 1-3 times per week in the evenings and would often perform in the Arbeiterheims (worker's homes). Here was the birth of Zipper's ideas about bringing music to the common man and not just the elite and fancy concert halls.

Zipper, like many of his friends, was a sort of musical gypsy in those days taking jobs wherever he could find them. For example, he was also the conductor of a Jewish Sports Association orchestra. The Association (called "Hakoah") had a terrific soccer team in a Vienna major league, but also had an amateur orchestra which performed all over town. He also conducted in the arbeiterheim throughout Vienna as many working class districts had pick-up orchestras composed of union musicians, some Academy students, and some local workers.

During these years Trudl would come to all of Zipper's performances when she was in town. However, by 1930 Trudl Dubsky had traveled all over Europe. Everywhere she went the press reports were glowing. Audiences were particularly enthralled with her astonishing leaps and elevation. She could fly through the air with seeming effortless grace and her leaps would cause spectators and critics as well to gasp. In the Slavic languages, Dubsky is a colloquial expression meaning "little fanny" so wherever she went it was misspelled: Disbsky, Dobsky, Doska, etc. In addition, at only 17 years of age she was invited to London to teach at the Bedford College for Women. She was asked to work with Miss Jeannette Rutherston in founding a dance school in London - the Rutherston-Dubsky School. Also, she choreographed a Handel ballet, "A Woman's Privilege" for Sir Thomas Beecham. Several times Zipper visited her in London and often accompanied her at the piano in dance recitals.

The early years of the 1930's were, for Zipper and Trudl, a time of exciting but hectic commuting between London and first Ingolstadt and later Dusseldorf. They would meet on both sides of the Channel and would spend vacations together. Also, they corresponded at least three times a week. By now they knew they would marry one day and both had given up any involvements with others. Their careers at this point made marriage temporarily impossible but they knew in time this would be resolved.

In addition to his conducting jobs Zipper also picked up extra money writing orchestra scores, as a sort of subcontractor, for another composer, who was also a bit of a character, Eugen Zador. Zador, a Hungarian born and Vienna-trained musician, received his Doctor of Philosophy in 1921 and settled in to teach at the Neues Konservatorium until the Anschluss in 1938 when he emigrated to America and became a successful and prosperous orchestrator of film scores in Hollywood. During the 1930's he orchestrated a steady flow of operettas, composed by "God knows who" mused Zipper, and Zador paid Zipper to orchestrate many of these. Zipper's memories of Zador are quite amusing:

> I don't recall when and under what circumstances I met Eugen Zador, the Hungarian-Viennese composer. It must have been sometime in 1924 or 1925 when he asked me to tutor a young, rather pretty girl, a student of the Vienna Conservatory who had difficulties with her studies of music theory and Zador felt that she may fail in her examination regarding functional harmony. I believe it must have been at that time when my rather extended working relationship with Zador started.
>
> He derived a considerable part of his income by orchestrating the music of a number of Vienna's operetta composers, the kind of work that quite a few of the "learned" Viennese composers did anonymously to earn part of their livelihood. Arnold Schoenberg was one of them.
>
> Zador who combined considerable charm with a good deal of Hungarian shrewdness regularly accepted or hustled more commissions than he possibly could deliver and it was in the middle of the Twenties when I became his "subcontractor."
>
> I never knew whose music I was orchestrating. I only could judge from its quality whether their author was a major or a minor composer. With the "minor's" music, more often than not, I had to correct faulty harmonic progressions.
>
> In later years and also after my return from Germany, I frequently became a ghostwriter for Zador's far-reaching connections. He combined his teaching activities at the Vienna Conservatory with a couple of days teaching at the Budapest Conservatory every other week. Judging from the number and the variety of orders I received for his Hungarian· interests, he must have had quite a few students or would-be composers there. These orders were of a rather serious nature and most likely were designed to help students to deliver the required number of works for their graduation. Of course, this was only an assumption on my part because Zador never told me and I never asked. Zador's order I received usually over the telephone in a very precise way. For instance, he would call me on a Monday morning ordering the first movement of a piano sonata in f minor, time signature 6/8, Allegro, style between Brahms and early Max Reger, minimum 8 pages, delivery the following Saturday not

later than 4:00 p.m. Or, last movement of a string quartet in D major, sonata-rondo form, time signature 2/4, Presto, French Impressionist style.

My working relationship with Zador provided me not only with some income but also with a great deal of fun. He never ceased to amuse me unintentionally. His style in practically everything was the opposite of mine and therefore attractive to me.

When Trudl and I met him again in Los Angeles (in the 1970's) we always had a wonderful time after a meeting recalling and discussing the charming, amazing "Hungarianism" of Eugen Zador.

One day he asked me whether he paid me well for the many scores I did for him and when I answered: "No, very shabbily," he said" "Hm, hm, I should have been ashamed."

When I inquired when and under what circumstances he left Europe, he said: "Actually I did not have to leave, but I wanted to, although, as is the case, I am nearly not Jewish." (N¯mlich ich bin fast kein Jude") This was vintage Zadorism!

Zipper's conducting career began to grow as he first took a full-time position in Ingolstadt in Bavaria and later, in 1932, in Düsseldorf on the Rhine. He was in Düsseldorf in 1932 when Albert Schweitzer traveled to Europe to pay tribute to the hundredth anniversary of Goethe's death. As a friend of long standing of Hans Weisbach, General Music Director of Düsseldorf and his wife, Schweitzer was invited to stay at his home while he was in Düsseldorf. Upon his arrival, Zipper, who often practiced piano at the Weisbach home, opened the door for him. Zipper vividly remembers the powerful impression his sheer physical presence made on him, his enormous, wide forehead, his penetrating eyes, the thick strains of hair, the bushy "Nietzsche moustache," the unusually broad shoulders. Everything about him seemed to be larger than life-size.

Zipper took Schweitzer upstairs to an exuberant reunion with the Weisbachs. Soon they engaged in a lively conversation about politics, the arts, Lambarene and Goethe. Schweitzer optimistically characterized the Nazi movement and Adolf Hitler as an aberration of the Twentieth Century which could not endure for long. In this connection the conversation turned to Richard Wagner whom Schweitzer characterized with these words: "What an overpowering genius! To write such original, significant and great works with so little talent."

Finally, he turned to Zipper asking him about his background, the position he was occupying in Düsseldorf, where and when he conducted and when Weisbach mentioned that Zipper was composing a great deal,

Schweitzer asked that he play something he recently had written. Schweitzer sat with Zipper at the piano, intently looking at the manuscript (of a 12 minute orchestral piece written for a ballet number based on "The Emperor's New Clothes") and afterwards making significant comments. What impressed Zipper most was Schweitzer's ability to involve himself for a time fully and exclusively with another person. He gave one the feeling that while he was asking questions and listening to answers nothing else in the world mattered to him, nothing could detract from his genuine interest in the person to whom he was talking. Schweitzer was a model in more ways than one.

The main purpose of Schweitzer's visit was to deliver a major address over the national radio, on March 22, 1932, commemorating the death of Goethe in his native city of Frankfort. On March 3 he gave a preview of this address at the intermission of a concert for which Zipper prepared the orchestra and chorus and which Weisbach conducted. Schweitzer, without specifically mentioning the Nazis, issued a stern warning against the rising fascist tide:

> After all what is now taking place in this terrible epoch of ours except a gigantic repetiton of the drama of Faust upon the stage of the world? The cottage of Philemon and Baucis burns with a thousand tongues of flame! In deeds of violence and murders a thousandfold, a brutalized humanity plays its cruel game! Mephistopheles leers at us with a thousand grimaces! In a thousand different ways mankind has been persuaded to give up its natural relations with reality, and to seek its welfare in the magic formulas of some kind of economic and social witchcraft, by which the possibility of freeing itself from economic and social misery is only still further removed!
>
> And the tragic meaning of these magic formulas, to whatever kind of economic and social witchcraft they may belong, is always just this, that the individual must give up his own material and spiritual personality and must live only as one of the spiritually restless and materialistic multitude which claims control over him.

Schweitzer, receiving cheers from his adoring audience of well-educated, concert goers, continued to show the relevance of Goethe:

> And now, a hundred years after his death, it has come to pass, through a calamitous development determined by events and through the influence of that development upon the economic, the social, and the spiritual everywhere, that the material and the spiritual independence of the individual, so far as it is not already destroyed, is most seriously threatened. We remember the death of Goethe in this most portentous and fateful hour which has ever struck for mankind. He is summoned as no other poet or thinker to speak to us in this hour. He looks into our time as one most out of place in it, for he has abso-

lutely nothing in common with the spirit in which it lives. But he comes with the most timely counsel, for he has something to say to it which it is essential that it should hear.

What does he say to it?

He says to it, that the frightful drama that is being enacted in it can come to an end only when it sets aside the economic and social magic in which it has trusted, when it forgets the magic formulas with which it deludes itself, when it is resolved to return at any cost to a natural relationship with reality.

To the individual he says: Do not abandon the ideal of personality, even when it runs counter to developing circumstances. Do not give it up for lost even when it seems no longer tenable in the presence of opportunistic theories which would make the spiritual conform only to the material. Remain men in possession of your own souls! Do not become human things which have offered hospitality to souls which conform to the will of the masses and beat in time with it.[26]

Prior to the intermission the orchestra played Handel's oratorio "Acis and Galatea," followed by Mendelssohn's "The First Walpurgis-Night" (Op. 60), a piece composed initially one hundred years earlier and based upon a poem of Goethe and the Walpurgis Night of *Faust, Part I*. After Schweitzer's intermission speech, the concert concluded with the finale of Mahler's Symphony No. 8 in E Major ("The Symphony of a Thousand") which is based on the final scene of Goethe's *Faust, II*. The juxtaposition of Schweitzer's warning of the impending and inevitable tragedy which results from humankind's abandonment of individual judgment to mass magic combined with the text of Goethe which Mahler wrote "draws us by its mystical force" was extraordinarily poignant. Particularly ironic was the experience of listening to the gorgeous musical expression of Goethe's text which glorifies the image of the Eternal Feminine as the resting place of the human soul at a time in history when the masculine force was beginning to express itself in one of its most ugly and barbarous chapters in the history of mankind.

Throughout Zipper's pre-Hitler-Chancellor days in Dusseldorf many other celebrities visited the big Weisbach house at the "Hofgarten." One day Zipper had dinner with Weisbach, Paul Hindemith (whose music Zipper had recently performed in Vienna) and Igor Stravinsky. Weisbach had purchased a toy electric train, quite an elaborate system, for his son. It spanned through three rooms and had three stations. Stravinsky was completely fascinated so it was determined that Weisbach would run the controls while Zipper, Stravinsky and Hindemith would each man one of the three stations. They also decided to set three trains in motion according to the elaborate schedule which Stravinsky, in typical fashion, would design. Stravinsky became totally and seriously involved and set meticulous and precise time tables. The slightest deviation, he warned, would cause disaster. Weisbach erred causing a huge collision. Stravinsky became quite upset, giving Weisbach a lecture on exactness while Zipper and Hindemith howled with laughter. The game continued well over an hour with Stravinsky demanding exactitude while the other three laughed until tears came to their eyes.

On another evening, Prokofiev exhibited his amazing piano technique playing a recent sonata. And on other evenings the guests included Darius Milhaud, William Walton, Kurt Weill, and many young composers including Zipper's friend, the young German composer, Wolfgang Fortner. More than 30 years later, in Manila, while Zipper was conducting a rehearsal of Schoenberg's *Transfigured Night* ("Verklärte Nacht") he suddenly heard behind him a loud voice exclaiming: "Herbert, you are still at it." It was the elderly Wolfgang Fornter standing with the equally elderly German composer Boris Blacher. (They were on a tour through the Far East.)

While in Germany Zipper attended Hitler rallies on at least six occasions in places such as Munich, Cologne and Düsseldorf. He was curious to understand the growing attraction of this man. However, he could not comprehend the appeal. He saw him as a vulgar, graceless, semi-illiterate maniac who spoke with bad grammar and little style. At this time he also read *Mein Kampf* and thought it to be stupid, simplistic nonsense. The book, however, made him feel uneasy for he could see its potential appeal to the semi-educated class which Zipper designated as "the middle slime." It was, nevertheless, terrifying to witness the growing anti-Jewish sentiment, particularly among people who knew no Jews.

Particularly disturbing was the book burning which Zipper witnessed in Düsseldorf in May of 1933. To stand and watch thousands of books go up in flames was to Zipper a terrifying atrocity against intellect, against civilization, against all that he valued. He watched books by authors such as Sigmund Freud, Sholom Asch, Erich Maria Remarque, Arthur Schnitzler, Karl Marx and Stefan Zweig trashed and burned as "junk." He could not, however, figure out why Maxim Gorky and Romain Rolland were included in the flames... The German poet Heinrich Heine had written in 1820, "this was but a prelude; where books are burnt human-beings will be burnt in the end." He was, as it turned out, a prophet one hundred and ten years ahead of his time.

On January 30, 1933 the die was cast and overnight the latent and growing anti-semitism became a national policy. General Kurt von Schleicher resigned as Chancellor of the German government and Hindenberg was persuaded to appoint as the new Chancellor, the leader of the Nazi party, Adolph Hitler. A French visitor to Vienna, Paul Painleve, upon receiving the news, said: "Today, perhaps, will mark the death of European culture. And this in the Twentieth Century... poor, poor Austria."[27] During that evening, January 30, 1933, Zipper had dinner with the Director of the Düsseldorf Art Academy and the Director of the Medical School. At one point in the dinner Zipper lifted his wine glass and said: "Let us raise our glasses for today marks the death-sentence of German culture." The five months after January 30 were for Zipper profoundly depressing. At that time, Zipper was living in a pension next to the music director of the orchestra. Living there as well were a painter named Moll, the director of the Art Academy, who was outspokenly anti-Nazi, and a police captain, a German nobleman also opposed to Hitler. But in the week that Hitler came to power the police captain began to "modify" his views. He said, "Of course I don't like him (Hitler) but at least now we know what to do! Life is becoming much simpler — I get clear orders and know exactly how to pass them on - no questions." Moll and his daughter exchanged knowing glances with each other and with Zipper. The owner of the pension agreed saying, "We are all going to be in trouble if we don't conform with the powers that be." It had begun.

Within two weeks the good people of Düsseldorf who had been Zipper's "friends" began avoiding their conductor on the streets. To illustrate, since coming to the Staedtische Musikverein and the conservatory in Düsseldorf Zipper had grown close to the general music director of the city, Hans Weisbach. He came to his house almost every day where they discussed the orchestra, the school, problems, music, and ideas. On March 27, 1931, Weisbach had written the following letter to Herbert Zipper's father, Emil Zipper:

Dear Mr. Zipper,

> It weighs heavily on my conscience that I did not yet inform you about the activities of your Herbert, but I assume that he himself reported to you what happened here since our return from Vienna. These were most difficult weeks! The worst, the sickness of my dear wife and the new fight with the city.
> After our return from Vienna, however, we experienced first great joy! From all sides, I heard how happy everyone was about the work of your son. He is very well liked everywhere and I had the beautiful surprise that the chorus was faultlessly prepared. Imagine that I was sick in bed until 2 days before the concert so that I could appear only at the dress rehearsal. If Herbert would not have prepared everything to the last detail I would not have been able to conduct the concert. It is unfortunate that one took just this concert as pretext to

attack me. I also was sorry for Herbert that we could not celebrate with unmixed joy the fruits of his work. However, besides Herbert's unusual musicality and artistry, we have learned to value him as a wonderful human being with a very firm character, so much so that I have to congratulate you for such a son. In the meantime, the events of the last weeks during which Herbert rendered the most valuable help to us and during which he proved to be a most valuable friend, so much so that, we grew together even more. There is much that should be told additionally but we are now involved with a great deal of work that for the moment I just want to tell you and your lovely wife that we are exceedingly happy to have your good son with us.

With my friendly greetings, your

Hans Weisbach

And after January 30, 1933, Zipper received a message from Weisbach not to come to the house again. He never saw or spoke to him again. Three weeks later one friendly member of the municipal chorus he was conducting came to his home at 10:00 in the evening and told him to leave immediately! That night he packed and traveled to Utrecht, Holland and stayed there for three days. Soon his friend called and said it would be relatively safe to return but that he should stay away from the chorus because there were "party members" out to get him. He resigned his position as conductor of the chorus.

In February 1933, Zipper received additional distressing news. Jeanette Ruthereton wrote him a long letter informing him that Trudl, after a recent performance, had come down with a high fever, had gone to a hospital where she was diagnosed as having tuberculosis. Zipper immediately set out for London and visited her for twenty-four hours. He found her in utter despair, fearing that her career was finished. He did his best to reassure her and then took the four-hour boat trip from Dover to Ostende. Later he traveled to Cologne to meet Trudl's father who was on his way to England to see Trudl. He then returned to his teaching post where he now felt like an outcast. In the summer of 1933, Trudl soon returned to Vienna to receive pneumothorax treatment from a specialist, Dr. Egon Waltuch. In 1934 she was able to resume practicing and in 1935 resumed dancing in performances with the Bodenwieser Company.

In late February 1933, he was warned again and once more left town this time for a week. On April 1, 1933 an official national Jewish boycott day was decreed and Zipper contemplated leaving for home. A sense of duty to his students and classes compelled him to stay in Düsseldorf until June. In June 1933 he left to return to Vienna. He went to the train station with a large number of other artists whose contracts had expired, refugees from the old Austrian Empire whose seasons were over in June and who were leaving the many theatres and opera houses to retreat to the apparent safety of Austria, Hungary, and Czechoslovakia. At every stop more artists would board the train; it was a strangely grim reunion among many friends and acquaintances of Zipper. To be an artist, a teacher, young and enthusiastic, passionate, to be forced to sneak out of town in the dark was to say the least discouraging. It was, moreover, only the beginning.

The years from June of 1933 to March of 1938 were for Zipper years of feverish creativity and profound dismay. It became increasingly clear that a plague was gradually infecting Europe. Zipper's response was essentially twofold: to use his creative gifts in celebrating the human spirit and to do what he could to oppose the growing intolerance and violence.

Now, at 29 years of age, he was back in Vienna. Because her mother was dying of cancer, Trudl had returned to Vienna and was again teaching and dancing for Madame Bodenwieser. Again they postponed marriage as their lives were too unsettled, jobs were scarce, there was very little money, and even less security. They were certain they would marry some day. Zipper was living at home while Trudl stayed at the Dubsky house with her brother where Zipper and Trudl would go to be alone. Meanwhile, the city was now bursting with musicians and artists who, like Zipper were fleeing the Nazi humiliations. Zipper and other musicians did not, however, return to a country free from the constrictions of fascism. Since the time Zipper had left for Dusseldorf in 1931, Austria had moved farther and farther to the Right. The Depression had brought latent tensions between the Socialists and the Right Wing Christian Socials out into the open. Engelbert Dollfuss who became Chancellor of Austria on May 20, 1932 managed in March of 1933 effectively to end parliamentary democracy in Austria. From then on he tried both to curb the rights of the Socialists as well as to resist the Nazi Party. However, in order to resist the Nazi pressure, Dollfuss had to accept a different kind of pressure from Italian dictator Benito Mussolini who promised to help against the Nazis on condition that Dollfuss would make radical reforms along more fascistic lines. Dollfuss also had to try to control the Right Wing extremist Heimwehr which was trying to wrest control from him and to provoke the Socialists into a civil war. Finally the tensions erupted in violence. The Socialists mobilized and announced a general strike. It was a dismal failure. For three days from February 12, to February 15, 1934 there was fighting in the streets of Vienna but the disorganized Socialists were easily subdued by the police and the army. The debacle ended with the shelling of worker's apartments, the execution of nine socialist leaders, and the dissolution of the Socialist Party. Karl Seitz, the mayor of Vienna, was arrested and replaced by a more right-wing politician and while the number of deaths was reported in the hundreds, some have estimated that there may have been over 1000 members of the Schutzbund killed. Red Vienna was virtually destroyed. Elias Canetti, winner of the Nobel Prize for Literature in 1981, was in Vienna in 1934 and describes his reaction to the events of February:

> Then in February 1934, the power of the Vienna municipal government was broken. Its leaders were despondent. It was as though all their work had been in vain. What was new and original in Vienna had been wiped out. What remained was the memory of an earlier Vienna, which was not far enough back to be exonerated from its share of guilt for the First World War, into which it had maneuvered itself. The local hope that had stood up to poverty and unemployment was gone. Many who could not live in such a void were infected with the German plague and hoped to achieve a better life by being absorbed into the larger country. Most failed to see that the actual consequence could only be a new war, and when the few who saw clearly pointed this out, they refused to believe it.[28]

As almost a footnote, one of those who refused to see or believe what was happening was one of Zipper's heroes, the formerly radical and progressive social critic, Karl Kraus. Kraus was one of the intellectual casualties of the events of February 1934. Canetti desribes very well the reaciton of intellectuals like Zipper and himself to Kraus's move to right. Canetti writes of his reaction in 1936 when he heard that Kraus had died:

> Karl Kraus has died recently and, true enough, I hadn't gone to his funeral. I had been terribly disillusioned after the events of February 1934. He had come out in support of Dollfuss and had said not a word in condemnation of the civil war in the streets of Vienna. All his followers, literally all, had dropped him. He still gave small, obscure readings that no one knew about; no one wanted to know about them, let alone attend them. It was as if Karl Kraus had ceased to exist.[29]

To Zipper that Karl Kraus would support Dollfuss was unthinkable. His only explanation was that old men sometimes do inconsistent and unexplainable things — Hindenburg and Deng Xiao Ping (1989), he cites as examples. But like Canetti, Zipper recalls discussing with his close friend, Eric Simon, and with others, the sadness of Kraus's defection from progressivism.

During the three days of fighting in February, Zipper himself had brought food to the Socialist forces but he had not participated in the fighting. For one thing he was both intellectually and emotionally opposed to violence. Ever since he had accompanied a hunting expedition at age thirteen and had observed a beautiful deer felled before his eyes, he had hated guns and violence. But more than that, in February of 1934, he was still more a political observer than an activist. He had just returned to Austria and was still intent upon becoming a conductor and a composer. In his eyes the arts were a means of transmitting culture, of providing elevating experiences, of enlightening men's souls. He did not yet fully embrace the connections between art and issues of the day. Thus while his sympathies were with the Socialists, he was not ready yet to take action. Rather than focusing his attention on politics, Zipper turned his attention to music.

For not the first and not to be the last time Zipper created a new orchestra. With the financial help of his friend Eric Simon's father and others - including noblemen such as Count Esterhazy, the Vienna Konzert Orchestra was organized. And the orchestra enjoyed a successful season until July of 1934. For this fateful summer season the orchestra had rented an outdoor performing area in the palace gardens (Burggarten) and had completely sold out their season tickets. However, on July 25, the day before the opening performance, Chancellor Dollfuss was assassinated by the Nazis who had made an abortive attempt to take over the Austrian government. The park was closed and placed off limits for the summer. All ticket sales were refunded, the orchestra was financially ruined, and Zipper was out of a job.

Characteristically, Zipper recalls some lighter moments. One morning, soon after his return to Vienna, Zipper was strolling with his friend and colleague the conductor Paul Breisach, on the Ringstrasse. When they passed the Hotel Imperial, the famous conductor Bruno Walter, on his way to the opera, joined them. The conversation immediately turned to the precarious political situation and Breisach complained that in contrast to Walter who was already an international celebrity greeted with open arms everywhere in the world, he and Zipper were at the beginning of their careers and their chances were very slim in and outside of a Vienna which was already over-crowded with returning artists from Germany. Walter abruptly stopped and offered one of his typically amusing and somewhat 'off-the-wall' epigrams: "One ought to open up Peru; also Spain is not yet fully musically saturated." ("Man m'sste Peru erschliessen; auch Spanien ist noch nicht ganz durchmusiziert.")

In the midst of growing restrictions on European Jews, Zipper still found it possible to travel. One trip took him to Russia in 1935. During the mid-30's there was a virtual procession of European Jewish conductors, all refugees from Nazi oppression, who lost their jobs in Germany and were offered guest conducting jobs in Russia. Among them were: Erich

Kleiber, former Generalmusik Director of the Berlin State Opera (1923-35); Fritz Stiedry, a Viennese who had been the music director of the Berlin Municipal Opera (1929-33); Eugen Szenkar, a Hungarian conductor at the Cologne Opera (1924-33) who married a non-Jewish daughter of a Rhine Ruhr industrialist whom Zipper recalls as one of the most beautiful women he ever saw. Another was Paul Breisach, former general music director in Mainz, who was a good friend of Zipper and who arranged for an invitation for Zipper to come to Russia as guest conductor of the Moscow Radio Symphony Orchestra.

At this juncture Zipper and Trudl decided that if he was offered a secure position, she would join him and they would be married. Had fate so decreed, they might have married and lived as emigrees in Russia. However, this was not to be. Nevertheless, although Zipper was forced to leave Trudl for four months, September - December, 1935, he was at least re-united with his friend Eric Simon who was already a clarinetist in the Moscow Symphony. Zipper stayed at the Moskwa Hotel but often visited Simon in the home where he was living.

One evening while visiting Simon, who had to leave early, Zipper told Simon's housekeeper, who they fondly called "Babushka" (old woman), that she need not fix him a meal as he was about to leave to see *King Lear* at the Stanislawski Theatre. "Oh wonderful," she said, "I've seen it three times already." Such was the democratization of culture in this Soviet State. *Lear* was for Zipper also a memorable event. In each actor, every gesture, every movement, was organically wedded to fit the text. It was as though the distinction between life and art were completely obliterated. So it was also at the Stanislavsky production of the opera, *The Barber of Seville* which ran for hundreds of nights, like a Broadway smash. "You almost forgot," Zipper fondly reminisces, "that they were singing on stage!" Rarely had he seen opera so non-artificial.

The orchestra he conducted was distinctly mediocre. One week he experienced difficulty teaching the orchestra a new piece by a Soviet composer. So he went to the Radio Commissioner to ask for extra rehearsals.

Commissioner: "So when is broadcast?"
Zipper: "Tuesday."
Commissioner: "So, will not be Tuesday, will be Thursday."
There were some advantages in a totalitarian state.

Just before Christmas, in December 1935, he returned to Vienna. He had received a tentative offer to become the music director of the new radio station in Stalino near Moscow. But the offer was changed to Khabarovsk, in Siberia. He respectfully said, "No, thank you." Remaining in Austria, he devoted himself to writing music for the political cabarets and for Radio Vienna, (RAVAG) a monthly half-hour broadcast "News of the Month" in the form of a cantata for orchestra, chorus and soloists. Some of these contained distinctly anti-Nazi implications.

In 1936, Zipper traveled to England to conduct a Ballet in Covent Garden. Jeanette Rutherston's husband, Christopher Powell, invited him to attend a session of Parliament where he heard Churchill imploring England to oppose Hitler now, "War," said Churchill, "will surely come if we don't act forcefully."

In September of 1937 the love affair of Herbert Zipper and Trudl Dubsky was again interrupted. Trudl was invited to take a one-year appointment in Manila to help establish a dance department at the University of the Philippines. They planned to reunite in the fall of 1938 in America. Zipper was now working on an opera. He had been commissioned by Paul Csonka, Director of the Salzburg Opera Guild, to compose the music for an opera version of Oscar Wilde's *The Importance of Being Ernest*, with libretto by Hans Weigel, for a tour to America. (Three quarters of the first act survives today.) The opera was to be performed by the Salzburg Opera Guild which had been invited to America by Sol Hurok. Zipper and Trudl planned, therefore, to be married in America. The Philippine adventure for Trudl was to be only a one-year appointment. Zipper took Trudl to the train station which would take her to her ship in Trieste. At Trieste, she found in her cabin a long letter and three dozen roses and she was met by a letter at every stop of her journey to Manila - Brindisi, Bombay, Colombo, Singapore, Hong Kong.

Zipper's main source of income during the years 1933-38 was as a composer for the remarkable underground theatres which sprang up in Vienna. Historian Joseph Gregor provides the setting for their evolution:

> Since public life in the Austria of those years was turning increasingly authoritarian it became simply impossible to gain admittance to the circle of existing theaters that were united through commercial interests and state financing; that is to say, it became impossible to obtain a license for a new theater. But the Theater could not be suppressed, and found different outlets. [30]

The main outlet was the underground theatre, referred to as Kleinkunstbühnen (little art theatres) held in basements of coffee houses which could partially escape government licenses and censorship by housing 99 people or less. In the wake of Herr Hitler's rise to power in Germany, Dollfuss had outlawed all open left-wing political and literary activity.

In his collection of works by contemporary playwright Jura Soyfer, Horst Jarka writes that:

Unconventional as these Little Theaters were, they never put on antiartistic airs. On the contrary, they were artistically extremely ambitious. This is evident from their repertoire and from the fact that several actors and directors who later became famous started their careers in these theaters. More significantly, perhaps, it is evident from the emergence of a new dramatic form which, initiated by the Viennese cabaret writer Rudolf Weys in 1934, soon became characteristic of the Little Theaters. In the conventional cabarets the program, though perhaps loosely unified by a common theme, essentially consisted of unconnected numbers: sketches, chansons, poetry recitations, and various other soli. In the programs of the Viennese Little Theaters such numbers no longer constituted the whole program but only its beginning and end. They were the frame around the core of the program: the "middle pieces" (Mittelstücke) which consisted of a sequence of connected scenes and formed a play that lasted about fifty minutes.[31]

In Vienna the main market area was the Nachmarkt located just a few blocks from the Cafe Dobner, opposite the Sessesion Building. In the basement of the cafe was the Literatur am Nachmarkt, the tiffany of the underground caberets. It offered the most sophisticated literature and the most serious music. Here Zipper was the 'home-composer' from 1934 to 1936. (After 1936 he focused his attention on writing an opera.) During these months Zipper would often work at the coffee house below the cabaret at the Literature Nachmarkt. The various writers would rush downstairs with the text and he would begin composing right there. Or sometimes someone would run over from the Theatre An Der Wien (where *Fidelio* received its first performance) next door to ask Zipper for an instant chanson for this or that cabaret and he would dash one off. Often he was given little time to whip out an entire two-hour show.

Zipper became good friends with several of the leading writers for the underground theatre - Rudolf Weys, Hans Weigel, Rudolph Spitz and Jura Soyfer. Weys, Weigel, and Spitz asked Zipper to write the music for many of their productions. Soyfer who was to play a more prominent role in Zipper's life in Dachau and Buchenwald, provides an interesting political contrast with Zipper. After the failure of the General Strike in February of 1934, Zipper was disappointed but not inspired to take action. Soyfer, however, disillusioned and angry with the ineffectual Socialist leadership, decided to join the underground Communist Party. He was arrested once in November of 1937 and kept in jail for three months without trial. By joining the underground theatre, Zipper had expanded his consciousness of the function of art from the transmission of culture to social criticism but he was still not comfortable with this function. He wrote his cabaret music under a pseudonym (Walter Drix) fearing that this kind of music would tarnish his emerging reputation as a classical composer. He was still the traditional Viennese serious musician, anti-facist in spirit and in theory, but not yet a political activist. While Soyfer sat in jail, Zipper composed cantatas and wrote cabaret music as Walter Drix.

Most of Zipper's music was, to his knowledge, lost during the war years. What remains are portions of a work he wrote with Hans Weigel, *The Song Of War* (1936). It was written just after Zipper returned from Russia in December 1935 at the time of Hitler's massive rearmament and six songs were preserved by Zipper's mother. The songs are in Zipper's files. Also, one of Zipper's first songs, "Die Kleinen Nebensachen," text by Rudolf Weys, (The Little Unimportant Things) survives somewhere in Munich since Zipper received a royalty in the 1960's from a Munich radio show.

Today, as Horst Jarka writes, "it is possible only to a limited extent to judge the literary merits of these plays because most of them were never printed. The only texts available in book form are two complete Mittelstucke and a few scenes by Rudolf Weys, and... four plays by Jura Soyfer."[32] Soyfer had first written dramatic texts for celebrations of the Socialist Party but after strict censorship laws were passed in 1934, he was forced to turn to the little theatres for artistic expression. "To see his plays performed at all Soyfer was obliged to couch his criticism in the traditional garb of old Viennese Popular Comedy, and in so doing he developed both his dramatic and verbal imagination." [33]

Zipper and Weigel collaborated on other works, one of which was named "Der Tag der Musikpflege" (The Day of Nurturing Music). It was a satirical piece setting forth a supposed Music Day, like Mother's Day or Veteran's Day. That Vienna with its rich history of Mozart, Beethoven, Schubert et. al., would need a day to devote to music was, of course, preposterous and was itself highly amusing to the Viennese. The play unfolded by having everything set to music - a family gargling and brushing their teeth musically, cooking a favorite recipe, (Kaiserschmarrn") dictating a business letter, eating in a restuarant, having stomach aches and going to the doctor, all sung in different opera styles. At one point a teacher in a classroom sings a grammar declension to his students in the rhythm of a tango. The incongruity of singing about trivia was hilarious to the Viennese. It was as though one dressed up in a tuxedo and top hat and wore tennis shoes. The play was one of Zipper's most popular and provided a welcome and humorous respite from serious social and political criticism and satire.

Josephine (Fini) Rudiger, a young cabaret and theatre actress (who later moved to California and became a noted artist, Fini Littlejohn) recalls that acting in Zipper's "Die Tag Der Musik" was a thrill. Zipper, she recalls, was a serious and glamorous composer whose musical satire was both elegant and hilarious.

The subject matter of these coffee house performances, while humorous, was deadly serious. Most of the thrust of the content was anti-fascist. One such piece was "The Newspaper Opera," Libretto by Spitz and music by Herbert Zipper. The final fuge (Schlussfuge) was sung to the following text (translated by H. Zipper):

> "Age old might whether right or wrong
> Remains victorious to the end of the song."

There was no dialogue; every song was filled with strong political implications. It was a biting anti-fascist satire and a condemnation of the press which bowed to the pressure of the time. Part of the text survives in Zipper's own archives. The cabaret programs changed about every six weeks. Thus Zipper was constantly writing new material often working until late hours. One piece contained such a vehement denunciation of Hitler that the police, who came to all dress rehearsals, feared a riot and refused to allow it to run. One song was a hilarious trio with Hitler, Goebbels, and Göring (played by a small actor with three huge pillows in his stomach) who were incompetently trying to knock down Jewish pins in a bowling alley. It was particularly insulting to the three Nazi top dogs.

Jarka sums up this period by saying:

> Perhaps more than any other in Vienna, the unfunded, makeshift Little Theaters proved that even in the gloomy years of the Depression the originality of the Austrian theater had not faded. It is true that these Little Theaters were short-lived, as short-lived as was the corporate state of the Dollfuss-Schuschnigg era whose fascist tendencies they criticized. Nevertheless, the five years of their activity form a significant part of Viennese theater life in the thirties that thus far has been denied the serious consideration it deserves. [34]

It was a unique period of creativity, improvisation, profundity and hilarity amidst the growing gloom.

On February 12 of 1938, as Herbert Zipper was writing what was to be his last cantata for the radio show, Chancellor Kurt Von Schuschnigg traveled to Hitler's Bavarian mountain retreat in Berchtesgarden. After hours of enduring Hitler's verbal abuse he secretly agreed to Hitler's demands for an Anschluss, a reunification of Germany and Austria. Zipper describes the events which followed from his perspective at the time:

> "When the news was broadcast that Schuschnigg was meeting with Hitler on February 12, 1938 in Berchtesgarden I was gravely apprehensive. When

Ernest Simon, Eric's father called me to solicit my opinion regarding the situation. I advised him to leave the country. He did with his family.

During the following weeks little leaked out of what happened behind the scene and rumors mushroomed.

On February 20, Hitler addressed the Reichstag in regard to the Austrian situation. He had some kind words for Schuschnigg, but those of us who were mindful of Hitler's insidious treacheries became aware of the underlying threats contained in his speech.

On February 24, Schuschnigg answered Hitler's speech with a highly patriotic address to the Austrian Bundestag. He mentioned that the concessions made to Germany in the past and recently have reached the limit and that Austria would never voluntarily give up its independence.

During these days I tried to focus my mind in vain on concluding the second act of the opera I was writing for the "Salzburg Opera Guild." I hardly could concentrate on my work and what I wrote then I had to discard. There was an oppressive atmosphere abroad comparable to the tension that is in the air before a thunderstorm breaks loose.

On March 9, Schuschnigg, who then was in Innsbruck, gave a speech that was nationally broadcast. He announced that he ordered a plebiscite to be held within four days, that is on Sunday March 13th. There will be only two questions to be answered; namely whether Austria should retain its independence, or whether Austria should become a part of the German Reich.

There was euphoria all over Vienna with an undertone of nervous apprehension. Nobody was in doubt that there would be an overwhelming majority for independence but at the same time there was fear that Hitler must be aware of the Austrian public's mood and may take drastic action to prevent the plebiscite.

After returning from Berchtesgarden, Schuschnigg had been faced with the most terrible decision of his life: to oppose Hitler and lead his country to a bloody and, no doubt, futile war or to accept annexation into the Third Reich. Like everyone in Austria the Zipper family was glued to their radio. Emil Zipper was in London on business. Rosie had gone to her bedroom and when the announcement came, during the evening of March 11, that the Chancellor would soon address the nation, the Zipper children - Walter, Herbert, Otto, Hedy and her new husband, Fritz Horwitz, gathered together with Rosie to listen. The plebiscite had been cancelled and Schuschnigg spoke, his voice trembling:

> Austrian men and women! This day has brought us face to face with a serious and decisive situation. It is my task to inform the Austrian people about the events of this day. The Government of the German Reich presented a time-limited ultimatum to the Federal President demanding that he appoint a

candidate chosen by the Reich Government to the office of Chancellor and also follow its suggestions when selecting the ministers to serve in that cabinet. Should the Federal President not accept this ultimatum then German troops would begin to cross our frontiers this very hour.

I wish to place on record before the world that the reports disseminated in Austria that the workers have revolted and that streams of blood have been shed, that the Government is incapable of mastering the situation and cannot ensure law and order, are fabrications from A to Z.

The Federal President has instructed me to inform the nation that we are giving way to brute force. Because we refuse to shed German blood even in this tragic hour, we have ordered our armed forces, should an invasion take place, to withdraw without serious resistance, and to await the decisions of the coming hours. The Federal President has asked the army's Inspector-General, General of Infantry Schilhawski, to assume command over all troops. All further orders for the armed forces will be issued by him.

So, in this hour, I bid farewell to the people of Austria with a German word and a wish from the bottom of my heart: 'God save Austria!'" [35]

The Zipper family was silent knowing in their hearts that they had just heard the death knoll of Vienna. After listening to the Haydn C Major ("The Emperor") Quartet (No. 3) for a few moments, Zipper got up and left his mother's bedroom to go to his own room. He needed to be alone. He was overcome with a feeling of despair and emptiness. He even had the urge to destroy every piece of music he had written, including the opera he was composing. Why bother to write music when Vienna and all that it stood for was lost? He had seen the Nazi rallies, the orgies of book burning, the fury and irrational hatred of the masses, the bigotry and hysteria. And having seen this, he knew that the glory of Vienna, the freedom to create, the creativity of this remarkable moment in history was coming to an end, probably forever. In a flash he had a glimpse of the future and he experienced, for the first time in his life true depression. He felt that he would never again be allowed to write music. He shoved all his music into a few drawers and for the next few months wrote not one note of music.

Franz Werfel, in a recently translated version of an unfinished manuscript from 1938-39, gives a novelist's view of the evening. In his novel *Cella* the narrator listens to Schuschnigg's speech in a coffee house:

> I sat in the Cafe Rebhuhn. I drank four black coffees. I heard the voice of the departing chancellor on the radio. His voice no longer sounded bombastically confident, it trembled and gasped. I noted a few sentences spoken by that heart-wrenching voice:
>
> "Since we do not, at any price, wish to shed the blood of our brothers, even in this earnest hour, we have ordered our army to retreat without resistance in case the Germans march in."

> And then, after taking a long breath, "And so I take my leave in this hour with German words and a wish from the bottom of my heart: Gott sch`tze Österreich! God protect Austria."
>
> I sat and drank my fifth black coffee. My pulse was racing. But, exhausted and uncomprehending, my head sank down almost to the marble tabletop. The voice on the radio yielded to a hollow silence. This silence was a gasping dread. This silence was the fate of the man who had spoken. Then came a solemn funeral march, to fill out the chasm between two eras, before a new voice began, presumably the voice of the twins. This music, by Haydn, blended with Haydn's old imperial anthem. Not only did the patrons of the coffeehouse vanish one by on, but so did the waiters, except for the hoary, gouty maitre d', who nodded at me knowingly.
>
> I found St. Stephan's Square bizarrely dead. All the people probably had their ears glued to radios. The evening was rather cold, the sky cloudless. The arc lamps seemed dimmer than normal. The black monster of the cathedral cowered as if trying to make itself less vulnerable to attack. The spire tapered off into invisibility.[36]

Another contemporary of Zipper's, George Clare, who was living in Vienna on this evening describes his reaction at the close of Schuschnigg's speech:

> They played the national anthem. After the last bars of Haydn's tune we all sat in utter silence for a few moments. Then, before any of us had had a chance to say anything, the sounds of hundreds of men shouting at the top of their voices could be heard. Still indistinct, still distant, it sounded threatening none the less. Those raucous voices grew louder, were coming closer.
>
> I rushed to the window and looked out into Nussdorferstrasse. It was still quite empty. A few moments. Then the first lorry came into sight. It was packed with shouting, screaming men. A huge swastika flag fluttered over their heads. Most of them had swastika armlets on their sleeves, some wore S.A. caps, some even steel helmets.
>
> Now we could hear clearly what they were shouting: 'Ein Volk, ein Reich, ein Führer!' they were chanting in chorus, followed by 'Ju-das verr-recke! Ju-das verr-recke!' ('Perish Judah!'). In English this sounds softer, less threatening, but in German, coming from a thousand throats, screaming it out in the full fury of their hate, as lorry after lorry with frenzied Nazis passed below our window, it is a sound one can never forget.[37]

The Nazi invasion of Austria occurred the next day, Saturday, March 12. Zipper and his family listened to the radio all day and didn't leave home in order to avoid physical danger. On Sunday they also stayed home. Monday, Zipper went to the radio station to collect his fee for his last composition and was thrown bodily into the streets. There he saw Jewish women forced to their knees to scrub anti-Nazi slogans off the sidewalks and walls. Most appalling was not only the scrubbing but the sight of the sidewalks lined with their fellow Viennese "citizens" cheering the indignities.

Observers have written that some of the worst anti-Semitic excesses in Europe took place in Vienna. An American newspaper correspondent witnessed the first days following the Anschluss:

> For the first few weeks, the behavior of the Vienna Nazis was worse than anything I had seen in Germany. There was an orgy of sadism. Day after day, large numbers of Jewish men and women could be seen scrubbing Schuschnigg signs off the sidewalk and cleaning the gutters. While they worked on their hands and knees with jeering storm troopers standing over them, crowds gathered to taunt them. Hundreds of Jews, men and women, were picked off the streets and put to work cleaning public latrines and the toilets of the barracks where the S.A. and S.S. were quartered. Tens of thousands more were jailed. Their worldly possessions were confiscated or stolen . . . Perhaps half of the city's 180,000 Jews managed, by the time the war started, to purchase their freedom to emigrate by handing over what they owned to the Nazis. [38]

During this time one of the Zipper cars was "requisitioned" by a Nazi gang. Friends lost their businesses. In one piano company that the Zippers knew, the non-Jewish technicians simply threw out the Jewish proprietors and took over the company. All Austrian passports were invalidated, taxes for a year in advance were now required to leave the country. Martin Gilbert, in his massive study of the period, *Holocaust*, describes the city after the invasion:

> Overnight, the Jews of Vienna, one sixth of the city's population, were deprived of all civil rights: the right to own property, large or small, the right to be employed or to give employment, the right to exercise their profession, any profession, the right to enter restaurants or cafes, public baths or public parks. Instead they experienced physical assault: the looting of shops, the breaking of heads, the tormenting of passers-by. A British journalist, G.E.R. Gedye, wrote, after the suicide of a young Jewish doctor and his mother in his own block of flats, 'From my window I could watch for many days how they would arrest Jewish passers-by — generally doctors, lawyers or merchants, for they preferred their victims to belong to the better educated classes — and force them to scrub, polish and beat carpets in the flat where the tragedy had taken place, while insisting that the doctor's non-Jewish maid should sit at ease in a chair and look on.'"[39]

The famous journalist William L. Shirer, who happened to be in Vienna at this time, writes of the cataclysmic takeover:

> And so Austria, as Austria, passed for the moment out of history, its very name suppressed by the Austrian who apparently never forgave it for not rec-

ognizing his true worth. Vienna becamse just another city of the Reich, a provincial district administrative center, withering away. The former Austrian tramp, now the mighty German dictator, had wiped his native land off the map and deprived its once glittering capital, which he thought had rejected him, of its last shred of glory and importance.[40]

Eugene Lennhoff, one time editor of the Vienna "Telegraph" published later in 1938 an account of these days in a book entitled *The Last Five Hours of Austria*. In this he quotes from a letter written by a friend who left Vienna just after the Nazi invasion. The letter is but one more first hand account of the nature of the times:

"Herr —, whom you know as a half-Jew and an active member of the Patriotic Front, has committed suicide. It is a tragedy, but he is one of so many of our friends who have met the same sad fate, that I should not be specially mentioning the case but for circumstances after his death which cause me to recount the story to all I can.

"After Herr —'s suicide the family had so little money that the funeral had to be of the very simplest character. The widow, who is also half-Jewish, and her two grown-up daughters, followed the hearse to the cemetery on foot. Along the road that leads to Simmering, they fell in with a party of Nazis, enjoying, as the song says, 'the free life of the Third Reich,' who stopped them and asked the ladies if they were Aryans. Obliged to admit that they were not, they were ordered to go down on their knees and scrub away the crosses painted on the pavement. The women burst into tears. The elder daughter begged of the men that they might first accompanying their father to his last resting place. The leader of the party glanced quickly at the tears, then said: 'Fall in, obey your orders at once and no nonsense. The dead can wait.'"[41]

During the night of the 12th to the 13th of March Emil Zipper called from London and said he was coming home. Fearing that his phone was tapped, Zipper replied, "Father, if you come home I'll never speak to you again." Father Zipper understood the double meaning. If he had come home, it would have been a catastrophe for the Zipper family. Outside Austria he could help — as, in fact, he did.

Zipper urged his family to leave the night Hitler's troops arrived. He still hoped to be reunited with Trudl in a few months in America. Although his family realized they must leave, they thought he was exaggerating the menace and, for the next two months, made preparations to leave, to secure visas and passports and to make the necessary arrangements. In the midst of these preparations on the morning of May 27th, 1938, a plainclothesman arrived at the Zipper home. He left with Otto, Walter, and Herbert Zipper.

Chapter V

Dachau

"Arbeit Macht Frei"

On May 31st, 1938, Herbert Zipper, the young composer, the conductor of the Dusseldorf Symphony, the Vienna Madrigal Chorus and others, the student of Joseph Marx, Maurice Ravel and Richard Strauss, the lover of Dostoyevsky and Goethe, the product of Europe's finest culture and education, found himself standing in the darkness of a boxcar, herded together with other confused men, nursing broken ribs and a swollen and closed eye and wondering what was to come. After the 13 hour ordeal, the train stopped at the Dachau concentration camp where the prisoners were chased out, a few stumbled out in the wrong direction and they were shot. They arrived at approximately 10:00 AM on a hot, sunshiny day and were ordered to stand in front of the camp without moving, eating, or pissing. Zipper, with the letter "Z" prisoners, was among the last to be admitted at sundown. Finally, they were sent to their assigned barracks and required to sign a paper saying they were now in "protective custody." One little man admonished, "Don't sign, you are signing your life away." He was dragged away and murdered. Zipper heard the guard say, "One breakfast less!"

The town of Dachau is situated just eleven miles northwest of Munich. The town stands on a hill at the summit of which is the Castle of the Wittelsbacher and the other sight is a parish church dating back to 1625. Prior to 1933 it had been a small cattle market town (first mentioned in 805 A.D.) with renowned breweries and comfortable taverns. Starting around 1870 it gained a new fame as a city which attracted painters and artists, hundreds of them, including names such as Carl Spitzweg, Max Liebermann, Louis Corinth, Ludwig Dill, Adolf Holzel, and Arthur Langhammer. Until 1933, it remained famous as an artists' colony. In 1914 a huge war powder factory was built to manufacture ammunition for the battlefields. After the war the factory was shut down and thousands were thrust onto welfare.

The presence of the empty factory was one inducement for Heinrich Himmler to choose Dachau as the place to erect his first Nazi camp. And on Wednesday, March 22, 1933 the following announcement appeared in the paper Münchner Neueste Nachrichten:

> "On Wednesday, March 22, 1933 the first concentration camp will be opened in the vicinity of Dachau. It can accommodate 5,000 people. We have adopted this measure, undeterred by paltry scruples, in the conviction that our action will help to restore calm to our country and is in the best interests of our people.
>
> Heinrich Himmler,
> Commission of Police for the City of Munich."

On March 23 the first sixty prisoners arrived. The facility was quickly enlarged to house large numbers of people. When Zipper arrived in 1938, there were already over 5000 prisoners: mostly communists and socialists (required to wear red stars), religious groups and 7th Day Adventists (the "Bibelforscher"), homosexuals (wearing pink stars and kept in a separate compound), a few criminals (wearing black stars), and only 225 Jews (wearing black and yellow stars). During the next month more than 1500 Jews would be sent to Dachau. And by the beginning of summer the population had increased to well over 9,000. The camp itself was a model of order:

> "The watchtowers on the wall which surrounded the concentration camp at Dachau allowed a striking view of the Bavarian Alps. The mountain peaks could be seen at times from within the camp as well. Along the inside face of the walls ran barbed wire fences, including an electrified one. Powerful projector lamps were set on the walls and on the inside fences, lighting the camp and its surroundings from sunset to dawn. The guards in the towers and those who sat above the single gate which led into the camp were armed with machine guns. The positions were guarded twenty-four hours a day. Armed patrols in black uniforms circled the camp on the outside, accompanied by terrifying guard dogs.
>
> Some thirty identical wooden barracks were built within the camp over the years, and served as living quarters for the prisoners. They stood one after the other, in two parallel rows separated by an avenue of poplars. Each barrack was meant to house about 200 prisoners in eight rooms, four for sleeping and four for daytime activity. Toward the end of the war more than 1500 prisoners were packed into each one. Other barracks in the camp served as sick rooms, a canteen, and work rooms. One was used for so-called medical experiments on prisoners, another as a morgue. During the course of the war a crematory was built by the camp and was used to burn the bodies of the dead. A gas chamber was also constructed, but at Dachau it was never used.

The staff quarters and its service facilities were built next to the camp, to the northwest. The Dachau camp was a model. As long as it was possible, exemplary order was preserved. The structure of the camp, its internal organization, and the conditions there were imitated by other concentration camps established thereafter."[42]

On Zipper's first night all were shorn and sent to their barracks. The following morning they were marched to a huge assembly area to hear a "welcome" speech from the Nazi commandant. He told them what to expect. Zipper recalls vividly the conclusion of his speech in the exact words, words he would never forget: "Everything in Dachau is prohibited," the commandant decreed, "even life itself. If it happens, it happens by accident."

Later this same day, Zipper met an old acquaintance, Arno Schirokauer, an essayist and literary director of the S.E. German Radio in Leipzig. (Zipper himself had received an offer, in 1933, to be the conductor of the Leipzig Radio Orchestra, largely due to a recommendation from Otto Klemperer, but he was unable to accept the offer when Hitler came to power.) Schirokauer was a left wing political writer. He was also a highly decorated German fighter pilot in World War I and had lost his left eye serving his "Fatherland." Upon seeing Zipper he said, "Herbert, you are very late!" Zipper inquired what he meant, and Schirokauer replied, "I've already been here for four years!" This meeting occurred at the end of the day when the prisoners were given thirty minutes of unsupervised time to lie around the barracks, feet up, to talk. Zipper also asked Schirokauer, "Before I make any wrong assumptions, what can I expect the future to hold?" Schirokauer replied, "When I came here, there were 245 Jews in my compound. Two were released; 180 have died. Those who don't die the first two weeks usually survive longer, these are statistics; you make your own conclusions." This was 1938, the fate of Jews in the years to come would be very different.

At that moment and in the next few days, a resolve came upon Zipper. He came to the realization that he would probably not get out alive. And, somehow, this realization washed away his fear. He resolved he would not give the Germans the pleasure of watching him exhibit cowardice, fear or despair. Many prisoners could not endure the pain and misery and terror and so committed suicide. The new education which began on the train trip deepened quickly during these first few days in Dachau. He quickly learned to rely upon his inner resources – there were no others. He was in the weeks to come to learn two important lessons. In the midst of the brutality, hunger, terror, humiliation and misery, Herbert Zipper came to know — at a level he could not have imagined before — the joy of giving to others and the immense power of the arts. "It was here, at Dachau," he affirms, "that I truly became a human being." Concurrently, he became quickly acclimated to day-to-day life in a concentration camp.

At the next assembly the Commandant explained to the prisoners the punishments. He emphasized three: first, for minor offenses there would be standing — without moving an inch, for six to twelve hours. No food. No opportunity to relieve oneself. The second was hanging. Your hands would be tied behind your back and you would then be hooked to a gallows and strung up. The duration of hanging would be anywhere from thirty to ninety minutes depending on the offense. Anything beyond thirty minutes usually would pull the arms out of their sockets and leave them paralyzed. A friend of Zipper's, Hugo Ebner who was condemned to hanging, lost the use of one arm except for his fingers while he was an inmate. The third punishment was flogging — a medieval practice of twenty-five strokes with a cudgel. This was followed by a week to a month in solitary confinement in a cell, named by the prisoners "the coffin." Curiously, a flogging was preceded by a medical exam since many prisoners died during the flogging. Zipper and the others were forced to observe many of these barbaric procedures.

After the explanation of these various punishments, the prisoners were marched to their first job: to dig a ditch, for twelve hours a day. This was to be the fare for the next few weeks. After five to six feet they would strike water but were ordered to keep digging, standing in the muck and mire. Although his eye and ribs healed, after several weeks Zipper contracted "Schippers Krankheit" (shoveling disease). "I couldn't lift my arms above my shoulders. They were numb, some muscles in the back were torn. This was, of course, a disaster. If you couldn't work, you were useless and in danger of being eliminated." He was, however, unbelievably lucky — the first of many such instances of fortune saving his life.

The next morning at the assembly during the line up, a Capo counted off the odds and evens and took Zipper and the other "evens" to a new job! Zipper was now to be a pack horse — pushing a cement cart. For this he didn't need to raise his arms but to push with his shoulders and chest. This he could do and kept this job for most of his stay in Dachau. This change of job probably saved his life. The new job, while enormously strenuous (twelve hours a day), had the advantage of allowing the "horses" to have conversations. Initially, Zipper could talk with Arno Schirokauer and later with Jura Soyfer.

There were even a few moments of pleasure in out-witting the guards. One hot August day, for example, the guards left them alone to work in the camp, whereupon one of the prisoners impersonated the Capo and screamed and yelled which enabled everyone to sit safely on the ground in the shade. As long as someone was screaming the S.S. assumed everything was normal and under control. Another day Zipper found a yardstick and decided to take a chance. The next morning, instead of going to his "horse" job, he took a pirated pencil and paper and leisurely walked all over the camp measuring everything he could find. He figured that the SS with their anal love of order would consider him to be on official business. So he spent a free day walking around while the SS looked at him and went about their business as he measured away.

The daily work was not only dismal and exhausting but the meals were disgusting. Evening meals usually consisted of meager portions of a slop-soup. It took Zipper a long time to endure it. Often there were worms floating on top of the "soup." There was a saying at the time: "Besser Würmer als gar Kein Fleisch" which translates as "Better worms than no meat at all." However, on Tuesdays they were served Kuttelfleck ("the cows stomach"); it was so awful smelling that he could not eat on Tuesdays. Sometimes, the evening meal was cooked in whale lard. The prisoners were required to clean their aluminum eating dishes after each meal and the whale lard was almost impossible to clean. Prisoners were issued cold water only and no matter how hard one rubbed and rubbed the lard wouldn't disappear. It also stank. Whenever Zipper saw the white residue of the whale lard floating on top of the "soup," he simply didn't eat. One particluarly bad day Arno Shirokauer told Zipper that it wasn't as bad now as it had been in the earlier days of Dachau when certain prisoners were forced to drink their own urine and eat their own excrement. Zipper stared at Shirokauer in complete disbelief but his friend only nodded his head saying, 'this is true.'

No one who lived in Dachau during these times will forget the word "Bettenbauen" - a German verb meaning literally "to build your bed orderly." During the first few weeks in Dachau the prisoners were required to sleep on sacks on the floor but the sacks were so itchy that Zipper slept on the floor. Later they were issued 3-tier bunk beds. Then began the constant inspections with the order shouted out "Bettenbauen!" Beds had to be made perfectly smooth. The command would prompt a wild, crazy scurrying about, prisoners put their feet on top of each others heads, in each other's faces, a few minutes of absolute bedlam while the over-crowded prisoners tried to make order! It was compulsive orderliness and rigidity pushed to German absurdity. At times Zipper could tolerate the sheer nonsense only by laughing. But for most of the prisoners it was a terrifying way to begin the day. Zipper had developed a quick technique of making his bed smooth as glass. He could do his own bed in just a few minutes which gave him extra time to help other frightened prisoners. Thus each morning he would quickly do his and then do the beds of Dr. Zerkowitz and Dr. Shey who could not do their beds to the Nazi's satisfaction.

Paul Berken in his official history of *Dachau, 1933-1945,* describes this time of day and confirms Zipper's recollections:

> Reveille was usualy at 5 a.m. in summer and 6 a.m. in winter. But there were times when men had to get up at 3 a.m. In any case squads appointed to special duties were paraded before the ordinary hour at all times. In the rooms reveille marked the beginning of a period of excessive activity, for a number of tasks had to be done in a very short space of time. In 1938, when there was still a discipline with which that of the later years could in no way be compared, prisoners rose at 3:15 a.m. in summer and a little later in winter. In three-quarters of an hour prisoners had to have washed, made their beds, tidied their cupboards, gulped down their 'coffee' and if possible visited the latrines. Nonsensical orders controlled the tidying of rooms, and it was impossible for newcomers to conform to them completely unless they were helped by an 'old hand' who showed them the 'tricks of the trade'.
>
> To make a bed according to the rules, the most skillful needed at least ten minutes. The palliasse had to be completely level and form a perfect rectangle with well-creased folds. The blue-and-white checked sheet covering the palliasse and the pillow had to be placed so that the squares where perfectly aligned, horizontally and vertically. The bunks were placed one on top of the other and joined together, and so the men had to agree in which order they did their bunks. It was well-nigh impossible for one who had the upper berth not to disarrange the tidied bunk of his neighbour below; the lower had to wait, and became impatient. This resulted in daily arguments, which degenerated occasionally into brawls. It was impossible to gain time by getting up earlier, for this was forbidden, and there was no lighting available before the official hour of reveille. Some were so afraid of being punished that they slept on the floor so as to avoid untidying their beds, but in doing so they ran risks for this too was forbidden...[43]

There were two other particularly memorable days that August. One day the camp received a visit from Herr Heinrich Himmler and his entourage who graced Dachau with an inspection. Photographers filmed the entire day. The featured event of the day was having the prisoners move a rock quarry from one end of the camp to the opposite end. Everything was, of course, done at bayonet point at a jog, "Laufschritt"! When every rock was moved, the prisoners were then ordered to put them all back. This day, Zipper recalls, was a particularly depressing day – the meaninglessness of it all, the uselessness. He couldn't sleep that night, not out of fatigue but out of soul-sickness.

The other day involved wheelbarrow running. One of the most excruciating jobs in Dachau was running with a full heavily loaded wheelbarrel, always with the SS chasing prisoners with their bayonets. Not only was this excruciating work but blisters formed, were rubbed off and one's hands became bloody raw meat. Zipper, as a pianist and conductor, was fearful for his hands. So he formed a plan. He stole a piece of rope and kept it hidden in his bed. When the inevitable happened and he was assigned to be a wheelbarrel runner, he was prepared. He had cut the rope to fit inside his shirt stretching from one hand across the shoulders and neck and down the other sleeve. It was not visible, but it could be coiled around the wheelbarrel handles so that the arms and shoulders were holding up the wheelbarrel like a harness and not just the hands. With this contrivance Zipper endured his day at the wheelbarrel. One day he saw an acquaintance — Judge Osias, who had handed out stiff penalties to fascists during the Schuschnigg regime — come away from the day with his hands a bloody mess. He was ordered to do it again the next day. Zipper gave him his rope but was unable to find out if it helped. He never found out what became of Judge Osias.

Two other startling episodes occurred early in Herbert Zipper's stay in Dachau. The former occurred one morning at assembly. All ten thousand as usual were lined up at the meeting square and the Commandant shouted the number of a prisoner who had to walk forward to receive a telegram. The Commandant read aloud "Ihre Mutter verreckt!" which translates roughly as "Your mother croaked" — the word "verreckt" being one you would apply to an animal. What kind of a person, Zipper wondered, could do this to another. He recalls that one day a friend said to him, "You know, Zipper, that book of Dostoyevsky (*The House of the Dead*) is a bedtime story compared to this place." At about this time a comrade in Walter Zipper's barracks received a letter from his wife urging him not to play cards too much and to save his money for when he got out!

The other incident occurred after the Nazi doctors became irritated at having to treat so many edemas — huge swellings of the head by exposure to the sun. The prisoners were issued caps, "Mützen." But, of course, ten thousand men standing in precise lines one could not just put them on and take them off. The Commandant insisted, in a typical Prussian love of order, that the ten thousand put them on exactly in unison on command. "Mützen auf!" "Mützen ab!" he would shout. Because sound takes time to travel from the front of ten thousand men to the rear, there was a wave effect of caps going on and off. This infuriated the Commandant. The prisoners were sent back to their barracks to practice in small groups. Of course, in small groups everything was precise. But when they reassembled as a group of ten thousand, again the wave effect occurred. Finally, at noon the frustrated Commandant called them "swine" and dismissed them in frustration. Zipper struggled to keep from bursting out in laughter. Walter Zipper, several rows away, was also convulsed.

There were, however, few opportunities for laughter in Dachau. In 1938-39, the Nazis had not begun their "final solution" policies of mass extermination, but torture, humiliation and death were the daily fare. The spate of books that have been published about life in concentration camps have given eloquent testimony to their horrors. The very names of these places conjure up images too grotesque to comprehend: Babi Yar, Auschwitz, Treblinka, Sobibor, Belsen, Vilna and, of course, Dachau and Buchenwald. The ultimate torture, however, for the living was not merely the starvation and exhaustion, the beatings and punishment, the constant humiliation. For Zipper the ultimate torture was the ticking away of time, the robbing of one's life, an endless succession of minutes being taken away. "I could," Zipper states, "endure running around with 100 kilo bags of beans on my back. What I could not stand was the theft of my life." This was one of the hidden horrors, the degradations often overlooked in prison camp literature. It was horrible enough to see one's body shrinking which gave physical confirmation to the psychological sense of withering away. But what was worse was the torture of not only losing the time of one's life but the very slowing down of time so that all one could do was focus upon this very loss as one was losing it. To have to stand and watch the clock slowly move, a second, a minute at a time, in these miserable surroundings was, in a very real sense, worse then the physical torture and humiliation.

What makes Zipper's experiences different and important to pass on are the positive lessons he learned amidst the starvation, brutality, degradation and death. To suggest that Dachau was valuable because of these lessons would be, of course, a blasphemy. Nothing can justify the loss of life and the breaking of spirit that was systematically inflicted upon the innocent. But for a time this was Zipper's reality.

Zipper was, in a sense, fortunate. He was present at a unique moment in history. He experienced the full degradation, pain and suffering of Dachau but he did so at a time when the Nazis were primarily interested in establishing control over the prisoners, in humiliating, dehumanizing, and demoralizing the Jews and other prisoners. They had not yet determined to exterminate them. Thus Zipper was one of several to observe a unique laboratory experiment in seeing how human beings would behave under such conditions. What Zipper observed was the spectrum of human behavior intensified by the very desperation of the situation. People rose to unexpected heights or conversely they reached the nadir of depravity and cowardice. The full range of human potentiality was enacted each day and it was clear to Zipper that even in the midst of the attempt to seek bare, minimal survival, there were still choices to be made. Zipper was not without rage and hatred for the guards and for the German people. He realized very quickly, however, that such feelings were useless and even dangerous. He also learned that survival depended upon being able to control one's feelings and to consciously focus upon potentially productive feelings. His natural bent towards self-control, combined with his Viennese proclivity toward order and restraint, both stood him in a good stead. He learned that he must govern himself carefully and help others to do similarly. He also learned that the arts were still possible even in this miserable place.

On the second or third night at Dachau after a paltry meal – usually a thin, watery, ugly soup and a small piece of bread – Zipper and another prisoner, Peter Ulanowsky, began to recite poetry. (Peter's brother Paul had been a schoolmate of Zipper at the Academy in Vienna and later was to become the accompanist to Lotte Lehmann). They were in front of their barracks and began reciting from Act I of Goethe's *Faust*. Zipper had, and to this day possesses, a remarkable memory. He began with some lines of Mephisto: "Glaub unsereinem der so manche tausend Jahre" and Peter joined in with lines he knew, and they went back and forth quoting lines, attempting to transcend the dirt and stupidity surrounding them, to satisfy their thirst for something which elevates rather than degrades:

> Believe me, who for thousands of years
> Has chewed this toughest of food, know
> That from the cradle to the bier
> No man can digest the ancient bitter dough.
> Trust one of my kind, this show
> Is made only for a god's delight
> He dwells in an ageless aureole,
> Us he has thrust in darkness out of sight
> And you are fit for only day and night.[44]

After a few moments people began crowding around them to listen, urging them to continue. Zipper recently described this experience in a hearing on the arts for the California legislature:

> "In June 1938, during one of my first evenings after a long day's work in the ditches of Dachau, I stood with a friend of mine in front of our barracks while scores of other inmates were scattered on the ground, exhausted, mute and hopeless. The chances for survival of any of us seemed practically nil.
>
> I have no explanation for what urged me then to start in a loud voice reciting passages from Goethe's "Faust." My friend Peter helped out whenever I got stuck and soon the inmates on the ground grouped themselves around us listening with obvious intensity. The dramatic change of mood that happened to all of us is still vividly in my memory. The following evenings an ever-increasing crowd urged us to continue our recitations and we obliged with the best of German poetry that we could remember. *Poetry did its intended work.*"

The next evening more people congregated and urged them to repeat their "performance" and so it went for several evenings, each night with a larger and larger crowd. Walter Zipper was in a different barracks and was unable to attend these recitations. During the intervening days Zipper struggled to recall every line he could possibly remember and he and Ulanowsky assisted each other. It not only enabled Zipper to endure the days but more importantly, it gave others something to look forward to, some sense of hope and dignity amidst the terrible suffering and ugliness. The crowds of prisoners who gathered to listen were not just Viennese intellectuals like Zipper and Ulanowsky. Many were simple, uneducated laborers, poor farmers, criminals, a motley crowd. For many it was their first exposure to poetry and literature. Yet they not only enjoyed it, they were fed and nourished by the experience. Prior to the advent and rise of Hitler, Zipper had viewed the arts as the highest expression of man's aspirations, as representing a continuity with the past which he gladly joined. After Hitler he came to view the arts as not only an expression of high ideals but as a down to earth means of protesting abuses of the human spirit. But in Dachau he came to see that the arts are not just an expression of important ideals or of political outrage; he came to see that the arts are essential to the very existence of life. Without the arts, the human spirit withers and dies. This was a lesson which changed him.

Often the arts are spoken of almost synonymously with entertainment. And, in fact, much concentration and death camp literature speaks of the art experiences that did find nooks and crannies of expression in the camps as helping the prisoners forget, giving them a moment's reprieve through entertainment. For example, Viktor Frankl in his book *Man's Search for Meaning* (formerly *From Death Camp to Existentialism*) writes:

> Earlier, I mentioned art. Is there such a thing in a concentration camp? It rather depends on what one chooses to call art. A kind of cabaret was improvised from time to time. A hut was cleared temporarily, a few wooden benches were pushed or nailed together and a program was drawn up. In the evening those who had fairly good positions in camp — the Capos and the workers who did not have to leave camp on distant marches — assembled there. They came to have a few laughs or perhaps to cry a little; anyway, to forget. There were songs, poems, jokes, some with underlying satire regarding the camp. All were meant to help us forget, and they did help. The gatherings were so effective that a few ordinary prisoners went to see the cabaret in spite of their fatigue even though they missed their daily portion of food by going. [45]

Certainly there was this element of focusing attention on something other than one's misery, but to Zipper the arts served a more crucial function. They enabled one not only to forget but to become more conscious of what one's bare, naked Self truly was. The Nazis stripped the prisoners of their hair, clothes, even their names became numbers and the problem became knowing who one really was. Zipper learned this by learning what is not essential - he learned by paying the closest attention to his own reactions to each experience.

After a few weeks in Dachau, around June of 1938, Zipper met several first-rate musicians (many Jews and some political prisoners), especially some very good string players. He learned that there were, somewhere in the camp, one or two violins and a guitar or two. And he concocted the idea, preposterous as it seemed, of making music. He began to compose music in his head, memorizing it as he plodded around at his daily "horse" labor. He also identified two good instrument makers in the wood shop (both long-term residents of Dachau) and he set them to work, surreptitiously, working with stolen wood. Next he needed strings. He had noticed that one of the SS men did a lot of loud shouting but was never physically violent. One day he came into Zipper's barracks and asked if anyone knew how to plant flowers? While he was standing there Zipper perceived a different manner and decided to take a chance. He asked the man for violin strings! The SS man said nothing. Two days later Zipper found a sack under his pillow filled with violin strings. (He found out later that the man was not a Nazi but a communist spy.) So by the beginning of July "Zipper's orchestra" had enlisted 14 players with a peculiar assortment of instruments. He had to compose music specially tailored for the capabilities and limitations of each. Soon there began the Sunday afternoon outhouse concerts.

The "orchestra" rehearsed for a couple of Sunday afternoons, a time when the guards usually did not come around. Various prisoners also took turns keeping watch. The "concerts" were held in an un-used latrine that had been built for expansion. Only the plumbing was in place so there was an open space with room enough for 20 - 30 prisoners to listen at a time. The prisoners filed in quietly. No one spoke, and during the short concert they sat in absolute silence in an atmosphere of conspiracy. There was also the feeling of excitement, of reaffirming something worthwhile, of exerting some freedom of the will. Here at least was a breathing space where the Nazis did not control everything they did. The seriousness of the endeavor restored a sense of human dignity, of not being the scum to which the Nazis tried to reduce them. For two to three hours the orchestra performed in shifts of 15 minutes. During the week Zipper wrote new music for the next Sunday. He wrote his music on "manuscript" paper made from strips of the margins of Nazi propaganda newspapers, cut and pasted together for him by "patrons" of the concerts. After a while the orchestra developed quite a repertoire of Zipper compositions. The composer was able to write late at night as a result of volunteering to clean the barrack's latrine for the duration of his stay in Dachau - this after a full 12 hour working day. Why, he was asked later, did he volunteer for such duty. "It was a time," he explains, "to be alone, to think, to be a human being." The latrine was quite big, 10 toilets, a huge stone basin, the cleanest place in the camp. Here Zipper could be himself; here he could sit amidst the toilets and reflect. It was brightly lit and some evenings he stayed there until midnight writing his music. It was, he believes, part of his salvation.

For some prisoners memory was a severe problem in concentration camps. "Probably as a result of malnutrition, mental anguish, and ambivalence toward the outside world, prisoners tended to forget names, places and events of their past lives. Often they could not recall the names of their closest relatives ... Prisoners were quite upset about this loss of memory for things past, which added to their sense of frustration and incompetence. This too was a process which had only begun for new prisoners, and was nearly completed in most old prisoners."[46] This was not, however, a problem for Zipper who exercised his iron will to maintain his sense of self. During the day, while performing mindless labors, he would think about his music, committing new songs to his memory which got better and better during his stay in Dachau. The music he composed for the inmates was not popular music; the concerts were not "entertainment." They were a means of keeping alive some small measure of civilization, of restoring value to their lives. Everything else in Dachau was dismal and degrading but here at least, for 15 minutes a week, one could reaffirm life itself. Two of the sons of the Archduke Franz Ferdinand, who was assassinated in 1914 at Sarajevo, were in Dachau at this time. Often Zipper arranged for the two to have "jause" (high tea) using watered-down coffee. They addressed him as Herr Docktor and he addressed them as "Kaiserliche Hoheit" (Your Imperial Highness). These two Hohenbergs were there on suspicion of "imperialism." One once said to Zipper in his strong Viennese accent: "If I owe anybody my sanity it is to you for this contribution to our lives." The younger son cried during the first concert. Like the legendary hero of his childhood, Der Liebe Augustin, Zipper brought music to the victims of this new plague. These times were for Zipper a decisive revelation of the life giving and life saving quality of the arts. The concerts lasted until the end of September.

The second lesson he learned during these months was equally important to him in the development of his character. He had always been a kind, polite and civilized young man. In Dachau he came to realize at a more profound level the joy to be gained from life by giving to others. The concerts were one such gift. The recitations of poetry were another. Each day he found ways to help others keep their spirits alive. He discovered, too, that true humanity is not a product of formal education. He observed highly educated men stealing bread from their comrades, while uneducated men could act like saints. Tillinger was such a man. Formerly, the owner of a small grocery store, 3 - 4 steps below the street level in a poor section of Vienna, this little Jewish man, 50 years of age, had not completed more than a 4th grade education. He could hardly read and just barely eked out a living in his little store. In Dachau he became a giant. His wise counsel, his daily acts of help and encouragement prevented scores of prisoners from committing suicide. He became the "little hero" of the barracks. Zipper never found out what happened to Tillinger, he only knows that this wise, small, simple man was for a time his teacher.

During this time the two Zipper brothers had little contact. They sensed that it was not wise to draw attention to oneself in any way so they did not let on that they were brothers. Anonymity was a key to survival.

In late June the poet and writer, Jura Soyfer, a friend of Zipper's from the underground theaters of Vienna, joined him. By 1938 Soyfer was already a well-known playwright. He was born in 1912 in Kharkow, Russia the son of a wealthy businessman in the Russian steel industry. He had a French governess from the age of four and became fluent in French and Russian. However, after the Revolution it was clear the Soyfers could not continue their life of ease and affluence and at the end of 1920 they went first to Turkey, and later to Vienna. In Vienna, Jura gradually became interested in politics and at the age of 15 joined a high school Socialist Association. He made a half-hearted attempt to be a student at the University of Vienna but spent most of his time devoted to political journalism and after the February 1934 showdown, like many other socialists who were disgusted with their leader's luke warm response, Jura quit the Socialist Party and joined a Communist underground group. Because the socialist newspapers were outlawed, Soyfer turned to the underground theatre where he met Herbert Zipper and collaborated on a few theatre pieces. He became well known for his thinly veiled criticisms of the Schuschnigg regime and when the German troops invaded Austria 1938, Soyfer, a Socialist, a Jew, a Communist, was a prime target. He tried to escape to Switzerland on skis but was captured at the border and was sent to Dachau. Soyfer's capture is recounted by a survivor, and friend of Zipper and Soyfer, Hugo Ebner:

> My decision to escape through the Montafon Valley was made, because during the year before (1937) I went there for skiing and knew the area. I also believed that I could justify, if need be, my presence near the Swiss border by posing as a harmless skier, an assumption that however proved to be erroneous.
>
> My friendship with Jura Soyfer started in 1929. Upon the resignation of the Schuchnigg government on March 11, 1938, we were pretty sure that we will be arrested by the Nazis. Since Jura did not have a passport – because when he recently was released from police prison his valid passport was not returned to him – we decided to take our escape through the western mountains.
>
> During the night from the 12. to the 13. of March 1938, we took the train to Bludenz. From there, we took the Montafon train up to the terminal where we boarded a bus for a short distance, we continued on skis toward the Swiss border. On the way we ran into a border patrol consisting of three gendarmes who stopped us. We produced our identification papers and told them that we were on our annual ski-vacation and that last year we had been in the same area and stayed in Gargelien from where we took our skiing tours and I even named the inn where we were staying. The leader of the patrol, an older gendarme, seemed to be satisfied with our explanation and wanted to let us go. One of the younger ones however, obviously a real Nazi, continued to ask questions and openly expressed his suspicion which eventually led to our arrest.
>
> We were led to St. Gallenkirch where they kept us overnight. On March 14, they took us to the police in Bludenz where we remained for two days and on March 16, we were transported to the court prison in Feldkirch where we were imprisoned until June 3. From June 3 to June 23, we were held prisoner in the police prison in Innsbruck and from there they shipped us to Dachau. [47]

Soyfer was assigned to join Zipper as a "horse," pushing carts of heavy stone. During this time they became much closer friends than they had been in Vienna. They found that they each viewed the Dachau experience in a similar way — each was able, or perhaps constitutionally inclined, to focus on the outside world and not on one's own inner fears or reactions. Both were observers of the environment and not victims of their own ego needs. Both were convinced that if they should get out alive they would never be the same. Soyfer was eager to write about his experiences; Zipper was eager to bring music to a wider community. Both were agreed that such an experience as Dachau was a decisive event and that being cut off from all normal conventions and amenities brought one face to face with ultimates. It was in the midst of one of these discussions one afternoon early in September while returning to their barracks from a days labor they happened to look up at the sign above the entrance "Arbeit Macht Frei" - Work Makes Freedom. Zipper said to Jura "that would make a good song." Jura said he would think about it. Jura was a marvelous young poet and playwright. A few days later he recited the words of a new song to Zipper. Zipper memorized the words and a week later *sang* it back to Jura - He had composed music to Jura's words. This song was destined to have a remarkable journey.

The next Sunday, in mid-September, Zipper set about to secretly teach the song to one violin playing Capo and 2 guitarists - all three were excellent musicians. The teaching was without written text or written music. Teaching the song was exciting for Zipper - to actually hear on instruments the song he had been composing. Just after dinner before the 9:00 sirens signaled lights out, Zipper and the three musicians sneaked back into the barracks, with Arno Schirokauer on sentry, and Zipper taught them the music. He knew he was about to leave Dachau and there was a sense of urgency to teach the song. He taught them the melody, the words, and the chord structure. All three were reliable and trustworthy (members of the Communist Party as it turned out). Soon, prisoners throughout the camp were singing this song, the "Dachau Lied." It was not a popular type song. It had a defiant, martial quality and it spoke deeply to the prisoners. The words of Jura Soyfer are printed here:

Dachau Lied

Words by Jura Soyfer
Music and Translation into English
by Herbert Zipper

Charged with death, high tension wire
Rings around our world a chain.
Pitiless a sky sends fire,
Biting frost and drenching rain.

Far from us is lust for living,
Far our women, our town
When we mutely march to toiling
Thousands into morning's dawn.

But we all learned the motto of Dachau to heed
And became as hardened as stone
Stay humane, Dachau mate,
Be a man, Dachau mate,
And work as hard as you can, Dachau mate,
For work leads to freedom alone!

Faced by ever-threatening rifles
We exist by night and day.
Life itself this hell-hole stifles
Worse than any words can say.

Days and weeks we leave unnumbered
Some forget the count of years
And their spirit is encumbered
With their faces scarred by fears.

But we all learned the motto of Dachau...

Lift the stone and drag the wagon
Shun no burden and no chore
Who you were in days long bygone
Here you are not anymore.
Stab the earth and bury depthless
All the pity you can feel,
And within your own sweat, hapless
you convert to stone and steel.

But we all learned the motto of Dachau...

Once will sound the siren's wailing
Summons to the last roll-call.
Outside then we will be hailing
Dachau mates uniting all.
Freedom brightly will be shining,
For the hard forged brotherhood
And the work we are designing
Our work it will be good.

For we all learned the motto of Dachau...

Somehow the Dachau Lied made its way out of Dachau to other prison camps - to France and Holland, even to England and Mexico. The song survived the war through the oral tradition and was published in East Germany in an anthology of antifascist songs of concentration camps. In 1953 Zipper received a letter from the East German Ministry of Culture asking if he was the H. Zipper who wrote the 'Arbeit Macht Frei' song. In the meantime the collected works of Jura Soyfer were published with the song included. It is clear, as so many other writers have noted, that works of art once created often have a life of their own. "Dachau Lied" was one such creation.[48]

In September of 1938 as Adolph Hitler made plans to first acquire the Sudetenland and later all of Czechoslovakia, the Nazis also made plans to expand their prison camps to accommodate the Jews and political undesirables they would be accumulating. Zipper and many of his fellow prisoners were told by their capos about a week before it happened that they would be transferred to Buchenwald.

On September 22, 1938, the day before they left Dachau, Zipper, Walter Zipper and the others were issued new "clothes." The thin synthetic clothes they had been wearing were most unpleasant when they were wet. Partially made from wood pulp there was a prison saying:

Pisch nicht an der Baum du Schwein
morgen kanns dein Anzug sein.

("Dont' piss on the tree, you swine,
tomorrow it might be your suit.")

The six foot, one inch Zipper was issued an old Bavarian police uniform about half his size. The sleeves came to just below his elbow and the pants to his knees. His friends laughed hysterically when they saw him. One friend commented that the uniform was sized for a dwarf. Although he looked ridiculous, he took some solace in the fact that the fabric was wool. Thus, while Hitler was preparing to meet with Chamberlain, Herbert and Walter Zipper, Jura Soyfer, and 4,000 others were carted off to their new home, concentration camp Buchenwald, near Weimar.

On September 23, 1938, after the prisoners gathered in the assembly area, the regular detachment of the dreaded SS guards who were in charge of the train trip from Vienna to Dachau marched off and a new, more elderly group took over. The prisoners waited for several hours. Finally, they were loaded into passenger trains, Zipper in the first train, Walter in the second. The curtains were drawn. Looking out the windows, like everything else, was forbidden. The train arrived at Weimar whereupon the prisoners were loaded into trucks and ordered to put their heads between their knees so that none of the citizens of Weimar would know who or what was being transported in these many trucks. Zipper and the others had no illusions that their new "home" would be any more hospitable than Dachau.

Photostat of Zipper's Admit and Release dates from Dachau. [49]

The Zipper family at home in Vienna. Walter, age 13 (standing); Otto, age 1 1/2; Hedy, age 8; and Herbert, age 11 (seated). Photo taken in 1915.

Family and friends aboard the craft designed by Emil Zipper for a boat decoration contest in 1931. From left to right: Hedy, Fred, Jeanette Rutherston, Herbert, unidentified, Otto, and Trudl.

Der Liebe Augustin, statue in Vienna.

Emanuel Westreich, Zipper's maternal grandfather. Engraving by Arthur Paunzen.

A breathtaking Trudl leap. Photo circa 1930.

A publicity photo of Trudl perched atop a telephone pole in Vienna, 1929.
The Spire of St. Stephens is in the background.

Passport photo of Herbert Zipper, March 1926.

Josephine (Fini) Rudiger Littlejohn was an actress in Zipper's Cabaret Productions. Photo circa 1930.

Helli Andis in Vienna, Girlfriend of Jura Soyfer. Photo circa 1937-38.

Jura Soyfer. Photo circa 1930-32.

Jeanette Rutherston (Mrs. Christopher Powell) founded a dance studio in London where Trudl taught. Photo taken in 1930.

Herbert Zipper, age 28, and Wolfgang Fortner in Dusseldorf in the spring of 1932 at the home of Hans Weisbach. Fortner joined Zipper in Manila in the 1960s.

Jewish citizens being arrested by German soldiers in Vienna, 1938.
Photo courtesy of Dachau Museum.

Sculpture photographed at Dachau concentration camp in 1988.
Photo courtesy of Clyde A. Joyce.

Prisoners in barracks yard in Dachau, 1938-39. Photo courtesy of the Dachau Museum.

A work crew of prisoners. The work day in Dachau lasted 12 hours, with little in the way of nourishment to sustain the interns. Photo courtesy of the Dachau Museum.

Prisoner barracks in Buchenwald, 1938. Photo courtesy of the Simon Wiesenthal Museum.

The entrance to Buchenwald and administration building. Photo courtesy of the Simon Wiesenthal Museum.

In August of 1939, Zipper conducted his first symphony in Manila. This photograph was taken by a Japanese soldier, one of 17 who would return in 1941 to arrest Herbert on suspicion of supporting the Allied cause.

Herbert Zipper in Paris, 1939, just before leaving for Manila.

TIME

Philippine Symphony

In Manila the music season starts just after the rainy season begins. In June wealthy Filipinos return from the country, children start back to school. By August Manila society is ready to converge on the cheesecakey Metropolitan Theater on Plaza Lawton, for the opening night of the Manila Symphony.

The music which dapper Conductor Herbert Zipper led his 86 Filipino musicians through last week had nothing remotely reminiscent of the rumble of a Moro tom-tom. Manilans have been elegantly enjoying their concerts and opera for nearly 300 years, and were ready 15 years ago for the organization of a full-out orchestra. With precision and grace last week it swung through Beethoven's *Fifth Symphony*, Strauss's *Till Eulenspiegel*, Glazounov's *Une Fête slave*. Jovita Fuentes, Filipino soprano who has sung *Madame Butterfly* from China to Nazi Germany, sang a set of Gustav Mahler's ivory-turreted Lieder.

Formed in 1926 by an expatriated Viennese musician named Alexander Lippay, the Manila Symphony at first had hard sledding, often played to audiences of fewer than 150 people, but by the time Pioneer Lippay died in 1939 it was playing to full houses of 1,500 and Lippay's Filipino symphonies all had regular contracts. Today playing in the Manila Symphony is a full-time job, pays from ₱100 to ($50) to ₱300 a month (as much as the starting salary of a government employee). Key men like four-feet-six Concertmaster Ernesto Vallejo have studied in Europe or the U.S. But most of the players, including a bassoonist who learned his instrument in a few days before his first concert, are naturally gifted natives who take to Beethoven like an Igorot to confirmation.* Conductor Zipper, also an Austrian, who fled to the Philippines from a Nazi concentration camp in 1939, arrived in Manila just in time to take up where Conductor Lippay left off.

With the help of his wife, a Viennese dancer named Trudle Dubsky, Zipper introduced Manila to the latest thing in modern ballet. Between seasons he took Manila's orchestra to the mile-high Luzon

CONDUCTOR ZIPPER
...

resort-town of Baguio, where it played symphonies for vacationing Manilans while puzzled Igorots in G-strings looked on from the sidelines. Zipper rehearses his men for 105 hours before each concert, sometimes has to teach them how to play their parts. But he claims that his musicians can grasp a trick of technique quicker than many a more thoroughly trained Occidental. Says he: "My first clarinetist could play with any orchestra in the world."

TIME, August 18, 1941

Wedding day, Manila, October 1, 1939.

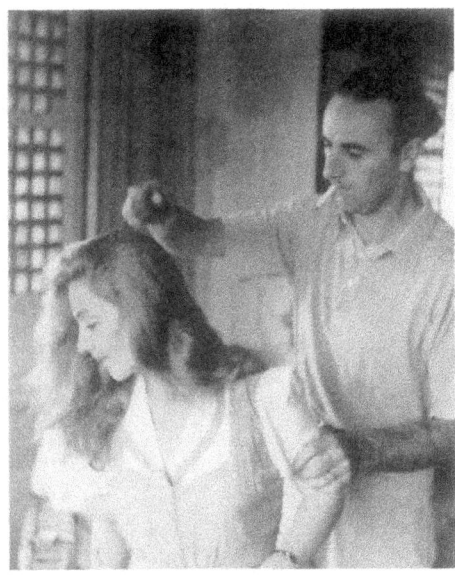

Newlyweds Trudl and Herbert sharing a moment together in Manila, 1940.

Igorot tribesmen in the Philippines, 1940. Photo by Trudl Dubsky Zipper.

Herbert Zipper with the members of the Manila Symphony Orchestra, 1940.

Trudl and Herbert with General Bonner Fellers in Manila, 1945, after the liberation of the city.

War-torn Manila, 1945.

Colonel Harry Disston, Chief of Special Services, U.S. Army. When Herbert suggested a symphony performance in Manila, Disston responded, "My dear Zipper, don't you know there's a war going on?"

Zipper in his dressing room at the Rex Theatre in Chinatown in Manila, late summer 1945. The army rented the Rex so that Zipper could give performances six or seven nights a week for 45 weeks.

Dr. Zipper conducts the Manila Symphony Orchestra for troops and residents, May 1945. Photo taken by U.S. Signal Corps.

The journey to America. The captain of the Liberty cargo ship *Russell A. Alger* (holding the Zippers' dachsund, Niddy) provided transport to the States.
Photo taken by Trudl in San Francisco harbor.

Back row: Herbert, Trudl, and Otto; front row: Mr. and Mrs. Zipper. This picture was taken by the U.S. Navy upon their arrival in San Francisco, March 1946. The U.S. Consul secured non-quota visas for the Zippers.

Hedy Zipper Holt, photo circa 1941.

Chapter VI

Buchenwald

> Here we were
> Surrounded by a forest,
> There were even trees
> Inside the walls.
> Between the kitchen
> And laundry
> Stood the Goethe Oak.
> Its inscription:
> "Above all the summits
> there is peace."
> Yet as though they knew
> This was no place for them —
> There were no birds,
> Not a one,
> In Buchenwald.
>
> — Paul Cummins

Buchenwald is situated on top of a hill of Ettersberg overlooking the city of Jena. It was a stone quarry not far from Weimar, the hub of German culture, where in 1937 this concentration camp had been constructed. The landscape and the view are beautiful. Between the prisoners' kitchen and laundry stands a huge, majestic and famous oak tree, known as the "Goethe Oak." There Goethe had written his poem, "Ein Gleiches" which begins with the lines: "Uber allen Gipfeln ist Ruh" (Above all the summits, there is peace.)[50] The irony of surrounding this oak, this inscription with this barbaric concentration camp was almost too painful to bear.

Apparently, the irony was not lost upon the birds of the Weimar district. Soon upon arrival, Zipper noticed that there were no birds in Buchenwald. Another inmate who was there at the same time was a journalist named Walter Poller, who after the war wrote an account of his two years in Buchenwald, *Medical Block Buchenwald*. In this account he too notes the absence of birds:

Long before I witnessed this tree hanging, (an excruciating torture of prisoners in which their hands were tied behind their backs and they were then hooked to gallows and strung up) I had once spoken to my friends on a Sunday, during our leisure hour, about the remarkable absence of birds in these woods, although there were coniferous and beech woods, high and low-lying forests, as well as brushwood in and around the camp. Among us was an ornithologist who suggested many plausible reasons for this fact.

In the camps of Neusustrum and Borgermoor, however, I had noticed that the birds which were previously not at home in these inhospitable areas soon settled down to live there. The reason for this fact was, I think, because of a kind of herd instinct which was due to the knowledge that the birds could depend on finding food about the camps.

Our ornithologist could not really explain the absence of birds in Buchenwald, despite the enlivenment of the inhospitable forest by human beings and great stables of all kinds, and as a responsible scientist he would not make a mere assumption an assertion.

After I witnessed the tree-hanging I needed no further explanation as to why the birds stayed away from this hellish place.[51]

In 1938 Buchenwald housed about 10,000 prisoners. Ultimately 238,379 prisoners would pass through the gates and, of them, 56,545 men and women would be murdered there.[52]

Unlike Dachau, where everything was "Ruck-Zug" (double-time), here in Buchenwald everything was slow. The ground was a soggy clay; one couldn't run or even move fast or one's shoes would get stuck. Zipper and his fellow inmates soon learned that walking in Buchenwald was more difficult than running in Dachau. In addition, the landscape was mountainous and the prisoners were always walking up hills. Zipper's stay at Buchenwald began with the normal roll call, followed by assignment to barracks. He was assigned the barrack where he had to join the column that he and others came to nickname as the "Eau de Kolonne." For they comprised the detail assigned to empty the latrines. In addition, for the next several months there was no running water in Buchenwald - not until January of 1939. The prisoners were fed a bilious soup, and twice a day, a miserable coffee: this was the total extent of fluids. Zipper and the others could not brush their teeth or wash for months.

The outdoor latrines were open-pits, twenty-five feet long, twelve feet wide, and twelve feet deep. There were four of these for thousands of prisoners. Zipper's job, along with twenty-three others, was to empty them all day, every day. To do this they had to carry five gallon buckets, lower them on ropes, scoop up the excrement, then carry it down the slope to the edge of the camp where they dumped it on the ground. Always, of course, under the supervision of armed guards.

The latrines had no ledges or seat handles to hold on to and nothing to lean back against. Sometimes exhausted prisoners, usually older men, would fall into the pits of excrement; some died. The one time Zipper witnessed this he was the only one willing to help the man out. He then had to clean himself as best he could - with no water. It is hard to explain why Zipper, given his fastidious nature, his immaculate middle class home background, his elegant education, would be one of the few able to endure covering himself in human excrement to save a fellow prisoner. When asked, he simply responds that he did what had to be done. But others saw what had to be done and often were not able to do it. Zipper, I believe, made on such occasions existential choices and the carrying out of these choices enabled him to preserve his sense of manhood and individuality within conditions designed to erase human feelings. Zipper was, I believe, not just saving others, he was saving himself.

Witnesses other than Zipper have given similar accounts. For example, Eugen Kogon, in his detailed account of the death camps, and Buchenwald in particular, (*The Theory and Practice of Hell*) describes the railings along the edge of the pits and recounts that "one of the favorite games of the SS, engaged in for many years, was to catch prisoners in the act of relieving themselves and throw them into the pit: In Buchenwald ten prisoners suffocated in excrement in this fashion in October 1937 alone."[53] Terrence Des Pres in *The Survivors* writes that these same pits, which were always overflowing, were emptied at night by prisoners working with nothing but small pails. Zipper was one of these prisoners. And Des Pres quotes Eugene Weinstock, another Buchenwald survivor who adds his account: "The location was slippery and unlighted. Of the thirty men on this assignment, an average of ten fell into the pit in the course of each night's work. The others were not allowed to pull the victims out. When the work was done and the pit empty, then and only then were they permitted to remove the corpses."[54]

Why one wonders was there such an emphasis placed upon subjecting prisoners to excremental filth. Des Pres suggests that it was not accidental but was "a deliberate policy which aimed at complete humiliation and debasement of prisoners." It was, he suggests power feeding upon itself, growing more and more hostile as its appetite was fed. Its aim was to destroy the soul. Des Pres argues that there was another logic served as well by this defilement. "In Buchenwald," recounted one survivor, "it was a principle to depress the morale of prisoners to the lowest possible level, thereby preventing the development of fellow-feeling or co-operation among the victims."[55] And there may have been a very different reason for this degradation — to so reduce the dignity and recognizable humanity of the prisoners that it would be easier for those who carried out the inhuman policies to do what they did. This was suggested after the war by the commandant of Treblinka, Franz Stangl.

Whatever the logic, this was the reality Zipper endured along with the other 23 members of the Eau de Kolonne detail. Most of the 24 were university graduates, and, fortunately for them the Capo (barrack leader) was a Mensch. He learned to scream and shout at the 24, a pose which helped to keep the SS away. In December several of the men were sent away (2 doctors, an engineer, etc.) and the Capo threw up his arms in mock dismay, saying, "Ich verliere mein ganzes akademisches Personal" ("What am I to do, I'm losing all my academic personnel" - How will I be able to carry on this complicated job?). There they stood, dressed like clowns, stinking, holding buckets of shit. Zipper and his comrades understood the Capo's grim humor and broke out into roaring laughter. The ability to laugh continued to be a means of survival.

Laughter on one occasion was provoked by an event both incongruous and bizarre. For reasons which no one could ever fathom there was a caged wolf in Buchenwald, a rather mangy, pathetic creature. One morning the Commandant, in a rage, announced to the assembled prisoners that the wolf had died: He shouted:

> Der wolf is g'storben. Die Juden ham den wolf umbracht. A Jeder Jud muss f nf Mark bezahlen f r an neuen wolf...
> ("The wolf is dead. The Jews have killed the wolf. Every Jew has to pay 5 marks so that we can buy a new wolf.)

Actually, the drunken Commandant simply wanted money to buy more liquor. But Zipper somehow found the whole incident so ludicrous that he could not help but laugh. Others did not find it so amusing but Walter and Herbert Zipper saw in this event the absurdity of the German authority.

Life in Buchenwald was strangely different from Dachau. In Dachau everything had been predictable, precision was an obsession of the Nazi leaders. The prisoners came to call it "organized Hell." Buchenwald was, by comparison, "disorganized Hell." The place was a mess; the camp commander, S.S. Obersturmbannfuhrer Rödl, "a stout man with a puffy face and clumsy, bearlike movements,"[56] was an illiterate, ignorant slob, often obviously drunk. He couldn't utter a single decent sentence. Zipper recalls one exact quote — spelled in phonetic German to capture Rödl's ability to murder the language:

> Wann I morgen an derwisch der was net g'schorn is, so kriegts der frisör und der andere.
> Translated: (If I catch one tomorrow who has not been cropped, the barber will get it and the other one.)

For the rest of their lives together Zipper would quote this to Walter and the two would collapse in laughter. Rodl was, however, not always so amusing.

One evening at the end of November or early December, at 3:00 A.M. the sirens went off - everyone had to report to the assembly area. It was freezing; snow covered the ground. The commandant appeared drunk, screaming incoherent obscenities, while machine guns were lined up in front of the prisoners. They were ordered to strip off all their clothes and to kneel down in the snow. Zipper got the giggles at this ridiculous sight - 10,000 naked men with their behinds sticking up in the cold winter air. Then the commandant said "you will all be shot." After a pause, he ordered everyone to put their clothes back on and to march back into the barracks. He was enjoying some drunken sport. For Herbert and Walter Zipper just noting the ignorance of this man and the stupidity of the place helped them keep their balance. They could remind each other of the grotesqueness of it all and laugh at it.

While Herbert and Walter Zipper were adjusting to their new "accommodations," Adolph Hitler was preparing his next moves. On September 30th at Munich, the British, French and Italian leaders acceded to Hitler's demands and the Sudentenland was to become part of Germany effective October 10. The die was cast for the imminent invasion of Czechoslovakia. And, on October 27, Hitler made the next attack. This time 18,000 Jews, although they had been living in Germany since 1914, but who had been born in the former Polish provinces of the Russian Empire, were expelled. One of these eighteen thousand was a man named Zindel Grynszpan who was sent to the Polish town of Zbaszyn. From there he wrote his son Kirsch a postcard describing the miserable treatment his family was enduring. The son, Kirsch, was so enraged he went to the German Embassy in Paris on November 6, 1938, shot the first German official he saw, Ernst Von Rath. As Von Rath lay dying, Hitler seized the opportunity to blame the deed on a Jewish-inspired world conspiracy against Germany and unleashed a 24 hour onslaught against Germany's remaining 300,000 Jews. The night of violence is known as the Kristallnacht ("night of broken glass"). That night synagogues and Jewish institutions were burned to the ground, over seven thousand businesses were destroyed, ninety-one Jews were killed, and more than thirty thousand -

one in ten of those who remained - were arrested and sent to concentration camps. Before most of them were released two to three months later, as many as 1,000 had been murdered, 244 of them in Buchenwald.

On November 10, 1938, Zipper and other prisoners were sent each day to Weimar to dig a foundation for a new police station. When they returned to the barracks, they saw a ghastly scene. Buses and trains had carried 10,911 Jews to Dachau, 9,000 Jews to Sachen Lausen, and 9,845 Jews to Buchenwald. The new arrivals were sitting on the ground, most of them with bloody heads. Subsequently, about 800 were stuffed into barracks designed for 400. Many suffocated and died. Others were tied to trees having gone insane due to their treatment. On that first evening Zipper and Jura Soyfer could hear them moaning out in the yard, particularly those tied to the trees. They were wretched beyond belief and were hungry and without water. Zipper and Soyfer could not stand the misery outside and decided, at great risk, to do something. After curfew they stole into the darkness, pilfered two buckets and managed to secure some water in the laundry to bring to the pathetic victims. Had they been caught, they would probably have been killed. The next morning Zipper helped carry out corpses, he saw 40 - 45 himself, many young boys 10 or 11 years old. Jura Soyfer, Hugo Ebner, and Zipper volunteered for several grizzly jobs just to see and experience what was going on.

As an added punishment for the Rath assassination in Paris, food rations for all Buchenwald Jewish inmates were cut in half. People began dying of starvation. Then a typhoid epidemic hit the camp. Because of the excrement dumping on the outskirts of the camp, nearby peasants and farmers also began contracting the disease. To alleviate this spread of the disease, lime was to be poured on the dump. Zipper volunteered for this job as well in order to gain a break from the daily routine of shoveling shit. November and December were dismal beyond belief.

There was no possibility in Buchenwald to form an orchestra or to organize other "Art" events. The only good works that Zipper could do here was to try to keep up the spirits of his depressed fellow prisoners. One such prisoner was Walter Zirner, the son of an old friend of Zipper's father and owner of one of Vienna's biggest jewelry stores. Almost every other day Zirner expressed his intention to commit suicide. On these mornings Zipper urged him along, yelling at him, once even slapping him in the face to get him so mad he would regain his fighting spirit. Zirner did survive, and although his leg froze on a particularly miserable December night, he did get out of Buchenwald. Eventually he had to have his leg amputated. But his life was saved by Zipper's fierce determination.

One sub-zero December in the afternoon the sirens went off and the prisoners were required to assemble. At the sound of the siren, Zipper was cleaning the typhoid latrine. He was the only one of fourteen assigned to this duty who did not contract and die of the disease. Of this he remarked, "Some people are somebodies, some nobodies; apparently I am an antibody." When all 10,000 were assembled, the commandant shrieked at them that two prisoners had escaped and that they would stand where they were until the two were captured - even if it takes a year. So began an ordeal of standing motionless - to move was to be beaten - from 5:00 that afternoon until about 12:00 noon the next day. Over 19 hours of standing in the freezing weather. Many prisoners died during the night. Some of the older men simply dropped dead in their place. Zipper recalls seeing over 60 corpses in the light of the morning. Everyone in his barracks except him suffered from frost-bite. Walter Zipper had badly frost bitten toes and fingers.

During this night Zipper was once again to learn how to rely upon his inner resources, to discover those powers that human beings possess but do not even attempt to utilize except in times of dire crisis. That evening he began to concentrate upon the blood flowing through his body, becoming conscious of each muscle, each part of his body and through sheer mind and willpower of his mind to keep his circulation flowing. He also concentrated on making slight movements in each part of his body, keeping his toes, fingers, every muscle in regular movement in ways that could not be detected by the guards who were moving about and clubbing people. In this manner he survived the ordeal without injury.

When, the next morning, the two prisoners were captured, the assembled were returned to their barracks to eat their half rations. Then came a call to carry out and bury the corpses. Zipper and Jura Soyfer volunteered. They were to put the corpses in paper shirts and stack them up outside the camp. Later they were then transferred to crematoriums and ashes were mailed to the home address - sometimes ashes would even be covering a pair of glasses! They had to give their identification number and those of the corpses as they left the gates. Zipper cannot remember how many they carried at that time, but it was between 50-60. He remembers that after they had carried several corpses through the gate the guard in attendance, seemingly moved by a residue of compassion asked: "All old men, aren't they?" Where upon Soyfer in a very defiant tone answered: "All in their best manhood."

Bruno Bettelheim had also been transferred to Buchenwald at this time and gives us his account of this grim evening.

> ... On a terribly cold winter night when a snowstorm was blowing, all prisoners were punished by being forced to stand at attention without overcoats — they never wore any — for hours. This was after having worked for more than twelve hours in the open, and having received hardly any food. The prisoners were threatened with having to stand all through the night.
>
> The reason for this punishment was that two prisoners had tried to escape. On such occasions all prisoners were always punished severely, so that in the future they would give away secrets they had learned, because otherwise they would have to suffer. The idea was that every prisoner ought to feel responsible for any act committed by any other prisoner.

Bettelheim's and Zipper's memories are essentially the same, although Bettelheim was more struck by the collapse of discipline and order in the dawn:

> After about twenty prisoners had died from exposure, the discipline broke down. The threats of the guards became ineffective. To be exposed to the weather was a terrible torture; to see one's friends die without being able to help, and to stand a good chance of dying oneself, created a situation similar to the transportation, except that the prisoners had by now more experience with the SS. Open resistance was impossible, as impossible as it was to do anything definite to safeguard oneself. A feeling of utter indifference swept the prisoners. They did not care whether the SS shot them; they were indifferent to acts of torture committed by the guards. The SS no longer had any authority; the spell of fear and death was broken. It was again as if what was happening did not "really" happen to oneself. There was again a split between the "me" to whom it happened, and the "me" who really did not care and was just a vaguely interested, but essentially detached, observer. Unfortunate as the situation was, the prisoners felt free from fear and therefore were actually happier than at most other times during their camp experiences.
>
> Whereas the extremeness of that situation probably produced the mental split mentioned above, a number of circumstances combined to create the feeling of happiness in the prisoners. Obviously it was easier to withstand unpleasant experiences when all found themselves in "the same boat." Moreover, since everybody was convinced that his chances to survive were slim, each felt more heroic and willing to help others than he would have felt in other situations, when helping others might endanger him. This helping and being helped raised the prisoners' spirits. Another factor was that not only were they free of the fear of the SS, but the SS had actually lost its power over them for the moment, since the guards seemed reluctant to shoot all the prisoners. [57]

Remarkably, In addition to Zipper and Bettelheim, a third inmate, Eugene Kogon has written of the evening. Kogon is even able to date the event:

> During roll call on December 14, 1938 two convicts turned up missing at Buchenwald. The temperature was 5 degrees Farenheit above zero and the prisoners were thinly clad — but they had to stand in the roll-call area for nine-

teen hours. Twenty five had frozen to death by morning; by noon the number had risen to more than seventy... oh, it is easy enough to write about now-standing like that after a full day's work, throughout the night and until next noon, without food. The cold death figures can be set down — but not the permanent damage suffered by hundreds who later perished of their effects. [58]

For almost a full week Zipper and Soyfer continued to be undertakers, carrying out victims of the terrible evening.

Life in Buchenwald was described in 1939 by the Central European Correspondent of the London Times who made a valiant but futile attempt to alert the world of conditions in prison camps. G.E.R. Gedye wrote furiously and published hastily a book entitled *Beytrayal in Central Europe* in which he described the conditions in Buchenwald in the fall of 1939. It appears as though he is describing the same evening Zipper and Bettelheim describes though Gedye's date is off by two months:

> Last October, when two prisoners escaped, the other prisoners were made to stand on parade from six o'clock in the evening until eleven the following morning. Several prisoners collapsed, and were punished by being deprived of food for three days. One prisoner, named Weinreiter, was found to be hiding in the carpenter's shop, and he was executed. Of the two prisoners who escaped, one got away altogether, the other was recaptured, and as he had killed his guard making his escape, he was handed over to the police, tried for murder, sentenced to death, and beheaded. [59]

Gedye continues describing everyday life:

> One morning the Camp Commandant asked for seven volunteers for some special job. No one responded, whereupon five men were selected and marched off to the front of the camp. Shots were heard. The men were never seen again, only their clothes, bloodstained and pierced with bullets, were returned to the camp. The names of two of the victims are Bischof, a Social Democrat and former municipal councilor, and Fischer. The names of the other three are unknown.
>
> The death of the lawyer Hans Litten, which occurred at Buchenwald, was reported some time ago. A load of heavy stones was tipped over him. He was carried off with a broken thigh and a damaged chest. It was from these injuries that he died.
>
> The "Bible students" are subjected to special illtreatment. Some have undergone a so-called "German baptism." They were placed in a barrel of sewage and asked "if they still believe in Jehova." The "Bible students" have shown a dour fervour in all camps and prisons, and at Buchenwald they refused to answer the question. They were then completely submerged in the sewage again and again.

> In the year ending last May, 145 prisoners were either killed outright or beaten to death or driven to suicide at Buchwald.*

(*Manchester Guardian: Special Correspondent, August 1938.) [60]

A further illustration of life in Buchenwald is the execution of Forster. This prisoner was a member of the KP (Communist Party) who had escaped to Czechoslovakia and supposedly had killed an SS guard. After the Munich Conference, he was captured in the Sudetanland and brought back to Buchenwald to be executed. It was just before Christmas, on December 21 or 22, 1938 and all the prisoners were brought to the assembly area. A gallows and a platform had been erected from which many speeches were shouted about what a swine this man was, what he did and so on. He was a very thin man, shivering in the cold, blindfolded with his hands and feet bound. He was carried to the gallows and hanged. He did not, however, die for at least a minute and was jerking and writhing in front of everyone. When Forster stopped jerking, however, the SS men who had been sneering with hatred and contempt during the speeches, now seemed different. They appeared terrified and seemed uneasy; they quietly wandered off in different directions. For Zipper this was a confirmation of his conviction that killing, even in the name of justice, affects the killer adversely and injuriously.

December was made even more depressing by the 'Z' incident. Z was a Viennese lawyer (whose name Zipper has withheld to spare embarrassment to any surviving family members.) He had been arrested and thrown in Zipper's train compartment on the Vienna to Munich leg of the trip to Dachau. He tried to explain to the SS that he was a loyal German, a decorated soldier in World War I, whereupon the SS guard slapped and beat him brutally. At some point Z decided to become an informer. After a few days in Dachau Zipper and his fellow inmates became suspicious: Z didn't have to work hard, he was given a typewriter and the Capo was told to leave him alone because Z had his own "assignment." Soon also, a few barrack mates were singled out for severe punishment. Whereupon Zipper and the others decided to isolate him. One day, Zipper recalls, the Capo, Tillinger, and others discussed what to do. Someone suggested "accidentally" killing him. Zipper opposed this saying that, killing is not our business and that if he were killed "our" barracks would be singled out. Besides, Zipper argued, the SS will eventually take care of him themselves. Zipper advised keeping vigilant and waiting.

Z was among those transferred to Buchenwald. Soon after arriving he made a fatal mistake. He informed the SS that some of their own men were accepting bribes from the prisoners. The SS decided to "have fun" with him. At this time Zipper and others were working in Weimar. Zipper speculates that the commandant was probably lining his pockets by supplying cheap labor. One evening after returning from Weimar, Zipper and a few others were emptying some shit cans when Zipper came upon a gruesome sight. Several SS men had taken Z to the edge of the camp and were beating him unmercifully trying to drive him to the electric wires surrounding the camp so that he would "commit suicide." He was hideously beaten. Finally, the SS dragged his semi-conscious body to the front of the barracks and dumped him there. Zipper and Soyfer carried him on a stretcher to the hospital but the Capo in command wouldn't accept him asserting he was an informer. They returned and laid him in the enclosed porch area between two barracks.

At midnight Zipper could hear him moaning. He also heard a creak in the porch door and got up and tiptoed to the barrack door, quietly opening it a crack to peer out. He saw two to three SS men with sacks of sand beating the man's head. And he heard this dying 40 year-old man moaning "Mutter, mutter." Zipper quietly retreated to his bunk thoroughly dejected. Though Z was a Jew who had informed on his own people, Zipper was appalled at this murder. He was unable to sleep that night, struggling with a growing rage against those men who could murder this pathetic, suffering man who lay begging for mercy. To see how men could be trained to surrender their humanity to an ideology, to regard other human beings as Untermenschen, "under" beings, was for Zipper particularly demoralizing. The next morning he did not discuss the episode with anyone. He knew the others would feel relieved to be rid of Z and that it would be foolhardy to try now to defend Z's right to life. Zipper also knew that survival required the suppression of normal feelings of anger and rage and that one's emotional energy had to be conserved in order to simply get through the next day. In any event, when Christmas came to Buchenwald in 1938, "full" rations were restored.

January of 1939 began for Zipper, literally, with the same misery. However, every other week the prisoners were allowed to write a letter. Before he was arrested, Zipper had told his mother that if something should happen to him his letters would be in code: everything he said was to be interpreted as its opposite. He also referred to Walter as Pepi and himself as Julia - after their own middle names of Joseph and Julius - leaving the impression to outsiders that these two are relatives in Vienna. By now the entire family was in Paris. At this time, as Martin Gilbert recounts:

Emigration still offered a way out for those Jews of Germany and Austria who were at liberty. More than ninety-eight thousand Jews, nearly half of the Jews of Austria, left for other lands. They were, indeed, encouraged to do so by the Nazis, and a special emigation office, the Central Office for Jewish Emigration, was set up in Vienna (in the Palais Rothschild) for them, headed by a thirty-two-year-old SS officer, Adolf Eichmann.[61]

In addition, if one could obtain a visa to an overseas country - not the USA, prisoners such as Herbert Zipper, who were then listed in a category known as "protective custody," could be released. In retrospect it seems as though Zipper lived a bit of a charmed life. Though he had the misfortune of experiencing Dachau and Buchenwald, he had the relative good fortune of being there during the pre-war Nazi pestilence. In addition, he had the doubly good fortune of having a prosperous father who just happened to be in London during the Anschluss and who was able to pull strings to secure the release of his sons. Securing this kind of release was enormously difficult for ultimately the Nazi State did not want to solve "the Jewish question" by deportation. For one thing they feared that strong Jewish interests would run counter to the German economy. A second reason went beyond economics: "the mere departure of the German Jews... could not satisfy the enormous potential of hatred accumulated by the Nazis. This potential would have to find other channels if all German Jews had been allowed to emigrate."[62] The "other channel" for six million Jews was to be wholesale extermination. It was Herbert Zipper's almost miraculous luck to have escaped the fate of the six million victims for by 1941 emigration was no longer possible. "During the first year after the Anschluss close to one hundred thousand Viennese emigrated. The Nazis stopped issuing exit permits to Jewish men between the ages of eighteen and forty-five in August 1939, and soon afterward all Jewish emigration from Vienna came to a halt. The last Jewish refugee group from Vienna, headed for Portugal, left at the end of October 1941."[63] Zipper got out just under the wire. In early February of 1939 Zipper learned that his father had secured visas for them to go to Uruguay. And, on February 19, he was told by his capo that he and Walter (the Nazi's still did not know that Herbert and Walter were brothers) and 12 - 14 others of the letter 'Z' were to be released.

However, the excitement of the possibility of gaining freedom was tragically diminished during the week before release. Zipper's dear friend, the immensely gifted Jura Soyfer had contracted typhoid and was rapidly weakening. This fatal illness was particularly tragic not only because Zipper would lose a good friend but because Jura was an enormously talented writer who wished to write about life in the prison camps, to give expression not only to the misery but to the instances of courage and affirmation of life.[64] Ironically he too was due to be released but it was too late. There was little medical attention for the ill. The last two days of Jura's life he failed to react to anything. His release from Buchenwald was to be through death.

The final days of Jura Soyfer are recounted by another survivor, Max Hoffenberg a friend and fellow prisoner in Dachau and Buchenwald. Hoffenberg's reminscences are published in a book by Horst Jarka, *The Legacy of Jura Soyfer*. He writes:

> But things got really bad for us when the "Judenaktion" began. The camp was not equipped to accommodate the great numbers of Jews that now came pouring in. And it was this overcrowding of the camp that resulted in Jura's death. Three of four weeks before the Jew hunt began five large barracks had been built in Buchenwald. Their interior equipment was as simple as possible - they had no sanitary installations whatsoever. When the first victims of the hunt arrived, approximately 10,000 Jews, the barracks were overcrowded immediately. The prisoners locked up in there were not allowed to leave their beds at night. The sanitary conditions were indescribable. Every day the S.S. and other criminals killed hundreds of Jews and stole their money and any valuables they could find on them.
>
> Soon typhoid fever broke out. In the "sick ward" more help was needed. Jura and I had to carry corpses. Jura was one of the first to get infected. There were not provisions for protecting ourselves. For five weeks we did not even have water to wash with. We carried the dead and soon after ate or smoked without being able to clean our hands. In spite of the unbelievable psychological strain of these weeks, Soyfer was mentally alert as ever. I remember that while we were working he gave me French lessons.
>
> Soon after I got typhoid myself and was put in the sickroom, where Jura was already lying. He had diarrhea and was in a bad way. His temperature was high. My sickness was still in the beginning stage and so I could take care of him a little, but nothing helped. Jura was too far gone. His lemon-yellow complexion frightened me. In the night between the 15th and 16th of February an orderly sat down on my bed and told me that Jura was in very poor condition. He got up to look after him again. When he came back he said, "Jura has died."[65]

It was Zipper and Hugo Ebner who were to carry him out, enclosed him in the paper shirt and place him in a box. This was one of the most painful moments in Zipper's life.

As release drew closer, Zipper was filled with apprehension. On his last morning, February 20, 1939, he was sent out with the other 25 men in his "shit brigade" to clean his last typhoid latrine. In those last few hours he memorized the addresses and a brief message to give to the families of the other 25 men. Again, his remarkable memory was to serve his fellow man. He remembered each address and was able to deliver each message exactly as it had been given to him.

After the morning's labor Zipper and the others to be released had to pass a medical exam. This was a major hurdle for any problem could doom one to stay. Zipper was extremely nervous for his brother Walter whose toes were still badly frostbitten. Walter kept his socks on during the examination and fortunately the doctors did not notice. The prisoners were then issued the same clothes in which they were arrested in Vienna. Zipper's still contained the blood stains from the train trip to Dachau. They were searched frequently, even belts were cut open to ensure that no messages were being smuggled out. The prisoners waited until about 4:00 P.M. when they were marched outside the camp to buses. It was a poignant moment. This place where thousands had already died and where, by 1945, over 56,000 human beings were to die victims of disease, torture, medical "experiments," and systematic genocide. It was, however, not a moment for exultation, knowing what those who were being left behind had yet to endure. They climbed aboard the buses and began their journey. The road was icy and the trip down the steep and narrow road to Weimar was dangerous. Walter quipped, "We lived through that hell and now we will be killed leaving." At the train station they were received by Gestapo plainclothesmen. Two old ladies in the train station recognized them as concentration camp prisoners and gave them their first decent cup of hot coffee in over a year.

The first train trip was from Weimar to Leipzig. At the first opportunity Zipper went into the toilet compartment not because he needed to use it, but simply to be alone. In Buchenwald one was never alone. The feeling of locking the door and being alone was at that moment a strangely luxurious feeling. During the next train trip from Leipzig to Vienna a waiter, who recognized the shaven headed, crumpled clothed, under-nourished travelers as concentration camp victims, brought them a free breakfast: their first real breakfast in over a year. Zipper and Walter sat in a compartment with a father and son, also from Buchenwald, named Zeitlin. Zipper had a mild argument with the elder Zeitlin, an orthodox Jew, who argued there were no good Germans. Zipper said his Capo had been a decent man. But for the most part it was difficult for Zipper to have any logical train of thought. The Dachau-Buchenwald experience had been such a shattering of his sense of continuity between past and future that he felt unable to concentrate. The sudden, unexpected release gave little time for acclimatization. For a time he lost his equilibrium. Still, it was distinctly pleasurable to be returning to Vienna. Arriving in

Vienna, on February 21st, Herbert and Walter Zipper proceeded as ordered from the train station to the Gestapo.

They took a taxi planning to pay from the money they were allowed to take out of their "account" at Buchenwald. They asked the taxi driver to take them to the Gestapo headquarters. When they arrived and started to pay, he appeared distraught and said, looking away, "No money from you." They were required to report to their local police station twice a day until they were able to leave.

Bruno Bettelheim often discusses the sense of guilt which prison camp survivors felt at leaving behind others, less fortunate, to suffer and die. Zipper, however, claims not to have experienced this guilt. Neither does he have nightmares about the camps. He has wondered if he is not somewhat of a "freak" for not feeling such guilt or because of his somewhat clinical view of the prison camps while incarcerated. For clearly, he sees that his experiences were a valuable education. In restrospect, he acknowledges his "good fortune" at being imprisoned in 1938-39 and not 1943-45; for in the early, pre-final solution days, he could experience it all without the virtual assurance that his stay would end in death. His attitude during his time in Dachau and Buchenwald was to observe and to experience all he could at this unique historical moment when humanity was laying itself bare at every level - jailers, prisoners, criminals, capos, doctors, generals — all were exposing a wide range of human responses. Partially as a survival mechanism and partially because of his own inner sense of self-confidence which helped him inwardly to look down upon his captors, Zipper was able to not only endure but to benefit from the experience. When he returned, his sister Hedy and others noted that he was decidedly a different person. He had always been a serious, industrious person but now there was an intensity and gravity and depth in his eyes which reflected the life time of experience he had just endured. No longer was he merely an elitist, intellectual, artist. A radical fire had been ignited and it burned in his eyes and in his soul.

The next order of business was to use the Uruguay visa to secure a German passport. This required a great deal of bargaining with the German officials. In the meantime Herbert and Walter Zipper took a room in a pension near the parents of their brother-in-law, Fred Horwitz. These few weeks in Vienna were a strange and sad time. This erstwhile capital of European culture, the pride of the Hapsburg Empire, had become a provincial city. Walter Zipper sent a postcard to the other members of the family in Paris. To illustrate, in code, what had happened to their beloved city, the fall from glory to vulgarity and mediocrity, he wrote on the postcard (which was a picture of St. Stephen's: "Greetings from Linz!" As one writer has put it, "Austria had ceased to be. Vienna became merely another German city, and not a very important one at that."[66] People's dress had become drab. Not only were almost all the Jews gone, but the important people had left for Berlin - the new seat of power. People that Zipper had known pretended not to know him and avoided him on the streets. Hans Knappertsbusch, the famous conductor, however, recognized Zipper late one afternoon on the Ringstrasse. He rushed across the street and threw his arms around him saying, "Oh, I'm so glad you are alive!" Zipper returned the greeting but warned his friend that "it might be dangerous for you to be seen with me." Hans replied: "The Gestapo can kiss my ass."

Konzentrationslager Buchenwald
Kommandantur

Weimar-Buchenwald, den 20. Feb. 1939

2457/3

Entlassungsschein

Der ~~Schutzhäftling~~ Jude Herbert Z i p p e r
~~Vorbeugungshäftling~~

geb. am 27.4.04 in Wien hat vom 31.5.38

bis zum heutigen Tage im Konzentrationslager ~~Buchenwald~~ eingesessen.

Auf Anordnung des ~~Stapoleit Wien~~ ~~Geheimen Staatspolizeiamtes Berlin~~ vom 17.2.39
~~Reichskriminalpolizeiamtes Berlin~~

wurde er nach Wien entlassen.

Der Lagerkommandant
i.A.
~~SS-Sturmhauptführer~~
SS-Hauptsturmführer

Kö.-

Zipper's Official Release (photostat) from Buchenwald. [67]

THIRD MOVEMENT

VII   Manila

VIII   Liberation

**The Manila Symphony Society
1945
Opening Symphony Concert**

in the name of Santa Cruz Church Plaza Santa Cruz

The Manila Symphony Orchestra

HERBERT ZIPPER

7 P.M. WEDNESDAY, MAY 9

Tickets: P10.00, P5.00, P3.00 all reserved
At the Office of the Society 1011 R. HIDALGO

Chapter VII

Manila: Reunion and a New War

"Zipper, you didn't omit a chance to be killed"

- Otto Klemperer

On March 15, 1939, German forces occupied the Bohemian and Moravian provinces of Czechoslovakia. The next day, March 16, Herbert Zipper and Walter Zipper made the 24-hour train trip to Paris. Visas had been finally secured by Father Zipper. In retrospect, the Zipper family came to realize that they had survived precisely because they had been dispersed and could therefore make arrangements for each other. Just ten months before Herbert Zipper had taken a very different train trip to Dachau. The trip to Paris was, needless to say, considerably different. In their compartment, Herbert and Walter Zipper were joined by a Hungarian diplomat who did not utter a word. However, once the train crossed from German-occupied Austria into Switzerland, the Hungarian echoing the sentiments of conductor Hans Knappertsbusch, turned to Herbert and Walter and announced with a heavy Hungarian accent: "Gentlemen, I don't mean to be indecent but now they (the Nazis) can lick my ass."[68] ('Meine Herren, ich will nicht unfein sein, aber jetzt können die mich im Arsch lecken!')

Zipper and his brother were greeted with great joy at the Paris train station by the whole family: Papa, Mama, Otto, Hedy and Fred. The family was surprised and delighted to see the two returnees looking reasonably well. They drove to their home at 8 Rue Borghese, Neully, in a car the clever Otto had managed to abscond with from Vienna. At home they celebrated with a festive lunch and talked mostly about the uprooted family and its current plans. It was an unspoken decision not to talk about the horrors of the concentration camp: it was too joyous a reunion to look backward. After lunch Zipper walked to the nearest post office to send Trudl a telegram: "Hale and sound, arrived in Paris with Walter, letter en route. Love Herbert." For twelve years now Trudl had been a daily presence in the life of Herbert Zipper. They were by now soul-mates, love and commitment were a mutual guarantee. The one-line telegram communicated volumes and held out the promise of a new life together — in a new world. He would soon be able to hold her and talk with her. For now, however, he would content himself with being alone. His overwhelming need was to be cleansed. After the metaphoric and literal dirt, crowding, mud, and shit surrounding and covering him, now to be alone was like taking a warm, refreshing bath and washing off the last year's filth.

On his first evening in Paris, he took a delicious walk down the Champs Elysees. From across the street he heard someone shout his name, "Herbert." The voice was that of a friend, Oskar Karlweiss a half French and half Viennese well known actor who had worked with Zipper in Vienna. Karlweiss, who had fled Austria in time, related that he had assumed that Zipper had died in Dachau and only yesterday he had told a friend that Zipper would have been just the composer they needed to compose the music for a comic opera they were producing! Just like that, Zipper had a job. The yo-yo quality of his life during this period was astounding to him even as it was happening. This was to be but another in the strange sequence of events which were to mark his life from 1938 to 1946.

Karlweiss said, "I've got the libretto. Can you write an opera in six weeks?" The answer was obvious: if they had asked for it in three days the answer would still have been "yes." They went to the actor's nearby studio where Zipper received the libretto — a political satire entitled *Le Paraplui* (*The Umbrella*). The main object of satire was Neville Chamberlain who always carried an umbrella. Zipper had arrived in Paris with the equivalent of $2.50 in his pocket and he set to work. In two weeks he had enough written so that rehearsals could begin. On May 1st, the opera opened in the Theatre Pigalle and ran until the Nazi invasion of Paris a year later.

While in Paris, Zipper sought and finally found Helly Andis, the girlfriend of Jura Soyfer. Helly had already learned of Soyfer's death but she insisted on receiving a detailed account of his last days. She wept throughout his telling of the story and was completely devastated for the two had been deeply in love. He dictated to her the text of the "Dachau Lied" without the music as copying machines were not available. Their meeting occurred just before he left Paris and, although she emigrated to New York, he never saw her again.

During this time Hans Weigel came into town from Switzerland to visit him and Zipper gave him a hand-written copy of both the text and the music of the "Dachau Lied." He asked Weigel to make a copy and to send one to Eric Simon in America. The single melody line version and text published in Eastern Germany after the war had made a separate journey through the oral network of prison camp songs.

Next he sought to discover the whereabouts and fate of other friends and was told that many refugees were gathering at the home of an old man who was giving money away. Zipper went there to make some contacts. There he witnessed a memorable scene. In his home there sat an old French rabbinical-looking Jew with a long white beard, speaking only French. He listened with profound grief to the sad stories of his guests and then gave money to each of the victims. The money was not official in any way; it was simply his own money given from the heart. The scene had about it an Old Testament quality and was indeed a moving example of the Torah teachings put in practice.

On May 3rd, Zipper received a telegram from the Philippines. The Viennese conductor, Alexander Lippay, founder of the Manila Symphony and Director of the Academy of Music of Manila, had died. Would he come to Manila as Lippay's replacement? The offer was a joyous one for Zipper on several fronts: To be able to continue his profession, to teach; to travel to an exciting new part of the world; and, most importantly, to be reunited with Trudl Dubsky.

Trudl had gone to Manila in 1937 to serve as director of a dance studio and to found a dance department at the University of the Philippines. In Manila, she had choreographed and danced in several of Zipper's compositions (with Lippay conducting) and so the faculty and administration of the academy were familiar with Zipper's musical abilities. Trudl, herself, had done more than a little "marketing" on his account.

Thus, on May 27 the intrepid Dr. Zipper began yet another adventure. He went by train to Milan. There he was joined by a former roommate from both Dachau and Buchenwald, Dr. Fritz Zerkowitz who later emigrated to the U.S. Years after, he told Zipper (in 1946 in Watersbury, Connecticut) that Zipper's sense of humor had helped him survive some of his darkest and most despairing moments.

On May 30th 1939, the steamer "Conte Biancamano" departed from Genoa on a 23-day voyage with many stops. One early stop was in Port Said which Zipper experienced as a hot, stinking city but with a fascinating culture. Zipper wandered the streets at night when the city came alive. They journeyed through the Red Sea, again in drenching heat. The passengers were all hot and wet and Zipper slept on the deck to seek some relief. The journey continued to the desolation and dry heat of Aden which had not had rain in three years. There were additonal stops in Bombay where Zipper was astounded by the poverty and to Columbo in Ceylon where he drove to the edge of the city and saw elephants and lions.

For a European and a recent concentration camp survivor the trip had an aura of unreality and fantasy. It took Zipper's mind partially off of Buchenwald and of the imminence of seeing Trudl. But it was not just the exotic and strange sights which enabled Zipper to place the concentration camp horrors into the cupboards of his mind. Unlike many who were shattered by their concentration camp experiences, Zipper was somehow able to conceptualize his experiences rather than emotionally internalize and be destroyed by them. In an almost freakish way he is able to clinically examine an experience even as he is experiencing it and thus is able to shield potentially destructive and raw emotions from the slings and arrows of life.

In Singapore he experienced two days of cool breezes which he thought were a preview of Manila. He also took time on board to write letters including the long letter to Eric Simon describing his train trip to Dachau. He practiced his English at every opportunity.

On June 23, the ship passed Corregidor only 17 miles from Manila and Zipper studiously packed and unpacked and repacked trying to contain his excitement at the prospect of seeing Trudl again. Finally they arrived on Pier Seven in Manila Bay.

Departing from the ship, Zipper experienced his first shock of the tropical Philippine enveloping heat. It was an unforgettable moment. He had, however, little time to focus on the heat for a huge reception committee waited at the dock to greet the new conductor and director of the Academy. There were members of the Symphony Board, musicians, dancers, photographers, and - most important of all - Trudl. When she had recommended Zipper for the job, she had discretely not mentioned that Zipper and she were lovers. Consequently, she did not rush up to embrace him. She noticed, however, that he was carrying an umbrella - a ridiculous appendage in the Philippines - so to avoid any photographs she sent her friend and roommate, Harriet Agens, up to Zipper to say hello and unobstrusively relieve him of the umbrella. Trudl stood there on the dock, dressed in a white and blue light summer dress, her long blond hair wafting in the morning breeze. "She looked very good to me," Zipper recalled. She then stepped up to greet him and they formally shook hands and, like a good Viennese gentleman, he kissed her hand. Zipper was wearing a light wool jacket which he was about to remove in the heat when he discovered that the heat had melted the red ink off of his ticket and his white shirt was stained in red. He kept his jacket on the rest of the festivities and was soon drenched in sweat.

Zipper and Trudl were eager to be alone, but that would have to wait. He was ushered from the dock to a Packard limousine of the Manila Symphony and driven to the cemetary to lay a wreath on the grave of Alexander Lippay. This was followed by a grand reception at the Academy of Music. Among those in attendance were Aurora Quezon, the wife of the President of the Philippines and Mr. Bocobo, the Secretary of Education. There were speeches, chamber music, and an impromptu speech requested of Zipper whose English was at this point still somewhat shaky. He was then officially installed as the Director of the Academy of Music of Manila. The reception was followed by lunch and finally, late in the afternoon, Zipper and Trudl were able to be alone with each other for the first time in two years. They walked to the bay and sat together looking out over the water. The June sunset was a glorious palette of red and orange. They sat holding hands looking at the sky and Trudl said, "I know you have much to tell me but I don't want to hear horror stories at the moment."

After their walk, they went to Trudl's apartment where they had dinner with Trudl's roommate, Hatty. After dinner, Hatty retired to her separate quarters and Trudl and Zipper were allowed complete privacy. Late in the evening he walked back to his new residence in a pension. There would be time for stories; now was a time for becoming reacquainted. The very next morning he went to the huge rehearsal hall to meet the orchestra for their first rehearsal. Together with the Board, they had decided to perform the Tchaikovsky "Symphony Pathetique" dedicated to the memory of Lippay. Maestro Zipper was soon to learn that he would earn his new pay. The Maestro smiled at his orchestra, and gave the downbeat. Instead of the bassoons' opening notes, he heard a most peculiar spitting noise. After a few more unsuccessful attempts, the bassoonist stood up and confessed, "Sir, we do not know how to play the bassoon." Though the orchestral instruments were all European quality products, many woodwind and brass orchestra members were new and virtually untrained. Until January 1939 the woodwind and brass members of the orchestra had been engaged from the well trained constabulary band. For whatever reason, late in 1938, the legislature passed a law disallowing these musicians any outside engagements. Whereupon the symphony society immediately ordered instruments from Europe and shortly before his death, Alexander Lippay had distributed them among music students and jazz players unfamiliar with symphonic instruments. The orchestra was at this time a mixture of experienced and relatively inexperienced players. All were Filipino except for the First Cellist, Vasili Prihodko, a Russian emigre from the 1917-18 exodus of Russian musicians who left for China, the Philippines and the U.S.A. With this orchestra, Herbert Zipper found himself not only conducting but teaching — a pattern that was destined to characterize his entire career.

Every afternoon he would meet with small groups — the "bassoonists," the French horns, et cetera — to teach his orchestra how to play their instruments. His patience, kindness, intelligence and humility were not lost on the orchestra members. A loyalty and love was to develop which paid amazing dividends in surprising and wholly unimagined ways.

And soon, almost miraculously, the orchestra was able to give several concerts in 1939. While he was still in Paris, Trudl had wired him to bring certain pieces of music, including the Mozart Requiem. When he arrived, Zipper asked her to tell him about the chorus for which she had ordered the Requiem. She replied, "Oh we don't have a chorus here, but I know wherever you go you must have one." The next day he set about to organize a chorus. It eventually grew to over a hundred and when President Manuel Quezon heard the Requiem he remarked to Mrs. Benito Legarda, "That's what I want played at my funeral."

From the very first weeks of his arrival in Manila, the Legarda family had become an important part of Zipper's life. Don Benito Legarda rapidly became a close friend. His grandfather was the first Philippine representative to Washington. The Legarda family owned a great deal of real estate in Manila and were a highly cultured, aristocratic family, many of whom had been educated in Paris. Benito's mother, Filomena, spoke excellent French. Benito was extremely knowledgeable about music. His younger brother, Jose, was and still is an excellent pianist. And, at the 70th birthday of Filomena, in 1943, Zipper helped organize a surprise 4-piano performance of the Bach-Vivaldi Four Piano Concerto. Benito and Jose played two parts, along with Benitos' son, Benito Jr., and Benito's sister, Mrs. Rosario Valdes.

On October 1st, 1939 Herbert Zipper and Trudl Dubsky were at last married. They had been in love for 12 years. They had been separated by work and by impending war, but now, finally, they were able to be lifetime partners. They had planned a civil wedding at city hall but the Manila Symphony Society insisted upon the full regalia. The wedding took place at the Arch-Bishop's palace with hundreds of spectators, including the First Lady of the Philippines. The wedding of Herbert Zipper, an Austrian Jew and Trudl Dubsky whose father was Jewish and mother a Catholic Austrian - was a full blown Catholic ceremony. Zipper didn't care, he was grateful to be alive and to be married. Afterwards there was a huge party at the University Club on the Luneta (the open space by Manila Bay) with flower girls and a traditional four foot wedding cake. The newlyweds honeymooned in their new apartment. The next day Zipper went to work at orchestra rehearsal and Trudl to her dance classes at the University, much to the surprise of their students and servants.

The orchestra season ended in March 1940, and the conductor decided it would be opportune to extend the season by taking the orchestra up into the cooler, mountain province city of Baguio, for a summer festival. There was no money for this in the symphony budget so he visited Baguio and met with thirty of the leading citizens. He told them he needed three thousand pesos and each pledged one hundred pesos. The five concerts were sold out and plans were made for a 1941 season.

After the concerts Zipper and Trudl stayed for an additional six weeks - their first real honeymoon. The symphony association owned a small house there near an Igorot village. The native women were all fascinated with Trudl's blond hair and wanted to touch it. The Zippers were, in turn, fascinated to learn that the Igorots carried out their courtship to music, without words. The men would carve gorgeous nose flutes and, at a kind of market, called ologs, with young girls lying on bamboo-woven beds, the young men would play music for the girls in low, soft tones so as not to disturb others. Zipper discovered that this remarkably creative people have no word in their language for 'art.' They are marvelous wood carvers, singers, dancers whose art is interwoven with their daily lives, not as entertainment, or economic product, not separate from work but as the very sustenance of life itself. Again, Zipper came to understand even more fully the essential nature of the arts, as being as crucial to the survival of the human spirit as are breathing and eating to the human body.

The universality of the arts was also brought home during the first rehearsal in Baguio. Zipper and his orchestra were rehearsing Mozart's "Jupiter" Symphony and he noticed his orchestra members looking uncomfortable, even frightened. The lowland Filipinos feel menaced by the mountain people. When Zipper looked behind him, he saw several hundred Igorot headhunters sitting there having left their spears and shields outside of the hall. They were quiet and happily enjoying the music, hearing for the first time a symphony orchestra playing Western music. They appeared practically every day. Eventually, Zipper asked one of their English speaking leaders what it was that attracted them, why they were coming again and again? The Igorot answered: "Because it is beautiful."

Meanwhile, the clouds over both Europe and the Pacific were rapidly darkening. While Zipper was rebuilding his life in the Philippines, the Nazi war machine was conquering all of Europe. On September 1, 1939, Poland fell and Britain and France declared war; on April 9, 1940, Hitler invaded Norway and Denmark, and on May 10, Holland, Belgium and France. By the end of June, France was under Nazi domination. And in June of 1941 when Herbert and Trudl Zipper returned to Manila to begin a new school semester, Hitler sent his troops into Russia. There was little sense of security in the Philippines, for the Japanese designs upon the Pacific were now clear. The Japanese were waging a devastating war upon the Chinese and were at the same time building up a huge navy. The navy was obviously not for defensive purposes; from whom, after all, need they fear an attack? Claude Buss, a friend of the Zippers, a high government official, and a leading historian of the Far East who lived in the same apartment building, said that a war with Japan was inevitable.

In June 1940 during this interim before war with Japan, Zipper went to a friend, Francis B. Sayre (the son-in-law of President Woodrow Wilson). As Sayre was the High Commissioner of the Philippines (that is, the representative of the President of the United States to the Philippines which was then a U.S. territory) Zipper asked him for help. Zipper's father, mother and brother Otto were still in Paris which was now under domination of the Nazis. His sister Hedy and her husband had emigrated to the United States in December of 1939. Walter was in England. Herbert asked Sayre to assist his family in Paris to secure visas in order to leave the Nazi controlled city. Sayre wired the U.S. Department of State and with his personal guarantee obtained for the Zippers visas to the Philippines with transit visas to the U.S.A. When they reached America, they stayed. Now all but Walter and Herbert were in the new country.

The period of 1940-41 was, as Herbert and Trudl Zipper realized later, for them a sort of "fool's paradise." A new exotic countryside, a foreign culture, a totally different architecture and means of transportation, radically different trees and flowers, visits from high government officials seeking his advice — everything was different. It was seductive to focus on the new, to become students learning every day new ways of being and relating to others and allowing oneself to forget the recent events. Zipper's idiosyncratic ability to compartmentalize and to emotionally distance himself from unpleasant realities was now reinforced by the strangeness of the new setting and by how much there was to learn. While Europe was going up in flames; while Russia was being invaded; while women and children were evacuated from Hong Kong as the Far East moved toward its doom; the newlyweds existed blissfully in their beautiful apartment looking out over the bay. On a clear day one could even see the island of Corregidor. They had a wonderful cook, Julio, and a comfortably strenuous life. Trudl performed with her dance company (Ballet Moderne) and enjoyed teaching dance at the Academy and the University. Zipper conducted his orchestra to sold out concerts, taught music theory, history, and chamber music, and directed the Academy. The time 1940-41 was as wonderful as 1938-39 had been ghastly. It ended on December 7, 1941.

On December 8, 1941 at 4:00 in the morning Far Eastern Time, Claude Buss called Zipper to tell him of Pearl Harbor. Zipper exclaimed, "They must be nuts!" but he was not altogether surprised. On December 5th he had conducted a concert commemorating the day of Mozart's death, 150 years before. After the concert, Zipper and Trudl went to their weekend house in Tagaytay south of Manila (where it was fifteen to twenty degrees cooler) and when they came back on the evening of December 7th, they noticed that the Pacific Fleet had left the harbor, including the flagship "Augusta" (a ship on which FDR would later meet with Winston Churchill in the Atlantic). "That's peculiar," Zipper had commented to Trudl.

After receiving the call from Buss, Zipper expected Nichols Airfield, which was not far from their apartment house, to be bombed that night. In the morning he hurried to the Academy and was telling his friend and treasurer of the academy, Benito F. Legarda, that he was expecting bombing at any moment. Just then the bombs began to fall on Cavite naval base. While Zipper and others, including the Japanese, had expected the American Air Force to be airborne and to resist attack, General MacArthur mysteriously did not act. Some historians have assumed that he was awaiting Congress to officially declare war. However, subsequently, other historians have puzzled over why, after receiving the news of Pearl Harbor, MacArthur did nothing for the next nine hours while the entire Air Force was destroyed upon the ground - a disastrous blow to America in the early months of the war. Perhaps, some have speculated, MacArthur did not grasp at first the nature of what was happening. He did seem to underestimate the Japanese war potential. For example, only three months before Pearl Harbor Zipper heard MacArthur give a speech in which he said he could defend the Philippines with a hundred P.T. boats. In any event while MacArthur deliberated for over 9 hours, the Japanese destroyed all the grounded American planes everywhere in Luzon. Almost the entire Far East Air Force was obliterated. Not a bomb was wasted. Japanese intelligence had been deadly accurate, for many Filipino-Japanese citizens were spies. An acquaintance of Zipper's, a dealer in pharmaceutical instruments, proved to be a rear admiral in the Japanese Navy. On the basis of many reports, Commissioner Sayre wired the U.S. State Department warning them of Japanese-Americans who might be spies.

On December 8, the State University was closed. Trudl was told she would receive two months pay. Zipper drove her to the Treasury building where they stood in line, but other waiting faculty members graciously offered her to go in first. She received her check and as they drove away, Japanese planes came and bombed the building they had just left, leaving behind many wounded and some dead.

One week later, Zipper met with his Orchestra Board. It was clear that the situation was hopeless: The fleet had been destroyed at Pearl Harbor, the air force crippled at Nichols Airbase and Clark Field, Admiral Hart had pulled out of Manila Bay with the remainder of the U.S. fleet. Manila could not be defended. Philippines President Manuel Quezon, declared Manila an open city and the American Army retreated to Bataan and Corregidor. There was nothing to do but to close the Academy, to disband the orchestra, and to hide the instruments and the library.

A new period in Zipper's life began. Having escaped the horrors of Dachau and Buchenwald, he now had to use his wits to prepare for the imminent Japanese invasion. He started by moving huge empty crates to the basement of the home of General Basilio Valdes, Chief of Staff of the Philippine Army. Zipper knew the Japanese would occupy this beautiful house and he had a plan in mind for later.

Next, he and Benito F. Legarda hid most of the instruments and the orchestra's library in the old abandoned distillery of the Legarda family. Although the distillery was inoperative for many years, a large quantity of alcohol was stored there. When the Japanese occupied Manila Bay, Ben Legarda ordered his employees to pour out into the estuary all the alcohol, some $250,000 worth. Legarda foresaw that the Japanese would convert it into fuel for the war effort. For the duration of the war, Zipper, in an almost ritualistic reaffirmation of his deep and old commitment to the arts, would slip out to the vat at least once a month to clean and care for the instruments.

On January 1st, 1942, the Japanese Army entered the city of Manila. Zipper and Trudl avoided leaving their apartment except when absolutely necessary. When the Japanese soldiers walked or marched through the streets of Manila, Filipino citizens were required to bow to them. If they did not, the soldiers would slap their faces. During the weeks before the invasion, Zipper found himself experiencing the same apprehensiveness he had felt on March 11, 1938. During this period of December 24-31, 1941, the Americans and Filipinos blew up ammunition dumps and oil refineries outside the city and an ominous curtain of black smoke surrounded Manila. One morning Zipper noticed their little canary was not singing. It lay dead poisoned by the fumes, a symbol of things to come.

About three days after occupying the city, the Japanese announced that all enemy aliens including Americans, British and French must report to the Rizal Stadium. Zipper and Trudl tried to go with them where they would be less conspicuous. But their passports were noticed (Herbert's was German and Trudl's was Czech) and they were sent home.

A few days later Zipper was looking out his apartment window when he noticed a Japanese troop truck drive up. Out jumped 17 soldiers and began clomping up the 3 tiers of stairs to the Zipper residence. At first Zipper thought they had come for a friend. The Secretary of the Manila Symphony, A.V.H. Hartendorp, an American, who had several children with a Filipino woman, was staying with the Zippers to avoid incriminating his children. Zipper quickly hid him in the bathroom but the soliders had not come for Hartendorp. When Zipper opened the door there stood, grinning, the photographer of Trudl's dance company - a Japanese spy dressed now in his uniform. He spoke English. Zipper inquired, "am I arrested?" He smiled and replied, "Yes." Zipper was loaded in the back of the truck surrounded by the soldiers with their fixed bayonets. The Japanese had known that Zipper was a friend of the American High Commissioner, Francis B. Sayre, and they knew of his friendship with Claude Buss who became the chief American representative after Sayre left for Corregidor and subsequently by U-boat to Australia. They also knew he had known MacArthur. He had also, 6 weeks earlier, delivered a speech to the Rotary Club of Manila bemoaning the cultural devastation that the Axis powers were causing.

Ironically, as the school building in Vienna had been turned into a detention center in 1938, the music conservatory of the University of the Philippines at Villamor Hall now had been converted into a police jail. Zipper's new "roommates" were McCullough Dick, a Scotsman proprietor of the Philippine Free Press, who celebrated his 70th birthday while they were in jail, and an American, Roy Bennett, the editor in chief of the Manila Daily Bulletin whose wife was also in a prison camp in Manila. When they arrived at the jail, they stood in line in front of a desk manned by a Japanese officer who took their personal information; Dick stood in front of Zipper, Bennett behind him. They were all told that they would be shot. When Dick's turn came for questioning, the officer shouted: "You, you owner of Free Press?" Whereupon Dick answered, "No, I am not the owner, I am the proprietor!" "No," shouted the Japanese, "you OWNER." "No," answered Dick, thoughtfully and somewhat pretentiously, "owner would be the wrong word; the correct word is Pro-Pri-e-Tor!" Bennett whispered into Zipper's ear: "Look, we all will be shot and there is Dick giving an English lesson to this Jap." Their prison room looked down on Taft Avenue. Zipper recalls one morning there was a great victory parade and all the Japanese tanks — small, medium and large — lined up. On signal, all the soldiers stepped out and bowed deeply to the east, to the Emperor. This incongruous juxtaposition of the modern tanks and the ancient tradition of bowing to the rising sun, was an unforgettable scene.

At one point during the interrogations the imprisoned Chinese Counsel (to the Kuomantaing) in Manila became ill. A Japanese officer took Zipper to serve as an interpretor. The Japanese doctor spoke German and the Chinese Counsel spoke English. As soon as the Counsel was able to move he was taken to Fort Santiago for further interrogations and was subsequently shot. Zipper became aware, increasingly, of the remarkable bravery of the Philippine people. Bravery is, perhaps, a quality found in all groups, tribes, nationalities, especially in times of tribulation but the Philippine people Zipper believes have a special, quiet toughness. One Filipino gentleman, Ramon Oriol, a friend of Ben Lagarda, was a sculptor of marble monuments for cemeteries. He expressed his intense hatred for the invaders and, because of his underground associations, was captured. The Japanese knew that he had knowledge of the network of underground workers. In 1942 he was sent to Fort Santiago and was severely tortured. He would not speak and almost died. He was allowed to regain a degree of strength and released. He could no longer walk and soon died from the torture. He had not, however, revealed a single name. This kind of bravery Zipper discovered was not unusual among the Philippine people.

In addition to their bravery, Zipper admired the honesty of the people. For example, one Filipino salesman at Oceanic Company Jewelry Store belonging to a French family, was sent off to Mindanao and Visayan Islands with a collection of jewels valued at over $250,000. He was off on his travels in the Fall of 1941 when the war exploded. In August of 1945 he showed up in Manila, returned to the Oceanic Company office, which miraculously survived the shelling, and returned the entire collection of jewels which the owner had long ago given up as lost. He apologized for having sold a couple of watches to stay alive. Otherwise the collection was completely intact.

On February 1st, the interrogations began: five, six days a week, for four weeks. Zipper was taken each day to Fort Santiago for the all-day questioning. The questions always began with the names and personal data of his grandparents, his parents, what did they do, endlessly repetitive questions. The Japanese knew that the evening before the High Commissioner Francis Sayre left for Corregidor, Zipper had dined with him; also, they knew that Zipper was friendly with Mrs. MacArthur. And, consequently, they thought he might have inside information. Actually, Zipper's friendships with both Mrs. MacArthur and Sayre were based on music. Zipper honestly had nothing to tell his interrogators. The first interrogator, a major, died after a week or so, and the second one became very ill necessitating a replacement. Zipper wrote to Trudl in one of his smuggled letters that 'maybe interrogating me is not good for their health!' They never hit or slapped him. Brutality would grow as the war progressed but in the early days the Japanese invaders were making some attempt to win the 'hearts and minds' of the local inhabitants. Enemy soldiers, however, fared poorly from the very beginning.

Zipper noted that there were radical differences between the German and the Japanese military. The Germans had carefully designed a system of brutality which each individual soldier, blackshirt or brownshirt, was required to obey on threat of death. There was no deviation from the cruelty which was officially and specifically prescribed.

Much has been written of the brutality and cruelty of both Japanese and German prison camps. Incidents and hundreds of complete books have been written of atrocities in Europe and the Far East. The differences have not, however, been carefully explored. Not only were the Japanese not subject to a comprehensive bureaucratic system of brutality, they had a concern for local opinion as well as world opinion. Initially they wished to use Zipper and his orchestra as a means of gaining support of the local populations. They were also more concerned with economic imperialism than with racial extermination or designing a comprehensive propaganda campaign. As frustrations of war and impending defeat in the Far East developed, more and more cases of atrocities and torture occurred but never was there national policy handed down from Emperor Hirohito as from the Fuhrer, Adolf Hitler. An individual prison guard might be cruel or kind. One man, a Lieutenant Yamamoto, was a gentleman. He hated the war. One day he showed Zipper about twenty cigarette burns on his back — the result of his resistance to a brutal command. He was a cultured man who spoke good English, French and German and who enjoyed playing chess with 'Dr. Zipper.'

After four weeks the useless questioning came to a halt and Zipper was left alone in his prison room. Soon, however, the interrogators began to pressure him to reorganize the Manila Symphony Orchestra and to give concerts. In exchange, they offered to release him. He said he could make no promise as long as he was imprisoned but if they would let him out of prison he would "investigate the possibility." A few weeks later he was released - just two days before the fall of Corregidor. He then began his plan of stall tactics. First he told them that his instruments were all in the crates in the basement of General Valdes' home. When the Japanese found that the crates (marked "Property of Manila Symphony") were empty, Zipper suggested that the Japanese soldiers who were stationed on the premises must have taken them. For weeks the Japanese interrogated their own soldiers. Then he told them he had no idea where his musicians were. Some, he suggested, must have been killed and others thrown in prison. Several times each month the Japanese officials visited Zipper and pressured him to get the orchestra going. Always he was polite, friendly, firm and evasive. Trudl said "When these men come to visit you grow a foot taller when you speak to them." On one occasion they threatened to shoot him, if he did not locate the instruments and orchestra members. He replied, "We all have to die one day. Well, do what you have to do; I can't find them." He had learned through wars, revolutions and concentration camps that one must face oneself each day and that essential decisions must be made on that basis. He learned that death is preferable to living one's life despising oneself. Trudl understood this and supported him in his wartime attitudes and activities.

While Zipper was being interrogated, an American couple, Grace and Ralph Nash and their children, were also incarcerated and remained in prison for the duration of the war. They were friends of Herbert and Trudl and, after the war, Grace Nash wrote an account of her families' experiences entitled *That We Might Live*. Throughout her book she mentions brief encounters with the Zippers giving further testimony to the kindness and unselfishness of both Zippers during this period. While both her husband and the Nash family were in prison, Trudl managed to "arrange" for Grace to secure music students when Grace was allowed out on passes and she also slipped money to Grace even though she had little to spare. For example, Grace Nash who then was expecting her third son, writes that in February of 1943:

> The next secret visitor who came to the island was Trudl Dubsky Zipper. She was like a fairy godmother, sneaking in when few dared, and risking the spying of the Japs who watched her and her husband's activities closely. Bearing fruits and sweets, she proceeded to tell me of her visits to Philippine General Hospital to see Stan (her son) and Ralph, and to Holy Ghost Convent to see Gale (her other son). She had taken him candy and cookies and told him stories while he lay in bed. Both Stan and Gale knew and loved Trudl and Herbert, so Trudl's visits must have cheered them and brought hope to Gale. The Zippers were teaching privately in their apartment, and Herbert, despite the Jap's weekly visits to check on his progress in reorganizing the Symphony, was still managing diplomatically not to do it! I knew they had little to eat

themselves, yet Trudl continued to bring fruits and supplies to us, plus bits of encouraging news."[69]

Trudl told her husband of the guards' regular schedule and he was thus able to sneak in the next day to visit Grace himself. On May 24, 1943, Grace Nash had just given birth to a third son, though she was still under Japanese arrest:

"It was just 7:20 the next morning when Trudl Zipper appeared in the door, smiling from her eyes to her toes. 'Grace,' she said, 'I have just seen your new son, and I'm on my way to Santo Tomas to sneak word in to Ralph,' She bent down and kissed me. Trudl always had a way of knowing my desires without my voicing them. Assuring her that I was fine, she left on her mission, bicycling the several miles to camp."[70]

This friendship that began in the Philippines was to continue for the rest of the Nash's and the Zipper's lives.

Meanwhile, after returning from prison to his apartment with Trudl, Zipper knew their days of occupying this particular apartment were numbered, for the Japanese would surely take it over given its location. On May 6, the night Corregidor fell, Zipper and Trudl were sitting on the porch of their apartment. It was an eerie night with intermittent explosions and flashes from across the bay; there was even an earthquake! "It was a clear evening," Zipper states, "but we knew the American and Philippine soldiers were doomed. Soon it was quiet and we realized it was all over."

The Zippers quickly moved to a new apartment on Herran Street in the Paco district of Manila. The new apartment building was owned by a Philippine woman physician, Doctora Guazon. Zipper also had his 1941 new Plymouth dragged there by a carabao cart. He had removed the distributor to render it useless to the Japanese. It was subsequently burned by Japanese during the Liberation of Manila.

In July 1942 a young man came to see Zipper, introducing himself as Lucio (his code name) and asked Zipper if he would join in helping to organize an underground intelligence unit. Zipper agreed and became part of a cadre of 32 men, mostly Chinese. (The Chinese, because of their well-justified, anti-Japanese feelings, were very effective in this kind of work.) Zipper's code name was Berting. Just a few blocks away there was a market and an old walled-in cemetery with huge trees and large gravestones - a place where Zipper was to hold many a meeting with his underground contacts.

Lucio had found out that they could hook up with MacArthur's wave length. Berting, having learned about radios from his brothers was able to help. He knew, for example, that the Japanese could detect their signals and therefore, that they must constantly move the radio. Usually they concealed the radio under cabbage or food and moved it around on a pushcart or a carabao cart. They had almost daily contact with MacArthur's headquarters, first in Australia, then in New Guinea. The Japanese knew of the existence of this radio-cart and constantly searched for it. A Japanese truck with a large antenna drove all over the city searching for the secret radio but never found it. The population knew where it was but were so thoroughly reliable that for the next three years no one ever betrayed them. Headquarters wished to know the nature of Japanese warships movements in Manila Bay. Consequently, Zipper went to the owner of a new 8 story building overlooking the Bay and secured a key to the unoccupied top story. The owner warned him that there was a Japanese machine gun sentry on the roof - day and night.

Herbert (Berting) Zipper who had no knowldege whatsoever about warships now needed two things: one, a good pair of binoculars and two, the 1941 edition of *Janes Fighting Ships* - a British publication with a thorough description and pictures of every naval vessel in the world. How could he get this book? Surely the Japanese admiralty would have one. He asked Lucio to bring him a couple young Chinese boys. Did they have any friends who were houseboys at the enemy admiralty? No, but they would check around. What did he need? He described the book and they left. A week later his morning newspaper was delivered with a copy of *Janes Fighting Ships* wrapped inside.

When Zipper began studying the book, Trudl inquired what was he doing? "Just canons," he replied, the pun intended. He never, for her own protection, told her what he was doing. He then secured a pair of Zeiss binoculars from the father of one of Trudl's dance students. And so, once or twice a week, with his binoculars concealed under vegetables in a Bayong (bamboo made shopping bag) he would go to his 8th story lookout post and with his newly acquired expertise he would record the number of ships, war or transport, and what kind they were - destroyer, cruiser, their class type, and would make a weekly report to MacArthur's headquarters.

One morning, in 1944, he was at his lookout position when he heard footsteps approaching him. He turned, binoculars in hand, to see a Japanese sentry approaching. His gun was in his holster. Zipper quickly decided, its him or me and planned to fight to the death. The soldier stopped and gestured as if lighting a cigarette and said: "You, you matches?" Herbert had some, gave them to him and the satisfied soldier left with a grin; Zipper's heartbeat went back to normal.

At about this time, while Zipper and his wife were living on Calle Herran, in the district of Paco, an ammunition truck stalled just below the Zipper's apartment window. They looked down from their third story window and saw an amusing scene unfold. The two Japanese soldiers driving the truck had lifted the hood and were unsuccessfully trying to get the engine to start. Soon a group of Filipinos gathered around and one man, a mechanic offered to help. He worked slowly, methodically, pointing out this and that to the two soldiers to occupy their attention. Meanwhile, a group of citizens had formed a human conveyer belt at the rear and completely emptied the truck of its ammunition, the loot disappearing into homes along a side road. The mechanic rattled on in Tagalog, the official Philippine language which the soldiers didn't understand, and finally in measured time completed the work. The soldiers thanked him and drove off, unaware that their truck was now empty. The Zippers enjoyed the show from their balcony seats.

Another incident is worth recalling. One day in 1944 two of the Chinese boys in Zipper's underground cadre came to him in their cemetery secret meeting place. They showed him photographs, taken at Nichols Air Field, of six Japanese bombers painted with American insignias: Sun bombers with the American star. Zipper immediately surmised the Japanese were planning to bomb Manila and blame it on the Americans. For the Japanese knew that the Filipinos were overwhelmingly pro-American and they wished to wage a propaganda counter offensive. Zipper showed the photos to Benito Legarda, Sr. and the two of them concocted a plan to inform the Philippine citizens. They determined to print the story on the back of 10 Centavo paper notes. (The Phillipine currency was printed during the war by the Japanese. Filipinos called it "Mickey Mouse money." When the U.S. Armed Forces returned, it became worthless.) Legarda provided 1000 of them and on a Sunday afternoon when there were no employees working, they went to his office. Zipper secured a stencil from the owner of his apartment building, (Doctora Guazon), and they typed their message on the stencils:

> FILIPINOS: BEWARE. THE JAPANESE ARE PAINTING 6 OF THEIR BOMBERS WITH AMERICAN INSIGNIAS. INTENT TO BOMB MANILA TO AROUSE ANTI-AMERICAN FEELINGS.

On the thousand notes they blotted on their message. It took them all Sunday afternoon.

The next morning they each took 500 centavo notes, Legarda went to the north of the Pasig River and Zipper to the south, and they dropped them on the ground in public places - markets, shopping centers, etc. Zipper cut a hole in his pocket and just let them drop out of his pants. They also slipped them into mailboxes of Japanese officials so that they would know their game had been detected. By 11:00 Legarda called to say he was okay, their code for "mission accomplished." In the afternoon of that day, Zipper's first music student arrived all excited. He had purchased a 10 centavo note with the message on the back for one peso. Already the notes were becoming collector's items. Zipper knew then it had worked. The next morning the Japanese controlled local newspaper carried an editorial denying the painting of the bombers and blaming the whole incident on enemy propaganda.

All was not, however, so adventurous during this time. Gradually the Japanese paid less attention to Zipper and their pressure to have him reconstitute the orchestra faded as the war heated up. Zipper continued his underground work and continued giving private lessons, some 60 a week, just to have enough food and rent to survive. In November of 1943 things took a turn for the worse. Until then food was scarce but now a terrible flood caused by a typhoon devastated almost all of the lowlands of Northern Luzon, including Manila. Water reached a height of 6 feet in front of the Zipper apartment. All electricity and gas was out. Zipper had stored some charcoal in the garage as a precaution. He swam to the garage, pried the door ajar. Out floated the charcoal. He shouted to Trudl to throw him something to collect with and he gathered up the charcoal cubes in a hat. That evening it took over an hour to dry the charcoal for Trudl to cook a decidedly unsavory mush. Later on there was a knock at the door: Dr. Stransky, a Viennese physician from the nearby general hospital, couldn't get home so he swam to the Zippers to spend the night. He took out his money, laid it on towels in the candle light to dry out. Trudl said he looked like Hogarth's "The Miser."

After the flood food was a critical problem. The growing hatred of the Japanese toward the Filipinos was now such that they would let the citizens starve. Increasingly the civilian populace became dependent upon guerillas to ambush and steal food from Japanese transports, push carts, trucks, cars - whenever they could. The Chinese boys came to Zipper and said they needed more small arms for the underground fighters.

Zipper discussed the problem with Ben Legarda who was able to secure six 22-caliber pistols from a relative. But he had no ammunition. Next Herbert went to Huang Cheng Yung the father of one of his piano students, Dorothy Huang (now an excellent piano teacher herself in Los Angeles). Huang had a drug store and with unusual resourcefulness was able somehow to secure ammunition. Before delivering his "gift packages" to the underground, Zipper wrote "For delivery to the Japanese Military Police" on the boxes of guns as a precaution in case he was stopped.

The food problem did not go away and many citizens died of starvation. In the old Spanish part of Manila, Intramuros - "inside the wall" there were 40,000 people living before the war. At liberation day there were 224 remaining. Many had died of starvation. Most were simply murdered by the Japanese. On March 1st or 2nd in 1945 Herbert Zipper looked into a burned out church building and saw the corpses of 700 people. The Japanese soldiers had herded them into the church and set fire to the building.

On September 23, 1944, Zipper was sitting at his desk at 9:00 in the morning. The house boy was cleaning and Zipper, still the musician, was writing the 3rd act of a ballet score. He became aware of the drone of airplanes but it was a different sound than he was accustomed to. He called to Trudl, "These are not Japanese planes - let's go to the roof." There they saw a spectacle. From out of the clouds came wave after wave of American planes - fighter planes from Halsey's fleet. They bombed the harbor and blew up practically every ship, scores of Japanese planes went down in flames. The whole bay was covered with black smoke. That afternoon Zipper went to his lookout place and reported the damage. The following morning, the Japanese Press carried the headline "Damage was of the slightest."

A week before the invasion Zipper saw that the 8 inch guns on the deck of a half sunk cruiser were being repainted and the ship was being loaded with ammunition, obviously to fire upon the city. He radioed in his observation and the next morning three U.S. fighter planes came and bombed the cruiser totally away. The liberation of Manila was now imminent.

Chapter VIII

Liberation: Dr. Zipper Gives a Concert

> "The arts live continuously, and they live literally by faith; their nature and their shapes and their uses survive unchanged in all that matters through times of interruption, diminishment, neglect; they outlive governments and creeds and societies, even the very civilizations that produced them. They cannot be destroyed altogether because they represent the substance of faith and the only reality. They are what we find again when the ruins are cleared away."
>
> - Katherine Anne Porter

As the people of Manila anticipated the transformation of their lives that the liberation would bring, an already transformed Herbert Zipper was leading a double life. Ostensibly he was just a local citizen scratching out a meager living, yet behind the shadows he was now an activist working for the underground. No longer was he the Viennese, coffee house intellectual, no longer the elegant gentleman, the graduate of the Academy. And, no longer was he a concentration camp survivor whose daily life for almost a year had been motivated by the desire to endure. Now he was changed. Now he was an activist working in the streets with the people; natives who trusted and depended upon him. The transformation was radical and permanent. The customs of social privilege and economic security with which he grew up had been obliterated in Dachau and Buchenwald and now in Manila. There could be no going backward. The seeds were set for his second life as a community worker. He had lost Europe but had gained a more global humanity.

In their day-to-day world, as 1944 ended and 1945 began, the Zippers continued their precarious life of teaching and attempting to maintain some creativity amidst the growing misery. He taught 60 students and with many he established barter arrangements for various necessities. In the midst of these unsettling days Zipper also managed somehow to compose music. His major undertaking was a full length ballet, "Veritas," for Trudl. She prepared the choreography, set designs, and gorgeous costume drawings and together they wrote the scenario. Unfortunately, in the bombing and shelling during the liberation of Manila the score was destroyed and the ballet was never performed. Only the scenario and costume drawings which were at Ben Legarda's office survive to this day.

One other Zipper possession survived the fall of Manila. Early in 1941 Zipper had purchased the Fourteenth Edition of the *Encylopedia Britannica* from a couple departing the Philippines. In January of 1945, when the American forces landed in Luzon, Zipper began to prepare for the impending battle by moving a few belongings to places he believed would be more safe. He had constructed a little pushcart by using old bicycle wheels and using this, he moved the encyclopedia to a friend's apartment in a large concrete building across the street from his apartment. A few days later he noticed the Japanese placing bombs in the vestibule of the building and so he moved the encyclopedia set again. This time he dug a hole in a neighbor's garden and buried it gambling on the relative certainty that it rarely rained during the first three months of the year. As he pushed his makeshift cart laden with the heavy books down the street an old Irishman leaned out his apartment window and exclaimed: "There goes Zipper with the wisdom of the world."

The liberation of Manila began on February 3, 1945. During the 30 days of fighting which followed the arrival of the American troops, Manila was virtually leveled. The destruction paralleled Dresden, Hiroshima, Warsaw. Of the 700,000 people living in Manila, over 100,000 died - at least six civilians for every soldier on both sides. The Japanese officer in charge of Manila, General Tomoyuki Yamashita, gave explicit orders to blow up military installations, to remove or destroy all supplies, and to establish a new line of defense outside the city. Historian William Craig gives an account of what followed:

> When MacArthur's troops arrived on the outskirts, it appeared that the Japanese had truly withdrawn. A communique was sent out to the world announcing the capture of the city. A triumphal parade was planned. The First Cavalry Division was accorded the honor of leading the procession into the capital. Uniforms were pressed. Speeches were prepared.
>
> Then observation planes flying over the peaceful streets noted large fires burning in the center of the city. Manila was in flames. The Japanese were staying to fight.
>
> American officers were appalled at the news. No one wanted to see the beautiful city become a battlefield. Many of the men around MacArthur had spent years in the Far East and looked upon Manila as one would a home town. To some it was a romantic mistress, to others an adventurous oasis from a former life. The Sixth Army went into battle with heavy hearts.

Up in the mountains, Yamashita assumed that his soldiers had left the capital. Cut off from the rest of his army, he could not know that a naval landing force had entrenched itself inside the walls and erected barricades on the streets in defiance of expressed orders. As usual in Japanese military circles, the Army and Navy seldom agreed on anything. Admiral Okochi, in charge of naval personnel, decided that Manila should be defended and sent Rear Admiral Iwabuchi into the still unmarked city with a vague plan to delay the Americans as long as possible. Iwabuchi and his desperate rear guard did a formidable job.

For nearly one month, into late February, Manila was a slaughterhouse, the scene of multiple atrocities, as Japanese marines fought insanely to defend the strategically unimportant city. In the hills of Luzon, Yamashita could know nothing of the extent of the carnage, but he was advised of the ridiculous rear guard action and ordered the Navy to leave. He even sent an Army relief column to help Iwabuchi's forces to withdraw. It failed to make contact, but the situation could hardly have been altered anyway.[71]

The 16,000 Japanese soldiers refused to surrender and gradually the city was reduced to rubble as one house, one building after another was destroyed by heavy artillery. Hundreds of people were caught in the cross fire between American and Japanese soldiers and artillery. The smell of death was everywhere. Monuments were destroyed; the beautiful old city of Intramuros was totally demolished. At some points in the center of the city one could see all the way to the bay - for there was nothing remaining but ground level debris.

William Manchester, in his biography of Douglas MacArthur describes the events of these 30 days vividly:

> The devastation of Manila was one of the great tragedies of World War II. Of Allied cities in those war years, only Warsaw suffered more. Seventy percent of the utilities, 75 percent of the factories, 80 percent of the southern residential district, and 100 percent of the business district were razed. Nearly 100,000 Filipinos were murdered by the Japanese. Hospitals were set afire after their patients had been strapped to their beds. The corpses of males were mutilated, females of all ages were raped before they were slain, and babies' eyeballs were gouged out and smeared on walls like jelly. The middle class, the professionals and white-collar workers, suffered most. Ironically, the chief survivors of the prewar oligarchy were the members of Laurel's puppet government, who were safe in Baguio and Yamashita.
>
> MacArthur blamed the holocaust on the Japanese general, but the guilt lay elsewhere.[72]

For as John Tolard writes:

"Unlike Corregidor, Manila was not to have been defended at all. Yamashita moved all except security troops out of the city, but no sooner had they left than Rear Admiral Sanji Iwabuchi reoccupied Manila with 16,000 sailors... and once there, against Yamashita's specific order, turned the city into a battlefield."[73]

Manchester speculates that

Either Iwabuchi had not received the order from Yamashita declaring the capital an open city, or he chose to ignore it. Once he had decided to defend Manila, the atrocities began, and the longer the battle raged, the more the Japanese command structure deteriorated, until the uniforms of Nipponese sailors and marines were saturated with Filipino blood.

GIs fought them hand to hand, room by room, closet by closet. Then enemy survivors retreated into the old walled city of Intramuros, whose stone walls, forty feet thick and twenty-five feet high, had withstood nearly four centuries of earthquakes.[74]

Zipper remembers those days as vividly as his days in Dachau and Buchenwald: "These were moments in which you knew you were living in epoch making times." Zipper's intelligence network had informed the American headquarters that the southern approach to Manila was heavily fortified and should be bombed prior to invasion. For whatever reason the report was ignored and consequently, many lives were needlessly sacrificed. As the Americans neared Manila, Zipper knew the Japanese would mine the bridges, so he instructed his underground team to cut the Japanese cables at night. Each day the Japanese inspected and replaced the cut cables. Zipper's efforts here ultimately failed as the Japanese finally blew up everything they could.

As American tanks and troops entered the city Zipper surmised that if there were street fighting he and Trudl would be trapped in their 2nd story apartment. He cut a hole in the basement wall so they could exit from the rear. To leave through the front door would have been suicide: there were machine gun nests lining the street. The Zippers had moved to this building, by carabao cart, in November of 1944, as he had heard rumors of friends being re-arrested. Now only Ben Legarda and a few friends knew where he lived. As it turned out this was a wise manuever. The Japanese did in fact come looking for him at his old address but no one knew where he had gone. Some acquaintances in his old neighborhood were be-headed in the streets in front of their home.

On the eve of February 6, Zipper and Trudl were in their living room. Trudl laughed loudly at something and, seemingly, in response, a bullet came whizzing in through the open window. The next morning, an acquaintance came to tell Zipper his friend, from Vienna, Dr. Markuson was dying of tetanus in the hospital. Lucio had come to the apartment that morning and was unable to leave because of the street fighting. So Lucio and Zipper helped each other climb over back fences to get to the hospital with anti-tetanus vaccine (which Zipper had obtained from a Spanish pharmacist down the street). At one wall the bullets sprayed by narrowly missing their heads and the two decided to return home. Now Zipper devised an alternate and outrageous plan. He borrowed a stethoscope and instructed Trudl to sew a red cross on his white shirt, whereupon he simply walked boldly up the street, passing Japanese soldiers, who were hiding with their guns within the foliage of the trees. He walked directly to the hospital where his friend received the vaccine, Dr. Markuson rewarded Zipper's efforts by a complete recovery.

After returning home, he and Lucio saw a body lying in the street in front of their building. It was that of a young Chinese boy. They brought him to the garden next door where they discovered a bullet hole in his chest just below the heart and an exit hole in his back. Although they covered him up with one of the Zipper's blankets, he was still shivering. They then further rolled him up in a small carpet. The carpet thus escaped the ensuing destruction and is one of Zipper's few surviving relics of the time. For the next 3 weeks they carried the boy everywhere and managed to keep him alive. The Zippers called him their mascot. On the 26th of February they finally located a U.S.A. ambulance and turned him over to the Red Cross. The doctor said he should have died. As it turned out, the bullet had entered his body, hit a rib, gone in a circular manner around his rib cage and exited - thus missing his heart. (When Herbert Zipper returned to the Philippines in 1951 this young man greeted him at the airport with flowers. The rug which saved the boy remains in Zipper's home.)

By February 6, a major problem to be solved, besides the gunfire, was where to find food. They had some Navy cans of biscuits and amongst the three of them - Zipper, Trudl and Lucio they allowed themselves 3 biscuits a day. Soon they found the artillery was increasing and they decided to retreat to the back yard next door where they had dug ditches. Zipper had, however, insisted no one return to the house, because he assumed that the entire street would be shelled by American batteries. On the 3rd day of shelling unbeknown to Zipper, Trudl and her houseboy Toni crept back secretly into the house to recover the ballet score and a book on counterpoint Zipper had written for Philippine students. Zipper's predictions materialized with a huge explosion - the entire front half of their apartment building had been blown away. Someone shouted to him, "My

God, your wife is in there." He raced to the building and found Trudl staggering out covered with dust and rubble. "It's okay," she mumbled - later he had to take 5 small pieces of shrapnel out of her hair. Miraculously she was unhurt though somewhat shell-shocked. Toni had a jagged glass cut in his arm and again Zipper was prepared. He happened to have sulfanilamide pills with which he made a powder to put on the wound. Later, a medic observed that this possibly saved the boy's arm from amputation. The apartment had been hit by a US-105 shell. Herbert Zipper's manuscripts were reduced to confetti.

They knew now that they must move from the yard immediately. They went up the street to a church courtyard and huddled behind a wall. The artillery barage and flashes of light continued non-stop. Trudl wondered whether they could possibly survive. He assured her, "Of course." Having survived the horrors of Dachau and Buchenwald, he had few doubts that somehow they would survive the Manila siege. He did, however, use his wits and employed his cool ability to objectively assess the situation and act accordingly. For the next few days they moved from place to place seeking relative safety, trying to avoid the heaviest barrages, all the while managing to carry the wounded Chinese boy with them. Eventually, they found shelter in a large bombed out, 7-story apartment building along with about 800 people who huddled together. Zipper installed Trudl, Lucio, and the Chinese boy and himself in a hallway which he felt would be safer than a room. He reasoned that American shells were impact coded and two cement walls provided relative safety. There was no water in the building and toilets were unusable. A group of predominantly Chinese men and Zipper designed and built a latrine. Zipper supervised the job: by now he was an expert in Latrines.

Next, having heard tales of Japanese soldiers killing and raping the citizens, Zipper called together 15 of the Chinese men and they organized a plan should the Japanese enter their apartment compound. A few days later, a company of Japanese soldiers appeared. The Japanese commander shouted, "Everybody down to the courtyard" and the soldiers stood facing the staircase with their rifles pointed. On a pre-arranged signal all 800 civilians appeared from all over the building. They came not just from the staircase but from every door and corner and they surrounded the 30 or so soldiers. Their plan, which the Japanese could easily see, was to rush the soldiers. Though some of them would die, they could overpower the Japanese by sheer numbers. The Japanese soldiers backed off and left. They did not come back.

Throughout his pre-war and wartime experiences, Zipper came to trust his instincts. He discovered that each of us has untapped levels of intelligence and means of apprehending the world. It is only in moments of crisis that we are forced to call upon these powers. As the war came to an end in Manila, two such incidents occurred within a week of each other which reaffirmed this growing awareness. The first occurred on one of his water-getting forays. He and two Chinese boys would crawl on their bellies, early in the morning each day pushing buckets in front of them while Japanese soldiers trained their machine guns on them. On that morning when they reached their water hole and were about to fill up their buckets, Zipper suddenly had an overwhelming urge that he must get away, that he could no longer bear the place, sensing impending disaster. Without thinking, acting on impulse alone, he jumped over a wall and within two seconds a shell landed directly where he had just been. The two boys were killed. He crawled back to the apartment.

The second incident occurred a few days later. Zipper and Trudl helped two women give birth. Neither of them knew what to do but somehow managed. Afterwards, Trudl said that she could no longer take the dust and filth. She must wash. He searched the building and found one empty apartment with a bathroom intact. There was, of course, no running water. He said to her, "All right you stay here with Lucio and I'll get water." As he was returning he heard an immense explosion and saw one corner of the building blown apart - the corner where Trudl was waiting. Zipper rushed back to the scene of the explosion. The bathroom was gone. Seconds before the crash, however, Trudl had had a premonition. She heard no sounds, no whistling of shells. She was simply overcome with a feeling that she had to move. She grabbed Lucio by the shoulder and dragged him into an adjoining closet. As she closed the door, the shell hit ripping away the street front wall of the room she had just left. Lucio had bloody scratches on his shoulder.

On February 26, 1945 at 4:00 A.M. in the morning, Zipper was crawling over the road from the bombed out apartment building when he realized the unusual quiet. There was no shooting. He looked to his left and saw helmets. He almost shouted for joy. They were not Japanese helmets. One soldier raised himself up a little and waved. Zipper leaped to his feet and ran to the barricade. An officer there, a captain, said "You look a little done in - would you like a cup of coffee?" Yes, he would. The Captain then asked, "How many people are in that building? We are going to shell it in 15 minutes." "No, you are not," an agitated Zipper exclaimed. There are 1,000 people in there!" The Captain asked how long it would take to get them all out and Zipper told him "an hour." The captain phoned the artillery and delayed his bombardment by 45 more minutes. Again, fortune intervened. Had Zipper gone for water 20 minutes later, he, Trudl and a thousand others would have been blown apart.

Zipper ran back to the building and set his Chinese messengers in action. The wounded boy and the two women who had just given birth were carried out and the boy wrapped in the carpet was turned over to the ambulance and Red Cross. As they walked behind the American lines, some of the group discovered a Japanese sniper hiding behind a bush. The sniper was a terrified young boy. They dragged him out and were about to beat him to death, when Zipper exploded. He screamed with a ferocity that surprised everyone, including himself, "don't do that. You will never live it down!" The crowd stared at him thinking he had gone crazy but they quietly turned the Japanese over to the U.S. soldiers. Zipper had looked into the pathetic boy's eyes and saw a misguided young boy doing what he had been ordered to do. Essentially, he knew that to kill the boy would be to reduce everyone to the lowest level of the war. For he had seen in Dachau, Buchenwald, and now in Manila that those who kill and degrade others ultimately kill and degrade themselves.

Where, I have often wondered, is this young Japanese soldier today? The president of an international relief organization? the manager of an arms factory? A doctor or teacher? Does he ever reflect upon the moment when his life was saved by a Viennese civilian-survivor of the fall of Manila whose ferocious defense of the value of human life overrode the prevailing lust for vengeance of a war-torn group of native Filipinos? Has that soldier ever reflected upon his personal choice of accepting his government's orders to conquer a foreign people and kill those who resisted? One wonders. In any event, Zipper's ability to live and act according to his code, according to his rational understanding of what is right, even at moments of the deepest emotional turmoil, is both remarkable and encouraging. For if he could and can do it, then why not others? Why not, ultimately, humankind?

That evening for the first time in a long while, Herbert and Trudl Zipper slept, unrealistically believing themselves safe, in a garden behind the American lines. The next morning Zipper led several soldiers on a tour of the area showing them where the booby traps were located. He then walked around South Manila and saw the full extent of the devastation. It was beyond belief. The city was almost complete rubble. Here a scalded tree, there stairs leading to nowhere, here a toilet suspended on pipes in mid-air, hanging upside down, there the remnants of a wall. At one point, a mile in-land from the sea, where a dense city once had existed, now one could see all the way to the beach - the city had simply been leveled. And everywhere the stench of thousands of bodies decomposing in the tropical heat.

Claude Buss described the grim scene in a report reprinted in Fortune Magazine:

> Manila is utterly destroyed. From Nichols Field to the Luneta, it is one heap of twisted, dusty debris. The lovely old houses along Taft Avenue and the Boulevard are gone — dynamited and put to the torch in one of the most senseless orgies of bestiality ever perpetrated upon a helpless people. The legislative hall, the Agriculture and Commerce Building, and the Finance Building have been blown to bits. Jai Alai is a ghastly scar. The Port Area is a shambles, the harbor a graveyard of sunken ships. The Escolta is tragically like a set of building blocks kicked over by a maddened giant. North of the river row upon row of houses have been so completely obliterated that not even the outlines of their foundations remain. And among the ruins there are hundreds — if not thousands — of charred automobiles mixed crazily with the skeletons of sewing machines, barber chairs, umbrellas, stoves, lathes, and iceboxes.
>
> Unsupported walls stand here and there in fragile defiance. In some places whole floors hang suspended by threads of concrete and steel. Dozens of leaning frames are silhouetted black and gaunt against the white tropical horizon. The University of the Philippines looks like the ruins of ancient Rome. LaSalle College and Letran are mere shells, and the General Hospital is a battered monument to the heroes who perished there. Intramuros has been pulverized. The sturdy walls of the ancient Spanish fortress have crumpled under artillery fire. The High Commissioner's Office, the Army and Navy Club, the Elks Club, the Manila Bay View hotels, once aristocratic and resplendent, are now gutted horrors in a neighborhood of tombs.
>
> The grass is not green in metropolitan Manila this year. There is no grass. The flame trees will not show their gorgeous colors; those giants have perished at the roots. Pet dogs and cats have disappeared. Nothing remains of the zoo except the blistered bars of the empty cages. Only a few scrawny ponies remain to pull the carromatas on Marnila streets. Manila, which was to the Philippines what San Francisco and New York combined are to the U.S., has been destroyed.[75]

At one point General Basilio Valdes asked Zipper if he had any possessions left. Zipper thought a moment and said that there might be a set of the Encyclopedia Britannica remaining. They drove through the stench of rotting bodies and debris of the city to the apartment building. There was nothing left, not even a wire from three totally demolished pianos. But miraculously all 24 volumes of the encyclopedia set were lying around the garden, all in good shape. These books and the small Chinese rug in which Zipper carried the wounded boy throughout the duration of the Battle of Manila were the only belongings that survived. All others that he had distributed to friends on their side of the Pasig River fell victim to the total destruction of South Manila.

Later that day Zipper, Trudl, Lucio, and "Niddy", the Zipper's little dog who had accompanied them through all the past adventures, marched toward the river and were picked up by an Army truck that took them over a Bailey-bridge (pontoon) to the still intact home of Dr. Alejandro Legarda, Ben's brother. There they were overjoyed to find thirty or so friends and relatives. At night, after dinner Herbert and Trudl quietly went into the private garden in the back. There was no water in Manila now but Dr. Legarda's home had a well with a bucket. There surrounded by mango and avocado trees, orchids and night-blooming jasmine - nullifying the stench of death from the air - They took off their clothes and poured buckets of cool water over each other. It was a quietly joyous and almost holy moment — a kind of baptism of survival.

The next day, March 1st, a nearly complete cease firing had been reached. Ignoring danger, Zipper went to find his friend Jim Halsema and found him in the tent of the Associated Press. Zipper was relieved to find him alive though he looked weak having been badly treated by the Japanese soldiers. Zipper asked him for a typewriter and some stationery with the Manila Symphony Society letterhead, as well as assistance in typing a letter. "To whom?" Halsema asked. "To General MacArthur," Zipper replied, "I want to organize the symphony orchestra right now." Halsema asked him if he lost all reason. "No," Zipper responded, "the city is devastated, the stench of death is all around, everyone is depressed and demoralized. We need something to lift our spirits." [76]

Zipper dictated the letter and that same afternoon at about 2:00 he walked down to MacArthur's headquarters and gave the letter to an M.P. who delivered it to the General. He then walked home. Zipper's letter to General MacArthur requested the aid of the armed forces for the purpose of reorganizing the Manila Symphony Orchestra that had been dormant during the Japanese occupation. In the letter he explained that the surviving population, having faced extreme deprivations after the traumatic experiences of occupation and the month-long fight for liberation, the complete absence of any civilized activity and the chaotic condition of the city, needed now an artistic expression of organized beauty, the rebirth of its symphony orchestra as a symbol of hope and courage.

At about 5:00 that same afternoon Brigadier General Bonner Fellers and Colonel Andres Soriano (a symphony donor and owner of the San Miguel Brewery) came to the Zipper home. Now what is this you are suggesting, they inquired? Zipper informed them that he wanted to call for an immediate meeting of the Symphony Board in order to reorganize the

Manila Symphony and to put on concerts - "tout de suite!" "I need," he told them, "strings, reeds, bows, and dozens of other items from America." They told him to bring a list to headquarters the next morning at 8:30. Zipper also told them his list would have to be teletyped to San Francisco and that he would need air priority. "That," said General Fellers, "is difficult."

That evening Zipper made his list and delivered it to General Fellers the next morning. The general went in to see Douglas MacArthur who stuck his head out the door and said to Zipper, "Hi, I'm glad you're alive. Good luck to you." Fellers soon came out of the office with the list signed by MacArthur. General Fellers told Zipper "with that signature you can go to God." Instead, Zipper went to Col. Harry Disston head of Special Services and handed him his list. The Colonel looked at it and said, "My dear fellow, don't you know there's a war still going on?" The Colonel inquired who signed this. Whereupon Zipper pointed to the signature. This produced an immediate response, "Okay, Okay." Disston provided Zipper with a jeep and an orderly. The teletype communication with San Francisco was arranged and 6 days later the musical supplies arrived.

Zipper then called for the first meeting of the Manila Symphony Board since 1941. Some members were dead, others were exhausted from the bombardment of Manila, and almost everyone thought the maestro was a bit off his rocker. Where, for example, would the concert be held? Zipper replied, "in the bombed-out Santa Cruz Cathedral." Where will the money come from? "I'll find it." Finally, Mrs. Legarda, the president and a very powerful and imaginative woman, said, "Let's do it."

The next major problem was to locate the members of the orchestra. The city was in ruins; there were no addresses. Some musicians were dead, some had fled to the hills. Undaunted, Zipper activated "the bamboo telegraph" - the word-of-mouth network. He also used the bicycle lent to him by Gen. Valdes and later the jeep that the Army had provided for him to drive around the city rounding up his old orchestra. One day he was out in Pasay, a suburb of Manila, looking for a cellist. At one stop an old lady approached him.

"Maybe you are Mr. Zipper?" she said.
"Yes." "Maybe you are looking for musicians?"
"Yes. I am looking for Agapito Cruz," he replied.
"Well," she said, "I think he's over there in that tree."

The conductor walked over to a huge, old tree, standing next to the ashes of what had been a house and a tennis court, and looked down into a hollowed out hole at the base of the trunk. He saw a small figure in there reading. Recognizing Dr. Zipper, the figure leaped out and exclaimed, "Maestro!" They embraced, and then he reached down into the tree hole and pulled up an object and said, "Look!" He was holding his cello - all that he had preserved from his home. He was thrilled with the idea of re-establishing the orchestra. "But," he exclaimed, "Sir, I cannot come, I do not have any pants." Zipper arranged for a U.S. Army truck to deliver khaki pants and shirts to several drop off locations for his re-emerging orchestra.

There were sad stories as well. His former violinist concert master, Ernesto Vallejo, had been among hundreds of citizens who where herded into a church in his home town and incinerated by the Japanese soldiers. When he located his first French horn player, Ramon Atilon, he said he would be glad to return but he was half-starved to death and too weak to blow his horn. Zipper immediately arranged for rice and canned foods to be delivered to him and to others. The U.S. Army soldiers took a particular delight in "feeding the musicians." Zipper also supplemented his orchestra with a few fill-ins, conscripted from the Army, for example, the composer Robert Kurka (who later wrote an opera based on *The Good Soldier Schweik*) played 2nd violin and the former concert master of the N.Y. Radio City Orchestra, Leon Zsawisha, also played violin. In addition, he acquired one first clarinetist and an Australian Lieutenant, Horace Samford (G2) who played cello, and a couple other "ringers." Later in June these ringers were ordered to rejoin their company and to move to the north for "mopping-up" duty. Again, Herbert Zipper wrote a note to MacArthur requesting their continued services because they - especially the woodwind players - could not yet be replaced. Request was granted for all who had joined the orchestra. A few days later came the news from the north that this particular company had walked into an ambush and was wiped out to the last man. Only the soldier musicians had escaped death.

Mrs. Legarda had secured permission from the Arch Bishop to hold the first concerts in the bombed out remains of Santa Cruz Cathedral, in the heart of the city. And on April 2, Zipper was ready to begin rehearsals. One obstacle remained: how to pay the musicians? He went to the head of the Office of War Information: Pacific War Office, Frederick Marquardt, an old friend, and said, "I need 3600 pesos (about $1800)" Marquardt said, "I have no authority to pay Filipino Symphony musicians - but I'll do it." He returned in a few minutes with the cash in an envelope.

Rehearsals began. By the end of April Zipper invited a few of the Big Brass, Colonels and Generals, to a rehearsal. They were amazed and asked him to plan a repeat concert for the Army. Meanwhile Zipper had a host of logistical problems to solve. For one, how to build an orchestra platform, where to get the lumber? U.S. "ingenuity" solved the problem. One evening, at midnight, three colonels took Zipper to the railway station and ordered the M.P.s to load lumber on their truck. No requisitions were issued. In effect, they "stole" the lumber from themselves. These were known as "Midnight Requisitions."

A new problem surfaced. The concert had been announced in late April through a few posters on walls. A few days later the tickets went on sale, at 7:00 A.M. By 8:00 A.M. a line - literally 10 blocks long had formed and by 10:30 in the morning they were sold out: 2400 seats. But there were no chairs in Manila. The Red Cross, somehow, managed to scrounge up 400 folding chairs but they were still 2,000 short. What to do? Zipper tried everything he could think of with no results. He even had the top brass, Generals, Colonels, looking for chairs - with no results. The word "chair" began to give him nightmares. Finally, acting both in desperation and on a hunch he to this day, cannot explain, Zipper approached the Australian Lieutenant Samford who had offered to help and asked him to drive him down to the rubble of what had been Manila's Chinatown. There were now only five days left before the concert. "What in the world," asked the incredulous Lt. Samford, "are we doing driving around at night looking for chairs in Chinatown with the concert five days away."

In Chinatown, Zipper observed two men leaning over the railing of a small bridge spanning a smelly canal. He told Samford to pull up. One of the men recognized the conductor and said, "You are Zipper." "Yes," Zipper replied. "What can we do for you?" "I need chairs." "Wait a moment," he said, and the two men disappeared into the darkness. It was virtually pitch dark. And Zipper and Samford stood on the stinking estero bridge, lit only by a small oil lamp, with its cork swimming in the glass, barely able to see each other, and waited. Samford wondered aloud what in hell was going on with Zipper? Had he cracked under the pressure? They waited five minutes, then ten minutes, nothing happened. Samford continued walking up and down mumbling to himself.

Finally after more than fifteen minutes had passed, the two Chinese returned accompanied by an old man with a short white pointed beard, with hair in pig tails and dressed in a kimono. He came up to Zipper:

What do you want?"
"Chairs."
"How many?"
"2,000"

Samford letting out a subdued giggle, turned and walked away shaking his head at the absurdity of the situation.

After a few moments of silence, the old man looked at Zipper with a completely poker face, thought a while and said:

"How much you pay?"

That question filled Zipper with hope and he answered:

"25 cents a chair."
"No, 50 cents."
"30 cents."

A deal was struck at 35 cents a chair with one condition: "There must be M.P.'s 24 hours watching. Otherwise, chairs get feet, walk away." Samford promised to have them commandeered. They shook hands and the old man walked away into the night. Samford was dumfounded: "You mean you think that's it? You shake hands with an old man you don't even know. You have no contract. Are you crazy?" Zipper smiled and said that a Chinese handshake is more secure than any written contract.

At 7:00 AM the next morning, May 6th, the old man, Mr. Lee, appeared at the Symphony Office, which then was located in the downstairs hallway next to the entrance of the 1011R Hildago Street, Legarda Bldg., where he received half of the rental (Pesos 350.) the other half to be paid upon delivery of the chairs at the church. Two days later, on May 8th, one day before the concert, again at 7:00 AM, a procession of rickety old trucks piled high with 2,000 chairs of all sizes and shapes, found its way to the Santa Cruz Cathedral. Zipper, Dale Pontius and others were amazed. When Zipper paid Mr. Lee the second half of the rental, he said: "Now Mr. Lee, please tell me, how did you get all these chairs?" Mr. Lee replied:

"Very simple. Schools in outskirts not destroyed, but kids stay home. So tell principals I give them 10 cents for a chair to lend me for one week. Good business."

Zipper's experience with Chinese had taught him that they were intelligent, resourceful, and utterly reliable. His Army friends and others who helped to put the seat numbers on the chairs were amazed.

The concert, May 9, 1945, was to become a legendary event. Even now over 45 years later, people remember it as if it were yesterday. As recently as the summer of 1986, while staying at the Friendship Hotel in Beijing, Zipper met a geophysicist from Colorado, Dr. Wallace Campbell.

Upon learning that Herbert Zipper was *the* Dr. Zipper who conducted that day in Manila, Campbell was overwhelmed with excitement. "I was there," he exclaimed, "on that day I came to love music."

As always it was a warm May evening, overcast, and the church was lit by Army searchlights. A young Army surgeon, George Shape, whose memoirs were published in 1989, described the scene: "That week the Manila Symphony Orchestra held its victory concert amidst the ruins of the walled city. It was a rather emotional setting: A beautiful sky above filled with billowing white clouds, some starting to accumulate in a threatening manner, seeming to foretell the future."[77] Before the concert Herbert Zipper stood in the corner of the front of the church waiting to go on. He recalls feeling a sense of unreality. Far from Vienna, in the ruins of Santa Cruz Church, with no roof over their heads, with Mrs. MacArthur sitting in the front row, in a city as badly devastated as Warsaw, 2,400 people took time out from the catastrophe of their lives in order to feed their spirits. They listened to Beethoven's "Eroica" Symphony No. 3. and Dvorak's "New World" Symphony. The symbolism of the titles of the two works escaped no one.

During the second movement of the Eroica (the "Marcia Funebre"), at moments of relative silence one could hear the distant rumbling of artillery fire coming from Antipolo, about 30 miles away - a sound which brought the reality of war and death back to everyone in the church. The Ostinato rumbling of artillery was an ironic commentary on the power of the Beethoven funeral march. Everyone in the audience knew from firsthand experience, often tragic experience, the reality of war. This life-affirming concert was almost asking a question: which is to be the ultimate reality - death and destruction and war? Or life and creation and peace? Zipper's own lack of international notoriety probably added to the concert's success. Had Toscanini conducted, the focus would have been on the great maestro. But because it was a relatively little-known conductor, the focus was on the music.

The next day news reached Manila that the war in Europe had ended. According to war correspondent, William J. Dunn, whose memoirs were published in 1988, the news of the Nazi capitulation was not particularly heartening to a city lying in rubble. Dunn does, however, give his own eyewitness account of a special concert he attended:

Eroica

There was one particularly moving exception to the near-indifference with which Manila greeted the news of the Allied victory in Europe. Dr. Herbert Zipper was a Viennese musician – a refugee who had spent twelve anguishing months in the notorious Dachau concentration camp. While a prisoner of the Nazis he made a vow that one day, somehow, he would mark the fall of Adolf Hitler and the Nazi regime by conducting a thanksgiving performance of Beethoven's Third Symphony, the Eroica. He never wavered from that vow, and on May 10, 1945, after twelve long years, he conducted that thanksgiving performance.

After escaping from Dachau, Dr. Zipper finally arrived in the Philippines, where he became conductor of the Manila Symphony Orchestra. The maestro was just beginning to realize some success with the orchestra when the Japanese invasion forced him to disband. The instruments and the precious library were secreted in a fireproof vault, everything but the score of the Eroica, which remained with the conductor through three years of occupation, an ever-present symbol of his vow.

Finally the Americans returned, but Dr. Zipper and his wife spent ten nightmarish days and nights evading the brutal Japanese guns and the sadistic firebrands that destroyed their home, their possessions, their community, everything but their indomitable spirit and the precious score that the maestro carried with him day and night.

When they finally reached safety and he announced he was going to reform his orchestra, most people thought he was crazy and said so. The musicians were scattered, many dead, and all were out of practice. But Herbert Zipper refused to be discouraged. With the aid of the U.S. Army special services branch, he located some seventy of his former one hundred plus players. He banded them together, provided them with instruments miraculously salvaged from the fires, and started rehearsals. Many of his men had just come down from the hills where they had spent three years as guerrillas. Others were still weak from malnutrition when the rehearsals started. All were rusty, fingers out of condition and unaccustomed to ensemble playing. Frankly, it looked like a hopeless task.

But the work went on for four weeks, Zipper tirelessly driving, begging, coaxing, teaching. Finally, out of it all, something began to emerge. The orchestra took form, and the rich, full themes of the Eroica gradually began to take on the life and vitality with which Beethoven had endowed them. After long deliberation, Dr. Zipper decided to use his cherished score to commemorate the liberation of Manila. The ultimate fall of the Nazis would merit a second thanksgiving. Then, as the date for the first concert was set and final rehearsals began, the Nazis fell as if on cue! Dr. Herbert Zipper's presentation of Beethoven's Eroica fulfilled his greatest ambition — commemorating the fall of Nazism and the end of more than a decade of forced exile from his homeland — in addition to celebrating the liberation of his adopted home.

The Eroica has been performed by many greater orchestras but never with greater feeling, and I have heard far greater orchestras perform the Eroica and produce far fewer moist eyes. You couldn't be critical when you knew that the former concertmeister had been killed by the Japanese, and that the leader of the woodwinds had suffered the same fate. The fact that the horns in the trio of the third movement were less than strong became unimportant when you learned that both the finest horn players in the Philippines had given their lives for their country. What remained of this orchestra performed the Eroica from a makeshift stage in the nave of Santa Cruz, what was left of one of Manila's most anciet churches, the music echoing between the shattered walls and soaring to the tropical sky that provided the only roof. It was at once a paean of joy and a prayer of thanksgiving.[78]

Two days later the program was repeated for the U.S. Armed Forces. Afterwards, the chief of the Manila Naval Base, Admiral Kaufman, requested another repeat of the concert. Then, after this concert, heaquarters called Zipper to a special meeting. The Army wanted the concerts to continue *every day* and for that purpose rented an old, large movie theatre, "The Rex," in Chinatown. And so for the next 45 weeks, after a four year drought, Herbert Zipper found himself conducting six rehearsals and, sometimes seven, concerts a week to culture-starved, war hardened, and deliriously appreciative audiences of soldiers and civilians. Every night the house was full. They changed the repertoire every two weeks, except for the Schubert Great C Major Symphony which was so popular it was repeated for three weeks.

On one of the evening concerts during one of those sublime passages of a Beethoven Symphony, Zipper heard a deep, collective sigh emanating from the audience. Moved and inspired by the response, Zipper told Trudl during the intermission that the audience seemed to be exceptionally responsive this evening and he cited the collective sigh as evidence. Trudl had also heard it and her explanation quickly brought the maestro back to earth. It so happened that during the sublime passage a giant cockroach settled on the back of Zipper's white formal coat and started slowly and steadily to creep upward toward the collar. The entire audience leaned forward, breathlessly watching the cockroach's progress. Just before reaching the conductor's neck, it flew off and with a sigh the audience settled back.

After the Liberation it was hard to find anything to drink, except boiled water. Zipper managed to locate an empty white label whiskey bottle during intermission which he filled with boiled water and brought to all rehearsals and performances. His practice was to drink half the bottle before and half after each session. One evening his dressing room door was open as he drank his customary half bottle. After going out to conduct Trudl overheard two nearby soldiers talking — one said to the other: "How does that guy do it? He drinks a half bottle of whiskey and then goes out and conducts. He must be made of steel!"

On April 11, 1988, in the *Christian Science Monitor*, a tribute appeared written by a woman who as a kindergartner had heard Dr. Zipper conduct in her school in Illinois and whose child now also a kindergartner heard him conduct in the same children's series in Los Angeles. This article prompted another letter to the editor by a person who had been in Manila in 1945. He writes:

> As a member of the U.S. Army, I arrived in Manila just after it had been liberated. My unit was stationed about 20 miles south of Manila. One day the first sergeant announced that several tickets for that evening's performance of the Manila Symphony were available. As a young music student, I eagerly took one.
>
> There was no organized public transporation in Manila at that time, so we hitchhiked to the Rex Theatre, located in Manila's Chinese quarter. On entering the theatre, we found standing room only. In a short time, a tall, thin, energetic, intense gentleman made his way quickly to the podium, and then began an evening of such extraordinarily beautiful music, which helped to erase from thought the depressing ugliness of the war's destruction which seemed to engulf all of us. The conductor was Dr. Zipper.
>
> The U.S. Army had entered into a contract with the Manila Symphony to provide a series of concerts for all military personnel on a regular basis. Each concert was repeated 8 times during a 2 week period, thus enabling as many GI's as possible to share in this musical "breath of fresh air."
>
> During the year I was in Manila, those who attended the concerts heard the major symphonies, many concertos (when soloists could be found), the Messiah at Christmas time, and many, many smaller pieces beloved by all.
>
> After several months, the concerts were moved from the Rex Theatre to what I would call a gigantic quonset hut provided by the Army. This meant many more GI's could be accommodated at each concert.
>
> Opening night in the new location was an occasion never to be forgotten. Dr. and Mrs. Zipper had choreographed, staged and produced as a ballet Mussorgsky's "Pictures at an Exhibition," the magnificence of which has never, for me, been equaled, before or since.
>
> The obstacles which faced Dr. Zipper daily in providing these concerts for the American GI's were enormous. Lack of transportation for the orchestra members in a war-ravaged city, rehearsals in a second floor room miles from the concert site, inadequate ventilation in both places, excessive heat at all times, Army red tape, insufficient funding, missing musical scores, repair of musical instruments, etc. plagued the Symphony continually. I never knew Dr. Zipper to go in any direction but forward.

The lives of thousands of GI's were touched by Dr. Zipper's indefatigable efforts with the Manila Symphony. It would be hard to measure how much comfort and refreshment he gave to the military personnel stationed in and around Manila.

I left Manila in 1946. For a time in the late 1940's or early 1950's Dr. Zipper came to the United States and was the musical director of the Brooklyn Symphony. In 1971 I saw him briefly in Wilmington, Delaware when he was travelling across the United States in order to assist and promote the activities of community music schools.

I was so happy to read in the Monitor article that Dr. Zipper is continuing to do what he has always done so generously for so many years - give, give, give.

- Worden Gifford
Philadelphia, Pennsylvania

It has been Zipper's faith that the arts are not only healing but inspiring, that they literally breathe life into a people. Out of the rubble and stench of Manila came a form of new life in the Zipper concerts of 1945-46. The music was not just entertainment or a separate moment set apart from the rebuilding of the city. The music became an integral part of the people's daily life where aesthetic expression becomes as natural as breath. Many of those who were in Manila in 1945-46 learned this lesson when they came to hear Dr. Zipper give a concert.

INTERLUDE

Interlude

Patriot of the Globe

"I am a patriot of the globe."

- Herbert Zipper

The Army concerts lasted until February of 1946. In December of 1945 President Osmeña called Herbert Zipper to his office and informed him that he had just created a Committee for the Cultural Rehabilitation of the Philippines. He invited Zipper to serve on the committee, make policy recommendations and travel to America to seek financial support. Trudl and Herbert Zipper began immediately to make arrangements. At this point both of them were "stateless," that is, they had no citizenship anywhere. But since his presence was now desired in America, within one week the U.S. Consul had secured non-quota, U.S. Visas. Next they needed a way to travel to the states. Because air travel was impossible, Zipper went down to the pier every morning to the shipping agency of Mr. Rocha, a member of the symphony committee.

On the morning of February 12, 1946 Mr. Rocha told him that there was room for two people on the Russell A. Alger, a "Liberty" cargo ship. It was not equipped for passengers but the vacant 2nd and 3rd radio operator's cabin could accommodate the couple. And, oh by the way, he informed him, it was sailing that afternoon at 2:00. Zipper rushed home and at 10:00 A.M. told Trudl that they were sailing to the USA at 2:00 P.M.

"Fine!" she said, "but you have to get me a truck." She insisted on returning various items they had borrowed from friends, since they had lost practically all their possessions. Zipper obtained an Army truck and they made the rounds returning this and that. At 1:00 they returned, picked up their few remaining belongings, loaded them and their little dog Niddy into the truck, and drove down to the pier where they stepped into the waiting motor boat that ushered them to the ship, anchored far out in the Manila Bay.

Zipper had lost almost everything in Austria and what he and Trudl had acquired in Manila went up in flames when their home was destroyed, first by American shelling and then what was left by Japanese arsonists. An old Sufi saying states that "you possess only whatever will not be lost in a shipwreck." Herbert and Trudl Zipper had learned this lesson well. On February 12, 1946 they climbed up a rope ladder to the deck of the Russell A. Alger with their set of the Encyclopedia Brittanica, the Chinese rug, with Niddy their little dachshund, and with each other.

The purser of the ship seemed irritated and until that moment unaware that he would have two passengers, the only ones on board. Then he asked: "By any chance, do you play chess.?" And, as Zipper said he would enjoy playing chess, he was quite happy. The ship's chief engineer used to have his daily chess game with the 3rd radio operator who, along with the 2nd one, was commandeered off the ship. Since then the engineer became melancholic and, because nobody else on the boat could play chess the crew was afraid of the engineer's state of mind. The chess playing Zipper brought relief. The trip lasted 31 days and for the first 23 days the engineer beat Zipper in their daily chess game. Then one day he loaned him a copy of Richard Reti's book on chess (Reti's brother, Rudolf a Viennese composer and music critic had been an acquaintance of Zipper). Zipper read the book for two days and won the next eight games. "I lent him this book," the engineer complained to the captain, "Now I can't win a game. Schlemihl that I am."

And such a joy to be able to read again. The boat, as it turned out, had a fine library and for the first time in a long while, the Zippers had the time and quiet and opportunity to read. The trip was also a glorious time for them to be together - in a world at peace. To talk, hold hands and simply look at the beauty of the ocean - not knowing what the future was to hold and not dwelling on the horrors of the past but in that moment, watching Niddy chasing sea gulls and simply being together, quietly.

This time for Herbert Zipper was a sort of intermission between the two acts of his life. He had just witnessed the collapse of the world community. He would not return to Austria. Not only was he still outraged at the behavior of the Austrian citizenry as compared with the loyal attitude of the Filipinos during the Japanese occupation, but he had seen enough to know that the old order was in ashes. Zipper could not imagine trying to restore the old world as many wished to do. What was needed was the restructuring of society. He envisioned not the restoration of old elitist, hierarchical, societal patterns but the creation of new values, new and more democratic ways of knowing and affirming human dignity.

The Second Act of his life was about to begin. In Dachau and Buchenwald, Zipper had learned several truths. He had learned to trust the depths of his own resources. He had learned that "although man can survive without the arts, he is not really alive without them and, under certain circumstances, the arts can help him to survive." And while he had learned the depths to which humans can sink, he had also seen new heights to which they might rise. Clearly there were choices to be made.

He chose, therefore, to put aside his earlier goals and to go beyond "the confining horizon of European traditions, European idiosyncrasies, and European prejudices of which (he) became fully conscious only after living for years outside of Europe." He decided, in addition, that "there were many more in Europe with my background who could do my work than there were outside of Europe and I felt much more needed in Asia and America."

Experiences from Dachau to Manila taught Zipper a lesson in the 1940's which America and Russia in the 1980's are still struggling to learn: that Nationalism is no longer an appropriate way to organize the planet; that national boundaries must be a step on the road to global citizenship. "I am," Zipper proudly affirms, "a patriot of the globe." The second half of his life, then, would become an effort to broaden the horizons of small communities in America and Asia, to expand the curricula of educational systems by including quality arts programs, and to raise the general level of cultural and mulit-cultural literacy in a host of schools and communities. The enemies from Dachau to Manila had been physical brutality and bestiality. For the next forty years the enemies were to be mediocrity and ignorance. Of course, the two themes are not unrelated. For it was certainly the mediocrity and ignorance of the "Middle-slime" which enabled a "gutter snipe," as Winston Churchill called him, such as Adolph Hitler to rise to power. In Dachau, Zipper had learned to do what was necessary to survive; he became a radical empiricist — observing and designing plans to achieve the necessary results. The strict structures and content of formal, traditional European education were useless in the prison camp; what was needed was imagination, ingenuity, self-reliance, and community spirit. These were the qualities Herbert Zipper brought with him as he and Trudl sailed into San Francisco Bay on March 14, 1946.

FOURTH MOVEMENT

    IX.   America

    X.   Chicago

    XI.   Manila Revisited

Chapter IX

America: From the New World Symphony To the New World

> "You have destroyed it
> The beautiful world
> - - -
> Build it again
> In your breast rebuild it."
>
> - Goethe, *Faust*, I

The trip from Manila to San Francisco took 31 days. With a good tail wind the Russell A. Alger plowed forward at nine knots an hour. Finally, on March 14, 1946, early in the morning, the Golden Gate Bridge became visible. It was a windy March day. The waters were choppy and the two Viennese expatriots stood on the front deck, brushing their hair out of their eyes, looking through a hazy, pale sun at the most moving sight imaginable. Sir Francis Drake could not have been more excited to see this new land. It took three hours to enter the bay of "the white city." At one point, her Manila experience still fresh in her mind, Trudl Zipper turned to her husband and exclaimed, "look, Herbert, all the houses have roofs." The ship anchored in the midst of San Francisco Bay and two immigration officers came on deck; they checked "interim papers" of the Zippers and left after a few minutes. The captain stood on deck cradling Niddy in his arms. He told the immigration officers she was his pet to avoid her being quarantined. When the liberty boat docked at Oakland, the crew of about forty rushed off leaving Zipper and his wife sitting on the deck. They looked around expecting other formalities but instead they were abandoned; no one came to check their belongings. After years of German fanatical slavishness to orderly papers, here they found themselves alone and free. It was at once discomforting and exhilarating. When they disembarked, Zipper saw a car at the end of the dock. Out stepped Papa Zipper, then Otto. Mama Zipper, not a good walker, stayed in the car. One could not have scripted a more emotional scene. The first few minutes were a confusion of almost incoherent emotion. Everyone embracing, talking, laughing and embracing again. Emil Zipper, an over-powering personality, was wild with joy. Zipper had not seen his parents and brother since leaving Paris in 1939. Hedy at this time was in Santa Monica and Walter remained in London.

That night the two emigres were taken to a hotel where the Navy had rented them a suite. Trudl was delirious: at last a bath tub! To take a bath was an indescribably sensual luxury. They were, however, unable to sleep on a soft mattress, having been accustomed to sleeping on hard stone floors. First they put the mattress on the floor - too soft still, and then simply slept on the floor - just right. The next day the Navy hosted a reception with the press for the two new visitors. Afterwards there was more time for the family to become reacquainted with each other.

The Zippers were expected in Washington, D.C. by the end of April. After two days in San Francisco, Otto drove the clan in a borrowed Cadillac down to Santa Monica to stay with Zipper's sister Hedy Holt, her husband, Fred and their children Lucy and Henry. Hedy's husband had changed his name from Fritz Horwitz to Fred Holt. He had been the proprietor of a book store in Vienna but in America had become a landscape architect. His brother, who had been a pianist with the NBC Piano Quartet, was asked to change his name so as not to cause confusion with Vladimir Horowitz. Fritz also "Americanized" his name to be consistent with his brother. During their four-week stay, Zipper and Trudl spent a little time to buy a few things - some clothes, for example! Otto Zipper, who was to become a well known automobile dealer (VW's and BMW's) in Los Angeles, secured them a second hand pre-war Studebaker Coupe with four new tires — an almost unheard of luxury at that time. Because of their travel commitments, they gave Niddy to Hedy and Fred. Niddy, the courageous little dog of Manila now became a great favorite in Rustic Canyon in Santa Monica.

After a marvelous family reunion with Zipper's parents, Hedy, her husband Fred and their children who also had not seen their aunt and uncle from Manila since 1939, Herbert and Trudl Zipper set off across America. They went from city to city making appeals on behalf of the cultural rehabilitation of the Philippines. There were speeches, press conferences, parties, from Flagstaff to Phoenix, Albuquerque, to Denver, Kansas City, St. Louis, Chicago, Cleveland, Cincinatti, Pittsburg, Washington D.C. and finally back to California. Zipper's goal was to raise 2-3 million dollars to repair the Manila Metropolitan Theatre, libraries, music, art schools and the like. These were exciting days of discovery and reflection. Discoveries of places such as the Grand Canyon and Yosemite, which were for Austrian emigres, staggering and majestic. Later, after his ninth or tenth visit to the Grand Canyon, Zipper mused "a pity that Beethoven rather than Ferde Grofe didn't immortalize it in music."

The Zippers' first impressions of this new land was of a crazy quilt of positives and curiosities. They were amazed by both the beautiful gardens and the filthy streets, the absence of fences and locked doors and the hodge podge of architecture, the friendliness of the midwest and the shocking rudeness on the streets of New York. They were awe struck by the space and distances and the extraordinary diversity of the landscape and the people. They were also surprised by the wonderful libraries but astounded by the level of cultural ignorance, vulgarity and most of all the naivete of the average person. The expansiveness of the land was matched by the expansive personalities they encountered. And then there was the speed of everything: the cars, the development of cities and industry, the acceptance and implementation of new ideas. It was this wild mixture which intrigued Zipper. The staid traditionalism of Europe ultimately was not suited for a man of ideas and of action. Here, he sensed, he could give his imagination free reign. Although elevator music and soap operas were the prevailing diet, the possibilities for change were enormous.

In October of 1946 Zipper left Trudl in Santa Monica and took the train, accompanied by Papa Emil, on a second trip to the East Coast. The day after he arrived, he was called by the head of the U.S. Division of the Philippine Cultural Rehabilitation Commission, J. Weldon Jones, the then U.S. Budget Director, who said: "Herbert, I have bad news. The rug has been pulled out from under us." There had been an election in the Philippines and a new regime under Manuel Roxas had decided to "postpone" the cultural rehabilitation program. Zipper was now stranded in New York with very few possessions and little money.

Zipper had no sooner arrived in New York than a group of former soldiers read in the newspapers that he was there and, having known of him and his work in the Philippines, approached him asking if he would revive the orchestra in Brooklyn which had been disbanded when Sir Thomas Beecham had returned to England. Once again (Vienna, Dachau, Manila) Zipper set about to build an orchestra – this time in Brooklyn, New York! He had also noticed something about America. It was not a singing nation. The arts were not a part of the fabric of daily life. The state of affairs fired his sense of creativity. How could he find ways to attack the problem? Accordingly, he set about to bring music to Brooklyn.

When he first arrived in New York, he sub-letted the apartment of Max Eastman near the New School of Social Research. In November, he called Trudl to join him and at Christmas they took a one-week skiing vacation with Eric Simon in New Hampshire. After Christmas they stayed in the Great Northern Hotel on West 57th Street for six weeks. Other guests staying there were his friend, Otto Klemperer, a world famous conductor, and Hedwig Kanner, a well-known and vitriolic Viennese music critic, a pianist, and the widow of pianist Moritz Rosenthal. The fare at the hotel was ten dollars a day for two. After their stay at the hotel they moved first to 96th Street and Broadway and then on March 1, 1947, they moved down to Brooklyn, eventually settling in at 35 Clark Street, next to the St. George Hotel. It was a comfortable, furnished two-bedroom apartment.

At this time he received a call from the New School of Social Research inviting him to teach a course, twice a week, on the history of the opera. Thus he began his work in America: teaching, conducting, developing new programs; combining his marvelous musical skills with his other unique attributes as an innovator, problem-solver and creator. Arriving in America, he saw very quickly that his most effective contribution to this new world would not be just as a conductor but as a cultural developer, an educator, a community builder. This was a lasting commitment which would lead him to turn down major conducting jobs in order to work with small and large communities in organizing and developing grass roots arts programs.

His wonderful, and often offbeat, imagination in creating programs was given early expression at the New School where, among numerous programs, he designed a music course for Expectant Ladies. The president was incredulous but the course was announced in the catalog, and on opening day fifty "large" ladies showed up. Zipper took a lot of kidding from the faculty. Undaunted, Zipper met his class and taught them songs to sing to their infants in the cradle and at nursing time and how to create a musical environment at home. In 1974 Zipper was lecturing at Washington University in St. Louis when a pretty young woman came up to him after the lecture and said, "May I give you a kiss?" He was thinking that this was certainly an enthusiastic response to his lecture when she continued, "Years ago my mother took your course for Expectant Ladies and she sang to me the songs she learned then and I loved it!" She said she was currently teaching these same songs to her sister's children. You drop a pebble in a pond and....

Most of the classes he taught were less idiosyncratic. His analytic course offerings included: The Beethoven Quartets, The Beethoven Symphonies, The Mozart Operas, The Bartok Quartets, and two others which warrant special comment. One course was entitled Thematic Logic in Music. Usually music history or form and analysis courses focus on form and harmonic structure. Zipper's courses began with the question how do the great masterworks evolve from their initial premise, growing seemingly as natural as a tree? The transformation of that initial idea into many different articulations, Zipper demonstrated, must give the listener what the German philosopher Helmholtz called "reasonableness" in music or what Leonard Bernstein described as "inevitability." A second course was entitled "Modern Times in Arts" and it explored the development of literature, music, philosophy and visual arts from the Renaissance to contemporary times. Zipper was the music specialist in a team of four teachers. Each taught one ninety minute lecture per week and all four came together with the students for a weekly two-hour colloquium. Zipper and the students alike enjoyed the course immensely.

His tenure at the New School coincided with the beginning of the Mc Carthy era. Full faculty meetings at the New School were held in a large lecture room on the top floor of the school building. Three walls of this lecture hall are covered with colorful murals of the "League of Nations" including the likeness of Stalin, Hitler and others painted by the Mexican artist Jose Clemente Orozco (1883-1949). The New School at this time was an exciting and colorful mixture of people known as the "University in Exile." There were many prominent European intellectuals as well as part-time lecturers such as Eleanor Roosevelt, Felix Frankfurter and Langston Hughes.

At one meeting in 1950 of about 150 faculty members, President Hans Simons (a political scientist and former German Social Democrat) was addressed by a faculty member who was a State Department official. He told the President that the New School was getting a reputation in Washington as being a "leftist" organization and that since many public meetings were held in this room, the Orozco Mural might cause trouble and he suggested that it be removed. Zipper sensed his blood rising in anger. President Simons suggested that since the mural was "rather overpowering and therefore distracting during lectures perhaps it should be covered with curtains. Zipper felt an all too familiar sensation rising again. In this room filled with university intelligentsia, none spoke up, none protested. Again the submission to fear. He raised his hand and stood up proclaiming that he had recently just watched mindless fear overtake Europe, had watched books being burned and art desecrated and he said, "If these murals are to be covered up, I go. And anyone else who feels this way should get up and walk out with me." About half of the faculty present started to get up, when President Simons said, "Whoa, you are absolutely right." The mural stayed uncovered and the next day President Simons called to apologize. He and Zipper became friends.

Trudl Zipper also very quickly found work. She visited Erwin Piscator, Director of the well-known Dramatic Workshop of New York and he, delighted with her qualifications, hired her to be the Director of his Dance Department. Although Piscator was an ardent left-winger, eventually he left New York during the McCarthy Era to return to Berlin. Trudl received her first paycheck before her husband. During her stay at the Dramatic Workshop she taught such actors as Walter Matthau, Paul Newman, and Tony Curtis (then Bernie Schwartz). In her last years in Brooklyn, she opened her own dance studio.

Very soon after beginning work in New York the Zippers made several tacit agreements. Given the disruption of their lives in Europe, the war on two continents, and their work commitments, they had decided for the time being not to have children. They also had an understanding that they would neither seek nor talk about money. Each had a savings account and with typical Austrian meticulousness, they set aside money each month which Zipper soon began to invest in securities. They decided not to invest in life insurance as Trudl's father, an insurance executive in Europe, had advised them against insurance: "Life insurance," he told them, "is good only if you are lucky enough to die immediately after you sign up."

These early years in America were for Herbert and Trudl Zipper busy and exciting years. The pace of life was hectic but their love was deepening and they were happy in their new adventure and with each other. They were also enjoying making new friends and renewing old friendships. For example, a fellow internee of Zipper's from the Japanese prison camp, Santo Tomas in Manila, now lived in Brooklyn. Edward Kephardt and his wife had moved there where Kephardt was a representative to the Far East for U.S. Steel. Before Zipper even had an office with the Brooklyn Orchestra, he used the Kephardt's address at 265 Henry Street in Brooklyn Heights, an old brownstone house.

The Zippers remained close to Eric and Ruth Simon. Eric was a dear friend of Herbert from Vienna and in the summer of 1947 the two couples rented a house in Sherman, Connecticut. Sherman, Connecticut was a refreshing respite from Brooklyn. It is a hilly, pastoral, wooded New England area in the Housatonic River Valley with large old houses widely scattered across the landscape. The town consisted primarily of an old wood frame city hall, a church, an A&P store, and a school. Poet Malcolm Cowley described the land in his poem "The Peppermint Gardens":

> In my country the big pines grow
> at the edge of the woods,

    in the heart of the woods,
wherever the autumn winds may plant them,
not in close order, row by row,
where acres are left that men will grant them,
and in my country the chestnut trees
scatter their harvest where they please.

About my country is nothing grand:
three gothic hills in lower case,
two valleys you could hold in your hand,
a church, a crossroad store, a school
standing no higher than your face,
a trout stream — so I catalogue
the magic of my country:
item, a grove of hickory,
item, a tumbledown factory,
item — damn my memory,
you must imagine the rest.[79]

The house, built in the early Nineteenth Century, an 18th Century pre-Revolutionary home, was owned by the noted author Matthew Josephson whose book *The Robber Barons* was a major contribution to American intellectual history. Zipper recalls that the house was an 18th Century pre-Revolutionary home. However, Josephson's biographer writes that "the house was built in the early Nineteenth Century and renovated again in 1848 in the Green revival style."[80] Josephson named the house Twin Willows and felt in touch with the spirit of Thoreau when he resided there. A beautiful little brook ran behind by the home which gradually widened to a place where one could swim a few strokes on hot summer days. The Zippers and the Josephsons soon became friends. Matthew and Hannah Josephson also introduced them to local residents Malcolm and Muriel Cowley and the well-known painter Peter Blume and his wife Ebie and together with the Simons the five couples spent many evenings discussing the arts, literature and politics - mostly politics, as all were rather radical. Sometimes it was a bit difficult to have a balanced conversation with Josephson who had become a bit hard of hearing and who often enjoyed expounding at length on a given subject. These stimulating evenings were enormously enjoyable for Zipper and Trudl. Zipper's last conversation with Josephson occurred during a party at Eric Simon's home. Somewhat out of the blue Josephson said, "You know, Zipper, the genius of Abraham Lincoln was his ability to construct a neo-biblical language with short decisive sentences and paragraphs which are unforgettable. He summoned forth religious feelings and grafted them on to politics." It was, he told Zipper, his intention to write about this but he died shortly after. Sometimes conversations turned to the Far East where Zipper's views were solicited. Zipper was quite surprised to discover how little American intellectuals knew about Asia. For Cowley, Josephson, and Blume, were uninformed and rather naive about China, Japan, the Philippines - their views and opinions primarily shaped by the mass media which, as Theodore White and Edgar Snow and others were later to show, was sadly distorted. Zipper found himself explaining to his friends that Chang Kai-Shek was not a hero and definitely not worthy of American support. Although Zipper subsequently moved to Chicago and later to Los Angeles, he maintained his friendship with Malcolm and Muriel Cowley and with Peter and Ebie Blume. Zipper also corresponded with Matthew and Hannah Josephson until her death in 1975 and with Matthew until his death, March 13, 1978. The evenings in Sherman with these remarkable couples provided a marvelous introduction to some of the elite of America's mainstream intellectual world.

Sherman, Connecticut was a striking contrast to Brooklyn Heights where Zipper and Trudl lived for almost seven years. They were fascinated by the neighborhood's international mixture of white Ango-Saxon Protestants and "New Amsterdamers," Irish and Italian Catholics, African-Americans, Jews from everywhere, Scandanavians, Armenians, Iranians, smoking water pipes and sitting on little Persian prayer rugs. There were the little old ladies with purple hair and old-fashioned hats walking their tiny pets, reminding one of a scene from "Arsenic and Old Lace." All spoke a peculiar brand of English, all rode the subways and bought things at Abraham & Strauss. But there were radical differences as well. They all spoke their own languages at home, published their own weekly newspapers and adhered to their own indigenous customs and cultural heritage.

Politically, Brooklyn Heights represented a microcosm of a wide range of American political thought. There were the traditionalists who carried on the spirit of Henry Ward Beecher, the celebrated minister of Plymouth Church who advocated the abolition of slavery, proposed women's suffrage and the teaching of scientific evolution, and embodied the spirit of Walt Whitman in the still-existing *Brooklyn Eagle*. There were the proselytizing supporters of the New Progressive Party of Henry Wallace who opposed the administration's cold war policy, who campaigned to cooperate with the Soviet Union, and who supported the administration of foreign aid through the United Nations and the reduction of armaments. They did not win anything in the 1948 elections but they drew more than 1 million votes. They were vociferously opposed by the "ultra-Conservatives," the "Blue Bloods" of Brooklyn Heights, the

Plymouth and Dutch descendants who considered all others "foreigners and riff-raff."

By 1948 Zipper and Trudl had amassed a new collection of books and needed some bookcases to be built. Somebody recommended a craftsman to them, an elderly Jew from Russia, who specialized in making bookcases. One evening he appeared, introduced himself, and without further ado went straight to the stacks of books, examining them one by one. When Zipper asked him what he was looking for, he sternly answered in a thick Russian accent, "Before I accept work for anybody, I must know what they are reading. I do not accept work for everybody, but you seem to be okay." Like the Zippers, he was an ardent supporter of Henry Wallace and charged the Zippers only $30.00 per bookcase. Zipper still owns these bookcases forty years later.

Zipper also learned that his vocabulary and comprehension of American English was hampered by his ignorance of baseball and, in particular, of the Brooklyn Dodgers. At an early meeting of the Brooklyn Symphony Board of Trustees, Zipper heard strange talk: 'could the Bums beat the Giants,' 'did you see Pee Wee's double steal yesterday?' "Do you think Duke can hit Sal the Barber?' and so on. Zipper, ever the scholar, approached a trustee-friend, Rembert Wurlitzer, and asked for a written explanation, followed by a 'field trip' to Ebbets Field. Zipper enjoyed the spectacle of people who took this strange game as seriously as Italians do their opera. He particularly enjoyed the motion of the pitchers which he found aesthetically akin to ballet. Zipper was, however, shocked when the Dodgers were sold to Los Angeles and was suprised also at how little outrage or protest there was in response to the sale. If a local soccer team had been sold in Europe, the townspeople would have protested the loss or rioted. For Zipper, however, a different loss was imminent.

One Saturday, April 12, 1952, the Zippers had driven from Brooklyn to Sherman, Connecticut to spend the usual weekend with Eric and Ruth Simon. During their visit Hedy Holt called from California late Saturday afternoon to tell Herbert that their father, Emil Zipper, had died of a brain hemorrhage. He had developed complications from an appendectomy six weeks earlier. Emil and "Rosie" had been married in 1901 when he was 26 and she 24. Though both were Austrian born, they had both come to love the United States and were now 'Americans.'

Like many Austrian Jews seeking acceptance and business success, Emil Zipper had been a political conservative until the middle of World War I. From that time until the advent of Hitler he gradually became a slightly-to-the-right of center liberal. By the time his son left Buchenwald and was reunited with his family in Paris, Emil Zipper had moved to the left of center. Upon arriving in America he became an admirer and supporter of Franklin D. Roosevelt. He was alone among his family and friends in insisting that Truman would defeat Dewey and took great delight in his correct prediction. Politically Emil Zipper's convictions were shaped by the cataclysmic events of his world and, to a degree, by the convictions of his radical son. On the other hand, Emil Zipper's influence upon Herbert Zipper and the rest of the family was profound. He was a true patriarch, with all that the word implies. He was respected by the family and was almost always positive no matter what the obstacle. He always seemed able to convince others of the value of his ideas and of moving ahead to seek and implement solutions to problems. This was the model Herbert Zipper received from early on. And, it was this model which fueled Zipper in the dark days of Dachau and Buchenwald. While others succumbed to despair, depression, and even suicide, Zipper composed music, organized secret concerts, memorized names. The heritage Emil Zipper engraved in his son helped to save his life.

The other side of the patriarchal coin was his tendency to be dictatorial. He also had an explosive temper which got the better of him from time to time. Both Zipper and his sister Hedy found this characteristic of their father unpleasant and in reaction to it vowed never to give in to fits of temper themselves. In fact both did manage to acquire a remarkable degree of self-control.

After coming to America Zipper's relationship to his father deepened. They wrote to each other with great regularity, they spoke on the telephone weekly, and they visited often. The call from Hedy Zipper on April 12, was like an electric shock. Zipper had spoken to his father only a day or so before to plan a visit on the next weekend. He put the phone down and told Trudl and some guests that he would not be home for dinner. He then went for a long walk to be alone and to re-order his inner world.

Zipper had learned long ago in the prison camps of Dachau and Buchenwald that one was essentially alone when confronted with human tragedy. He had learned to deal with the unbearably painful events of life by sublimating the grief to work and creativity. Perhaps there was a trade-off of stifling some emotion and suppressing some feeling.

As would become a pattern in his life, Zipper responded to the loss of his father by immersing himself in his work. The New School for Social Research was for Zipper an astounding place and helped him deal with his sadness. Its open spirit and diversity were healing and inspiring. Intellectual refugees from all over the world found a home there to teach. At this "University in Exile" Zipper found almost no accent absent. Alvin Johnson had founded the school in 1918 as one of America's first significant adult education centers. And now, after the war, the student body was increased by GI's hungry for learning and for meaning in their lives. Zipper was inspired by the G.I.'s to design an educational plan for the armed forces.

Having observed war at first hand and having witnessed the dehumanizing effects of war, Zipper submitted a plan for the cultural and educational enrichment of enlisted servicemen. In 1951 he thus presented Anna Rosenberg, Assistant Secretary of Defense, with his plan. She liked it and invited Zipper, accompanied by Dean Francis Sayre — son of the High Commissioner of the Philippines and grandson of Woodrow Wilson — to meet with several Generals of the U.S. Army. Zipper traveled to the Pentagon and was ushered through the maze of rooms into a room with a long table where the generals and colonels sat in steely silence. Sayre introduced Zipper who set forth his proposal.

Remembering the Dachau concerts in the latrines, his idea was that off-duty soldiers be encouraged to participate in a variety of artistic, social and cultural activities. The military, he argued, often focuses upon means of destruction. The World War II experience followed by the Korean conflict required this focus. "But," Zipper exhorted, "let us not only teach soldiers how to fight, but teach them the deeper values supposedly underlying the conflicts of ideologies." Let us, he urged, encourage soldiers to: 1) Write and edit their own newspaper; 2) Organize political forums and debates; 3) Rehearse and produce theatrical productions; 4) Prepare musical programs; 5) Practice arts and crafts; 6) Expand shop and vocational arts; 7) Prepare radio and television programs; and, 8) Participate in neighboring community arts programs. His plan called for a coordinator for each company, chosen from among the servicemen and a number of civilian specialists attached to each regiment.

The big brass listened and informed him they would take the ideas "under advisement." Anna Rosenberg, several months later, told Zipper it was unlikely they would act on his proposals. This proposal and the others that Zipper has designed that have not materialized are as interesting and potentially valuable as many that have come to fruition. No matter the results, he continues to dream his dreams. There is, however, one practical explanation as to why many of his dreams have not come true.

Zipper had trained most of his life to be a musician. The war however, was more than an interruption, it was an extraordinary education and a period of radical transformation. Zipper is truly appalled by human cruelty and irrationality and cannot comprehend why men are not more rational. The events he observed in Dachau, Buchenwald, and Manila demonstrated the frightening possibilities of chaos and disorder. Perhaps it is Zipper's innate sense of order or his need for neatness which have, in a curious way led him to want to solve problems on a larger scale and to do more than just conduct. He has an over-whelming desire to try to tidy up the world's messes, to reorder it all. Consequently, Zipper arrived in America with a new commitment to a larger community than that of the classical music world. His first-hand knowledge of hunger from both wars; his love of the mountains; his witnessing of the destruction of cities, the erosion of culture and decency; and his widespread interests and reading led him to new concerns.

Shortly after arriving in New York he began reading the works of Fairfield Osborn, an ecologist and environmentalist whom I once characterized to Zipper as "a man ahead of his time." Zipper demurred, "A man, he said, "is not ahead of his time; rather, he is aware of his time. It is the culture and the government and society which is behind its time." Zipper read two of Osborn's books, *Our Plundered Planet* (1948) and *The Limits of the Earth* (1953), and - well before Rachel Carson, Paul Ehrlich, Jaques Cousteau and others - became an advocate of ecology movements. Reading Osborn in 1988 makes painfully clear the lost opportunities of the preceding 40 years. For Osborn's warnings were clear and absolutely accurate:

> The discovery of nuclear energy marks an epoch in the history of man. On the other hand, it becomes a meaningless incident if we do not intelligently conserve, use and develop the life-supporting elements of the earth - its soils, forests and water resources - and at the same time measure the numbers of people who can be supported by the productivity of the earth. Impressive beyond comprehension are the technological advances of this era. The stark fact remains - nuclear energy means nothing to the man whose body is starving.[81]

Inspired by the writings of Osborn, Zipper proposed, in 1959, to Dr. Hans Simon, President of the New School for Social Research, that the University sponsor a series of public meetings to develop a platform to bring to legislators on key issues of the times. In Zipper's opinion these issues were: Space exploration, the control of nuclear proliferation (there were then only three nuclear powers), river control, re-forestation, the control of waste, and the overall education system in the U.S. The university agreed that these were critical issues but failed to follow through on Zipper's recommendations and was, in essence a microcosm of the Federal Government which also failed to heed the early warnings of a Fairfield Osborn or a Rachel Carson or a Herbert Zipper. Yet though some say it is already too late to avert nuclear or ecological doom, Zipper remains hopeful. Choices people have made had created our present day problems and there are choices to be made to resolve them.

In words which Zipper read over forty years ago, Osborn posed a question which today takes on even more immediate meaning:

> ... we still must ask ourselves, "Is the purpose of our civilization really to see how much the earth and the human spirit can sustain?" The decision is still ours to make, assuming we recognize that the goal of humanitarianism is not the quantity but the quality of living.
>
> If we evade the choice, the inevitable looms ahead of us - even sterner forces will make the decision for us. We cannot delay or evade. For now, as we look, we can see the limits of the earth.[82]

The dedication to Osborn's *The Limits of the Earth* echoes the essence of Zipper's life and efforts: "To all who care about tomorrow."

Meanwhile the Brooklyn Symphony was taking shape and the initial concerts went well. The season generally consisted of a fall and winter series with programs changing every two weeks. One concert would be held at the Brooklyn Academy of Music and the others at local schools. Zipper used his connections and salesmanship to attract such soloists as Issac Stern (violin), Brenda Lewis (soprano), Robert Merrill (baritone), Grant Johanneson (piano), Arthur Balsam (piano), and Zino Francesscatti (violin). In addition, he staged an opera recital of the fourth act of Verdi's *Don Carlo* with Regina Resnick and Giorgio Tozzi. He also learned that all is not joy in leading an orchestra. He soon discovered that fund raising is a constant drain. Eric Simon, then a clarinetist in the City Center Orchestra, formerly conducted by Leopold Stokowski, introduced Zipper to the Center's new conductor, a very young Leonard Bernstein. Together Zipper and Bernstein commiserated about the demands of fund raising.

Zipper was not content to simply play for the concert hall audiences and he began immediately a practice which he has pioneered and promulgated ever since these early years. He said to his Orchestra Board of Trustees, "We must take our orchestra and our music out into the local high schools. We must build audiences for the future!" No one had done this before but Zipper began taking music out to the 16 local Brooklyn high schools. The students and adults alike loved the concerts. This was an idea he was to promote in Chicago, Los Angeles, and Manila as well as in the many cities where his national guild work took him.

Initially, he experienced some difficulty with his Symphony Board for his bold and innovative practices and for the composition of his orchestra which included eight women and four blacks. The women were a much higher proportion than was customary in symphony orchestras and their were no blacks in any other symphony orchestra at this time. Jackie Robinson had just broken the color barrier in professional baseball. In fact, a big article in the Sunday Tribune on the new Brooklyn Orchestra showed individual pictures of *only* those 12 members thus making it appear that the Zipper Orchestra was composed of only blacks and women. Though it was a mixed population, Zipper has always been an outspoken champion for the rights of minorities, women and the underprivileged. Several Board members were quite out-spoken in the views that the symphony existed to serve a white, upper-class, tail-coat and white-tie audience. Zipper wanted to serve "the people." One Board member once said, "Why cast pearls before swine?" Zipper was infuriated and was restrained from exploding by his friend and fellow Board member, Rembert Wurlitzer. Zipper, in fact has never enjoyed particularly good relations with boards of trustees because of his desire to do it his own way.

It was at this time that he became friends with Langston Hughes from whom he learned a great deal about Black America. Zipper had asked the Vice President of the New School why there were no black students in attendance? She replied that they won't come down to 12th Street. Zipper said, then why don't we go to them up in Harlem? Too dangerous, was the reply. At Dachau Zipper had lost his sense of fear and he approached Langston Hughes and had him arrange a meeting with a pastor in Harlem. Zipper offered to provide lectures on music and the History of Europe and, the very next week, he gave his first lecture in a church social hall. It was scheduled for one hour: he stayed an additional three hours answering questions. The lectures were free and Hughes was thrilled. Zipper returned many times and enlisted others to do so.

His relationship with Langston Hughes grew even more close in 1949 as a result of a collaboration. A young German composer, Jan Meyerowitz, had collaborated with Hughes in writing an opera, *The Barrier*. Originally the opera was to be called *Mulatto*, based on an earlier play of that name, but it was changed to *The Barrier*. The opera dealt with the theme of miscegenation and filial rejection. Meyerowitz worked hard writing and rewriting the score throughout 1950 and by November it was ready to open in Washington, D.C. There was considerable controversy about the subject matter but the publicity did not help advance sales. As Arnold Ramperssand, a biographer of Hughes writes:

> The critics were almost uniformly hostile. In a typical response, the Washington Post reviewer called the show "altogether disappointing . . . . I don't believe such a story in the least"; the play made for "a sordid, depressing evening." Milton Berliner of the Daily News dissented. Noting the depth of

critical hostility, he later argued that only a powerful production on a disturbing subject could have driven his colleagues to such extremes. Indeed, other critics had alluded to the stark, Greek-like tragic tone, the overwhelming sense of hopelessness in the end. In any event, *The Barrier* closed after five performances. In a memorandum to the producers, Hughes himself blames not racism but a tendency as old as the original Broadway production of *Mulatto*. Although the current production was stronger and more beautiful in some respects than the previous stagings, something of its "simplicity and directness" had been lost, replaced by "a kind of bombastic melodrama" in which brutality and even sadism, "rather than a tragic self-defense," dominated the stage.

Later, Meyerowitz (who conducted the orchestra) blamed the fiasco on the shabby group of musicians assembled by Michael Meyerberg, and on Lawrence Tibbett. "Musically it was very bad. Meyerberg wouldn't spend any money, so we got these hacks who simply couldn't play the music. As for Tibbett, the poor man was past his prime and had no voice left."

Muriel Rahn's husband, the veteran producer and singer Dick Campbell, later weighed the matter differently. "Muriel and I thought Tibbett fine, although the role had been sung better at Columbia. He was quite nice and affable to everyone in the cast, and everyone liked him. The problem was the music. The critics just didn't go for the music." [83]

Zipper believed that the score was fairly good but that Meyerowitz's orchestration in relation to the human voice needed retouching. The opening, in Washington D.C., had also demonstrated that Meyerowitz was not the right conductor for his own work. Immediately Eric Simon and the publisher of the opera called Zipper to come down and help. He agreed to do so. Meyerowitz made some changes in the score and Zipper and Simon thinned some of its orchestration. Zipper then worked hard with everyone for two weeks and they reopened first in Brooklyn and then the Bronx for about 20 performances. The audiences loved it. Ampersand writes that "Lawrence Tibbett missed several performances," but Zipper, who believes this is incorrect, recalls that Tibbett never missed a performance. In any event, they prepared to open on Broadway, November 2, 1950, at the Broadhurst Theatre with Herbert Zipper conducting and with the lead roles to be sung by Muriel Rahn and Lawrence Tibbett.

General Omar Bradley was in the first row and was so moved he was crying at the end of the first act. Again the audience loved it. But the critics, mostly drama critics, tore it apart arguing that it exaggerated negative relations between blacks and whites.

... Meyerowitz's music was damned by Brooks Atkinson (who had reviewed *Mulatto* with sympathy in 1935) as "overcivilized and as remote from lynching and the blood lust as anything could be; and it is European in its artistic derivation"; Hughes's libretto was "hardly distinguished enough to sustain the complicated texture" of the score. In the Daily News, John Chapman praised the libretto, but found "little poignancy, little heartbreak, in the music." A few reviewers admired the show. "There is magnificence in it," Arthur Pollack claimed in praising the plain honesty of Hughes and Meyerowitz; "the season's hits look like nonsense compared with 'The Barrier'." He was decidedly in the minority, and the opera lasted only three days at the Broadhurst. "Such is show business," Langston gloomily concluded after his latest failure to recapture the glory of *Street Scene*.

To Meyerowitz, the reasons for the failure were clear. "These Broadway producers are born black-mailers," he confided many years later. "I advise you to have nothing to do with them, if you can help it. If we had the Mansfield Theatre, as in our contract, we could have made a go of it. But the CBS money was too big. As for my music, well, I think maybe it was too Jewish. I listen to it now and it sounds awfully Jewish to me. It is also Negro, but maybe not enough for the show."[84]

Zipper is somewhat amused by this notion of Meyerowitz. Certainly, he agrees, the music was not written in a jazz medium or with the qualities of Negro spirituals, and certainly it has traces of Mahler here and there, but it was not particularly "Jewish." Besides, Zipper observes, is *Falstaff* English musically? *The Barrier* folded after three days because the bad review killed any additional funding. As Zipper reflects, "the press can't make a piece of art but they can kill it." Nevertheless, the experience of the opera was an important one for him: It served to heighten his awareness of and commitment to the cause of racial equality and social justice in this new country.

During this period of growing familiarity with American culture, Zipper became more involved in the American public school system. After one of his lectures at the New School in which he had explained the importance of the arts in education, a young woman came up to him and asked if he would be willing to speak to her father - a public school principal at P.S. 51 in the Bronx. Soon Zipper met Mr. Levine who was a dynamic vital man with fiery eyes and a passion for his work. He told Zipper that his school, where he was newly appointed, was a disgrace - there were daily fights, rapes, a near murder, and constant racial tensions between blacks, Jews and Puerto Ricans. Every other week there was a story in the newspapers (especially in the *Daily News*) about incidents in this junior high school. "I have the idea," said Mr. Levine, "that we could turn this school around through the arts." Together they secured permission from the Board of Education, and received a free hand to hire a faculty and to design a curriculum - just as long as they would keep the school out of the newspapers.

Levine and Zipper turned this school into a Music and Art Junior High School. Levine transferred teachers out; they hired new full-time arts, music and drama teachers (all without certification); and, they set to work transforming the school into a Music, Theatre, and Art School. Within two months they had restored peace to a badly torn up school.

Three years after the critical period of transforming the school Zipper returned to visit Mr. Levine. The school was number two in attendance in the city, number four academically, and vandalism had all but disappeared. *Life Magazine* visited to do a story but the School Board killed the story - it would have been a disaster they argued. Everyone in New York would want such a school. They asked Levine, correctly: "Could you duplicate this quality of your faculty to service 500,000 children." "Of course not!" was his answer. The experience, however, merely whetted Zipper's appetite to bring the arts into the public schools. The opportunity to do so was not long in coming.

Later that year, in November of 1952, Grace Nash called Herbert Zipper from the Winnetka School of Music where she was then teaching violin. Grace Nash had met Herbert and Trudl Zipper in the Philippines where they became close friends. Zipper had visited Grace, her husband Ralph and their three sons in Chicago in 1946 and now she was calling to invite him to consider becoming the new director of the school. He flew to Chicago and was met at Midway Airport by Grace Nash and a trustee of the school, Richard D. Colburn. Colburn was a salesman equal to Emil Zipper and he fed Zipper dreams of creating a school which would be a model for the nation. Zipper, who was certainly susceptible to such a line of reasoning, was strongly influenced by the persuasive Colburn.

The next day they were visited by Harrison Collins the superintendent of the Northfield Public Schools. He told Zipper he was appalled by the state of music and the arts in public schools and would dearly wish to cooperate with him if he would take the directorship. Zipper's recent experience with Levine in New York made this offer an intriguing one. Initially, for Trudl the offer was less exciting. She was deeply involved in work at her own studio and at the Piscator dramatic workshop. The two of them discussed the move at length but finally they decided it was an opportunity to learn more of America. Moreover, it was, again, a new adventure, a chance to grow something from a seedling. Given his developing interest in building communities, combined with the possibility of joint venture projects with the local public schools, Chicago was too tempting to resist. Vienna, Dusseldorf, Vienna, Dachau, Buchenwald, Vienna, Paris, Manila, Brooklyn, the Zipper odyssey would now lead to Chicago.

Chapter X

Chicago

"We went for a fish and hooked a whale"

—Benjamin Rumage, Trustee
of the Music Center of North Shore

Down the north shore of Lake Michigan from Evanston to Winnetka to Wilmette to Glencoe, and Highland Park, there is little distinction between the towns. Like many American villages, and unlike most European towns, there is no center, there are no spires of a church or towers of a town hall. Rather there is a comfortable, leisurely placement of large two-story homes up and down streets lined by lazy elm trees and weeping willows shading well-trimmed lawns. Herbert Zipper accepted his new position in March of 1953 and on May 15, he and Trudl moved to Winnetka. Exit the colorful quilt of Brooklyn's international neighborhoods, the radical mix of urban affluence and squalor; and, enter the world of Chicago's North Shore, the ladies "who," as e.e. cummings wrote, "live in furnished souls and have comfortable minds." Enter the Jewish, Austrian radical onto the conservative stage of suburban, exclusive country clubs and what Zipper himself initially described to Trudl as the "homogeneity of cultural mediocrity."

Zipper and Trudl had two weeks to get settled and then on May 30, departed for his yearly summer position with the Manila Symphony. Since 1950 he had been enlisted to return to help rebuild the orchestra which had languished from 1946-50 during his absence. In 1951, he had returned to give concerts in the Rizal Memorial Coliseum and he and Trudl staged a ballet version of Mendelssohn's *A Midsummer's Night Dream*. Given this arrangement with the Philippines, Zipper negotiated a 9-month contract with the Winnetka School (mid-September to June 1st) and it was agreed that Grace Nash, as Assistant Director, would run the summer school.

The Winnetka School of Music, as it was called at that time, was a community school serving children and adults primarily during the after-school, afternoon and early-evening hours. It was and is part of a nationwide network of community arts schools all across the country. Originally founded in 1931 by David and Dorothy Dushkin, the school was situated in an old farmhouse in an apple orchard. The Dushkins made instruments in the school basement, baked bread for the children, and taught a variety of instruments. Somewhat ahead of their time, the Dushkins, believed that children have a natural impulse toward music - a premise now being confirmed by educators who have found that three-month-old infants can learn how to match pitches. The Dushkins encouraged parents to begin their children's lessons very early. At age four or five students were taught the recorder and within a few months were able to play in ensembles.

After three years they moved the Dushkin School to the corner of Willow and Glendale and it was renamed the Winnetka Music School. The enrollment grew modestly and the school became a familiar part of the North Shore community. After 22 years, the Dushkins decided to move to Vermont and Grace Nash, who had joined the faculty after being freed from the Japanese prison in Manila, recommended Herbert Zipper for the position of director.

In September of 1953 an enthusiastic 49-year-old conductor-composer-educator returned from the Philippines to assume his first directorship of a school in the U.S.A. The Zippers took residence in an apartment which the Dushkins had formerly occupied in the school building. It was cozy and convenient, a welcome contrast to the Brooklyn years living in congested quarters and battling subway crowds.

Zipper had observed the Dushkin's operation prior to accepting the position and quickly determined that he had a substantial job to do. The Dushkins were lively charismatic people whom the children enjoyed but the overall quality of the music programs was woeful. The musical ensembles were, at best, mediocre and the out-of-tune playing (on recorders made by the children) was, to Zipper, ear-assaulting; the rhythms were erratic, and the intonation, says Zipper, "took your shoes off." In addition, the enrollment was down to only 94 students and the private instructors were, in Zipper's view, not of desirable quality. He inherited twelve instrumental teachers but by the end of the year he had replaced all but two. The replacements were top-caliber, professional musicians. In fact, several Board of Trustee members were upset with Zipper accusing him of "professionalism" and several resigned at the end of the year. Fortunately, many Trustees - led by Richard Colburn - did understand and recognize real musical quality and supported Zipper's efforts. Whenever Zipper discussed musical standards, Colburn, a violist himself, was enthusiastic in his support. The Trustees believed, correctly, that Zipper was trying to change their quaint cozy little 'mom and pop' school into something much greater than they bargained for. One husband and wife, who were even friends of the Zippers, were disturbed because their daughter had been so inspired by the new teachers that she was now practicing two and three hours a day. They were concerned that she was becoming "too serious" about music.

Zipper also set about revising the curriculum. He added a comprehensive music theory program, expanded chamber music offerings, and, under Trudl's leadership, inaugurated a brand new dance department. One trustee warned that the dance program would attract "a bunch of fairies" and inquired if it couldn't be called something other than 'Dance.' But 'Dance' it remained and by the end of the year the closing dance concert attracted an enthusiastic full-house of over nine hundred people. Thereafter, each year the end-of-year dance concert was a huge success. Zipper's problems were, however, not limited just to faculty and curriculum development. No sooner was he on the job than he was hit smack in the face with a logistical crisis.

Upon his return from Manila in September, Zipper received in the mail a large legal document informing him that the school was located in an illegal zone and that it must close. The school was scheduled to open in two weeks. It appeared as though there had been some peculiar dealings of which he had not been previously informed. David Dushkin had apparently been given the assurance that as long as he was the director, the school could remain at its present site. However, upon his retirement, the zoning variance would expire and the city ordered the school to be closed. As the Winnetka school was across the street from Skokie Jr. High School it was hard for Zipper to understand the zoning problem.

Fortunately, there were several powerful figures on the Winnetka Board of Trustees. In addition to Richard D. Colburn, other Trustees such as Howard Fisher, William Lloyd, Lynn Williams, Kenneth Montgomery, president of the Winnetka School Board and an ardent supporter of the Music School, intervened with the city and obtained a two year postponement. Another powerful force was Denison Bingham Hull, who subsequently became a good friend and composition student of Herbert Zipper. He was a highly regarded, wealthy, former U.S. Senate Candidate. He became the next Chairman of the Board and in that capacity was invaluable in helping Zipper develop the school.

They secured only a two year reprieve, but where to go? On a dreary Sunday morning in November '53, Zipper received a phone call from the headmaster and founder of the nearby North Shore Country Day School, Perry Dunlap Smith. "I've heard your speeches," Smith said, "and I want to talk to you." He explained to Zipper that his school had a large campus with an unused slope of land fronting on Green Bay Road. If one were to level the plot, a large school could be constructed there. This was indeed an exciting proposal since Green Bay road was a main traffic artery with bus lines up and down the north shore.

Zipper called for an immediate meeting of his Executive Board and fund raising plans were drawn up. Denison Hull provided the leadership, assisted by Richard D. Colburn and others. The new school building would cost approximately $125,000 - $135,000. Denny Hull promised to secure a loan contingent on the Board's raising, in addition to the value of the old school, the sum of $25,000.

The Board of Trustees set about to raising the money but in 1954 $25,000 was a much larger sum than at present and as the year wore on the fund raising bogged down. One Sunday afternoon, in November of that year, Denison Hull phoned Zipper explaining that he had just had a meeting with some of the trustees and that they needed to come over to talk to him. Shortly afterwards Hull arrived at Zipper's door with Howard Fisher, Charles Kaufman, and Lynn Williams. These four men were the pillars of the Board who had the well-being of the school genuinely at heart and upon whose good judgment Zipper relied. Their gravely serious manner signaled that he was about to hear bad news. In a fund raising campaign a Board of Trustees must lead - providing anywhere from 25% on up of the total goal. The four were aware of this and told Zipper that the Board had been able to raise only $8,200 of the $25,000 needed. The school would have to close in June of 1955.

Zipper listened attentively, said little, but calculated what he would need to do. He had lived through too many crises to let the school be closed down. A crisis was simply an invitation to find a solution. The solution in this case came from five women on the Board. Upon receiving a letter to the Board from Herbert Zipper informing all the Trustees of the crisis, these five women set about to raise the needed $16,800. One must remember that $16,000 in 1954 was more like $160,000 in the 1990's. Furthermore, they had little time for they had to do in about two months what the full Board had failed to do in nine. The deadline was February 1, 1955. On another Sunday, January 30th, Lucy Montgomery, Carol Sopkin, Ruth Roberg, Jean Evans (Mrs. Bergen), and Ellie Martin arrived at Zipper's doorstep and, in a burst of unrestrained jubilance, they emptied their handbags - cash, checks, pledges - totalling exactly $16,800. They danced around the table which probably had never seen such a feast while Zipper and Trudl laughed and laughed and embraced with joy. The Music Center of the North Shore was born on that day.

In truth, Zipper had never doubted that somehow the crisis would be averted. In fact, during the fund raising drive he even launched a new program which required additional funds. In early January of 1954, Zipper met with Harry Collins, the public school superintendent who had helped lure him to Chicago. They discussed the general cultural climate of the North Shore and agreed it was rather bleak. No children could be seen carrying violin cases, cello cases had to be kept at school for no children would risk ridicule by carrying them home, there was little music in the schools, and virtually no quality classical music. Zipper said to Collins, "You can't build from the top with adults; you must work with children. We need to bring professional orchestras to the elementary schools." Collins slapped the table and exclaimed, "That's it, that's what we have to do."

Zipper prepared and presented a proposal to his trustees. Some of the board members said it was a great idea but given their present financial constraints necessitated by the building fund campaign it was utterly out of the question. Then the conservative wing immediately began to question the "why" and "how" and the wisdom of the plan. This forced Zipper to explain in detail the rationale for his proposal. In time he learned to appreciate the conservatives as a needed element. They made it imperative for him to thoroughly think through every innovation. To his disciples he used to explain that every vehicle needs a great deal of power to move forward; but it needs also power to be able to stop, perhaps a little less power but brakes all the same. A board of trustees he came to see needs 'motors' and 'brakes'.

Nevertheless, he was determined that no one put the brakes on his "children's concerts." He explained to his board that symphony orchestra concerts for children held in big symphony halls reach a total of less than 1% of the elementary school population and that going to the concert hall becomes the main attraction rather then the music. In-school-concerts, he explained, are entirely different educationally and physically. The meeting ended with little board support and Zipper went home slightly deflated but still determined to make the concerts happen.

One trustee, Ruth Roberg, was enthusiastic and committed to the idea. She approached Zipper the next day and said, "Symphony concerts in elementary schools - that would be a dream come true!" So she set about to organize a speaking series for Zipper - luncheons, teas, women's clubs, Rotary, Lions Clubs, service organizations of all kinds. Her attitude was, "Let's see what happens." One day in February of 1954 Zipper spoke at the Winnetka Women's Club. That evening at 7:00 Zipper was sitting at his desk when the phone rang. "My name is Arnold Maremont," the caller announced. "My wife heard you speak today and I would like to talk to you. Can you come tomorrow to our home for dinner?" Zipper replied, "Of course." He then called Ruth Roberg and told her, "A man called Maremont called me and asked me to dinner. Who is he?" Roberg was astounded, "Maremont called? Don't you realize who he is? Why he is a major manufacturer, art collector, and philanthropist!" She was thrilled and was eager to see the results of the dinner. The next evening Zipper drove to the Maremont address in Winnetka and found himself in front of an imposing but tasteful mansion. He was greeted by a maid and immediately observed a Braque and a Picasso. Then he was led to dinner with Maremont and his wife Adelle. Maremont was a slight, dark-haired man with penetrating eyes and a strong chin which immediately conveyed an aura of determination. For almost an hour at dinner Zipper held forth. Maremont asked most of the questions. "How much will the concerts cost?" he asked. Zipper explained the costs and presented a projected budget. Maremont then said, "Go ahead, I'll underwrite the whole project. Also," he said, "let's have a Saturday evening free concert for parents and I'll explain to them what our plans are." And on May 5, 1954 at Skokie Jr. High the children's concert series was launched with a preview concert for the parents. The following week 10 concerts were held at elementary schools in Northfield, Winnetka, Wilmette with Highland Park, and Northbrook eagerly joining at a later date. The orchestra comprised a first-rate group of professionals. Zipper was convinced that children need to hear great music performed by quality musicians.

Barbara Polikoff, in her monograph-chronicle of the Music Center of the North Shore, describes the project:

> "We went for a fish and hooked a whale," one resistant board member commented when confronted with Zipper's in-school symphony proposal. But a majority was persuaded, and Zipper received authority to establish the program he sought. He formed a professional orchestra of 33 musicians including teachers from the Center as well as other local professionals, and he called it the Music Center Orchestra (later to be renamed the North Shore Philharmonic). In 1954, the project was launched in ten schools with a total enrollment of 4,000 children. Just a few years after its inception the program was self-supporting, with two-thirds of the expense borne by the parents (at a cost of about 50 cents a concert) and by PTAs, and one-third by the Music Performance Trust Fund.
>
> The orchestra visited each participating school three times a year and played a 30-minute program. Two weeks before the concerts, classroom teachers were sent background material on the music to be played. Zipper had a special talent for planning programs that covered chronological periods in

symphonic literature while keeping within a length of no more than seven minutes for any one movement or piece.

"We played in so many gyms they all began to look alike," Louise Burge recalls. "It was a job getting to three schools in one morning, finding our way in winter storms, missing meals. But when we arrived we were dressed in concert attire and even if half the kids were sleeping at that early morning concert, we had to play at the very top of our skills."

The children began to look forward to the transformation of their gym to a concert hall where 33 musicians dressed in formal black, led by the conductor with the rather glamorous foreign accent, brought music to them. The Music Center Orchestra became "Dr. Zipper's Orchestra." After the concert children gathered to talk to Zipper and the orchestra members and ask for autographs. Classroom teachers reported that performance in all subjects went up on the day the orchestra was to play and continued to be higher than usual for the day following. There was an air of excitement, exhilaration. An instrumental teacher in a school district of 2,000 wrote in a report supporting the program that only 53 children were studying orchestral instruments the year Zipper first brought the orchestra to the school. Three years later the number had increased to 252, and the largest group was the strings. It seemed possible that Ruth Roberg's hope for bringing more string instrumentalists into the world was being partially realized.[85]

From the beginning, the concerts were impressive and are one of Zipper's major contributions to education. Concerts for children were not a new idea. For many years before Zipper came on the educational scene, and even since, symphony orchestras all over the country have provided concerts for children. These concerts are usually held in the main concert halls of cities. But, Zipper, believes, what children remember are the beautiful buildings and the plush red carpets. They remember the special, strange terrain but not the music. Zipper's novel idea was to bring the music, the symphony orchestra to the children's schools. He would bring the concert to the gymnasium where the children would sit on the floor, close up to the instruments, in an intimate setting. His idea was to break down the barriers between children and performers, to narrow the distance between music and place. The idea worked and continues to work in city after city where the idea is put into practice. A year after the concerts began in Chicago, the *New York Times* picked up the idea and ran the following story (February 7, 1955):

SERIOUS SYMPHONY FOR YOUNG URGED

Chicago Music Director Says 'Gimmicks' Are
Not Needed to Foster Appreciation

Symphony concerts for children need not be accompanied by "cute entertainment gimmicks" to keep the youngsters amused and occupied. That is the opinion of Dr. Herbert Zipper, director of the Community Music Center of the North Shore in Chicago and conductor of the Manila Symphony Orchestra in the Philippines.

Dr. Zipper offered this comment during a recent interview on a visit in this city.

He believes serious music should be given to children "seriously." He is convinced that concerts with professional musicians should be brought to the schools, where youngsters are in a learning situation.

In a large, strange concert hall, he said, there is an atmosphere of overexcitement. This, along with "fun gimmicks" distracts a youngster from real appreciation of the music, he declared.

Dr. Zipper bases these conclusions on the results of a musical education program he has been conducting for the last year at public and private schools throughout the North Shore area in Chicago. He has conducted programs before 1,100 children, from kindergarten through the eighth grade, in twenty-two schools. Four concerts are given during the school year, with the total cost to each youngster averaging from 70 to 75 cents a program.

Today's youngsters hear too much electronic or "canned" music, he declared. This, he added, cannot begin to give the children a serious appreciation of good music that a "live" concert experience does.

The younger a child is exposed to live concert experiences, he maintained, the more the child will learn to appreciate good music. This has been indicated, he emphasized, by the quiet and absorbed response of even young kindergartners. The only restlessness shown among the children, he maintains, has been merely in the form of imitating the orchestra — from motions of playing the drums and fiddling make-believe instruments to conducting.

Dr. Zipper's concerts, where possible, are held in gymnasiums — not on stages — where children can sit on the floor all around the orchestra. The concerts take place during assembly time and are never longer than forty-five minutes.

Zipper himself saw the concerts as a tribute to America where you can have an idea, almost any idea no matter how outlandish, and you have a chance to pull it off. Dr. Zipper's Orchestra, as thousands of children came to call it, was one such successful idea.

In addition to the hard work there were pleasant surprises. One such surprise was a phone call Zipper received in early 1954. Clara W. Mayer, Vice President of the New York School for Social Research in New York, telephoned to tell Zipper he was the recipient of the Louis S. Wise Award for his contributions to education. At this time, although living in

Chicago, he was still lecturing at the New School every other month (until 1957) and so on May 20, 1954 he attended a dinner party in New York to receive his award. The award was made even more poignant by being handed to him by Francis B. Sayre who attended especially to honor Herbert Zipper. Sayre read the inscription which read:

> "As a musician, a teacher, and a humanist he brings his great gifts to bear on communal life both in America and Asia and makes a significant contribution to the education of the adult."

The next morning his old friend Eric Simon called Zipper to ask if he knew he had won $1,000 as part of his award? Zipper said, "No." "Well, said Simon, "I just read it in the New York Times." Five minutes later President Hans Simons of the New School called, embarrassed that he had forgotten to give Zipper the check and said that he would mail it promptly.

Zipper's greatest reward during these years and ever since 1927 was his deepening relationship with his wife Trudl. They worked and laughed side by side, refined programs, and took pleasure in the growth of the school. Barbara Polikoff offers her first-hand account of Trudl's work at the school:

> At that early board meeting when alarm had been expressed about hooking a whale instead of a fish, it might have been added that the whale was of no mean proportions. Zipper's new ideas included a dance department to be headed by his wife. Trudl Zipper had been a child prodigy in Vienna and had danced in Continental Europe, England, and the Philippines. She was a tiny woman with long gold hair and a dancer's body that seemed as ageless as her spirit. A mother of a young dance student once asked Zipper how Trudl managed, in a rehearsal with 150 students of all ages, to see that each one knew exactly how to do the right thing at the right place at the right time. Zipper responded, "Because Trudl combines just the right mixture of the spirit of freedom with the discipline of a benevolent master sergeant."
>
> Officially, Trudl Zipper taught modern dance, or as she characterized it, "the free, expressive use of the entire body unhampered by any formalism." But Jean Pettibone (now the director of the Evanston branch of the Music Center), whose three daughters studied with Trudl, observed that she actually added ballet to the modern dance, just leaving out the French names. Pettibone's daughters, one of whom continued her studies with Martha Graham, and another of whom now dances professionally with Eric Hawkins, confirmed that as they moved into advanced studies they realized that Trudl had been training them in ballet all along.
>
> Dance recitals were major events at the Music Center. Rehearsals often continued into late night hours, as testified to by George Banhalmi who did the

accompanying. (A reliable authority reports that during the marathon rehearsal sessions, Banhalmi's small transistor radio would be tuned into the baseball game as he played the same phrase for the 20th time.)

An accomplished graphic artist, herself, Trudl Zipper painted the backdrops that transformed the recital hall to a magic forest or a toy shop. Under her direction, mothers sat for hours sewing buttons and seams for a fairy princess, witch, or shy dragon while their children rehearsed. Those costumes, too rich with memories to discard, are still stored away in many a North Shore attic. (Jean Pettibone still can't part with the cloud costumes her daughters wore when they danced to a Chopin etude.) Many of these dancers, now in their twenties and thirties, still remember those recitals as times of high exhilaration. As one put it, "Trudl had a magical ability to pick out for each of us what we could do best. She gave each of us the chance to feel beautiful." [86]

After work the Viennese couple explored Chicago, its restaurants, concert halls, and general culture. The rough edges of their relationship had been worked out during a twelve-year courtship. During these years they had their fights and learned to deal with each other's idiosyncrasies: For example, Trudl's tardiness and Zipper's fastidiousness. When they were finally married, each was more mature than the typical newlywed. They were also bound together by the common experience of learning to live together first in the foreign culture of the Philippines and then during the hardships of war. And after this they came to yet another strange culture, America, and the craziness of Brooklyn as their first exposure to America. Living now in the North Shore of Chicago, in a cozy suburb, in a comfortable apartment on campus with no problems of commuting to work may have seemed to others boringly harmonious. But to the Zippers it was a refreshing change from chaos and adversity. The Chicago years seem to have been fruitful and happy ones for Herbert and Trudl Zipper.

Of course, one wonders if the marriage was as blissful as Zipper, in his eighties, reflects upon it. Some friends and family member believe he may have idealized the marriage through the distillation of memory, creating his own myths, his own legends. To Zipper's way of thinking they never argued except about matters of artistic taste or professional choices - which set design to use, how this piece should be paced. Other family members say that it was not quite so; that Trudl could be sharp and sarcastic on occasion and that she could be quite critical of her husband. Often, for example, Zipper would fade out of a conversation, drifting off into this movement or passages of this or that symphony, and then return to the conversation obviously having missed its essential development. Whereupon Trudl would poke fun at his artistic dreaminess. Zipper, however, seemed oblivious to her humor or criticism and it all rolled off him.

Allowing for the possibility that they may have argued and fought more often than Zipper remembers, the relationship was, nevertheless, the single and most compelling communion in his life. Henry Holt says they had "a major passion" for each other. With Trudl he could reveal some recesses of his carefully ordered and, perhaps even repressed, inner life. Zipper maintains that his conflicts have never been within himself but only between him and the external world. Certainly he reveals little of his inner world to anyone so it is difficult to verify his contention. It may be that the combination of his Viennese upbringing, his natural bent towards order and neatness, and his dramatic experiences in Dachau and Buchenwald have impelled him to keep a tight rein on his inner world. And it may be that he is simply a remarkably secure man, not at war with himself. In either case, with Trudl he could let go and be silly as well as share what he chose of his inner life.

Besides each other, Herbert and Trudl Zipper made many new friends. One such friend was Trustee, Richard Colburn. Zipper had been immediately impressed with Colburn who was both knowledgeable and passionate about music. They played chamber music together, as Colburn was an accomplished violist. In addition, Colburn was helpful in a variety of ways, including securing instruments whenever Zipper needed them.

Zipper did, however, make mistakes with his Board of Trustees. On one occasion he grew exasperated with a Trustee's child who missed music lessons with Zipper himself, so he informed the child's mother he was too busy to wait for her son to show up to lessons and was therefore switching teachers. The father, a Board member, was furious and began some subtle and other not-so-subtle measures to work against Zipper. Eventually the Trustee's plotting was discovered and he was asked by other Trustees to resign. Zipper, however learned a valuable lesson: do not mess with Trustee's children.

On several occasions Zipper's disregard for rules, regulations, and majority opinions also caused trouble. In his eagerness to see things happen quickly he would often move without the full support of his board or committees. One such example was "the truck incident." When, in May of 1954, Zipper was setting up the first series of Concerts-in-the-Schools, a trustee's wife, Mrs. Howard Fisher, volunteered to cart timpani from concert to concert. This was a makeshift arrangement and so a truck was donated to the school. After some years it began to fall apart and Zipper asked the Board for a new truck. Two of Zipper's antagonists located a used-truck from a downtown dealer with the arrangement that Zipper rent it each week which would have forced him to drive miles downtown several times a month to pick it up. On the first outing Zipper drove the old truck to the concert whereupon it broke down. Rather than follow his Board's directive to rent a truck each week, Zipper decided instead to buy a Volkswagen van. He put up $500 of his own money as a down payment and bought the van for $1600. The old truck was carted off for $100 and Zipper had his new little bus. He then wrote the President of the Board and told him he would rent it to the school for interest only — half of what the other rental would have cost. The President of the Board, Ben Rumage, who had suggested the truck rental in the first place, asked Zipper why he had disobeyed the Board directive. Zipper explained why his decision was better. The conservative wing of the Board was furious and never forgave Zipper.

Trudl, on the other hand, who attended Board Meetings as an observer and provider of refreshments, urged her husband to be even more forceful in his opposition to the conservatives. She, in fact, egged him on in matters which were administrative and really beyond her knowledge or experience.

Nevertheless, the Board was successful in raising enough funds to own the land and buildings of the Center without debt, and, on January 31, 1960 Zipper attended a party with the Board of Trustees celebrating "the burning of the mortgage" on the school. There were over a hundred people present, all in high spirits. Late in the evening Arnold Maremont, who was by now an influential trustee, said: "Herbert you are in trouble! You have overcome a major hurdle, the Board members are satisfied with their accomplishments, they will go to sleep unless you can dream something up that will stir them up." Zipper told him not to worry, that a memorandum to the Board was already in the mail with a proposal for the next Sunday Board Meeting.

Zipper had prepared a four-year Development Plan for the Community Music Center of the North Shore which called for expanding the In-School Concert Series, expanding the range of instrumental instruction at the school, organizing an extension music program in private homes, and engaging the Fine Arts Quartet as a "Quartet in Residence" at the Music Center. The Fine Arts Quartet, one of America's leading string quartets had been enlisted to give a series of seminars at the Music Center and had just returned from their first European tour where they had enormous success as the first American quartet to tour the continent. The press, including *Time Magazine*, published glowing accounts of their concerts. Yet they came home broke. They sought out Zipper and described their financial plight. They could not see any alternative but to disband and to seek other work. After all, they all had to support their families. Zipper persuaded them to hold fast while he thought for a few weeks of possible solutions.

Before the upcoming Board Meeting Zipper called the women trustees who were the real movers on the Board and who appreciated the quality of the Fine Arts Quartet. He called to enlist their support for his "Quartet-in-Residence" idea. The women, Lucy Montgomery, Ruth Roberg, Jean Evans, and Ellie Martin were all enthusiastic about the idea. Their enthusiasm was not just for the Fine Arts Quartet but for Zipper the man. Perhaps Zipper's Viennese charm and masculine vitality were not lost on these women. At any rate these four women believed in Zipper's ideas and enjoyed working on the project with him.

The special meeting of the Board was held on February 7, 1960 and it lasted until midnight. There were heated debates and Zipper had to hear, again, the well-worn phrase: "Herbert, this is too rich for our blood." However, the women and Dennis Hull and a few others carried the motion and one of the first major American chamber music quartets-in-residence was born. And soon a major subscription series followed. The *Chicago Daily News* (September 30, 1960) picked up the story:

CULTURE WINS

> THE PROSPECT of four musicians seated on a stage and playing the masterpieces of chamber music has not in the past been one to cause audiences to stampede boxoffices. So, the unparalleled success of the internationally respected Fine Arts Quartet in attracting Chicagoans and suburbanites to its newly launched series of 28 concerts is cause for congratulations.
>
> Behind the musicians themselves and Herbert Zipper, musical director of the project, has been another quartet: Mrs. Bergen Evans, Mrs. Albert R. Martin, Mrs. Kenneth Montgomery, and Mrs. Leo Roberg. They rallied about themselves a group whose enthusiasm has floated an enterprise that seemed fool-hardy to some seasoned observers.
>
> If the Fine Arts project puts down permanent roots here, Chicago will be able to look any musical capital in the world in the eye with respect to chamber music, one of the most rarefied forms of artistic expression.

In 1962, Zipper conducted, for the first time in 40 years, Schoenberg's Pierrot Lunaire. He collaborated with the forces of the Chicago Music Center (Louise Burge, flute & piccolo; Chester Milosovich, clarinet and bass clarinet; Abram Loft, violin and viola; George Sopkin, cello) with Alice Howland doing the sprechotimme and Gilbert Kalish as the pianist. Abe Loft often provided comic relief. Before a performance, artists often experience a special kind of nervous tension, mixed with supressed anxiety and lowered well-being. On the evening of the first "Pierrot" performance in Chicago's Studebaker Theatre, the performers and the conductor all assembled at the stage entrance. Abe Loft who faced the demanding assignment of playing alternately violin and viola suddenly turned around and exclaimed: "So, what's wrong with teaching?" The performance was, by all accounts, superb and it led to a recording later by Everest Records.

Because of the major disruptions in their lives and in the world, Zipper and Trudl made the decision as early as the Philippines not to have children; nevertheless, their lives have been centered around children. They did, for two years at least, have a young relative live with them. From 1955 to 1957 Zipper's nephew, Henry Holt, lived with them while attending Northwestern University. He took classes at Northwestern, taught classes in clarinet and piano at the North Shore School in the afternoon, and played 2nd clarinet in Zipper's children's concert orchestra. Holt remembers the years fondly, particularly enjoying moments of gaiety and levity during the after hours. "We would," Holt recalls, "work 13 and 14 hour work days and then gather together, the three of us, at 11:30 and sip sherry and act like silly children." The silliness consisted of sometimes playing nonsense word games. Or sometimes Zipper would pretend to be a mannequin and Henry Holt and Trudl would move him from position to position or he would do his 'glass eye' routine, affecting a frightening pose. Or sometimes they would chase each other through the halls of the school.

Mostly, however, the years from 1953 to 1967 were spent chasing from one project to the next. He carried out several full time jobs simultaneously. Because he has always been at heart a teacher, he carried a heavy load of teaching. And finally, in addition to his teaching, administration, and development of new projects, Zipper also conducted three orchestras. There was the Chicago Businessmen's Orchestra which he conducted from 1955 to 1962. The orchestra was composed of half professionals and half amateurs. It gave some wonderful concerts, in a variety of concert halls, and featured soloists such as Janos Starker and Sidney Harth. Zipper finally quit when he found himself over-extended in projects. There was the orchestra he organized to give concerts to children, which grew to where it was visiting 85 schools annually, playing to an unduplicated audience of 40,000 children a year. And, there was the Manila Symphony Orchestra which he managed and conducted each summer. As if this were not enough, he soon became involved in a 16-year struggle to bring a cultural center to the Philippines.

Chapter XI

Manila Revisited

> "But what is uttered from the heart alone
> will win the hearts of others to your own."
>
> - Goethe, *Faust I*

In December of 1945 when Herbert Zipper was appointed by Philippine President Sergio Osmeña to a committee for the cultural rehabilitation of the Philippines, he began dreaming of a plan to build an Art Center for the Performing and Visual Arts in Manila. This center would rise out of the ashes of Manila like a Phoenix. However, in the fall of 1946 the committee was disbanded and Zipper had to put his dreams on the back shelf. During the following years the absence of adequate performing facilities became increasingly detrimental to the cultural life of the city. Nevertheless, the economics and politics of the time ruled out any hope of erecting such a costly structure.

Then in 1953 an ill-conceived plan for the Philippines, originating in Washington, D.C., gave Zipper the opportunity to once again pursue his dream. Thus began a 16-year struggle on the part of Zipper to bring a Performing Arts Center to the Philippine people. As he was to do often in America, he played a behind-the-scenes role, avoiding publicity and refusing pay in order to keep politically clean and beholden to no one but to the muse and to the project at hand.

In 1953 the U.S. Congress, having been lobbied by a former U.S. Ambassador to the Philippines, Emmet O'Neill, approved the construction of a "Bataan-Corregidor War Memorial" to be erected at the cost of $7,500,000 on Corregidor Island. A War Memorial Commission was created under the chairmanship of O'Neill in Washington, D.C. and a counterpart Philippine Commission was organized in Manila. After years of discussion, in 1957, an architectural contest was held in the U.S. with the unexplainable exclusion of any Filipino participation and a design was selected as the winning one by a jury consisting also of Americans only. The Philippine Commission politely concurred officially, but privately the members voiced angry feelings to Zipper. Then when the entire plan and winning design was published in the Manila press in 1958, a storm began to brew against the design, the location and the insensitivity to Filipino ideas. Yet nobody felt comfortable to oppose Washington and even the American Ambassador, Charles Bohlen, who was genuinely appalled about the entire concept, could not take any steps against a plan that was adopted by both Houses of Congress and supported by President Eisenhower. But Zipper was free to act.

At this time Zipper was President of the National Guild of Community Music Schools and as such a member of the congressionally chartered National Music Council. Returning from his summer session in Manila in the fall of 1958 and after having consulted leading personalities in Manila, including Ambassador Bohlen and the Chairman of the American Chamber of Commerce of the Philippines, Zipper prepared a memorandum and a resolution which he presented to the National Music Council (on December 18 of 1958) condemning the project. Under Zipper's careful shepherding the resolution was unanimously passed. Zipper then mailed both the resolution and the supporting report to members of the Congress and mailed a cover letter to Rep. Frank Thompson, Jr. (New Jersey) who then was a leading personality with regard to all matters concerning the arts which came before the House. Also, after the National Council meeting, Zipper presented the issue to Aura Smith, an editorial writer for the *New York Times*, asking him for his editorial support but without mentioning a cultural center, because if Smith had mentioned building an Arts Auditorium it would have revealed who gave Smith his information. Smith proceeded, February 26, 1959, to publish the following editorial:

THE CORREGIDOR MEMORIAL

> Protests are being made in Manila against the plan to spend $7,500,000 to erect an elaborate Corregidor-Bataan Memorial in honor of the Filipinos and Americans who died there together. It has been suggested that the actual memorial be much more modest and that part of the funds be used for permanent projects in the public interest. In this country it has been suggested in some quarters that the memorial fund might endow a much-needed cultural center.
>
> These objections to the memorial plan are valid. The monument to the men of Bataan and Corregidor ought to be a living thing, not some collection of lifeless marble. The money can be spent in a way that will do even greater honor to the men who are memorialized.
>
> An attractive alternative is the construction of a good children's hospital and a convalescent home. "Topside," on Corregidor itself, would even be a

possible location. These services are badly needed and their provision, surely, would be an ideal way to pay our tribute to the dead on behalf of the living. The Filipinos, we are convinced, would be in complete agreement with this viewpoint.

The resolution, Zipper's report, and the *New York Times* editorial were read in the House by Rep. Thompson and printed in the Congressional Record and caused the demise of the 7-1/2 million dollar war memorial on Corregidor Island. At the same time the idea of an Arts Center went into eclipse on the government levels. Zipper, however, did not give up. He continued to talk about the idea at every opportunity. And in July of 1959 when he was honored with the Philippine Presidential Award in a ceremony at Malacanan Palace, he seized the moment to discuss with President Carlos P. Garcia the importance to the Philippines of a cultural center in Manila. Zipper found Garcia not only receptive but enthusiastic about the idea. Zipper had also been able to find willing ears at USIA. Subsequently, the Philippine and American governments (represented by the USIA) got together to create in January of 1960 the Philippine-American Cultural Foundation. The Philippine government donated a valuable tract of land in Quezon City (a district of greater Manila where the Campus of the University of the Philippines is located) and conferred tax exempt status to the Foundation. The Board of Trustees consisted of a number of Zipper's friends, including Benito F. Legarda. At the same time USIA requested from the Congress an appropriation of $1,365,740 for the Foundation. Zipper wrote many letters of support and organized a letter-writing campaign to members of the Senate and House Appropriations Committee and in July of 1960, Zipper received a letter from Senator Leverett Saltonstall informing him that the amount was approved. A seven-year battle appeared to have been won.

With the money apparently secure, the U.S. State Department provided for the Foundation an Executive Director, Mr. E. V. Niemeyer and an architect was appointed, Leonard ("Lindy") Locsin to design plans for the building. Zipper was named as artistic consultant, which he accepted on a voluntary basis. However, in 1961, President Garcia was defeated in the national election by Vice President Macapagal who was inaugurated in December of 1961. His administration promptly lifted the foreign currency control and as a result of the U.S. dollar being traded on the open market, caused the exchange rate to cut the dollar value against the Philippine peso. Consequently, the American fund that was made available to the Foundation in pesos ($2,800,000) lost half of its dollar value. This turn of events appeared disastrous to Zipper and his dream of the Cultural Center. The funds were now ($800,000) insufficient to fund the originally planned building and the Board of Trustees reluctantly decided to cut down the building to fit the available funds. They notified Zipper of their new plans in early December of 1962. He was distressed but unwilling to admit defeat. "I decided to move heaven and earth to bring to realization the original concept of the center."

Once again Zipper had to shift gears. From consultation to acoustics and the artistic design of the building, Zipper now had to fight to keep the building from being reduced in size and scope. He immediately prepared a counter-report arguing strenuously against reducing the capacity of the auditorium from 1200 to 600-800. He argued that such a reduction would be uneconomical, a duplication of existing facilities, and a long range disservice to the Philippine people. He also argued that the exterior of the building should not be compromised but should impart to the viewer "the dignity and loftiness of the building's purpose" and that its exterior features, although contemporary, "should give the impression of timelessness." Zipper concluded his arguments about the exterior with an important argument against economic thrift at the expense of aesthetic beauty:

> ... To substitute this with a more "utilitarian" design may be rather detrimental to the effect the building should create. Many contemporary edifices devoted to the arts, recently constructed, including Philharmonic Hall in New York, have been severely criticized by competent experts in the most important publications in the United States because their appearance differs very little from the utilitarian character of contemporary department stores, airport structures, office buildings and shopping centers.

He sent his report to several key figures including the Washington Post Editor. Vic Niemeyer's tour of duty came to an end and his replacement was less effective. Nevertheless, the USIA was still helpful. The real problems developed through the representatives of the Department of State and the succession of cultural affairs officers there who were oblivious to the prevailing mores of the Philippines. The last officer involved in the project, a Mr. Esterline, did his utmost to scuttle the project. He even opposed Zipper's proposal to postpone the project, to invest the existing peso fund at the high interest rate prevailing in the Philippines until the fund would grow sufficiently to allow construction of the original plan. However, the project was postponed and Zipper continued his behind-the-scenes lobbying to keep the original design intact.

In this project, as in all projects of Zipper's life, Trudl continued to be his supportive partner, excited about every venture, offering insightful suggestions, helping him to refine his ideas, reading his letters and memos and reports. Over the years they developed an after-work ritual which both enjoyed immensely. Zipper would come home and say, "I've been thinking about — some author or idea — may I read this to you?" And Trudl would drop whatever she was doing, would move to a comfortable chair, light a cigarette, and curl her shapely ballerina's legs under her. Zipper would then read to her. One day it might be Walt Whitman — a favorite of both of them, another day it might be the poet Heine or the scurrilous, sarcastic German poet Joachim Ringelnatz whose poems were barred by the Nazis and whose collected poems Zipper was able to buy only after the war. Trudl was a voracious reader but, in a wonderfully childlike way, loved to be read to. Often they would discover it was 8:00 or 9:00 and they had not prepared dinner. Since Trudl never much liked to cook, Zipper would often run out and get something simple or they would eat oatmeal. Neither were much for gourmet food or restaurants. They were usually happy in each other's company.

Often on long car trips Trudl would say it's nice to be here together in our "schneckenhaus" (the shell of a snail), in our little protective hideaway from telephones and responsibilities. Both enjoyed these long quiet times together, in silence or in conversation. On one Saturday afternoon in 1962, Zipper was at work at his desk busily preparing a composition to meet a Monday deadline and to have ready for the 4:00 mail. Trudl came home from her teaching at about 2:00 and in great consternation said to her husband, "Herbert, do you realize we are all out of cigarettes?" Whereupon Zipper jumped up, drove to the corner drug store, and ordered two cartons - his favorites and hers. As the counter salesgirl went to retrieve them, Zipper had a moment of sudden realization, or epiphany. He realized he was a slave to this habit and in a flash he made a resolution. The salesgirl returned and he purchased only one of the cartons. When he arrived back home, Trudl noticed he had only one carton. "Where is yours?" she asked. He said: "I don't smoke anymore." And that was that. In a typically rational and self-centered manner, through a forceful expression of self-will, Zipper was able to simply end a major addiction in a moment's decision. An addiction of many years was dismissed just like that. After this he tried time and time again to persuade Trudl to quit but she never quite managed, a tragic weakness on her part.

Quitting addictions 'cold turkey' seemed to be a Zipper family trait. As it turned out, Papa Emil Zipper had had an addiction to gambling, horse-racing to be specific. In his late teens and early twenties he frequented the horse races betting on almost every race. He was quite knowledgeable and usually came out a little ahead. On one Sunday he had lost every race and went to the window to bet on the last race. He waved a 100 crown note and said, "I'll bet 10 crowns (worth about $2.00

then) on horse X." The teller saw the 100 crown note and rang up a 100 crown ticket. Emil Zipper protested, "No, 10 crowns." The teller said, "It's too late, I've already rung it up." And on and on they argued until the teller said, "Look at the board, I don't know why you are arguing, your horse won!" At the odds Emil Zipper had won over $2600. But he was distraught. He had won through another's error and it was pure luck not knowledge that saved his day. Whereupon he quit betting forever.

Otto Zipper, after coming to America became "addicted" to his Whiskey soda at the end of every work day. But one day driving home from work he realized he couldn't wait to get home to have his drink. When he realized he was dependent on the drink, he quit and never drank again.

Brother Walter, a deeply-addicted smoker, in 1962 saw a visual presentation on the physically harmful effects of smoking and he quit. It would seem that this ability to exercise the will over physical need or even addiction was a Zipper family trait.

Addiction to projects is also a Herbert Zipper trait. In 1965 President Macapagal was defeated by Ferdinand Marcos in a bitterly fought campaign and Zipper saw a new opportunity for the revival of the Cultural Center idea. Marcos was inaugurated on December 30, 1965 and in January of 1966 Zipper wrote a new memorandum on the Cultural Center which he mailed promptly to President Marcos and to the U.S. State Department. Marcos turned over all cultural matters to his wife, Imelda, and Zipper's memo landed on her desk.

Imelda Marcos, recognizing an opportunity to erect a monument to herself, immediately went to work full speed enacting her own ideas. She bought all the plans from the Philippine-American Foundation; she turned the parcel of land in Quezon City back to the government; she decided to drop the War Memorial concept; she excluded any American participation; and, she decided to build the Center at the edge of Manila Bay on Roxas Boulevard. This proved to be a costly decision because a great deal of land had to be reclaimed from the bay and the bedrock was much deeper than was initially estimated. But this did not deter the determined lady. The Center had to be built on this spot and money was not discussed. To this day nobody knows just how much it cost to erect the Center.

Early in June of 1965 Zipper arrived in Manila to resume his annual summer conducting duties. Soon after his arrival Mrs. Marcos requested to meet the four teachers and to meet Zipper regarding the Philippine Culture Center (PCC). One morning they all met at Malacanan Palace and after an exchange of pleasantries, Imelda brought up the PCC. She informed Zipper that she was retaining the architect, Leandro Locsin, and that the original design would be executed. She said, however, that the size of the auditorium was still under discussion and she asked Zipper for his opinion. He recommended that if cost were not a decisive factor, the seating capacity should be increased to at least 1800 and a maximum of 2000. Imelda Marcos decided on the 2000 figure. She also asked Zipper to continue his consultation on all acoustical matters. During the four succeeding years of construction he was in continuous contact with the architect Locsin and Russel Johnson of Bolt, Beranek, and Newman in Cambridge, Massachusetts until the opening of the Center in September 1969.

When completion of the Center was in sight, the U.S. Embassy until then excluded from all matters concerning the PCC - offered to provide an American soloist to perform in the opening symphony concert under the direction of Conductor Herbert Zipper. It was finally agreed that the U.S. Department of State would sponsor Eugene Istomin as a soloist to play two piano concertos. The Embassy also contributed a printed program which, however, completely and unbelievably omitted any mention of the fact that this concert was the grand opening of the P.C.C. To Zipper's mind it was a cheap and undignified demonstration of displeasure about the exclusion of the U.S. Government from the Center project. The Manila Symphony Society together with the PCC administration printed a second program acknowledging the historic event - a celebration fourteen years after Zipper's liberation concert in the ruins of Santa Cruz of the cultural rehabilitation of the Philippines. Despite this pettiness of the U.S. Embassy, the concert was a gala occasion. As he raised his baton to conduct Beethoven's "Prometheus Overture" (followed by the Beethoven Piano Concerto #4, the Mahler 3rd Symphony and the Chopin Piano Concerto #2) in this beautiful new building, Zipper had a special feeling of accomplishment for this concert represented the fulfillment of sixteen years of work.

Zipper, as he consistently has done since his early years in America, also gave regular symphony concerts in public and private schools in Manila. The American school there, a private elementary and secondary school that serves mainly the foreign communities of Manila, subscribed for many years to these concerts. Once, at the conclusion of a concert in 1965 at the American School, a good looking high school girl approached Zipper introducing herself in unmistakable Viennese German and telling him that his name was known to her family. Her manner of speech, her looks, especially the expression of her eyes suddenly reminded Herbert of a drama student he had known at the State Academy, in the early 1920's.

She was a colleague of his with whom he had carried on an intimate relationship. Prompted by the striking resemblance Herbert asked the girl, "By any chance is your mother an actress?" "No," answered the girl, "That's my grandmother. She's the only actress in my family." This was somewhat of a jolt to Zipper but not to his wife, who listened to the conversation with delight and had the time of her life for the rest of the day referring to her husband as "Grandpa."

During one of his annual summer visits to the Philippines in the early 1950's, Zipper conducted a concert featuring the Prologue and Coronation scene from Mussorgsky's opera, *Boris Gudunov*. In the coronation scene there is a dramatic pause that is filled with glorious ringing of church bells. Manila at this time was still half destroyed from the war, and, look where he might, Zipper could find not a single church bell. He remembered, however, a basic principle from his days of seeking chairs: When in need, ask the Chinese. Again, he contacted his friend Huang Cheng Yung who recommended that Herbert seek help from a Chinese man in the tenor section of the chorus, Mr. Chua Egan.

The next morning Zipper went to the electrical shop of Mr. Chua Egan. Zipper asked him whether he would know where he could borrow some church bells.

EGAN: Church bells? What kind of church bells?
ZIPPER: Bells that ring at the services.
EGAN: How many you need?
ZIPPER: Many. Maybe 10-15 or even 20.
EGAN: Oh, that is very difficult to find; for what you need?
ZIPPER: For the coronation scene! For our Mussorgsky performance.

(Egan's interest immediately became aroused as he was a tenor participant. "Wait a minute," he said and disappeared into the storage room of his shop. After a while he came back with a short piece of steel rod and a hammer, striking the rod with it.)

EGAN: Won't that do?
ZIPPER: Sorry, no. Sounds just what it is.
EGAN: Too bad. Let me think. Give me your telephone number. I call you when I have idea.

(Five days later he called:)

EGAN: You have transportation?
ZIPPER: Of course, our jeep. Why?
EGAN: Come tomorrow morning, pick up bells.

They arranged to meet at Mr. Egan's electrical shop. He called his 'boys' who brought out 25 bells - real bronze church bells - of all sizes. When Herbert asked where on earth he had procured them, Egan told him that he had installed electrical church bells in the convents as loaners and borrowed the real bells for two weeks. Ask the Chinese the impossible, Zipper chuckles telling the story, and it will happen. When Mr. Egan returned the bells after the performance, many of the convents liked the electrical bells so much they bought them. His good deed turned a nice profit.

In March of 1966 as Zipper was just leaving for the airport to Oklahoma to interview applicants for the Philippine Fellowship Project, his sister Hedy telephoned with sad news: "Rosie" their 90-year old mother, had died. She had lived with Hedy in the Santa Monica home which housed for many years three generations of the family - Emil and Rosie, Fred and Hedy Holt and their children, Lucy and Henry. Up until the last two years of her life she had been a vital, cheerful woman loved by all who knew her. After coming to America she had changed somewhat. She became an ardent patriot, deeply devoted to John F. Kennedy, and an enthusiastic reader. She read the newspaper thoroughly and read widely in general literature. She was particularly pleased on her 80th birthday to receive from her son the collected works of Herman Hesse. She was also a fine musician who was a major force in Zipper's musical growth. When he practiced the piano, she listened and called out constructive criticisms. Zipper fondly recalls in the 1930's in Vienna an evening ritual of returning home at about midnight or 1:00 a.m., Walter arriving at about the same time, and finding Rosie waiting for both of them with a snack. She particularly loved having her boys review the evening for her. All of Herbert and Walter's friends adored Rosie and often became her friends as well. In fact, she seemed to prefer her son's friends to people of her own generation. Often the boy's girlfriends became close to Rosie. For about two years Herbert Zipper dated the beautiful blond Ilse Furtwangler, a niece of the famous conductor, and she was devoted to Rosie. After having had four children "Rosie" - itself a nickname - became rather rotund and acquired a new nickname, "Kugerl" which means "little ball." Rosie loved meals with her children's friends and her husband also delighted in their presence.

In her last few years Rosie was confined to a wheelchair and gradually became less and less lucid. With her death, Zipper's last strong bond to the old world of Hapsburg Vienna was gone. As would become a pattern for him since the tragedies of Dachau, Buchenwald and Manila, Zipper attempted to deal with grief by immersing himself in work. By the time that the succession of family deaths began, Zipper had learned how to steel his emotions and to ignore or repress his inner grief by immersing himself in the external world.

During these years administration could easily have been a full-time job itself. For he not only conducted on two continents but had to administer the logistics of the three orchestras, the arrangements for the lectures, workshops, the series by the Fine Arts Quartet. There were the inevitable requirements of fund-raising. His newly acquired skills as a fund raiser were also required on behalf of the Far East. By 1965 Zipper realized that the Manila Symphony had hit a plateau and needed the infusion of new teachers and performers to reinvigorate it. Since he needed to bring in oboe, bassoon, bass, and cello teachers, he designed a proposal for the JDR-3rd Fund (John D. Rockefeller, III President). He met with Porter McCray, Director of the fund and he soon received a $68,000 two-year grant.

The positive results of the Philippine Fellowship Program encouraged the JDR 3rd Fund to branch out with similar programs into other East Asian countries. Consequently, they requested Zipper to investigate and eventually to take charge of projects in Taiwan, South Korea, Hong Kong and Thailand.

These programs took place during the years from 1969 to 1974 during which Zipper also conducted the symphony orchestra of Taipei and Seoul. While these two cities could boast of well established and respectable music schools for occidental music, and sizeable audiences for the European classics, Thailand, by and large, was artistically little influenced by the West and cultivated mainly its own indigenous art.

In 1969, during his Manila summer season, Zipper received from the JDR 3rd Fund Director, Porter McCray, a request to investigate in Bangkok the local condition of music education because McCray received a request from the Thai government for assistance in the form of providing the music school of the state college with competent music teachers.

Arriving at the Bangkok airport, Zipper was greeted by the administrator of the music school, escorted to the Hotel Oriental, and there he was informed about the needs of the school. When he asked to see the school, the faculty and the students, he met with embarrassed evasion. Upon his insistence and mention that without a thorough inspection of the school, he would have to return immediately to Manila and report to New York their refusal to let him inspect the school, it was reluctantly agreed to show Zipper the school the following morning.

Zipper was brought to a large courtyard containing a number of impressive buildings. He was asked to wait for a while inside a large Buddhist temple with a high ceiling, a huge golden Buddha on one end, and the acoustical quality of a Cathedral. A few moments later, about 200 students appeared carrying various instruments, strings, woodwind, brass and percussions. They assembled in groups according to their instruments, along the walls of the temple.

Zipper first assumed that this was a roll call, but soon he was proven wrong. A group of tired old men appeared who joined the students. Up to this moment, everything proceeded in complete silence. Punctually at 9:30 AM, the old men raised a little stick and the students began to play, different etudes, scales and rhythms, *all of them at the same time*. The shock of this earsplitting attack was more than Zipper could endure and he fled out into the open, followed by the group of administrators.

The Thais are very sensitive and gentle people and it took Zipper quite a few moments to regain his civility and to hide his anger. But he explained that the temple situation would be unacceptable to any foreign teacher, and if there could be no other place for the school, his report would have to be absolutely negative. "Is there no other place to house the school?" Zipper asked. One gentleman pointed at a large modern building and explained that its fourth floor was completely empty but it was not available to the music school. Zipper asked to look at it. This floor consisted of a very large room without partitions. However, by installing sound proof partitions, at least 10 good sized studios and two classrooms could be constructed. Zipper then asked to see the top government official in charge of the entire compound and he received an appointment on the spot. A representative of a Rockefeller finds open doors anywhere, even in Thailand. Within the hour, Zipper found himself sitting at a large desk opposite Mr. Sariman to whom he explained the situation and the problem. Mr. Sariman understood. Either an adequate place for the school or no support from America; he made a number of phone calls and before lunch time, permission was granted to the music school to occupy the fourth floor and to construct the partitions according to Zipper's specifications. Before returning to Manila, he promised to come to Bangkok in six weeks to inspect the completed work and to submit a long range plan of music education to their government and the JDR 3rd Fund.

Upon returning to Bangkok, Zipper was led by the beaming school director with the elevator to the fourth floor. He opened the elevator door and Zipper was struck with horror. The same earsplitting sound chaos that he experienced at the temple was repeated here. It so happened that the installed soundproof partitions did not reach the ceiling but were short by approximately 1-1/2 feet. Instead of the partitions, Zipper hit the ceiling. But, he realized that everybody at the school was so used to the temple pandemonium that they were satisfied with the physical convenience of the new location and disregarded the acoustical disaster.

The architect was summoned and realizing the mistake, had the partitions extended to the ceiling within 24 hours with satisfactory results. Back in America, Zipper engaged four string teacher-performers with the idea of starting first a string institute for the students and at the same time, organizing a string quartet to regularly perform for the students and faculty of the college and the public at large in order to create interest in occidental music.

For four years the Bangkok string quartet, with some change of personnel, was active in Thailand. Every year, Zipper spent a few weeks in Bangkok only to observe a minimum of progress in spite of the superhuman efforts of his four appointees. The students continued to scratch on their instruments with acid intonation and stiff bowarms, and the small public interested in occidental music remained small. It was time for Zipper to admit that the Bangkok project was a grandiose failure and to recommend discontinuance. At his last visit, and before leaving Bangkok, the Minister of Foreign Affairs gave a banquet in his honor. He concluded his kind and flattering remarks with the following words, "Some years ago, another Austrian musician was active here who had ideas for us similar to yours. He died of frustration."

John D. Rockefeller III once visited a Zipper site. When Zipper remarked that the success was owed to the fine teachers, Rockefeller congratulated Zipper saying: "Don't forget Zipper, this whole civilization of man has been built by very few people - and I'm talking to one." Zipper's goals in the Far East were the same as his efforts in Chicago as they have been all his life - to raise people's awareness of what is acceptable and what is not. All his life he has labored to help people set their sights above mediocrity, to help people understand true quality.

During the period after the war, Zipper and his wife thought often of their homeland. Finally, in May of 1956, just one year after the end of the Allied and Soviet occupation of Austria, they arranged to leave early for the Philippines and scheduled a trip to Vienna to visit a few friends and to see their birthplace for the first time since 1939 (1937 for Trudl). It was an unsatisfactory visit, for the painful memories interfered with feelings of nostalgia and reminiscence. What remains from the trip is a prose poem Zipper composed on May 13:

> Like an old, splendid palace
> Vienna,
> Where princes, kings and emperors lived.
> They died long ago;

Their crowds of courtiers
Now are memories.
Their remains transformed
An establishment of servants, lackeys,
Maintaining floors and sidewalks —
The spirit that reigned supreme is vanished.
Successors shuffle by, heads lowered,
Ever ready to turn obsequiously,
To retrieve a stray gratuity.
Scraping and bowing,
They trod on each others toes
With whining loathsomeness,
Bemoaning consequences of their own misdeeds.
In the hirearchy of the petty,
The highest rank is occupied by those
Who with fading, gilded lettering
On ancient, decaying sign boards,
Boast of their lineage
To providers of the court.

The highpoint of Zipper's return to Vienna was a reunion with Zipper's former teacher from the academy days, composer Joseph Marx. Before Zipper and Trudl went up to his apartment in the Traungasse, Zipper said to Trudl, "It will not take long, I'll bet, before Marx will talk about Debussy." And sure enough, the Zippers had hardly sat down when he explained, "You know, Zipper, Debussy was the only really pagan composer in all of the Western Civilization. His music is completely untouched by the Judeo-Christian traditions." The force and the manner in which Marx said this made it obvious that it was quality which accounted for his kinship with Debussy. It was the last time he would see Marx who died on September 3, 1964 in Graz.

During the visit Zipper also had a chance to visit with a former cabaret collaborator in the 1930's, Rudolf Weys, and to find out something of his war experiences. Weys, who was not Jewish, lived in Vienna throughout the war and managed to keep his wife, who was Jewish, hidden and safe. His wife was an excellent interpreter of cabaret chansons for whom Zipper had composed a song during the 1930's. Weys kept alive his feeling of resistance by holding secret meetings in his home where people met to express, at least, their anger and their sadness of what was going on, the loss of Vienna as a cultural center and the vulgarity and barbarism of Nazism.

During the 1956 visit, Zipper and Trudl ventured out of Vienna through the gorgeous countryside for a few childhood vacation sites including Zell Am See, St. Wolfgang, St. Gilgen, and Kitzbuhel. While in a coffee house in Kitzbühel, Zipper asked the waiter if, by any chance, his old friend Alfons Walde — a skiing companion dating back to 1925 — was still alive and still living nearby. "He's over there," said the waiter, pointing to the back of a man sitting two tables away! Zipper approached him, "My God," said the surprised and delighted Walde, "I thought you were dead." The two embraced and returned to Walde's studio where they downed two bottles of red wine and reminisced. They had not seen each other since 1934. Walde, by now a well-known local painter and ardent socialist had been jailed twice during the Nazi nightmare but had been released and had secluded himself in his studio and continued to paint. He died two years later in 1958 but has in the 1980's become recognized as a major painter whose works command high fees and high respect.

Returning to Vienna, Zipper visited a favorite coffee house, the Cafe Museum, for breakfast. He sat down. An old waiter shuffled in from the back, looked at Zipper and shuffled back out into the kitchen. He returned in 10 minutes with the exact breakfast (a soft-boiled egg, 2 pieces of toast, butter, marmalade, and coffee melange) Zipper used to order in 1936, twenty years before! He set the meal in front of Zipper and said, "You haven't been here for awhile."

After concluding their brief stay in Austria, Zipper and Trudl returned to the Philippines and to a new project in the works. Actually, it was a project he conceived in 1953 one evening while looking out at the magnificent sunset from the Legarda's home. Zipper's idea was to produce the opera *Carmen* by moving the scene from 19th Century Spain to the 19th Century Philippines and to present it in Tagalog, the national language. Zipper said to Mrs. Legarda, "You know, it's all there: smuggling, even bullfighting" (which was outlawed in Manila only as late as 1918). The Legardas considered it and about a year later the project was approved. It took some time to find appropriate translators. In fact, Zipper asked a Filipino writer to find translators. The writer, who did not speak Tagalog, tried to do it himself — with his cook checking his grammar. The translation was inadequate and, in late May of 1956, with opening night only a few weeks away, Zipper set to work with two new translators. Together they worked, sometimes until 4:00 A.M. translating French into Tagalog. The original writer protested being fired and the press picked up the controversy — much to Zipper's delight — for by opening night the opera was sold out.

The opera opened in August and four performances were scheduled. It was such a success that it was extended to eight nights. One performance was nearly cancelled because of a typhoon and heavy rains. There were three feet of water in front of the theatre but Zipper would not allow the opera cancelled and Filipino boys were hired to carry ladies across the street. (In some cases two boys to a lady if she were excessively well fed.)

Zipper's *Carmen* in Tagalog was reviewed in the local *Free Press*. People speculated that the author of the unsigned review was writer, Nick Joaquin, whose words captured the magic of the Tagalized *Carmen*:

> ... – for here was the world's famous opera being sung, not in the usual foreign gibberish, but in homely, racy, luminous Tagalog. And so effective is the translation of *Carmen* from her Sevillian world of majos, gypsies, the Giralda and the Macarena to the 19th century of Manila of mestizos, tulisanes, the muralla and the Roasario that it almost seems hardly a feat, so naturally does the Sevillana fit into their new Binondo setting. But it was a feat – a feat that the Manila Symphony Society, the Zippers, and Tagalog librettists Manuel Car Sangiato, and Vicente Liwag accomplished with magic and elegance.
>
> "For Filipinos, the Tagalog *Carmen* had an extra dimension. We find ourselves looking into our past from a different angle, and with fresh astonished eyes. We have peopled it so completely with agonized heroes and frail fainting Maria Claras that we need to be reminded that it contained a lot of ordinary folk like this cigarette girl and her silly, love-sick guardia civil. We are sternly bidden not to romanticize the past but perhaps there is no need to do so; the past may really have been romantic, in spite of all the nastiness that happened in it. Anyway, the Zippers' *Carmen* is unblushingly the exuberantly romantic (though the details, from the costuming to the wine posters on the tavern wall, are painstakingly accurate: and the curious thing is that, nevertheless, for Filipinos, it offers, again and again, the great shock of recognition.)
>
> "The smugglers may look picturesque but they could have stepped out of today's front pages, with their contraband of textiles from Hong Kong and jewels from Bangkok. The horrid modern slum of Binondo suddenly recovers the magnificence with which it glittered for our grandfathers, and fascinating vistas unfold behind such hackneyed place-names as Sta. Ana, Paco, Ermita and Tagaytay. And Carmen – how vividly we realize that we know her, and we have met her and seen her and heard her a thousand times outside the tobacco palaces of old Manila, along with the silent, solemn audience of males that collected on the Binondo plaza or on Calle Isaac Peral at five o'clock in the afternoon to watch the cigareras pouring out of their splendid factories. Arms akimbo, eyes flashing, through the factory gates they streamed: pert, young and lusty old women, the majas of Manila, reeking of the black leaf. Along the street, the men waited, solemn and silent before the female uproar. Husbands fell into step with their wives; lovers trained the group girls, who would break into a run, screaming, to catch the streetcar at the corner. It was one of the great scenes of the old Manila: his evening exodus of the cigarette girls.[87]

The opera was so popular that Zipper was asked to repeat the production first in 1958 and then again in 1979-80. How can one go wrong with such a winning ticket: to bring music to the people and to do so in a manner which honors their indigenous culture.

Zipper returned from the Philippines in the fall of 1956 and in 1957 he was elected to a four-year term as President of the National Guild of Community Music Schools. During his term as President he had come to see that the Guild needed a full-time Director. By the mid-sixties when the Cultural Center of Manila appeared to be secure, Zipper turned his fund raising skills to seek a grant from the National Endowment of the Arts, then headed by Roger Stevens who later became the President of the Kennedy Center for the Performing Arts in Washington, D.C. He submitted his grant proposal to the NEA in early 1967 and, just before leaving for Manila in late May, received a call from Fanny Taylor, the Music Program Director of the NEA, telling him that they were favorably inclined to make the grant but that they believed the Executive Director should be chosen from within the Guild. "In fact," she said, "the Endowment would like you to be the Director." Zipper told her he would consider the position but that he would need an official offer before notifying the Board of Trustees of the North Shore School. He was then concerned about possible difficulties with a couple of opponents on the Board. In July in Manila he received a cable from Charles C. Mark, then the Chief Operating Officer of the NEA, telling him that it was official. Because NEA grants were one-year grants, Zipper wrote the North Shore Board informing them that he would like a one-year leave-of-absence to organize the National Guild's executive office. He also told the Board he had located an ideal one-year replacement for himself. However, when Zipper returned to Chicago in September, he was informed that they had hired a new Director - the piano teacher of a Trustee, a man who had no administrative experience. Zipper was appalled and tried to dissuade the Board, arguing that the center had become a complex, quality organization which required an experienced and skilled administrator. By this time his relationship with some Board Members had deteriorated and his arguments were ignored. Soon the new director took over and Zipper moved on to his own new position. By spring, however, the center was having serious problems and Zipper was approached for advice. He recommended a few candidates and called one himself, Kalman Novak, Director of a Boston Community Music School, and encouraged him to apply for the position. Novak applied and the Board hired him.

Meanwhile Zipper and Trudl moved to a house they rented in Wilmette, and, on November 1, 1967 Zipper began his new position as Executive Director of the National Guild. His work consisted largely of day-to-day problem solving for all the member schools (some 40 in 1967). However, the founding of two new community schools stand out as typical Herbert Zipper adventures. When he took the newly created position as Executive Director of the Guild, one of his major goals, agreed to by NEA and the Office of Education, was to develop techniques for the organization of new schools in areas where such opportunities in the arts were not available. To begin with, three models were envisaged: one in a large city, one in a middle-sized area, and one rural. Zipper, never one to seek easy jobs, decided to first start a school in an area where classical music was educationally unavailable.

After identifying a region of Arkansas as their target, Zipper called his friend Porter McCray and asked him to arrange a meeting with Governor Winthrop Rockefeller of Arkansas. The meeting soon took place and Mrs. Rockefeller offered to help. She organized a research team with the State Superintendent of Education. When Zipper returned in three weeks, they had selected six school districts.

The six participating school districts were located in three southeastern counties of Arkansas: Ashley (population 24,220), Drew (population 15,213), and Chicot (population 18,900). The total school enrollment of the six participating communities was approximately 9,000 of which 5,730 were white and 3,270 black. The median family incomes ranged from $2,013 to 3,432. Zipper argued that "rural America neither participates in nor contributes to the performing arts to any appreciable extent. Rural life needs to be made more attractive and dormant artistic potential must be awakened." Zipper recognized that small, isolated rural school districts could not afford to engage specialists in the various arts disciplines. But he determined that "a mobile unit supported and shared by contiguous school districts (could) make this extremely practical." He reasoned that if you couldn't transport widely separated children to a single arts center, then why not bring the arts to the children. It was, in a sense, a variation on his 'In-school Concerts' then.

Accordingly, he went to a local bus body manufacturing company and explained to the President his idea: to equip a secondhand school bus with electric pianos and other instruments, air conditioning, and to travel around giving music and dance classes. The President was so intrigued that he donated a second hand bus and refurbished it. Zipper then arranged with the Wurlitzer Company for 6 pianos to be loaned at $1.00 per year. The teachers' salaries were paid by ESEA 65 Title I and III Funds. Zipper then arranged for Michael Saltzman and his wife Wilma McCool to be transferred from the Northfield Schools in Illinois (a suburb of Chicago) and to become director of the project and Orff teacher respectively. That very summer the school began. It was an instant success. Black and white children working together; black and white mothers serving together. When the project was fully funded and operational, Zipper offered some thoughts before moving on to his next project. His thoughts are as relevant now as they were in 1969. And while one may marvel at Zipper's insights and vision, it is somewhat discouraging to see how little concern and effort has been or continues to be expended on the cultural life of vast sections of the nation. Always the optimist, Zipper concluded the Mobile Project with these reflections:

> Migration from rural America to the cities is the cause of some of our major problems. Improving the quality of rural life may stem this tide and ultimately benefit our cities.
>
> Mass media are bringing some measure of sophistication to our hinterland but also exert a leveling influence. Networks, for the sake of nationwide consumption, sacrifice regional expressions, preferences and sensitivities. Rural academies, such as envisaged by this program, can help reverse the trend toward a monochromatic civilization and can stimulate indigenous artistic creativity. Conversely, artists, becoming residents in rural areas, may well find new challenges, motivations and inspirations.
>
> The black population of America has contributed in a large measure to the performing arts. Yet, for lack of opportunity, many art disciplines remain inaccessible to them. There are, for instance, very few black string players in the United States. Given the opportunity of expert instruction in early childhood black people can be expected to help meet the growing shortage of string players.
>
> For active participants, as well as for audiences, the pleasures derived from the arts transcend every human barrier. In our heterogeneous society the performing arts can be a unifying agent second to none.
>
> Political Democracy is a reality. Economic Democracy is in sight. Cultural Democracy is still a distant goal. The urgency for its vigorous pursuit is apparent. Plans for its realization must include Rural America.

The next school to be founded, also in 1968, came about in Newark, New Jersey. Stella Argand Lass, who heard about Zipper's activities, was the daughter of a Polish tailor who emigrated to America to make more money so his daughter, an aspiring concert pianist could go to Przemysl to study music. He came to America alone, worked in a garment sweat shop and sent home $20.00 a month for Stella's piano lesson. Stella's father had served in the Austro-Hungarian army and so Stella attended a German elementary school in Poland. However, the school was abolished when the Polish army defeated the Austro-Hungarian army in World War

I and an underground German speaking school was created where Stella finished high school. She then had to attend a convent school to secure a legitimate diploma. After high school, her father brought her to America and she began her studies in Newark, New Jersey.

In 1967-68, Stella Lass in addition to being the one of ten city-wide accompanists in the Newark Public Schools also taught piano actively. She was, however, appalled by the cultural wasteland. She heard of Zipper's appointment as Executive Director of the Guild and called him. They met in New York and she asked his help to found a community school. Together, somehow, this remarkable pair pulled it off. She with her passion and energy; he with his imagination and knowledge. The pattern was the same as before - secure donated pianos and other instruments, locate donated space, arrange radio and T.V. appeals, negotiate loans, donations, and provide hard work.

Stella Lass soon saw that the school was going to grow and she located a medical building for sale. It would take $25,000 to buy it. She called Zipper for advice. He told her to go to the local bank and ask for a loan. She took $200.00 and a great deal of chutzpah as a down payment. She secured the loan. She managed to secure a grant of $5,000 from the Englehardt Foundation, primarily due to the interest of one trustee of the foundation who was Adlai Stevenson's niece and was the wife of the Governor of New Jersey. With this $5,000 she convinced four other banks to loan $5,000 each.

The Newark Riots had begun in late 1967 and when the school opened its doors in mid-January of 1968, some fires from the riots were still burning. Lass was told it was folly to begin the school during such times. But in the cold winter, a line of people stood at the school's doors and the school was formed. Instrumental lessons were 10 cents, but everyone had to pay. For the next few years Zipper provided Lass with a great deal of help — writing grants, defining goals, learning how to administer a school. Mostly, he gave her the encouragement to persist. The school became a success and has persisted on into the 1990's.

Two incidents in the early days of the school epitomize for Herbert Zipper the importance and value of such schools. At the first registration day in Newark when the school opened, sometime after 5:00 p.m. a black truck driver came in with his three children. He pointed to his children and announced: "I want her to learn piano, him cello and him violin." When asked why, he replied that he had heard this piece on the radio and he loved it. After Zipper hummed a dozen or so main themes from various trios, they determined it was the Beethoven C-Minor Trio.

Another day in Newark at 6:00 in the evening, in winter, Zipper found a large group of people standing outside of the school. He asked were they waiting for their children? No, they had no children here; they were just listening. One man said, "We heard the sounds coming out of the window - it's the only hopeful thing in this town."

In addition to Newark and Arkansas, Zipper helped to organize many other schools during these years which included locations such as: Washington, D.C.; Worcester, MA; Waukegan, IL; Mountain View, CA; Oakland, CA; Claremont, CA; and, Vancouver, Canada. The President of the Guild Board at that time, Harris Danziger, used to call Zipper: "Our Johnny Appleseed of the Arts."

FIFTH MOVEMENT

XII   California

XIII   China

Chapter XII

California

> "What is good in people - and consequently in the world -
> is their insistence on creation."
>
> - E. M. Forster

In the 1950's and the 1960's, the Zippers often visited California: to see their family in Santa Monica, to visit guild schools, and to see friends at USC who included musicians such as harpsichordist Alice Ehlers and pianist John Crown. On one of these visits Zipper met Grant Beglarian. Beglarian had come to USC in 1969 to be Dean of the School of Performing Arts. Shortly after this meeting they began communicating, exchanging ideas about music, education, and community. Beglarian recalls thinking of Zipper as "a remarkable activist in the music scene."

In the summer of 1970 Beglarian suggested that Zipper come work at USC where several things were percolating. USC already was operating its own secondary, preparatory school. The school was designed as a non-degree awarding pre-college institution to serve students of all ages. USC had also been approached by a neighboring public school, the 32nd Street School, seeking a formal connection. Zipper's commitment to quality education for children had impressed Beglarian and thus in 1971, when Zipper returned from another trip to Asia, Beglarian made a formal offer: that Herbert Zipper come to USC to be Projects Director for the School of Performing Arts.

Beglarian and Zipper were a unique team. Both were dreamers and visionaries, both men of keen intellect, both composers and men of letters, yet both were tough-minded, practical implementers. They inspired each other and led USC to become involved in the surrounding community in ways that few universities have attempted.

Trudl and Herbert Zipper came to California in July 1972 where they had bought a house the year before in the Pacific Palisades. And in 1991, Zipper is still living in this home in the hills overlooking the Pacific Ocean.

He began work at USC in September. One of the first orders of business was to attend the USC School in Idylwild. In 1967-68 Max and Beatrice Krone had willed to USC a summer school of the arts in the mountains above Hemet and Palm Springs. The school, called Isomata, had been a money drain for the University and Beglarian asked Zipper to look into upgrading it. The challenge a welcome one - to help bring the arts to a small rural community. One of his first problems, he discovered, was to deal with an undercurrent of suspicion felt by the townspeople toward the University. Zipper approached the Idyllwild community not merely as an Ambassador for USC, but as an advocate for involving the arts as an integral part of the town's daily life.

Zipper's plan was to hire an energetic, creative, and dynamic young musician, an artistic ombudsman, to begin organizing and leading community involvement. This person would have to develop a community choir, help with the local church music, lead instrumental ensembles, teach at a local elementary school, cooperate in the program of nearby Redlands University, and be actively engaged in the summer session of the USC Isomata School. Zipper envisioned this program as a prototype of national significance for the development of local cultural resources in rural communities. He also saw the project as providing USC students with a training ground for careers in community service. Not for the first time his idealistic vision was to exceed what was realistically possible; nevertheless, the Isomata project achieved a great deal.

Terry Danne was selected to direct the program and Herbert Zipper provided his experience, wisdom and the resources of USC in assisting Danne. Their goals were to involve local families, schools, churches, and community clubs and organizations. It was not all smooth sailing but overall the experiment worked moderately well. Programs flourished, and not only did Isomata grow and become accepted but the cultural opportunities of the town were expanded. A guest artist concert series, choral groups, a dixieland jazz ensemble, improvements in local schools' arts curricula, musicals, solo concerts and recitals by local artists — these and many more activities were the results of Zipper's behind the scenes work and support. Even an excellent new arts high school, The Idylwild School of the Arts, eventually came into being under the leadership of William Lowman who received good advice and inspiration from Herbert Zipper. One other specific project at Idylwild deserves special mention.

One day, in 1971, while discussing American art with a USC ceramicist, Susan Peterson, Zipper opined that the real indigenous American Art is Native American ceramics. Susan in turn mentioned the name of the famous ceramicist, Maria Martinez from the Pueblo of San Ildefonso in

New Mexico, who was once invited to the White House by President Franklin D. Roosevelt.[88] Zipper suggested inviting Martinez and her family to the 1972 USC Summer program for youth and adults held in USC's Idyllwild campus. They determined they would need about $10,000 for the first summer. Never one to let grass grow under his feet, Zipper promptly flew to Washington D.C., and spoke to Nancy Hanks and others at the National Endowment of the Arts. Three weeks later USC received a grant for $10,000.

As summer approached, Susan Peterson told Zipper she was nervous whether the Indians would indeed show up on schedule. Zipper said, "Then let's go pick them up." He reserved by phone a U-Haul truck, and flew with Trudl to Santa Fe, while Susan drove her station wagon to San Ildefonso, New Mexico. They returned with Maria Martinez, her son's wife, Santana (also a fine artist), Maria's grand daughter Barbara, and several children. Zipper, accompanied by Maria's son Adam, drove the truck carrying the equipment and several sacks of cow dung, which would be burned to achieve the characteristic black coloring of the pottery. They drove back with this motley assortment of people and "materials" over 1000 miles to Idyllwild, California, to make certain the project was launched. Beglarian recalls the project with a belly laugh: "Here's this Austrian, for Christ's sake, tooling off to New Mexico to pick up an Indian pottery-maker and drive her to Los Angeles." It proved to be a terrific program; one that Herbert Zipper to this day speaks of with a sparkle in his eyes. Furthermore, the program has continued into the 1990's with other native American artists coming each summer to Idyllwild.

Another project on which Zipper worked with Beglarian was the creation of the Schoenberg Institute. Beglarian was the guiding force, while Zipper's role was to facilitate communication between USC and Germany and Austria. Zipper had met the famous composer in 1921 in Schoenberg's home and had attended many of Schoenberg's workshops at his Society for Musical Private Performances ("Gesellschaft fur Musikalische Privat-Auffuhrungen"), formed to study and play the works of Schoenberg and other composers of various periods. Fifty years later, Zipper was pleased to assist in the creation of a new Schoenberg center in a new country!

Schoenberg was one of the many prominent Austrians who fled the Nazi regime and relocated in California. Some formed little cliques and others, Zipper among them, worked mostly independently although occasionally making social or vocational contact with each other. The "Hollywood clique" included Erich von Stroheim, Billy Wilder and Otto Preminger. Zipper had known Preminger in Vienna where Preminger was a friend of the Dubskys. Zipper met him there often as part of a group of young intellectuals. Also, Emil Zipper had been good friends with Emil Kiesler, Director of the Wiener Bankverein. Kiesler often brought his little girl, Hedwig, to the resort at St. Wolfgang where the Zippers stayed. Zipper recalls having been struck by her young beauty. The little girl became an actress, whose nude scene in a Czechoslovakian film, "Ecstasy," in 1933, caused a sensation and disturbed her proper Viennese father. Nevertheless, she went to Hollywood in 1937 where she became famous as Hedy Lamarr. Another Hollywood acquaintance of Zipper was Erich Wolfgang Korngold who became a prominent film composer. On one occasion when conductor Otto Klemperer visited California, he was told that Korngold was in California writing music for Hollywood. Without missing a beat Klemperer replied, "Didn't he always." Other Viennese notables in California included Fritz Kortner, an actor and director; Leon Askin, an actor and director; Elizabeth Bergner, an actress; Hans Jaray, a playwright; Harry Horner, an Academy Award winning set designer; Kurt Herbert Adler, a musician who became General Manager of the San Francisco Opera; composer Erich Zeisl whose daughter married a son of Arnold Schoenberg in Los Angeles; film composers Eugen Zador and Max Steiner; Max Reinhardt, famous stage director and noted filmmaker and his second wife, Helene Thimig, a well-known actress. Trudl Zipper danced in some of Reinhardt's shows in Vienna, including *The Miracle*. Of the Austrian emigrees in Los Angeles, Zipper was closest to composer Ernst Toch who called himself "the world's most forgotten composer." Zipper believes Toch to have been a first rate, although unjustly neglected, composer. They spent quite a lot of time together and in 1965 Zipper made an English to German translation of Toch's last opera, *The Last Tale* ("Das Letzte Marchen"). Toch died the next year in 1966. As of 1990, *The Last Tale* has not yet been performed publically, an omission which Zipper finds regrettable. At one point the Zurich Opera did request to perform it but Mrs. Toch did not give permission, perhaps hoping for a more prestigious opera house for its premier.

During the years of 1972 to 1975 Trudl continued her working partnership with her husband teaching dance in a variety of projects and schools. One of these joint venture was at an unusual public school, the 32nd Street School. The school had been destroyed by an earthquake in 1971 and the Los Angeles Board of Education invited USC to become involved in the re-building. Zipper was asked by Beglarian to join the feasability study committee. He heard many proposals, none of which he liked. He made his own proposal to the diverse committee of 30 people that the school develop an arts emphasis and that a long-term research project be designed to study how teachers could learn and enhance their own classroom skills by working with competent arts teachers. In 1973 the Los Angeles Unified School District and the University of Southern California had agreed to develop an art-oriented approach to elementary education at the 32nd St. Elementary School, which is in close proximity to the University campus. Zipper first secured a planning grant from the Rockefeller Foundation and, after an intensive planning period from February 1974 through June 1975, they were ready to launch the program with children in the fall of 1975. For two years, under Zipper's direction, classroom teachers participated with children in art classes taught by professional artists and art specialists. Trudl was one of these teachers. One of Zipper's major goals was "to explore the extent to which classroom teachers, even without previous education in the arts and without any specific propensities for the arts, will be able to acquire through inservice instruction by talented and experienced art specialists, the necessary skills and techniques that will enable them to practice daily the arts with their students." Zipper has been convinced that this is the only way that the arts can become a viable force in American schools. Certainly few public or private schools have been willing to fund salaries for enough arts teachers to have any significant curricular impact.

Actually this project was not a new idea for Zipper. The origin of the 32nd Street School project dated back to 1969-70. While in Arkansas implementing the Mobile Academy (discussed earlier), Zipper received a call from the Chairman of the Michigan Arts Council who had read the printed description of the "Academy" and wanted Zipper to meet him in Hancock-Houghton, a city in the copper-mining district of upper Michigan. Hancock-Houghton is on the Keweenaw peninsula of Lake Superior. Fifty percent of the population is Finnish and thirty-three percent was then unemployed because of the closing of the copper mines. Not one to pass up an opportunity to implement his ideas, Zipper set off on a nine-hour, milk-run flight from Chicago to Hancock-Houghton. He arrived in midwinter, 1970, and walked down streets lined with walls of snow taller than his six-foot frame. He went to visit the school superintendent, a middle-aged, bright woman, and he explained to her his ideas of having classroom teachers and students learn from arts teachers and then incorporate this learning in their classrooms. She was excited by his ideas and the next day had him speak to her teachers. Zipper was encouraged by the prospect of implementing ideas with a stable faculty - there was little turnover of teachers and students here. In order to gain community support he was put on the radio and answered live call-ins. Because the response was so enthusiastic, he returned two weeks later to give a talk in the local

Calumet Theatre, an abandoned opera house built in the 1870's for copper magnates. Jenny Lind had sung there. When he arrived, the place was packed - 600-700 people. The superintendent said that 95% of the parents in the district must have come - all to hear this Dr. Zipper from Vienna talk about the importance of the arts. The excitement was so high that they launched the program within weeks. It was an effective program that is operative to this day. And not only was all this accomplished, but Zipper helped to convince the Federal government to declare the opera house a national monument and to have it refurbished.

Thus when the USC 32nd Street School project began, Zipper had his Hancock-Houghton experience to draw upon. And, as one would have expected, during the initial years of the project, Herbert Zipper was the guiding force behind this extraordinarily ambitious project: meeting upon meeting, tutoring children and teachers, teaching and conducting, refining specific curricular, goals and plans, but mostly inspiring his team of educators by his passionate commitment to teaching and to the arts.

The project was then extended beyond USC to a school uncontaminated by proximity with USC Thus the Commonwealth Avenue Elementary School was selected to serve as a testing ground for ideas developed at the 32nd Street School and yielding a great deal of research about the potentials and the limitations of the average classroom teacher and the beneficial effects achieved through the infusion of the arts into the daily classroom experiences. It was a promising program which has been adopted elsewhere, for example, in Newark, New Jersey and in Canada. Zipper has demonstrated not only that teachers who are inexperienced in the arts can learn how to teach using the arts, but also that the joint venture of student, arts specialist, and classroom teacher is immensely stimulating for all involved. Zipper's evaluation included two sentences which have profound implications and which one can only hope the educational world will come to understand: he wrote, "This [process described above] in our judgment seems to be the *only* way through which the arts can become an integral part of elementary education. Only if there is some daily practice and only if the arts are not separated from all other studies can we hope that they will occupy the place in education they ought to occupy."

In addition to the 32nd Street School, Zipper was heavily involved in another school - the USC Prep School, which was to become the USC Community School of Performing Arts, then renamed as the Community School of Performing Arts (independent of USC), and finally renamed in 1988 as the Richard D. Colburn School of Performing Arts. This evolution was a dramatic one, and one which involved other schools as well.

Bruno Walter welcomes the new Brooklyn Symphony Orchestra conductor to New York, March 16, 1949.

Brooklyn Symphony soloist Brenda Lewis and Herbert Zipper with Metropolitan star Giovanni Martinelli, preparing for a performance of *Don Carlos*. Photo taken in 1949.

Herbert Zipper and Eric Simon in New York. Photo circa 1950.

Zipper returns to Vienna in May 1956 for the first time since 1939.
Pictured with his beloved teacher, Joseph Marx.

Herbert pictured with Mrs. Trinidad F. Legarda, the president of the Manila Symphony Society, and President Ramon Magsaysay, 1956.

Zipper being awarded the Philippine Presidential Medal, July 4, 1959, presented by President Carlos P. Garcia.

A Zipper extravaganza.

The Native American ceramic artist Maria Martinez. While serving as Projects Director for the School of Performing Arts at the University of Southern California, Zipper arranged for Martinez to participate in the 1972 summer arts program at the Idyllwood campus.

To the left of St. Stephens Cathedral, was the home where Herbert Zipper was born - Am Graben no. 31. Etching by Luigi Kasimir.

The same building as it stands today. Photo taken in 1987.

Trudl with Ben Legarda, 1952.

Zipper pictured with composer Ernst Toch, 1962.

Trudl, seated in center, with friends Ralph and Grace Nash in 1975.

Walter with brother Otto in California, 1975.

Herbert and Trudl in 1974 with Marta Feuchtwanger, widow of Lion Feuchtwanger.

The poet Malcolm Cowley and his wife Muriel, friends of the Zippers from Sherman, Connecticut, where Herbert and Trudl rented a house as a respite from life in Brooklyn.

Lovers and friends after 45 years. Photo taken in 1972. Trudl would later lose a battle with lung cancer; she passed away on July 3, 1976.

Herbert and Grant Beglarian at Zipper's retirement party, June 17, 1980. Beglarian, Dean of the School of Performing Arts at USC, was responsible for luring the Zippers from Chicago to Los Angeles.

Vienna comes to China. Herbert conducting a rehearsal with the Beijing Symphony Orchestra in 1981.

A playful cultural exchange backstage before a performance.

Herbert striking a Wagnerian pose while clowning for Trudl in a hotel room, 1975.

Herbert with members of the Central Conservatory of Music in Beijing at the Great Wall in 1981.

Zipper embraces Rudolph Serkin after a performance at USC in 1983.

Herbert, seated third from left, pictured with (from left) the author Paul Cummins, Bruno Bettelheim, and Crossroads music teacher Warren Spaeth.

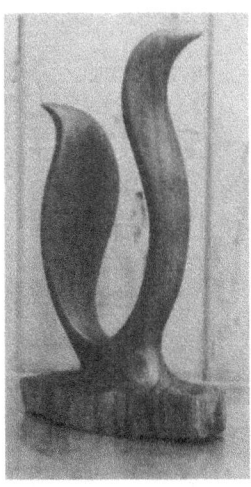

More than music: a wood sculpture by Herbert Zipper.

The author with Herbert in Vienna in 1988.

Zipper at the Goethe monument in Vienna.

Herbert with the author's wife, MaryAnn Cummins, in 1990.
Painting by the Chinese artist Yu Juang.

Zipper with friend and associate Richard D. Colburn in May, 1991.

Photo taken in Santa Monica in 1990 with Bruno Bettelheim.

The war remembered: Herbert conducting the 50th anniversary performance of "Dachau Lied" at the Autumn Festival in Graz, Austria on September 23, 1988.

Herbert Zipper in 1991.
"I have promises to keep and miles to go before I sleep, and miles to go before I sleep."

The USC Prep School was founded by Dorothy Bishop, a USC piano teacher who started an after-school instrumental program in the early 1960's. Noted musicians Michael Tilson Thomas and Gary Carr were among the early graduates. In 1971 Nancee Cortes was appointed Director of the school and soon after Herbert Zipper arrived at USC, Beglarian asked him to help professionalize the school. Zipper assisted Cortes and together, with the help of a talented assistant, Fran Zarubick, they rapidly rebuilt the faculty and increased the enrollment from approximately 200 to 800 students. Zipper soon found that in order to help improve the school and raise its standards and the quality of its faculty, it was necessary for him to do a great deal of proselytizing on behalf of the school at all levels of the USC administration. The school began to improve steadily. Zipper's policy was to remain in the background to be unobtrusive at the school, never to undermine the authority of its top administrators (who to this day speak of him with admiration, respect and love), and to back them up vis-a-vis the USC administration.

One of the team's (Beglarian, Cortes, Zipper) early ventures was to expand their approach and establish branches of the school to reach wider student audiences and to bring more music to the culturally starved Los Angeles public schools. The 32nd Street School was a sort of branching out as was a joint venture with a private school in Santa Monica, the Crossroads School. In the mid-1970's Nancee Cortes and I, as Headmaster of the Crossroads School, met from time to time and discussed the need for an arts high school in Los Angeles. Finally, in 1977, we hit upon the idea of school-within-a-school at Crossroads. I had met Zipper a year before and had enlisted him to serve on the Crossroads Board of Trustees as an arts advocate. (The arts, one notes, always seems to need advocates in America, since they are not regarded as intrinsically valuable in educational curricula.) Zipper, Cortes and I met to launch the idea. Marianne Uszler, a piano and music-theory teacher at USC, was soon enlisted along with my wife, Mary Ann Cummins, a private piano teacher and music-theory teacher at Crossroads, and David Colloff, a drama teacher at Crossroads, to help design the curriculum.

The Crossroads Board of Trustees was apprehensive of the idea, fearing that an infusion of "arts students" might lower the academic quality and reputation of the school. In fact, as Zipper and I predicted, the opposite occurred, and music majors have proved to be among the top academic students in the school. Zipper's enthusiasm and intelligent advocacy for the arts helped influence the Crossroads Board. Also, in order to really sell the idea, Zipper went out on a limb and committed USC to a joint venture with Crossroads. He had no authorization to do this and was later reprimanded by a USC Vice President. But Zipper took the chance, and in 1977, with school logos intertwined, the Crossroads/USC Performing Arts Majors program began on the Crossroad campus. Since then Crossroads has come to be recognized as one of the finest music, drama and visual arts high schools in the country. In receiving an award from the U.S. Department of Education in 1984 as one of 60 Exemplary Private Schools in America, the Crossroads arts programs were singled out for special commendation.

In addition to branching out, Beglarian, Zipper and Cortes were concerned about the long term funding of "the Prep School," which had become a member of the National Guild of Community Schools in 1970 when Zipper was the Director of the Guild. It was renamed the USC Community School of Performing Arts. The name "Prep School" had created the false perception that its task was to prepare students for college, while in fact its raison d'etre was to offer education in the performing arts to all who sought it without any preconditions and at the earliest possible age. When Zipper arrived at USC, the school was receiving its funding out of the USC general budget in the amount of about $60,000 a year. However, during the 1970's it was becoming clear that in order for the school to survive and flourish, it would need its own independent budget, board, and funding. Patrons would be needed and Zipper and Cortes both suggested courting Richard D. Colburn whom Zipper had worked with in Chicago.

Richard D. Colburn is an impressive businessman with a strong love of music. He had come to Los Angeles on May 1, 1965 and had met Beglarian before Zipper was hired. He enthusiastically described Zipper's concerts-in-the-schools program in the Chicago area and volunteered to help Belgarian fund a similar program in L.A. Thus when he came to L.A., Zipper was put in charge of the in-school-concert programs and began a three-decade history of managing, fund raising and conducting classical music concerts for children in culturally diverse areas. It is a magnificent program which has touched over 120,000 school children who would otherwise have been deprived of classical music. An account of one of these concerts recently appeared out-of-the-blue in the *Christian Science Monitor* (April 11, 1988) and is included here:

> Dr. Zipper never missed a beat
>
> > In the auditorium of the Third Street School in Los Angeles, I watched the kindergartners through third-graders enter, teachers attempting in vain to keep order and quiet among the fidgety children who were thrilled to have escaped

their classrooms for a few minutes. The neat lines gave way to masses of children poking, prodding, and teasing each other. I was perched in the back on a folding chair trying to catch a glimpse of my child.

The more curious children eyed the stage where musicians and their instruments were scattered. The others concentrated on finding seats next to their best friends.

I craned to spot Katie, my kindergartner, as she made her way down front. Her whole class plopped itself down on the cool linoleum floor in front of the auditorium seats. Her teacher, reminding the students one last time to sit Indian-style so that children behind them could see, retreated to find her own seat.

In that scene I saw myself as a kindergartner 30 years earlier filing into a noisy gymnasium in Evanston, Ill. I, too, sat right down front on the shiny gym floor to get the least obstructed view of what was about to take place before me: the annual Dr. Zipper Concert.

I remember wondering in those moments before the concert began — would he be a doctor like Dr. Seuss? Or would he wear a white jacket? Where do you suppose his zippers were? My six-year-old imagination was cut short when, at last, the "unknown" Dr. Zipper emerged and buoyantly leaped onto his podium, brandishing the thinnest of wands in his right hand.

Much to my disappointment, he looked absolutely normal. He was tall and lanky, with a high forehead and prominent nose. I remember it was his hands that immediately caught my attention. Long and slender fingers were in constant motion. He was sometimes hard to understand, but what he lacked in clear enunciation he more than made up for in energy and enthusiasm. He acted as if he were going to let us in on the greatest secret of mankind. And in many ways he was: the world of classical music, the composers who gave it to us, and the instruments that continue to translate it.

He held the children in rapt attention as he stepped up to his music stand. With three short taps he magically turned the gym into a concert hall. The melody of Strauss's "Blue Danube" floated out. "1-2-3, 1-2-3," I listened for the beat Dr. Zipper had told us about.

Then it was on to an exploration of how characters or moods could be introduced by instruments. Prokofiev's "Peter and the Wolf" provided the medium for this message. We picked out the violin playing Peter; the bassoon becoming the wise old grandfather; trills on the flute, the little bird; and of course, the rat-tats on the kettledrum, the gun shots of the hunters.

We listened to marches. He taught us what "pizzicato" and "pianissimo" meant. We were amazed to learn that a very famous composer lost his hearing but went on composing. And we saw and heard the differences in a violin, viola, cello, and bass viol.

I've happily remembered so much that Dr. Zipper shared with me as a child. His enthusiasm became my appreciation. Now I sat curious, nervously twisting my wedding band as I wondered about the Dr. Zipper about to emerge from the wings of *this* auditorium. It just couldn't be, could it?

> The musicians took their seats gathering up their instruments, the students settled themselves and fell quiet, and a very familiar tall man with a receding hairline bounded up onto his podium and in a thick Austrian accent introduced himself to my child as Dr. Zipper.
>
> The same man 30 years later still sharing his love for knowledge of music with elementary school children. The wonder of it all. Here, thousands of miles away from the school in Illinois where I first made his acquaintance.
>
> And now my daughter is about to be let in on that most wonderful secret I first heard about some 30 years earlier. With three taps of his wand the familiar strains of the "Blue Danube Waltz" filled the auditorium. And this time I just sat back on my tippy chair, listened, and loved.
>
> Carolyn Doepke Bennett

However, for all of his programs like the concerts-in-the-schools which have been successul, Zipper has conjured up dozens of programs which were either still born or simply failed to take hold. His idealistic, often excessively optimistic nature impels him to keep trying although at some level he must know his chances of success are often slight. Nevertheless, like a Don Quixote he continues to charge off, often getting slammed to the ground. He has just enough successes though to continue dreaming his dreams and hatching new ideas for programs, schools and legislation. He has also often played the role of a facilitator. During the mid-seventies Cortes and Zipper further approached Colburn about becoming the "patron saint" of an independent community school by purchasing it from USC It was now clear that USC would not fund the community school indefinitely within its general university operating budget. Colburn says, with a twinkle in his eye, "they were looking for a pigeon and I was it." Colburn had, in fact, wanted to start a school himself, and Zipper convinced him that the USC Community School was a ready-made opportunity. Colburn agreed in principle.

The negotiations began in 1978 and took 3 years to complete, with Zipper playing the role of ambassador and facilitator between USC and Colburn. The negotiations were difficult at best and Colburn became increasingly frustrated with the USC bureaucracy. On July 1, 1980 the day that marked Zipper's official retirement from USC he was told that the deal was off for good. The two parties could not see eye to eye, not only on substantive matters, but also in regard to seemingly irreconcilable differences of their negotiating styles — the bureaucracy versus the captain of industry. Zipper became frantic. Saving the existence of this school became the number one priority at that moment in his life. For nearly two months he spent a good part of his time commuting between downtown, USC and Colburn's home in Beverly Hills, carrying with him a continually changing contract document and making every effort to forestall and avoid direct confrontation between the two parties. Executive Vice President Kraprielian of USC jokingly referred to Zipper as "our Kissinger."

By this time Nancee Cortes had left the school to become the Director of the Performing Arts Department at the University of Utah and was succeeded by Fran Zarubick. Toby Mayman was the Executive Director working tirelessly with Zipper and others to close the deal. She was over eight months pregnant as the negotiations became critical and Zipper told her *not* to deliver until the contract was signed. When Zipper finally procured the signed document, everyone shouted "Hallelujah" and Zipper set off to USC with the first down payment. This was late in the day on August 26th and before leaving, Zipper said, "Toby, now you can have your baby." The next day, on August 27th, 1980, Toby Mayman had her baby, in a sense her second baby in 24 hours for the day before the Community School of Performing Arts was born as an independent community school.

The years at USC were not, however, simply years of success and joy. They were marred by the loss of dear friends, by the growing realization of time's inexorable passage, and by one loss in particular. Ever since he had first seen her as a vital, beautiful young girl in Vienna, Herbert Zipper had been deeply in love with Trudl Dubsky. She was, he says, "my mistress, my child, my companion, my co-artist of at least equal standing." Further reminiscing he muses, "She had an astounding maturity in some ways, in others she remained a child." In all their years together, over fifty, they had few serious arguments - usually about some artistic matters: should the ballet corps enter here or there, does this passage fit or not. "We were both," he believes, "absolutely free of jealousy." He remembers one time in Kowloon, for example, when Trudl suggested they go sit on a bench in front of the "Star-Ferry" to Hong Kong Island. She said, "Let's go there so we can look at the beautiful girls going to work in Hong Kong."

In conducting over a dozen interviews with close friends and acquaintances, I corroborated what Zipper has affirmed. He and Trudl were unique soulmates, who were devoted to each other, and whose relationshp was founded upon respect and trust. It was truly a rare and passionate love story. From Vienna to Manila and ultimately to Los Angeles they remained partners and lovers. In 1990 Herbert Zipper still remembered her phone number in Vienna when they began dating: B-15-276.

Trudl, like her husband, had a wonderful memory. Eric Simon used to call her "the woman of total recall." She was also an avid reader who would devour books and then tell her husband their content. In this respect she was his researcher, teacher, and main reader - synopsizing book after book culling their essence for her husband. "While we were married, we were actually conscious of how lucky we were to have each other. We were also conscious that we needed to work on our marriage each day. Each day we would do something nice for each other. When I traveled, I called her every day."

The beginning of the end of this life partnership occurred in March of 1975. Having experienced some discomfort in her lungs, Trudl, a heavy smoker, had a biopsy and gray spots were discovered on her lungs. The doctor told Zipper it looked bad. The next day the verdict came down - oat cell cancer. That same afternoon, Herbert went to the USC Medical School and procured a pamphlet on Oat Cell Cancer. It said of 10,000 recorded cases that only one person had survived. The life expectancy for Trudl was from two months to two years. As it turned out, she lasted for 16 months.

They had a few good months together, traveling in July to Seattle to see Hedy's son, Henry Holt, conduct his first Wagner Ring Cycle. They drove back together down the Pacific Coast and had a wonderful time. But soon the effects of the radiation and chemo-therapy treatments became severe and she would be terribly sick after the treatments. In February of 1976 Zipper traveled to New York for a few days. When he returned, Trudl looked changed. "Herbert," she exclaimed, "they found a new spot." She then began feeling pain in her hip. The cancer was starting to metasticize.

Zipper responded to this emerging tragedy in his life by putting his feelings into a deep freeze. He gave Trudl the feeling that he shared in her hopes. "You are," he recalls, "hard on yourself, soft to the loved one." On July 3, during her last night, her every breath practically shook the room. Only 24 hours before, she had whispered her last words in Herbert's ear: "I'm going to lick this."

When it became obvious that Trudl was in the last few hours of her life, Zipper asked the doctors to leave him alone in the room with her. He climbed up on the bed and put her head on his lap and stroked her head. He wanted her to feel she was not alone. He writes of these last moments:

July 1976

> It was still dark when the last death rattles faded into silence. Trudl's heart had stopped; her right eye was not fully closed. Softly, I put the lid over it as I withdrew my arm under her head. Trudl was dead. The terror of this last night was over.

California

I was numb. I could not feel anything. It was as if everything in me was frozen. I sat there and stared at the beloved face, at the wasted body. I was fully awake but unconscious. I don't know how long I sat there. It dawned. I called the nurse; she called the doctor. Another nurse appeared. They began to pack the body in white paper. I took the ring, our wedding ring, from Trudl's finger. On a stretcher they wheeled her out. In the remaining emptiness I gathered a few things, not everything; perhaps for not accepting finality.

I drove home through the empty streets. Emptiness, emptiness, emptiness. I called Eric in Connecticut to tell him. When I put the receiver down, the frozen inside began to thaw. An indescribable pain took hold of me. I wished, oh how I wished I could cry. I could not; the pain was bottled up.

For many months I knew this would happen. For many months I knew how terrible it would be. Yet, I did not imagine how terrible it was when it happened. To have to accept the finality of death is a most painful process. But the way death came to Trudl is a crushing experience that will remain with me as long as I live.

How I wished to spare her the agonies of the last two months! Though she seemed to have some happy moments, they were islands in a sea of pain and fear. I knew it, though she never showed it. The day before she died, she whispered into my ear – her voice had failed her for many days – "I am going to lick it, believe me, I'll lick it." These were the last words I heard from her lips. Sometimes I played with the thought to end her life myself before she would enter the last phase of suffering. On May 23rd, six weeks before her death we went to a party given by Betty Foley. Trudl insisted to attend although she had to be carried up the stairs to the home entrance. She was the life of the party, happy throughout. On the way home from Pasadena I felt that emotionally and physically she was near collapse. I seriously contemplated then to kill her. I could not do it, of course.

Life without Trudl! The world without Trudl! It was hard to imagine. For this reality, that I had to expect, I was not prepared; I guess one cannot be prepared. Now that she is gone a void stares at me with all its ghastly immensity. I have lost not only my love, my lifelong love, I have lost the one being through whom I could see myself, through whose reaction to me I could judge myself. I lost the only valid mirror that showed me my true identity. Yet, how fortunate I was that I could love so much, that I could trust so much.

The loss of a loved one carries with it the loss of parts of one's own personality. What one can be with a person very near to one, in many instances, cannot be duplicated in relation to anyone else.

Often after a day of hard work, a long rehearsal, a performance, I could amuse Trudl with all kinds of buffoonery, talking pure nonsense, indulging in the indigenously Viennnese activity called "Blödeln." Trudl on such occasions used to call me her "Kasperl," her court jester. She responded with a special kind of laughter that still rings in my ears. There is no other person in the world for whom I could act similarly; and there are many other such losses, a human relations shrinkage, I now have to accept.

In retrospect, Zipper wished that he could have let go and cried and sobbed. But he did not - fearing that he would become enmeshed in depression. Instead, he carved a wonderful piece of sculpture transmuting his feelings into the wood and graceful shapes. His nephew, Henry Holt, looked at the finished work and said, "Oh, that's a self-portrait." It was. Trudl was in many respects a deep part of Herbert Zipper's self.

Chapter XIII

China: Toward the 21st Century

Anniversary of A Train Ride:

When the evening of this day will spread its shadows, fifty years will have gone by since one evening turned to the darkness of my life's most dreadful night. Hardly could I imagine then that I would be alive on this or any other anniversary, even less that I would spend this day with Mozart, Beethoven and Brahms in Mukden of Manchuria, China.

- Herbert Zipper, Shenyang, May 30, 1988

Men and women, listen to my words of truth. What makes people happy is activity, Achieving useful things and able to transform The evil into good by its divine effect. Get up, then, at the break of day, and though you may find yesterday's constructions crumbled overnight, set to like busy ants and clear the ruins out. Devise your plans anew, employ new ways and means. If then the world itself be out of joint and race To its destruction of its own accord, you shall rebuild it once again, for everlasting joy.

- Goethe

With his friend, companion, playmate, his lover for over thirty-five years, his Dulcinea, his artistic confidante and advisor now gone, Zipper turned to his work for sustenance. He still had Walter, Otto and Hedy with whom to share some of his inner world and he had friends, such as Eric Simon to talk to each week, but the better part of each day was spent working. Each morning, after his long morning walk he attended to his various projects: Letters to senators, correspondence with friends and associates all over the world, grant proposals for any number of educational projects, composing music for students, conducting his concerts-in-the-schools, composing ensemble music for children, and dozens of other ventures. Working always with a fierce integrity and a total absorption in the project at hand, he gradually anesthetized himself to the loss of Trudl. Though, there has not, he says, been a day during which he does not feel her absence, his vision of a better world and his self-image as a productive worker keeps him going.

Many people who have met Zipper in his 70's and now 80's wonder if he is as he seems. Is he always so un-trivial, as deeply concerned with large issues, so responsible, so productive, so rational, so seemingly uncomplicated? The answer would seem to be, yes! Clearly he is a creature of habit and order is dear to him. Perhaps there are demons lurking in the far, dark corners of his psyche but he has kept the lights of reason burning so brightly, for so long, that there is little darkness he must consciously or even unconsciously confront. He is not unaware of irrationality. In his 85th year he coined this aphorism: "Logic and reason are the inventions of a few intellectuals who have been completely out of touch with reality." Zipper knows of the reality of irrationality; in Dachau, Buchenwald, Manila and, recently, Beijing he has witnessed atrocity and massacre. He believes, however, that men have choices to make and while acknowledging the reality of violence, he has chosen to follow the path of reason. He has sought to find avenues for the unconscious to find creative rather than destructive expression. The unconscious will have its say but its forms of expression are a matter of education and choice. Zipper is remarkable in that he has been consistent and persistent in applying and implementing his code of reason. Fin-de-Siecle Vienna where Zipper was born was a curious mixture of conservatism and radicalism and so too is Herbert Zipper. As an educator he has concocted a mixed brew of idiosyncratic, experimental and imaginative ideas. Yet he remains the Viennese gentleman; he shaves every day without fail, dresses neatly for his routines. He is meticulous in removing spots from the counters or floors of his home. He may have his dark moments but he has so conditioned himself to productive work that he keeps chaos and the void at a healthy distance. Unlike many prison camp survivors who came to focus upon man's dark and unreasoning instincts, Zipper emerged with a fierce dedication to strive for a rational world in which such barbarisms would never reoccur.

Zipper's politics are also a curiosity. The general human pattern seems to be that one is radical in youth and more conservative as one gets older. Zipper, however, grew up in a relatively conservative, middle-class, family headed by an entrepreneurial patriarch and during his youth moved to a more socialistic political stance. From the days of his encounter with the poet Thorn during World War I, Zipper has remained a socialist-humanist whose comprehension of global interdependence far outstrips younger radicals and certainly far outstrips the Congress and Presidency of America. In any given week one will find Zipper writing this or that Senator or Congressman urging more bold, courageous and innovative responses to a changing and deteriorating planet. He is, for example, infuriated by a President seemingly more concerned with the use and abuse of the American flag than with the preservation of the earth or the solutions to problems such as drugs, homelessness, crime, poverty, and AIDS. Zipper, were he President, would vigorously and boldly attend to these issues; he cannot understand why any man would do any less. During a recent visit to China, I could not but help compare two 85 year-old men: Zipper traveling to China to urge an expansion of vision and action and Deng Xiao-Ping responding to expressions of optimistic growth by retreating into a reactionary repression.

In any event, three years after Trudl's death, Zipper lost another dear friend, his brother Otto who died in Florida on February 3, 1979. He died in his sleep of a heart attack. Otto was attending the Daytona car race where one of his own cars was entered. He would often loan his personally trained crew to actor Paul Newman. Otto had had warning signals of impending heart problems and Zipper urged him not to go to Florida. His wife, Carol, called Zipper to tell him the sad news. While the two brothers did not share many common interests, their sense of humor, their bonds to Vienna and their sense of their mutual heritage were strong.

After Trudl's death Zipper had continued working on the 32nd Street School Project, refining programs and policies, as well as conducting his school concerts. The success of the program was given testimony in 1978-79 when the 32nd Street Public School in partnership with USC became a "magnet school for the arts and sciences." With his pet program at the 32nd Street School now fully established, Herbert Zipper decided to retire from full-time work at the university. He was now 76 years old and eager to pursue several new projects. "Retirement" was, as one could have predicted, a misnomer.

Within a few weeks of his announced, so-called "retirement," he was approached by a group from the Ambassador Foundation who were organizing to revive an elementary and secondary school in Pasadena, California, known as the Imperial School. They asked him if he would serve as their consultant in planning the arts component of the new school. Zipper said he didn't work for money anymore but only to see his convictions implemented. Over the years he has certainly formulated deep convictions. One conviction is that much of the universal deficiency of human beings might be the result of what he calls "the lost five years," the first five years. For while post-kindergarten education is successful for many people, for others it is a painful process and many frustrations come from the discovery of what has been irretrievably lost in earlier years. Here was a chance with the Imperial School to see if that loss could be prevented. Therefore, Zipper accepted the invitation. However, he imposed several conditions: that elementary classes receive a music lesson (singing and music literacy) *every day*, based mostly on the Kodaly approach; that he would choose the teachers; that he design the curriculum; and, that they begin an experimental program in the arts for a group of two-year olds!

The conditions were accepted and now Zipper, just two weeks after his farewell party at USC, began helping Ambassador College. One of his first acts was to hire Pamela Wade to direct the program. Pamela Wade, from South Africa, had been teaching music in the Pasadena Unified School District for two years. She had also studied the Kodaly Method of teaching music from Katinka Daniel, a prominent disciple of Kodaly. When Zipper called Katinka looking for a music teacher, she recommended Pamela. On September 1, 1980 Wade had her first interview with this man whom she had never heard of. Zipper laid out his plans and when she told him she had not been a music major in college, he told her he cared not about degrees but about intelligence, talent, and willingness to learn. Then he leaned forward and, with a spark in his eyes and voice, told her he had a rather special project in mind: he wanted to begin an experimental program with young children. Wade thought he meant 4-5 year olds. He told her people of this world live far below their potential and we waste our children's most potent years of learning. It was infants Zipper wished to teach. With so many women working, children plopped in front of T.V. sets, and fathers off pursuing their jobs, the children are not guided to develop their innate qualities, including their musicality. Pamela Wade, startled and a bit scared, told Zipper she had no experience with 2 year olds. "Good," said Zipper, "you won't have any pre-conceived ideas." Zipper told the Ambassador Foundation he wanted a 20 year study of these children to determine the impact of this early training on their subsequent development. One cannot help but smile at the situation: an 80 year old man initiating a 20 year study!

The program began with Wade teaching a class of 6 children: two four-year olds, one three-year-old, two two-year olds, and one 17 month old infant. A parent of each child was required to attend and to keep a written record of what they observed in class and at home. Initially, Wade recalls, it was a chaotic nightmare trying to learn how to teach this odd assortment of ages. But she learned. And the program, called the "Infant and Parent Learning Center," now has 105 children which meet in groups of 15, twice a week, in groups of 1-4 year olds. Some parents keep returning with new children.

This project, teaching music, dance and poetry to children from *two weeks old* on up to four years of age is a typical Zipper project - radical and unique. Its value for children is now, Wade and others are convinced, clearly established. Beginning with the prenatal listening, there is some evidence that the music has a calming influence. Children ages 2-6 weeks absorb everything unconsciously while nursing, sleeping, or just listening. As they become more aware of the environment, they "participate," crawling around, developing curiosity about the instruments (drums, xylophones, rhythm instruments) and sometimes clapping in rhythm to the class activity. During the ensuing months from 6 months to two years, they develop an incredible internal sense of rhythm and melody but it is not consciously or formally taught; rather, it is internalized naturally and organically. Often one can see them doing activities subconsciously attuned to the beat of the classroom activity. From two years on they receive more formal instruction in singing, sight-reading, and making music with the Orff instruments (instruments designed by composer Karl Orff to teach music to young children). They learn to feel the rhythms of words; they learn social skills (often older students help teach the younger ones — a feature which Zipper believes to be especially important); and they learn to create their own songs and patterns. Zipper and Wade also agreed on several principles: that they would emphatically urge parents not to push their children, not to be more ambitious than their child, and not to compare their child with others in the program, either negatively or positively. Both Wade and Zipper always called attention to the fact that there are innate differences in the rate of progress in children, in fact in all people, and that the speed by which accomplishment is achieved is immaterial, especially for children.

Zipper has also been concerned ever since coming to America in 1946 that America is not a singing nation. By comparison to European children, American children do not learn to sing at an early age in their communities, with their families. *Making* music is not part of the American cultural life. At the Imperial School, at the Community School, and the 32nd Street School in Los Angeles, and in community schools all across America, Herbert Zipper has tried to show a better way: to immerse children in the arts, to allow them to express their innate creativity and joy through the making of music and art. He was, however, soon to be called upon by a country where the arts are an organic part of the people's lives and where his wisdom was to be enthusiastically solicited.

In 1980 as Zipper was preparing to retire from USC, he was informed of a visiting Chinese delegation at the University led by Lin Mohan, Deputy Minister of Culture (the second in command but the main force in cultural relations with the West in the Post-Mao, post cultural revolutionary China). Zipper was asked among others to give a speech to the Chinese delegation at a dinner. After dinner Lin Mohan approached Zipper and said: "You've been all over the Far East, why have you never come to China?" Zipper replied that he had never been invited. To which Lin Mohan responded, "Well, we will then!"

Two months later Zipper received an official letter, signed by the Director of Art Education of the Ministry of Culture, Wang Zicheng, inviting him to come to China and teach in Beijing and other cities and to conduct concerts. A trip was arranged for May of 1981: two months in Beijing, 3 weeks in Tianjin, and one month in Guangzhou.

He prepared for this trip with excited anticipation. His travels through the Far East, his many Chinese students, and his reading had provided him with considerable knowledge and a deep interest in China. As early as 1941 he had met and become friends with Edgar Snow, who was at the time revising his important study *Red Star Over China*, originally published in 1938. He mentioned on one occasion, while staying at Zipper's home for two weeks, that Chiang Kai-Shek was a crook and that Mao represented the future of China.

Coincidentally, while Zipper was in China in 1988, an article appeared in the China Daily (China's English language newspaper) written by Harrison Salisbury (June 15, 1988) commemorating the 50th year anniversary of the publication of *Red Star Over China*. Salisbury wrote: "Even in China, Snow's work established for the first time the existence of what would become the most powerful political movement of modern times, that of Chinese Communists... The effects of "Red Star" were not only profound in a political sense but they changed the standard for American reportage for all time."

Zipper was also friends with Theodore White whom he had met when White interviewed him for *Time* Magazine. In fact, Zipper believes White and Snow may have themselves first met at the Zipper's home in 1945, which was a refurbished garage on 97 Balmes Street in Manila (a street which no longer exists). White was the Chief of the Pacific War office of *Time* Magazine assigned to cover MacArthur's headquarters. After the fall of Manila, Zipper recalls Teddy White showing him an article he was about to send into *Time*. White said, "Read this and then see in a few weeks what they will actually print." White was becoming progressively angrier and angrier at not only the re-writing of his articles but at the rewriting of history. Men like Edgar Snow and Theodore White, Zipper believes, were not ideologists; they were men who were passionately devoted to reporting reality as accurately as possible regardless of political systems. They believed in truth. White was ultimately to break with *Time* Magazine and Henry Luce. At one point White posted a sign in the shack that served as his *Time* office in Chungking which read: "Any resemblance to what is written here and what is printed in *Time* magazine is purely coincidental."[89] In effect, Luce had determined in the face of a mountain of conflicting evidence that Chiang Kai-Shek was a hero whom America should support, while White was sending in reports in 1944, stating that:

> "Neither the Nationlists or the Communists were democratic in the American sense...to aid Chiang against Mao was to commit us to a disastrous 'meddling' in a civil war in which we could only lose."[90]

White, of course, proved to be somewhat of a prophet and it was only in the 1980's after Nixon had opened doors and Carter had established diplomatic relations, that America and China began to re-establish, or perhaps it is more accurate to say, to build for the first time meaningful relations.

Zipper arrived in China for the first time on May 15, 1981. He was met at the airport by Prof. Huang Feilih and Prof. Chen Yi Shin, both conductors. A woman from the ministry of culture (now retired), Ms. Yu recognized him from a picture he had sent them. During the one-hour drive from the airport to his hotel in downtown Beijing, they gave him his schedule for the next few weeks which included: teaching conducting classes, teaching composition classes, and rehearsing each morning with the Beijing symphony orchestra. He asked if his schedule included teaching the students about chamber music. They replied that the students played little chamber music but that if he wished to start some groups that would be wonderful.

His first morning in Beijing was spent walking along boulevard after boulevard all lined with trees - two rows on each side - and filled with thousands of bicycles going in opposite directions. In 1981 there were few cars and everyone was dressed in either a dull blue or green uniform-like dress, all with the same drab caps. Men and women all dressed alike - remnants of the cultural revolution and the Mao era. Zipper observed that in just 5 years this all has changed radically: the dress became colorful and Chinese women began to adopt Western fashions. The streets became filled with not only bicycles but masses of automobiles. Traffic jams, unheard of in 1981, became commonplace. In 1981 it was difficult to get a taxi; by 1986 there were droves of taxis, mostly made in Japan.

On his two hour walk that first morning, he also noticed that the streets were clean. Invariably one would find two women sweeping towards each other from opposite ends of the street. As he walked he was constantly stopped: "You speak English? May I speak to you?" People were eager to practice, for in 1981 a foreigner still caused interest; five years later it was less common. Flowers, Zipper observed, play a prominent role in China. Always there were flower exhibits in the various cities. And once, after a concert in July of 1981, he found a beautiful vase of flowers in his dressing room with a poem written by an anonymous member of the audience. A large bouquet of flowers was presented to him on stage after the conclusion of every concert. In the many concerts he conducted in various cities he never saw an empty seat.

In between his 1985 and 1986 trips to China, Zipper had to deal with another loss. With Trudl gone in 1976 and then Otto in 1979, for a time only Hedy and Walter remained. And by the end of February in 1986, Walter took a final turn for the worse. He was now 84 years old. X-rays showed a block in his intestines; it was cancer. Herbert prepared to watch another loved one endure the ravage of the disease.

Walter Zipper and his wife came to America in 1948 from London. Herbert Zipper picked them up at the boat in New York and they had a grand reunion, not having seen each other since Paris in 1939. Soon Walter came to Los Angeles where he began his work as an inventor. He was never wealthy but always managed to get by. He had married in London, was divorced, and later remarried the same lady, Betty Maureen Upjohn. They had no children. Walter and Herbert Zipper were close friends. Their relationship to each other was irreplacable. They could giggle and fool around together and see life's absurdities with a relaxed, immediate mutual recognition. When Walter lay dying in the hospital, Zipper visited him at his bedside. Walking around the bed in mock Nazi manner, he affected a militaristic tone and said, "Walter, you forgot Bettenbauen." Walter smiled. Walter was the only person with whom the work-driven Zipper would go to a movie. Walter in turn would accompany his brother to almost every concert he gave — every children's concert, every orchestra performance at USC When he died, on April 4, 1986, another empty space was created, next to Trudl, in the twilight of Herbert Zipper's world.

Shortly after Walter's death, Zipper returned to China and resumed his affectionate relationship with the Chinese people. Zipper speaks of the Chinese with obvious respect. They are, he believes, a remarkable people. In June of 1986, for example, he was in Tienjin, about to conduct a rehearsal of the Brahms Violin Concerto, when the orchestra manager rushed in with a cablegram. Zipper read it and informed his inquisitive orchestra that his grand-niece had just given birth to a son. Whereupon the orchestra went wild - cheering, blasting their instruments, clapping their hands. "you cannot imagine such a commotion," Zipper reports. It lasted for a full five minutes. Zipper was amazed. What he learned was that this was "the year of the tiger" and the birth of a boy in this year was particularly significant. He would grow up to be strong and important. Herbert Zipper honored the tradition by buying 100 eggs, had them hard-boiled in the orchestra kitchen, and had a red dot put on them according to custom. The next day at rehearsal he would distribute them to the orchestra - again, according to custom. When he arrived at the podium the next day, he found a table full of gifts for the child and another lovely poem.

Another custom which he learned from experience was that the Chinese always walk a guest to his or her car or to the door and that when a guest arrives he is taken to a room to sit, have tea, and rest. It is, Zipper observes, an act of consideration to the human spirit, not just for the comfort of the body but for the mind and spirit. Wherever he went in nine cities, he was accorded this respectful custom. Once at a train station he expressed concern that they would miss their train, "Don't worry," his host told him, "you rest and we will hold the train."

During his first week in 1981 when he visited a concert of the BBC Orchestra from London, he observed the President of the conservatory riding his bicycle to the concert. Owning a bicycle was for the Chinese the equivalent of an American owning an automobile. He also observed that there was no theft. Day or night one could go anywhere and feel safe. For a major crime, trials were held in stadiums in front of 20,000 to 50,000 people. The accused would be led in with his head down. At sentencing his head would be lifted up - a form of public humiliation which Zipper was told by the Chinese officers is a deterrent to crime.

After his walk, he went to his first rehearsal and asked the orchestra to perform a piece with which they were familiar. Initially the intonation of several wind players was so off that it "took one's shoes off." But even more startling was how rapidly these musicians learned. One gentle example, one word of criticism, one suggestion was sufficient and immediately, rapid improvement occurred. After the first full rehearsal, Zipper followed the practice he had adopted in the Philippines: he became a teacher. He would work with one section at a time, teaching first the strings, then the brass, the winds, etc., and even breaking them down further into groups of individual instruments. Other conductors would come to Beijing, wave their baton and leave. Zipper sought to help, to teach. And respond they did! They loved the sectional work; they loved analyzing the music, they loved the fact that they were learning so much. They came to call him "Papa Z". During his 1988 trip to China a dinner (a welcome and a farewell banquet is traditional in every part of China) was held in Zipper's honor. One Chinese official leaned toward Zipper and said, "do you know why we always invite you back?" "No," he politely replied. "Because," the official continued, "you once said in 100 years Chinese symphony orchestras will reach the level of the best European and American orchestras. In China, a hundred years is a short time."

In the meantime the arts are an organic part of the Chinese culture. Not only is poetry a commonplace form of expression, but the visual arts are revered as well. In every city Zipper has visited he has been asked if he wishes to see the current art exhibitions and to visit the art academies. And, of course, he has been most eager to do so. Consequently, he was introduced to Zheng Shengtian a superb artist at the Art Institute in Hangzhou and to Zheng's student Yu Juang who has also become a respected and well-known artist. In Beijing he met Liu Chunhua who is the Director of the Beijing Art Academy and one of China's most famous artists. Zipper's home is now a mini gallery of contemporary Chinese representational art. In his living room, over his Steinweg grand piano, is a massive Liu Chunhua traditional Chinese water color of the great Chinese poet Xu. In his bedroom are two smaller water color paintings by Liu Chunhua, one of two young girl flutists and the other of a painter trying to coax a bird to come to him from a tree above. In his anteroom off the front door is a scroll painting inscribed to him by Wu Zuo Ren the famous painter of Chinese pandas. And, in his study is a lush, large oil painting of Chinese girls standing in sea water, shoveling brine. This latter painting is the work of Yu Juang.

Zipper's observations about China are further expounded in a letter written on June 8, 1988:

> It is here in Shenyang (Mukden) capitol of Lianoing (Manchuria) that I became fully aware of the reality of Chinese life. More so than I did in other cities and in previous years.
>
> What it takes to navigate through the daily problems of life in China is well nigh superhuman. Just to go and to come from work, to gather the necessities of the day, to care for their children and their old people and to exist in their tiny, over-crowded quarters is unimaginable for the average Westerner. The traffic is so dense, the crowds everywhere so huge, life's rewards so minimal that considering all circumstances one wonders how much zest for life can remain to want to survive.

Yet, there they are, moving about with obvious equanimity, taking everything into its stride, pedaling without haste and without bumping into each other in an uninterrupted, constant stream of bicycles through the endless streets of this vast city; finding the time to buy and to read books and to crowd into art exhibitions and to retain a healthy sense of humor.

This absence of resignation might be based on a spirit of hope. There is no real poverty now in China as I have seen in other far eastern countries. There is sufficient food for everyone, a place to stay for everyone, though miniscule; nobody starves and nobody is homeless. The improvements of the past ten years are enormous. Still, there must be more to the prevalent spirit than hope. Can it be that it is just wisdom?

Shenyang, they say, has a population of four million; to me it looks like ten. The over-population is glaringly obvious. I am really very angry at the Western critcism leveled against the Chinese population control policy. This is a most courageous experiment for which they ought to be admired. The many people to whom I have talked in China do approve this effort without exception. They want to have their grand-children live a decent life and they know without this control it will be impossible. There are many other issues that Europeans and Americans will have to become much less ignorant about. More about that verbally!"[91]

During his visits to China Zippper has met many students whom he has subsequently helped come to America and to enroll in American university graduate and undergraduate programs. One, a student of English Literature who in 1982 had been his interpreter, wrote a touching poem in English to her new teacher, "Papa Z."

No Need For Words
To my dear, dear Papa Z.

Why should true love be mute
When our two voices
Could speak enough words
To overflow a thousand leaves?
Yet with silence we often make a trio,
And leave our hearts feeling their way through a soundless duet.
Does the boundless sunshine of our souls

Refuse the confines of utterance?
Then fret no more at the stumbling passages of speech
Nor care about the power of these inadequate lines,
But let the internal music flow forth
From eye to eye, and hand to hand.

— Chang Jie
Oct. 27, 1982

Jie had been assigned to "Papa Z." as a translator on his second trip in 1982. She met him at the airport and it soon became clear that she was unfamiliar with the vocabulary of music. Zipper expressed concern but she reassured him: "Don't worry, I'll be better tomorrow." The very next day the growth of her knowledge of musical terms was staggering; by the end of the week she was virtually a musicologist. She had simply given herself an intensive crash course and had absorbed it all. Zipper was flabbergasted. Her capacity to learn was astounding. Subsequently, he helped her to apply for a Fulbright study grant and by 1989 she was at Berkeley working on a Ph.D. in English Literature and teaching freshman English. Zipper has also sponsored a number of Chinese students and teachers to study in the U.S. but he doubts that they will return to their homeland.

Part of the Zipper modus operandi is to inaugurate programs in deserts. For example, during his 1981 visit to China, while conducting in Tianjin, he noticed an outstanding young violinist, Miss Guan Wen-Ning, in the recently-formed symphony orchestra. He offered to help her musically and the following year he began introducing her to the subtleties of chamber music. She was enraptured. Zipper returned to Tianjin in 1984 and 1986 and each time he worked more with her, teaching her how to approach chamber music, sometimes working until midnight after a full day of conducting. Armed with her newly-acquired passion she was able to convince the local government that the city would benefit from a chamber music program and that she should develop a string quartet. Consequently the city determined to send her to America in 1991 to learn more literature and technique. Thus a new genre of music will come to a major city. Miss Guan Wen-Ning will be its director. The spirit behind it all will be Herbert Zipper, having provided the inspiration and the means and having done all this behind the scenes.

Zipper learned, through Jie and Guan Wen-Ning and many others, that in China wisdom is venerated in ways we cannot imagine in the West and their poets and painters are folk heroes. The driver of his car in Guangzhou passed his time while waiting for him by reading an anthology of Chinese poetry; the elevator boy in the Friendship Hotel in Tianjin was reading a Chinese translation of Tolstoy's *Anna Karenina*; a taxi driver in Beijing was in awe to be driving Zipper to the home of a famous painter. Zipper also learned that the Chinese learn differently. They believe in complete absorption, total concentration. You sit next to people reading in the park and they are enthralled. They would not hear a bomb going off. However, since 1981, Zipper has noticed the signs of a change here, too. For as life has become less stressful and more comfortable, the tremendous motivation which grows out of deprivation and the need to develop one's own inner resources seems to have decreased. Miserable poverty is, of course, destructive to the human spirit, but so too is too much comfort.

On one particular Sunday Feilih, Chen Yi-Shin and the head of the composition department Prof. Jiang Ding-Xian, drove with him to the Great Wall.

> "We climbed up to the top-look-out-post where one's eye could follow for miles the ups and downs of the winding structure.
>
> From the Wall we drove to the Ming Tombs where we had an outdoor lunch at a little restaurant. From the time going down the Wall, driving the considerable distance to the Tombs and during the meal, I became rather quiet and taciturn, so much so that Ding-Xian asked me whether I felt well. 'I am fine,' I said, 'but, you see, the "Wall" depressed me.' This caused much surprise and I had to explain. The sight of the Wall brought to my mind the useless, enormous expenditure of human efforts and lives over the milleniums, always for the same misguided judgments. It brought to my mind 1914 memories of the Liege fortress in the West and the Przemisl fortress in the East, of the Maginot Line, the Atlantic Wall, the Siegfried Line, the various present-day atomic silos and the "defense and standing tall" foolishness of our own, new government. Is there no way to develop in the minds of humanity a better memory?"

Zipper is also concerned by the rapid Westernization of China which is, for example, reflected by the growing number of television sets. He is disturbed by the inevitable passivity, escapism, materialism, and dissatisfaction with oneself as one is, which television engenders. These concerns have led him to not only teach music, but, at every opportunity, to convey a message to the Chinese. He is attempting to warn the Chinese of the dangers of industrialization, the inherent perils of technology. He has, and continues to explain to them that they are now in the beginning stages of their own industrial revolution and, that by observing what has transpired in the West, China can learn and not repeat the massive problems with which the West has saddled itself. The large scale alienation of workers from their jobs and consequently themselves, the absence of satisfaction in one's job with the paycheck being the only reward, the wasting and befouling of the environment, the neglect of human resources in favor of technological advance - these and many other disasters of industrial civilization are not inevitable, Zipper argues.

China, he explains to the Chinese and to anyone who will listen to him, has an historic opportunity: to by-pass the 20th Century. To go from feudal 19th Century China to a glorious 21st Century without experiencing the whole array of 20th Century ills. China can look down the highway the West has traveled and construct a different road. However, the challenge, as Zipper has presented it to numerous officials, is to clearly define their own spiritual goals. The West, he never tires of pointing out, has created the first model of industrial civilization. First models are never, can never be perfect. China now has the opportunity to create its own model, learning from the pitfalls of the first model. If the goal is simply technological efficiency and material wealth, the road will lead to the same dilemmas, the same alienation the West is suffering from. In preaching this message Zipper has restated and refined the ideas of the charismatic Chinese writer, Liang Ch'i-ch'ao (Liang Qichao, 1873-1929) who wrote:

> I therefore hope that our dear young people will, first of all, have a sincere purpose of respecting and protecting our civilization; seondly, that they will apply Western methods to study our civilization and discover its true character; thirdly, that they will put our civilization in order and supplement it with others so that it will be transformed and become a new civilization; and fourthly, that they will extend this new civilization to the outside world so that it can benefit the whole human race.[92]

During his trip to Vienna in 1987, Zipper presented a lecture in which he stated:

> "The Occident created the first model of industrial civilization, a model that with all its great achievements and advantages, carried with it also severe damages. The West today begins to become conscious of this fact and it seems to be superfluous to enumerate the long list of these damages. Only a few that appear to be among the most serious ones I should like to mention: the alienation of people from each other; the break-up of the family causing the decay of this germ-cell of human society; the absence of the satisfactions from work for a vast majority and the resulting flight into narcotic escapism; and, above all, the systematic destruction of our planet.
>
> I have justified reason to assume that the Chinese today at the beginning of their industrial development observe the occident with a critical eye. The Chinese are a people of learners. Everyone who comes to China as a teacher immediately realizes that teaching there is a paradise and a pleasure. The Chinese lust for learning creates a constant joy for teaching.
>
> The contemporary mood in China is formed by the concept of truth through reality, the supremacy of reason. At the same time an effort is made to preserve the most valuable parts of their tradition. The static condition that prevailed in China for centuries changed recently into a state of constant motion.
>
> The possibility exists, and I hope it is not a mere pipe-dream, that China now departing from feudalism, realizing not only the blessings but also the curses of Western industrial civilization will make the giant leap over the 20th

Century and will create a new social order for the 21st Century that, unlike any existing one, may serve as a guide post for humanity everywhere."

Let us, Zipper proclaims to the Chinese, be a warning to you. It is, to be sure, a message they do not often hear from visitors from the West. During each visit to China, Zipper has urged the Chinese *not* to follow blindly our ways, but to look to their own traditions and values; to learn Western techniques to add them to their own ingenuity and imagination and to create their own forms, their own modes of beauty. Thus his message leads back to the arts where the human spirit is developed, preserved, and expressed. He looks forward to each new trip to China with the anticipation and eagerness of a child, the hope of a prophet, and the passionate commitment to the arts that has characterized his entire life.

Postscript: China, June 1989.

This chapter was to end with the preceding sentence. However, Zipper, with his seemingly uncanny instinct for being in history-making places at just the moment of crisis, had traveled to China in May of 1989 and was staying in the Minzu Hotel, within walking distance from Tiananmen Square. He had been invited by the Ministry of Culture for the sixth time to conduct and teach in several cities. Arriving on May 18, he spent two days in Beijing meeting with officials at the Conservatory of Music and making plans for future visits. On May 21, he flew to Chang-Chun in Jilin Province where he rehearsed for several days with the city orchestra and then gave two concerts on May 28 and 29. The program featured Beethoven's Egmont Overture and Violin Concerto and Brahm's 1st Symphony. On May 30th he returned to Beijing for two rehearsals; one on Friday morning, June 2nd and the other on Saturday afternoon, June 3rd. The concerts were scheduled for June 15 and 16, with the Beijing Philharmonic, a veteran and competent orchestra.

On June 1st Zipper had walked through Tiananmen Square and was quite exulted by the spirit of celebration and the expression of democratic passions. He wrote to his sister Hedy that "this is the most interesting time I have had in this country. The political debates are intelligent, non-ideological, realistic and most important of all, absolutely non-violent. Students and the people in general are behaving maturely and with a sense of responsibility. During all these weeks all over the country nothing has been destroyed and not a single shot has been fired. The Prime Minister, Mr. Li Peng, is pretty much discredited and most likely will not retain his post much longer. Deng Xiaoping is not much discussed; people, however, believe that he is too old. Although he is exactly my age

(85), they say I am not too old. But then I have a few less responsibilities than Deng." As for the issue of age there was a joke circulating during Zipper's visit which ran: "In China today the 80 year-olds tell the 70 year-olds which 60 year-olds they should retire."

And in this spirit of apparent openness and political growth Premier Li Peng even met with student leaders and allowed a dialogue to be reprinted in all newspapers. For example, in the *China Daily* of May 20, 1989, in an article entitled "Li Peng Meets With Student Leader," Li Peng is quoted as saying:

> "Neither the Central nor the Party Central Committee has ever said that the students are arousing turmoil. We have been affirming the students' patriotic enthusiasm, and many things you have done are right. Many questions you have raised are just the ones that the government hopes to deal with. Frankly speaking, you have actually helped the government to a certain degree in the solving of these problems..."

At this time Zipper's spirits were high. He had written: "This is a real revolution and one can only wish that it will remain as bloodless as it has been thus far." He went on to say "New leadership has not yet crystallized and one can only hope that it will not fall into the wrong hands as it has happened so often as a result of upheavals in the past." [93]

After his Saturday, June 3rd rehearsal, he had a pleasant dinner with the new president of the Beijing Central Conservatory and neither of them felt any sense of foreboding. After dinner Zipper went to bed early. He was awakened just before midnight by a sound with which he was all too familiar — the sound of gunfire, rockets, tracer bullets, tear gas canisters, and the screaming of frightened people. Just below in the street and plaza in front of his hotel, a few blocks west of Tiananmen Square, through the darkness and tear-gas haze, he saw flashes of light and bodies lying all over the street. He could also hear and see shooting throughout the city.

It was a profoundly sad sight for the 85 year-old optimist, an evening recalling feelings of despair similar to those he felt when Hindenberg named Hitler Chancellor, when the Nazis invaded Austria, when the Japanese marched into Manila. At 6:00 the next morning he ventured outside. Most of the bodies had been removed in army trucks but one remained on the hotel steps and, a block away he saw the bullet-riddled body of a 9-10 year-old little girl. He walked through the city and saw more bodies, burned cars, and rocks littering the streets. He hid in doorways when army vehicles drove by.

That evening several friends called advising him to leave but he had no intention of doing so. He wanted to see for himself. He also received two calls from students eager to explain what happened in Tiananmen Square. One told him: "I saw. No matter what they say, it was a real massacre. At least 2,000 dead bodies everywhere."

The next morning, Monday June 5th, a car came to take him to the Philharmonic rehearsal but only the manager and four musicians showed up. He was driven back to the hotel, a long drive, and saw more burned cars. There was more shooting in front of the hotel, so they dropped him off several blocks away and he slipped back to the hotel on foot. By the next evening, Zipper was the only remaining guest. The chef served him meals for the staff had virtually disappeared. From the 6th to the 13th he was the only guest in the hotel. The streets were deserted and the shooting had subsided. Zipper recorded his observations in a journal he had begun on June 1st which reveals the level of optimism prevailing up to midnight of June 3rd:

> The experiences that I gained through my various Chinese engagements during the 1980's made me believe that China is reaching out toward a new level of political maturity in which controversy, dissatisfactions, disagreements, grievances and even social unrest could be resolved without recourse to violence and bloodshed. During the month of May my belief was strengthened by the obvious restraint practiced by the government and the people and the open and uncensored information about developments that was available through all the news media.
>
> The verbatim transcript of the conversation that Premier Li Peng had with some of the student leaders that appeared in the Chinese newspapers on May 20, 1989 added fuel to my hopes. Especially the remarks made by Wang Chao Hua, a postgraduate student from the Chinese Academy of Social Sciences were most encouraging. He said and I am quoting:
>
>> "I believe that the students are staging a democratic movement of their own accords *to gain the rights stipulated by the Constitution.* This is the point that I wish to make. If it were only patriotic enthusiasm anything might have happened with such enthusiasm. Otherwise no one could explain the sober-minded person, restraint and good order of this movement."
>
> Referring to the growing public support of their movement, student Shao Jiang of the Beijing University said, and I quote:
>
>> "The student movement may have become a people's movement. The students are relatively reasonable. But we cannot insure that a

people's movement can be reasonable. I like to hear your opinion on how to cope with this situation."

He asked Premier Li Peng (Mr. Li however evaded this and all other direct questions.)"

After the events of June 3-4, Zipper, alone in his hotel, returned to his journal and, in a very different mood, continued:

> It was during the night from Saturday, June 3, to Sunday, June 4, that my expectations and hopes turned out to be mere dreams from which I was rudely awakened by rifle and machine gun fire, rockets and tear gas spraying by the Chinese army shooting at unarmed civilians. I could watch it all from my hotel window a few blocks from Tiananmen Square. The violence continued on and off for over 3 days soon creating violent public reaction, mostly in the form of rock throwing and burning of scores of parked military vehicles.
>
> Until this day, June 11, Beijing is a dead city. Public transportation is practically unavailable. Economic activities are at a standstill. For the past five days I have been the *only* guest in this huge, 10-story hotel and I am told that other hotels have not even one guest. The economic loss must be staggering. China largely depends on tourism for its foreign exchange needs. The foreigners are gone, even the Chinese from Hong Kong. Schools and universities are closed. There are no newspapers. The newsstands that used to carry foreign publications are empty. Only the information that the government releases is available to radio and television and to a tabloid that began to appear on June 8. The *China Daily* and other publications have ceased to appear. To say that the information that the government releases is not reliable is a ridiculous understatement. What everyone has seen as it really happened is either not reported of completely distorted. I was overcome by feelings of depression similar to those I experienced when Hitler assumed power in 1933, when he marched into Austria in 1938 and when the Japanese marched into Manila in 1942. I again felt a sense of despair about the mindlessness of government to use bullets instead of ideas. Now they claim that they had to crush a counter-revolution, propaganda that nobody is swallowing, because everybody knows that what the students and eventually the public wanted is an implementation of the constitution that thus far has remained only on paper to a large extent, and also an end to the rampant corruption among public officials.
>
> The significant gains on all fronts made during the decade of the eighties, the building up of hope and confidence in the future have all been heavily changed. Whether or not beyond repair only time will tell.
>
> The government instead of offering news following the massacre, a positive program of reform and improvements offers instead a stupid propaganda and a description of the recent events as they did not happen which nobody can believe. I have talked to many Chinese of all walks of life and I found no one who did not express disdain of the brutal government actions since June 3 and a propaganda that spits truth into its face.

I have watched Deng Xiaoping three times addressing the assembled government officials on the T.V. screen and I gained the impression that his speech was impaired. Twice a person next to him, but not seen on the screen, had to help him out with some words that he did not get over his lips. Some of my Chinese friends confirmed my impression. It might be that Deng was not fully informed of the events and that he lacked the strength to investigate for himself and that he was pushed into a situation without considering its consequences, just like old Emperor Franz Joseph I of Austria was pushed into a war he did not want and old Hindenburg was pushed to embrace Adolf Hitler misjudging the consequences. Whatever the truth may be, history will not exonerate Deng as it did not some others who at the sunset of their lives committed fatal errors. Some important leaders just don't know when to die. Some of my Chinese friends would disagree with my analysis. They maintain that at heart Deng always was a dictator in spite of his proven abilities of leadership in matters of the economy. It might well be that a combination of both views led to the tragedy.

I have been asked by many Chinese of all walks of life the question: What now? What can we do to rid ourselves of a government that discredited itself in the eyes of its people and the whole world? (Who am I to give advice?) Yet, I feel that the crystalization of a universal world opinion together with a shrewd diplomacy capitalizing on the existing strong dissensions within the Chinese government may solve the problem (thought interrupted by gunfire)...

* * *

Incidentally, the events of the past week awakened in me 55 year old memories. In the summer of 1934 I, as co-founder of the Vienna Concert Orchestra, participated in the organization of "A Week of Opera" to be be held on the outdoor stage on the grounds of the Imperial court park (Burggarten). Days before the scheduled opening all seats were sold and everything was ready when a couple of days before the first performance the Austrian Nazis attempted a putsch that failed miserably because Mussolini rushed a huge number of troops to the Austrian border. However, the Bundes Chancellor Dollfuss was assassinated The entire palace grounds immediately were declared off limits, the opera season had to be cancelled and the tickets reimbursed. We lost a lot of money. Similarly in 1989 the concerts scheduled with the Philharmonic in Beijing on June 15 and 16 and the "Beethoven Festival" in Shenyang scheduled for June 27 and 28 naturally all had to be cancelled. (All to be under his direction.) I stayed on until June 13 in Beijing because I wanted to gather as much information as was possible.

Another matter came to my mind – Li Peng's opening remark at his conversation with the student representatives included the following sentences:

> "Today we will talk only about one thing: how to get the fasting students out of their present plight. The Party and the government are deeply concerned and worried about the matter of their health"...
> etc.

> He and his government had been so deeply concerned about their health that a few days later they have been shooting them.
>
> Li Peng then continued to say: "You are all young, no more than 22 or 23 years of age. My youngest son is older than you. I have three children. None of them engage in official profiteering"... etc. (Nobody ever accused him that they had.) The French say: "qui c'excuse, c'accuse!" Another more recent quote comes to mind: "I am not a crook!!"

June 4th and its aftermath has been a disappointment for Zipper. In addition to his own musical projects and programs which he has taken great delight in bringing to the Chinese in past visits, he has developed a genuine affection and respect for the country and has come to see China's future in rather idealistic and sanguine terms. To some of his friends his hopes have even seemed excessively optimistic. Perhaps Zipper and other American and European friends who shared his optimism needed to heed the warning of Edgar Snow in his last book, *The Long Revolution*, completed in 1972, just before Richard Nixon arrived in Beijing. Snow wrote: "The danger is that Americans may imagine the Chinese are giving up Communism — and Mao's world view — to become nice agrarian democrats. A more realistic world is indeed in sight. But popular illusions that it will consist of a sweet mix of ideologies, or an end to China's faith in revolutionary means, could only serve to deepen the abyss again when disillusionment strikes... "[94]

Zipper, however, was under no illusion that Marxist Socialism would be abandoned. Socialism in June of 1989 was not the issue; the issue was the oppressive presence and style of the bureaucracy — and this Zipper did understand clearly. In any event, the military crackdown with its reversal of the recent liberalization process was profoundly discouraging.

Zipper left China on June 15, and returned to Los Angeles. He was greeted at the airport by his nephew, Henry Holt, with more sad news. Hedy, Herbert Zipper's beloved sister and his life-long friend and soulmate, had suffered a stroke and died while Zipper was preparing to leave China. Hedy Holt had traveled with a friend to South Africa. On June 6 she had enjoyed her last evening with friends, had gone to sleep, awakened to call for help, suffered a stroke, slipped into a coma and died. She was 82 years old. For the preceeding twelve years, since Trudl died, they phoned each other each morning; they dined together almost every evening at the Holt residence where Hedy provided her brother with a Viennese cuisine redolent with the smells and tastes of their shared heritage. Theirs was an intimacy of love, respect, and mutually shared values. With the news of Hedy's death Zipper was now truly alone - father, mother, and siblings — all were gone. His response to this newest loss in his life was, again, to rely upon his iron will and spend his days not in mourning or reminiscence but in labor.

His grief was given poetic expression in a beautiful and moving duet for cello and violin — an exquisite little vignette which he composed for my daughters, Anna and Emily, to play at the memorial concert for Hedy which was held on July 16, at the Schoenberg Institute at USC. He also set to work to prepare for a July-August trip to the Philippines to conduct a 50th year anniversary concert honoring his becoming the conductor of the Manila Symphony; to finish composing pieces for a concert to be held in Graz in October of 1989; to prepare for the next series of Concerts-in-the-Schools; to prepare his next trip to China; and to work on a host of other projects. In a curious way Zipper has turned the appalling Nazi slogan, which was written over the Dachau entry gate, "Arbeit Macht Frei," into his own working code. Work has always set him free, or relatively free, from grief, depression, and despair. In his commitment to work he has found meaning to life and made order out of the chaos of history and of the 20th Century. The American novelist Reynolds Price once said: "Prepare, strip, divest for life that awaits you; learn solitude and work; see how little is lovely but love that." Since the days of Dachau, Herbert Zipper's life has been an unbroken application of this concept.

CODA

Coda

Return to Vienna

An aged man is but a paltry thing,
A tattered coat upon a stick, unless
Soul clap its hands, and louder sing
For every tatter in its mortal dress.

- W.B. Yeats

For only some grand theme will have the force
To stir the deeper reaches of mankind.
Man's thought is shrunken by a narrow round,
But as his aims are great, so he grows.
Now to its solemn end the century draws,
When poetry finds matter in the real,
When we behold the clash of mighty souls
Over a worthy goal, when struggles rage
For what is greatest among human themes,
Freedom and domination. And now art
Upon its shadow stage may set itself
To reach for higher flights – indeed it must,
Or else be put to shame by life's own stage.

- F.V. Schiller

The home of Herbert Zipper, a modest middle class dwelling, sits above the Pacific Ocean. His garden offers a rich palette of colors and gorgeous roses and camelias and other flowers which he attends to with the meticulous care which characterizes his every endeavor. Driving away after our long talks and interviews, I have often been struck by the peculiarity of this setting. To find this man – a Viennese Jew born in the Hapsburg Empire in 1904, educated in the Viennese Academy, a conductor in Germany, survivor of Dachau and Buchenwald, a conductor of the Manila Symphony Orchestra – living in Pacific Palisades overlooking the Pacific Ocean. As I complete this biography, Herbert Zipper is 87 years young, a vigorous man passionate about music, education, politics, ecology, life. I once asked his friend Dr. Eric Simon, what do you think of first when you think of Herbert Zipper? As his vision is impaired and his handwriting obscure, Dr. Simon sent me a cassette. I was expecting a flowery, profound response. "When I think of Herbert," said this friend of some 50 years, "I think of his nose!" I could hear the twinkle in his voice. Zipper does indeed have a prominent Vladimir Horowitz sort of nose. He also looks at you over this nose with intense eyes. He listens carefully and responds to questions with thoughtful, serious answers. I have met few people in my life who are less trivial. The Viennese accent is strong yet the English sentences are lucid with an excellent sense of the mot juste. He stands with a pronounced stoop to his shoulders and he sometimes jokes about how he has shrunk from his former 6'1" stature. Each Sunday for four years (1987-1991) I have driven to his home at 8:00 a.m. (if I was late he would call to see if everything was all right) and I have walked to the front door through his lush garden. The path is lined with freshly-watered, full rich roses which Zipper trims with a surgeon's care, and is also laced with beautiful greens and azaeleas. Off to the side are large wooden sculptures, some carved by Zipper. When I arrive at the front door, he looks up through the window, rises from his study desk, and comes to unlock the door for me. The interior of his home is a reflection of his orderliness, a testimony to his own aesthetic tastes and sensibilities, as well as being a small museum of almost a century-long life. The walls are covered with paintings from the Philippines, China, Austria; there are tables filled with artifacts and sculpture from all over the world, including the outer provinces of the Philippines; there are photographs of Trudl, of his family, his grandfather; and there are carpets and chairs of native artisans. We sit each Sunday in an indoor garden room filled with cymbidiums, and other orchids, a living tree indoors, and always a clearly polished marble floor. The garden room is adjacent to the living room with a Steinweg grand and bookcases filled with favorites such as the complete works of Goethe as well as volumes written by friends such as Edgar Snow, Theodore White, Claude Buss, Malcolm Cowley and others. Notwithstanding his age, he is up at 4:30 - 5:00 a.m. to begin each day with a vigorous walk in the hills above his Pacific Palisades home. He returns from his walk often to compose classical chamber music pieces for elementary school children for whom the traditional classical literature would be too difficult. He also composes children's chamber music programs at an elementary school he has helped develop over the years. He then writes letters to friends and associates all over the world and then frequently drives to one school or another where he conducts concerts for school children. Two days a week he teaches counterpoint at Crossroads School where he insists on not being paid. His days are more full at 87 than those of most hard working people I know. He is bothered only by the knowledge that he has relatively little time left to do so many things.

In fact, this very biography is a project Herbert Zipper would never have thought to do. He is too busy with today and laying groundwork for tomorrow to busy himself with yesterday. And, though I think he was slightly flattered by my desire to tell his story, I know he consented to the project out of his eternally optimistic hope that some people might be willing to consider and perhaps to benefit from his ideas. While his life has been fascinating and quite remarkable, even more important is his absolute commitment to a few simple truths and values. His life has exemplified a rapidly evaporating belief — that people *can* take control of their lives and by an act of will, choose to live meaningful, significant lives of service to others and to a better future.

Writing a biography of his life, however, has been difficult. Recently I told him, "You know, you are a biographer's nightmare." "What do you mean?" he inquired. And I gave him an example. I came to his home this one Sunday (July 17, 1988) to try, once again, to steer him into a discussion of his darker thoughts, his regrets, sadnesses; to coax from him some of his reveries, fantasies, dreams, the ghosts of years past who walk with him on his 5:00 a.m. strolls in the hills above his home. In my mind I could see him in dialogue with Trudl, with Jura Soyfer, with brothers Walter and Otto, with the historical figures of his life. I was, of course, seeking a little more drama and pathos in offering up the account of his life.

And so I asked him what he thought of on these walks. He closed his eyes, paused, and said, "Well, I usually take a theme of Brahms or Bach or Beethoven — just the other day the first four measures of the 5th Symphony — and then I try to re-write it and take it in a different direction." He then launched into a discussion of the development of melodies and motifs in various composers. His eyes were intense, his conductor's arms gesticulating wildly, his voice becoming more and more animated about the difficult and creative balance between 'the expected and the unexpected' in the arts. I began chuckling to myself. I had wanted to contact those things which haunt him. But he does not dwell in the past. He deals with ideas and themes, with politics and educational programs. Trying to dig out a dark past has been nearly impossible; Zipper is healthy, in love with the arts and with human possibilities. He is quite incapable of dwelling on himself.

From Manila to Brooklyn to Chicago to Los Angeles to Beijing and dozens of other cities, Zipper has sought to build his vision of a new world. The scale of his lost world — the loss of an Empire — has led to the scale of his life, trying to build and rebuild culture in America and Asia. The safe, sophisticated, tradition-bound world of Vienna and Europe was shattered in 1938 and his own personal routines and goals were obliterated. A Viennese by election, he was relegated to the role of the Jewish prisoner and would-be survivor. The security of childhood, family and Austrian culture vanished overnight in a violent crash and so he sought to replace it. In the 'New World' like many 'Adams' before him he has sought to re-create Eden, to teach a new language of aesthetics, arts, music — a language all people, rich or poor, could understand. Underneath the actions of great men there is often a personal need they are playing out. There is no mysterious "Rosebud" in Zipper's story. Dachau — Buchenwald — Manila radicalized a genteel young conductor. To ensure his own safety and the safety of everyone else he would seek to establish conditions of democracy, reason, culture and decency. Rarely has he looked back on Dachau with a 'never-forget' focus; instead, he is always looking forward to try to create situations and programs directly contradictory to the Nazi experience. Not 'never forget' ugliness, but 'always remember' beauty has been his code. And so motivated is he to see that Nazism never occurs again that his focus has been upon youth, education and posterity. He has successfully transferred a personal need and transmuted personal pain into a global vision.

Along with his seven trips to China (as of 1991) and the ongoing work in Los Angeles conducting his children's concerts and carrying on a host of projects, Zipper has returned to his birthplace three times. The second trip took place in October of 1987. He had visited Vienna once before in 1956 but this October trip was different. For this was an aged man returning to his home from a distance of almost a century with a half-century perspective — he had left Vienna for good in 1939. In part he was returning to see what his life might have been if he had gone back in 1946 - as many had urged him to do. He was, in a very real sense, returning to see what his destiny would have been: the destiny for which he had been so thoroughly educated and prepared and which he had rejected.

The young Herbert Zipper's Vienna (fin-de-siecle - 1920's) had, in some ways, a strong impact upon him and in other ways he seems to have been unaffected by the time and the place. Bruno Bettelheim in his *Freud's Vienna* (1990) gives eloquent expression to the emergence of psychoanalysis in Vienna at the time Zipper was going to school and growing up. Yet while Freud was discovering the depths of the unconscious and the degrees to which all people are shaped and driven by irrational forces within that unconscious, Zipper was forging his own selfhood along very rational lines. Observing his father's often violent temper, Zipper determined to control his own — and did so. Observing and reading about people whose sexual passions destroyed them, Zipper determined to have a healthy, happy sex life but not to be its slave. Observing others controlled by their passions, Zipper determined to control his own and be the observing monitor of his own passions. Consequently, he has always felt himself partly a participant and partly an observer of his own experiences. Generally speaking, this would seem an undesirable or even unhealthy exercise of self-control, perhaps even a defense mechanism against pain, yet it has served Zipper well. Much has been written of the latent conflicts within Viennese society — the sexual repression, the sterile conformism, the war which Freud described between eros and thanatos. Hilde Spiele, one of Austria's foremost writers today and one of Europe's leading cultural journalists, for example, writes of the period (1900-1920's) as:

> "a time of strong emotions, an era of melancholy; the inherited gloominess of all Jewry — 'the weariness of long-forgotten peoples', as Louis called it — combined with a tendency to dejection, to taedium vitae, to capricious ill-temper which affected the most sensitive and the most gifted Viennese. This was further nourished by the mood of impending doom which was steadily gaining ground in spite of the assumed air of high spirits prevailing during the last years of the Hapsburg Empire." [95]

Zipper grew up in this world, the world of composers such as Gustav Mahler who gave expression to "the conjunction of high tragedy and light amusement," the quality which Spiele refers to as "laughing despair, the macabre gaiety inherent in the native Viennese character," a quality given earlier expression by the legendary Augustin's cheerful refrain: "Alles ist hin" ("Everything's gone.") Yet somehow Zipper was not caught up in this Zeitgeist; rather, he was a cheerful, responsible young student whose major form of rebellion against the repressive side of Vienna was to become a free thinker and a political liberal. But to what degree Zipper was a product of Vienna, was unaffected by his Viennese milieu, was simply his own person coded or destined to become who he became is finally — as is the personality of each person — a mystery.

Returning to Vienna in 1987 was a depressing experience. It was depressing to go from book store to book store and to see primarily books about the old days, Vienna in its turn-of-the-century splendor. The mood of the city, he sensed, was one of looking backward, looking back to the glory that was the Empire. Portraits of Franz Joseph were omnipresent. He found little evidence of artistic experimentation or cultural renovation or simply of vitality. It was not a city anticipating; it was a city reminiscing. Hilde Spiel describes the decline which began in 1938:

> At the time of writing the Second Austrian Republic has well overtaken the first, not only in its life-span but also in its health and wealth. To suggest that the pendulum was swung again, however, would be wrong. While the boundaries of the city, unreasonably expanded during the Hitler era and reduced after its end, now compare roughly with those of 1938, the population is steadily decreasing. Those spacious government buildings, designed to administer a far-flung realm, which were taken over by the bureaucracy administering the rump state left after the peace treaty of St. Germain, are now filled to overflowing with civil servants increasing according to the principles of Parkinson's Law. The huge state theatres, monuments to Austria's former grandeur, are subsidized far more heavily than those of London, Paris or New York. But in the midst of all this splendour, the Viennese, busily bustling about like ants in their efforts to maintain their present political, social and economic stability, have to a great extent lost their former urban refinement and universal outlook. The lion is dead. And what was known as the concordia discors in the centre of a multinational state has been replaced by a uniform provincialism.
>
> If this judgment sounds harsh, it is borne out by the number of petty family squabbles in public life, the general low standard of the press and the absence of stimulating intellectual controversy. While music is still played and performed, if not created, to perfection, and while the visual arts may be said to thrive moderately, neither the literature nor the philosophy nor the science in the Vienna of today can compare with those of the years before the Second World War. In the light of these facts, that uniquely fruitful period in Vienna's history, lasting more or less seventy years from its gestation to its decline, is thrown even more sharply into relief. An attempt to describe the characteristics of Vienna's inhabitants and its various districts must be confined to the period in question: its results are not applicable to present-day conditions. In the field of culture, at least, the Anschluss in 1938 was a greater watershed than the collapse of 1918.[96]

Vienna in 1987 was also a city feeling uneasy about its own response to the historical challenges which the 20th Century had presented to it. Few wished to discuss President Kurt Waldheim's alleged collaboration with the Nazis. Revisionist historians have been eager to highlight the worldwide overall atrocities of the 20th Century to make the Nazi experience seem just one of many. During his 1987 trip, Zipper did meet, however, one man whose memory was clear and honest.

While walking to the Ministry of Foreign Affairs with the former ambassador to China, Dr. Wolte, Zipper chanced to meet an old acquaintance, Milan Dubrovic, a journalist and editor of various newspapers in Vienna from 1927 to 1977, whose book *Embezzled History* had recently been published. Zipper and Dubrovic discussed what had happened in the 1930's and how it could have been allowed to happen. Dubrovic himself offers a poignant passage in his book which captures the sense of guilt and helplessness many felt in Vienna as the Nazi tragedy played itself out:

Spring - Stroll at the Ring Boulevard

It was a glorious Sunday - weather, a soft breeze blew wool-like fleecy clouds across the blue sky. The rich green of the Ring-boulevard presented a southern picture of unburdened joyfulness; the deceptive appearance of a peaceful, conflict-free world took hold of the mood of the strolling pairs and idlers.

Suddenly an unusual noise destroys the idyllic holiday spirit. Three huge trucks, closely following each other drive with suspicious speed, rattling and rumbling through the street, fully loaded with people. They stand closely with pale faces drawn in fear.

Like a transport of slaughter cattle these trucks roll along driven by young SA - men. One of them stands watchful with pointed rifle toward the intimidated cargo.

With their own eyes the aroused strollers can see what is happening: the prisoners on their chest are carrying a yellow star. Is there among them one whom one knows, a person close to one or possibly even a friend? This thought strikes one like lightning. Too fast are the rattling vehicles going by to recognize among the crammed heap of prisoners single faces.

Some, not all of those, until their happily strolling boulevard - idlers stop apprehensively, looking after the vehicles that disappear in the distance like an evil phantom.

"Now one ought to cry out loud," my wife exclaims, "running after the trucks, protesting, throwing oneself in front of their wheels."

But nobody does it, we did not either. Why not? The heroes, the martyrs, where are they?

Thoughts, that will never disappear, that always will act as an everlasting admonition, as remembrance of failure, of our anguish and fear of the fall into absurdity.

That drama, this conflict of conscience became a component of everyday life.[97]

In retrospect, Zipper sees himself as one of the fortunate. He was not placed in the position of being a helpless bystander; he was at once a victim, a participant, and an active rebel. While at prison camp he volunteered for the jobs no one else cared to do. He wished to see and experience it all in its fullest measure. If fate was to thrust him into hell, then he would feel the full heat of the fire. If fate were to take him out of the

Academy, then he would learn all he could from his new "classrooms." Walking around Vienna in 1987 (and again in 1988), Zipper could imagine the life that might have been. He had few regrets. He had moved beyond a life of cultural elitism to become a believer in cultural liberalism. He had been transformed from a citizen of Austria to a citizen of the world.

Zipper's third trip back to Vienna and Austria occurred in September of 1988. My wife and I accompanied him first to Vienna and then to Graz where he had been invited to conduct the world premier of his "Dachau Lied" at the annual autumn festival of the arts in Graz. We arrived in Vienna early in the evening on September 19, and promptly set out for a walk through the old city. As we walked, he pointed out this and that building each reflecting a childhood memory. This was the building where his father worked; that was the apartment house (13 Mahlerstrasse) where he rented (60 schillings per month in 1928) a room for him (age 24) and Trudl (age 15) to carry out their love affair. This restaurant (St. Urbani-Keller) was where Leo Slezak and Zipper laughed and wrote cabaret music together; that one (Griechen Beisl) was a place Brahms frequented. "This street used to contain a number of Jewish merchants - now there are none;" that street housed a series of high class "Ladies of the Night:" "I used to take a few for coffee to hear their entertaining and hilarious stories of customers and experiences," he mused. As we walked along we came to a narrow passage with an old bronze plaque at the entrance. Translated it reads:

> PEDESTRIANS LOOK OUT FOR HORSEDRAWN WAGONS!
> Proceed with crawling pace!
>
> Coachmen of heavy wagons have to guide the horses by the rein or an accompanying adult person has to be sent on ahead to warn the pedestrians.
>
> Proclamation of May 8, 1912 Municipal Dept. IV
> Z2050

We concluded our walk at an espresso cafe located in the same building (the subject of an etching by the contemporary artist Kasimir) where he was born. It still, as it did 80 years ago, accommodates a bookstore which then was the only commercial store in the building.

Sipping delicious espresso and enjoying sacher torte at this nostalgic coffee house, we talked for a while of the fate of the Austrian Jew. It had always struck me since I met Herbert Zipper, that his identity was very little tied up in being Jewish. He had grown up in a home which paid scant attention to Jewish customs and religious observances. He has been a lifetime agnostic and his allegiance has never been ethnic or national so much as universal or international. His story was not untypical of many middle-class Viennese Jews at the turn of the century. His family and most Jews he knew considered themselves foremost as loyal Austrians dedicated with pride to the cultural and intellectual glories of the city. Stefan Zweig in his poignant reminiscences of these times, *The World of Yesterday*, explains:

> ... Because of their passionate love for the city, through their desire for assimilation, they had adapted themselves fully, and were happy to serve the glory of Vienna. They felt that their being Austrian was a mission to the world; and - for honesty's sake it must be repeated-much, if not the most of all that Europe and America admire today as an expression of a new, rejuvenated Austrian culture, in literature, the theater, in the arts and crafts, was created by the Viennese Jews who, in turn, by this manifestation achieved the highest artistic performance of their millennial spiritual activity. Centuries of intellectual energy joined here with a somewhat effete tradition and nurtured, revived, increased, and renewed it with fresh strength and by tireless attention. [98]

Zweig explains also that it was not only as leading artists and intellectuals but also as patrons that the Jews served Austria. Under Emperor Franz Joseph, the state had withdrawn financial support of the arts:

> ... To maintain the Philharmonic on its accustomed level, to enable the painters and sculptors to make a living, it was necessary for the people to jump into the breach, and it was the pride and ambition of the Jewish people to co-operate in the front ranks to carry on the former glory of the fame of Viennese culture. They had always loved this city and had entered into its life whole-heartedly, but it was first of all by their love for Viennese art that they felt entitled to full citizenship, and that they had actually become true Viennese. [99]

At the time of the Anschluss, March 12, 1938, there were 185,000 Jews living in Austria, 170,000 in Vienna alone. In addition to the patrons were the leading intellectual figures of the time - Freud, Wittgenstein, Zweig. By the time the war broke out over 120,000 were terrorized into leaving and another 6,000 left by the end of 1939. Of those who remained, an estimated 90% were murdered during "The Final Solution." As Hilde Spiel writes of the dead and departed:

> ....Nobody cries for them in present-day Vienna. Nor, in the city they lived in for so many generations, is there left an awareness of the immense diversity of its former Jewish inhabitants. Just like the hierarchy of non-Jews, they had their social scale from the loftiest, most refined and worthy human beings down to the black sheep, the money-grabbers, sharks and criminals.
>
> In writing this account of a great cultural epoch, I would have preferred not to have to point out which among the men and women who helped to

create it were of Jewish descent. What they themselves would have wanted was to be accepted simply as Austrian poets, painters or composers. This was and still is a Utopian wish. For that reason one may do well to rouse the collective memory and stress the fact that it was due to a unique moment in history, to an unrepeatable symbiosis, that Vienna's great era came about. To profit from it in retrospect, as the city now does, would seem to oblige its inhabitants to pay more than lip-service to the memory of its banished or murdered Jews, and to respect those few left of the same faith who still trust them to the extent of once more living in their midst.[100]

Herbert Zipper came back to "their midst" in Austria only to conduct his Dachau Song ("Dachau Lied") and to show my wife and me the place of his childhood. He regards the city, like Rome, Venice, Athens, as an imperial museum and the story of its past glory and its fall useful only if man will stop repeating history long enough, instead, to learn from history.

After two days of sightseeing in Vienna, the three of us drove to Graz where Zipper began a series of rehearsals and interviews preparing for the September 23rd concert. The odyssey of the "Dachau Lied" and my own journey of writing this biography were coming fittingly to a full cadence in Austria where 50 years earlier Zipper was arrested and sent off to Dachau. Originally Zipper had been invited to conduct the "Dachau Lied" at a 50-year memorial of the Anschluss planned for the Vienna State Opera in March 1988. Apprehensive of this invitation given the enthusiastic embracing of Hitler when he marched upon Austria in 1938, Zipper replied asking who and what was to be 'memorialized'? Who was to be present? It was rumored that Kurt Waldheim was planning to attend and this was unacceptable to Zipper as to others. The March event was fraught with such problems and Zipper finally declined to attend. But from this exchange came a second invitation: to conduct a revised and expanded orchestration, by Zipper, of the "Dachau Lied" as the opening piece at the 1988 Autumn Festival in Graz, the Steirischer Herbst, '88."

The concert in Graz, was one of those magical events, where disparate but related forces converge to create a special vitality and drama. Young reporters brought a heightened awareness that this premier of a 50 year-old prison camp song, conducted by its composer, was a rare opportunity to look back, to experience some of the pain of Dachau, and to remember some of the history. For three days prior to the concert the reporters interviewed Zipper building an increasing anticipation for the concert. The opening concert itself was built upon a theme: "Schuld and Unschuld der Kunst/the guilt and innocence of art." And in his introduction to the concert program, festival director Peter Vujica set a high tone, writing: "Guilty are those who demand forgiveness and expiation from art for what they once committed themselves... Great and innocent is all art that depicts and says what will or could be tomorrow." Present in the audience was the 90-year-old sister of Zipper's friend from his Vienna days, composer Hans Gal. Hans Gal had died on October 3, 1987. His sister 89-years old, Erna, who has resided in London since 1939 when she fled the Nazis, read that Zipper was to return to Austria for this concert and so she made the trek for a personal reunion with her old friend. She had seen Herbert the day he returned to Vienna from Buchenwald in 1939 and recalled how shocked she was to see him. "He looked," she said, "like death warmed up." Finally, it was important for Zipper to have two friends, my wife and me, journey with him to his homeland for the concert. These forces, combined with Zipper's own memories of the times spent in Dachau, the burial in Buchenwald of his friend Jura Soyfer (after whom Zipper learned only on this trip, a theatre has been named in Vienna); the chance to conduct and hear in person for the first time the piece he and Jura Soyfer wrote just before being transferred from Dachau — the song prisoners in Dachau would secretly sing to themselves but which Zipper himself never heard them perform... these were all added ingredients to give the concert the kind of intensity and meaning the song and its history truly warrant.

The concert was held on Friday, September 23, at 4:00 in the afternoon in an open-air amphitheatre high in the cliffs over-looking the Gothic, Renaissance and Classic Architecture of Graz, formerly a metropolis of the Holy Roman Empire. The choice of this outdoor theatre for this world premier of the "Dachau Lied" was particularly appropriate in that it had once been a prison in a large fortress in pre-Napoleonic Austria. Napoleon, enraged by Austrian resistance to his plans of conquest, conquered the fortress and destroyed the prison leaving only the two huge walls which framed the 1988 concert. The open-air brick walls lined with ivy called to mind another Zipper concert, the celebration of Manila's liberation in 1945 held in the bombed out, open-air church of Santa Cruz.

The concert began with a gray sky outlining the two parallel brick walls, partially covered by a canopy. The sky lay behind the stage like an added set. Then during the singing of the Lied and the ensuing public interview with Zipper, the late afternoon sun began to shine through the gray on its journey to setting as if to say that while darkness and death may be the final reality, the light insists on having its moment. This concert was such a moment.

The "Dachau Lied" was sung by a male chorus of 30 vigorous young men, non-professionals recruited from local Styrian villages, all united by their love of music and the thrill of performing in a world premier.

Accompanied by 15 guitars, 3 celli, 2 double basses, and 2 percussionists, the song begins with a march-like percussion ostinato. The combination of guitars, celli and basses along with the snare drum ostinato unite to produce a powerful Brechtian sound appropriate to the bitter beauty of making song in the midst of death. The militaristic drum cadence suggests impending death but over this emerges the male voices, noble and proud in their celebration of defiance and of the superiority of real men to barbarians. Beginning in a minor key, the song moves to a major key in the final refrain, symbolizing the ultimate triumph of the human spirit:

> But we all learned the motto of Dachau to heed
> And became as hardened as stone
> Stay humane, Dachau mate,
> Be a man, Dachau mate,
> And work as hard as you can, Dachau mate,
> For work leads to freedom alone!

Witnessing this 84 year-old survivor being honored and conducting his own composition written during one of humanity's most shameful and darkest times was more than just thrilling; it was an affirmation of man's creativity. The Third Reich has left nothing of value behind. Only the bones of millions of innocent human beings and the ashes of Hitler and his grisly gang litter Germany and Europe. There remain no lasting Third Reich achievements, no monuments, no contributions to political thought, no works of art to benefit mankind. What does remain are the works of Nazi victims, the works of art which give truth to the Nazi lies, a diary of an Anne Frank, an Elie Wiesel novel, a "Dachau Lied," which proclaim that in the final assessment hatred destroys itself and its worshippers, while the victims of hate, the creative spirits of this world ultimately triumph. Dachau has become synonymous with evil and hatred. Herbert Zipper did in his hour of horror and pain what men of courage and goodwill must do: to make song out of Dachau.

Endnotes

1. Translation by Herbert Zipper and Paul Cummins.
2. Berkley, George, *Vienna and Its Jews*, p. 367.
3. Berkley, p. 29.
4. Berkley, p. 30.
5. Berkley, p. 33.
6. Berkley, p. 32.
7. Berkley, p. 54.
8. Berkley, p. 55.
9. Lansdale, Maria Honor, *Vienna and the Viennese*, pgs. 14-15.
10. Zeman, Zab, *Twilight of the Hapsburgs*, p. 64.
11. Esterhazy, Christa, *Vienna*, p. 37.
12. Morton, *Thunder at Twilight*, p. 12.
13. Masur, *Prophets of Yesterday*, p. 3.
14. Schorske, Carl, *Fin-de-siècle Vienna*, p. 31.
15. Zweig, *The World of Yesterday*, p. 213.
16. Dubrovic, *Embezzled History*, p. 23.
17. Taylor, *The Hapsburg Monarchy*, p. 241.
18. Marek, *The Eagles Die*, pp. 465-66.
19. Szeps, Berta, *My Life and History*, p. 226.
20. Szeps, p. 249.
21. Vergo, *Art in Vienna*, p. 237.
22. Szeps, p. 272.
23. Quote of Oskar Kokoschka, as quoted in Kallir, Jane, *Austria's Expressionism*, p. 34.

24. Kallir, p. 35.

25. Whitford, *Egon Schiele*, pp. 35-36.

26. Schweitzer, *Goethe: Two Addresses*, pp. 56-57.

27. as quoted in Szeps, Berta, p. 315.

28. Canetti, Elias, *The Day of the Eyes*, pp. 248 - 249.

29. Canetti, p. 289

30. Joseph Gregor as quoted in: Jarka, Horst, *The Legacy of Jura Soyfer*, p. 21.

31. Jarka, pgs. 23-24.

32. Jarka, p. 24.

33. Jarka, pgs. 26-27.

34. Jarka, pg. 23.

35. as quoted in: Clare, *Last Waltz in Vienna*, pgs. 176-177.

36. Werfel, Franz, *Cella*, pp. 111-112.

37. Clare, George, pgs. 176-177.

38. as quoted in: Levin, Nora, *The Holocaust*, p. 98.

39. Gilbert, Martin, *The Holocaust*, p. 59.

40. Shirer, William L., *The Nightmare Years*, p. 317.

41. Lenhoff, Eugene, *The Last Five Hours of Austria*, pgs. 261-262.

42. Segev, Tom, *Soldiers of Evil*, pgs. 22-23.

43. Berben, Paul, *Dachau*, pgs. 60-61.

44. Translation by Herbert Zipper and Paul Cummins.

45. Frankl, Victor, *Man's Search for Meaning*, p. 61.

46. Bettleheim, *The Informed Heart*, p. 167.

47. From a letter written to Zipper by Ebner in November of 1989.

48. The "Dachau Lied" has been reprinted in: Jarka, Horst, *The Legacy of Jura Soyfer*, and in: *Leider Aus Den Faschistichen Konzentrations-Lagern*. The German words to the song are given in the appendix to this book. Also, see John Lehmann's memoirs *In My Own Time* and his poems of 1930-1951 published as *The Age of The Dragon*. In both works, Lehmann's translation (originally published by Lehmann in *Folios of New*

Writing under the pseudonym of Georg Anders) of Jura Soyfer's words to the "Dachau Lied." Lehmann's translation is printed here:

Pitiless the barbed wire dealing
Death, that round our prison runs,
And a sky that knows no feeling
Sends us ice and burning suns;
Lost to us the world of laughter,
Lost our homes, our loves, our all;
Through the dawn our thousands muster,
To their work in silence fall.

> But the slogan of Dachau is burnt on our brains
> And unyielding as steel we shall be;
> Are we men, brother? Then we'll be men when they've done,
> Work on, we'll go through with the task we've begun,
> For work, brother, work makes us free.

Haunted by the gun mouths turning
All our days and nights are spent;
Toil is ours — the way we're learning
Harder than we ever dreamt;
Weeks and months we cease to reckon
Pass, and some forget the years,
And so many men are broken
And their faces changed with fears.

> But the slogan of Dachau is burnt on our brains, etc.

Heave the stone and drag the truck,
Let no load's oppression show,
In your days of youth and luck
You thought lightly; now you know.
Plunge your spade in earth and shovel
Pity where heart cannot feel,
Purged in your own sweat and trouble
Be yourself like stone and steel.

> For the slogan of Dachau is burnt on our brains, etc.

One day sirens will be shrieking
One more roll-call, but the last.
And the stations we'll be seeking —
> Outside, brother, prison past!
Bright the eyes of Freedom burning,
Worlds to build with joy and zest
And the work begun that morning,
Yes, that work will be our best!

For the slogan of Dachau is burnt on our brains, etc.

There have been several recordings of the Dachau Lied. A 1988, fifty-year anniversary of the song was performed in Graz, Austria, and a video was made by the Austrian radio and T.V. for the Steirischer Herbst. Also, a record of songs and poems (including the Dachau Lied) of Jura Soyfer was produced in 1981 entitled, "Verdrangte Jahre: Osterreich Zwischen den Kriegen," performed by Die Schmetterlinge and produced in Austria at Almuttergasse 5/6, 1090 Wien.

49. Photostat from the Museum of Dachau.

50. Goethe as translated by Herbert Zipper and Paul Cummins, (4-28-90).

> Above all the summits
> The bliss of peace,
> In the tree tops
> You can scarcely feel
> A breath stirring.
> The little forest birds
> Are silent. Wait!
> Soon you too
> Shall rest.

51. Poller, Walter, *Medical Block Buchenwald*, p. 214.

52. As taken from Rosenberg & Myers, *Echoes from the Holocaust*, p. 377:

This table shows the numerical expansion and the death rate of the concentration camp Buchenwald during the years 1937-45. It was compiled from several lists, given in *Nazi Conspiracy*, vol. 4, pp. 800 ff.

Year	Arrivals	Camp Strength		Deceased [b]	Suicides
		High	Low		
1937	2,912	2,561	929	48	—
1938	20,122 [a]	18,105	2,633	771	11
1939	9,553	12,775	5,392	1,235	3
1940	2,525	10,956	7,383	1,772	11
1941	5,896	7,911	6,785	1,522	17
1942	14,111 [c]	10,075	7,601	2,898	3
1943	42,172	37,319	11,275 [d]	3,516	2
1944	97,866	84,505	41,240	8,644	46
1945	42,823 [e]	86,232	21,000 [f]	13,056	16

[a] These were of course mostly Jews.
[b] The total of deceased is certainly higher and is estimate at 50,000.
[c] This figure shows the influx from the Eastern Occupied Territories.

d The difference between arrivals and camp strength, or between High and Low no longer indicates liberations but transports to other camps or to extermination camps.
e Only for the first three months of 1945.
f Camp strength at moment of liberation.

53. as quoted in: Des Pres, Terrence, *The Survivors*, p. 64.

54. Des Pres, p. 65.

55. Des Pres, p. 66.

56. Poller, p. 63.

57. Bettelheim, Bruno, *Surviving and Other Essays*, pgs. 64-66.

58. Kogon, Eugen, *The Theory and Practice of Hell*, p. 80.

59. Gedye, G.E.R., *Betrayal in Central Europe*, p. 334.

60. Gedye, pp. 334-5.

61. Gilbert, *The Holocaust*, pgs. 62.63.

62. Poliakov, Leon, *Harvest of Hate*, pgs. 27-28.

63. Hoffmann, Paul, *The Viennese*, p. 258.

64. In writing of his career as a dramatist, Leon Askin (*Quietude and Quest*, p. 153) writes:

> Jura Soyfer left an indelible imprint on the era of the "little art theatres" of Vienna during the period 1936-1938. A leading newspaper carried the judgment of its critic: "Jest, satire and deeper meaning were the best that one could buy in Vienna in those days — and at bargain-basement prices." After World War II a group of us who had escaped or survived the Holocaust arranged an evening in memory of Jura Soyfer. We called the presentation "The Statue of Liberty for Two Bits," (*Die Freiheitsstatue um 5 Schlling*), sponsored by a coalition of Austrian-American groups. Soyfer had been one of Austria's leading candidates to continue the literary legacy of the late nineteenth- and early twentieth-century Austrian literary traditions and he, like so many of the candidates, was dead and gone.

65. Jarka, pgs. 348-350.

66. Hoyt, Edwin P., *Hitler's War*, p. 74.

67. Herbert Zipper's official Release (photostat) from Buchenwald, February 20, 1939.

68. The Hungarian diplomat's sentiment, as well as that of Hans Knappertsbusch, was within a respected tradition of epithets which dated back to Goethe, and specifically to Goethe's play *Goetz von Berlichingen*. Goetz (1480-1562) lost his right hand in battle in 1504, and his hand was replaced with an iron fist. Thus he is known as Goetz von

Berlichingen "with the Iron Hand." In Goethe's play it occurs that the Emperor's forces have surrounded Goetz's castle. A messenger of the imperial forces calls to Goetz who is standing at an open window, demanding his surrender. Goetz replies:

"Sag deinem Hauptman: vor Ihro Kaiserlichen Majestat hab ich,
    Wie immer, schuldigen Respekt. Er aber, sag's ihm,
        er Kann mich im Arsch lecken."

which translates as: "tell your captain: as always I have due respect for his imperial majesty, however, tell your captain that, he can lick my ass."

Ever since then in the German speaking world a "Goetz Zitat" (Goetz quote) is generally understood to refer to the specific insult that Goetz hurled back at the messenger and the expression "Goetz Zitat" is used by all who shun outright vulgarity.

69. Nash, Grace, *That We Might Live*, pgs. 97-98.

70. Nash, p. 35.

71. Craig, William, *The Fall of Japan*, pp. 266-67.

72. Manchester, William, *American Caesar*, pp. 482-83.

73. Toland, John, *The Rising Sun*, p. 765.

74. Manchester, p. 483.

75. Buss, Claude, "Report from Manila," *Fortune*, July 1945.

76. Halsema is currently completing a biography of his father, the former Mayor of Baguio, as well as writing his own memoirs.

77. Sharpe, George, *Brothers Beyond Blood*, p. 212.

78. Dunn, William J., *Pacific Microphone*, pp. 332-34.

79. Cowley, Malcolm, *Blue Juanita: A Life*.

80. Shi, David, *Matthew Josephson*, p. 129.

81. Osborn, Fairfield, *The Limits of the Earth*, p. 225.

82. Osborn, p. 226.

83. Rampersand, Arnold, *The Life of Langston Hughes, II*, p. 184.

84. Rampersand, pgs. 185-86.

85. Polikoff, Barbara, *An Affectionate Chronicle*, pgs. 17-19.

86. Polikoff, pgs. 17-19.

87. From the Program Notes of Herbert Zipper's 1979 performance of *Carmen*.

88. Peterson, Susan, *The Living Tradition of Maria Martinez*.

89. Seagrave, Sterling, *The Soong Dynasty*, p. 417.

90. White, Theodore, *In Search of History*, p. 277.

91. Letter to Paul Cummins, June 8, 1988.

92. Tu Wei-Ming, "Iconoclasm, Holistic Vision, and Patient Watchfulness," *Daedalus*, Vol. 116, No. 2, Spring 1987, p. 78. The quote is taken from William Theodore de Barry, et al, comp., *Sources of Chinese Tradition*, 2 Vols. (New York: Columbia University Press, 1964), Vol. 2, p. 6.

93. Letter to Paul Cummins, May 19, 1988.

94. as quoted in Mathews, Jay, "Edgar Snow Told You So," *The Washington Monthly*, July/Aug, 1989, p. 54.

95. Spiel, Hilde, as quoted in *Gustav Mahler in Vienna*, p. 42.

96. Spiel, Hilde, *Vienna's Golden Autumn*, pgs. 25-26.

97. Translated by Herbert Zipper from: Dubrovic, Milan, *Veruntreute Geschichte* (Embezzled History).

98. Zweig, Stefan, *The World of Yesterday*, p. 23.

99. Zweig, p. 21.

100. Spiel, Hilde, *Vienna's Golden Autumn*, p. 236.

References

The following categories of books are not intended to be a comprehensive bibliography. It is a personal collection of books used as references for this biography. It may, nevertheless, be useful to some readers as suggestions for further reading. The books will be donated to a Herbert Zipper Library Collection at Crossroads School, Santa Monica, CA, and will be available to those interested.

I. General Histories of Europe and the Modern World

Anderson, Eugene. *Modern Europe in World Perspective: 1914 to the Present.* New York: Rinehart and Company, 1958.

Armstrong, Hamilton Fish. *Memoirs: Peace and Counter Peace from Wilson to Hitler.* New York: Harper & Row, 1971.

Buell, Raymond. *Europe: A History of Ten Years.* Chatauqua, New York: The Chatauqua Press, 1928.

Chambers, Frank P., Harris and Bayley. *This Age of Conflict.* New York: Harcourt Brace and Company, 1950.

Craig, Gordon A. *Europe Since 1914.* Hinsdale, Illinois: The Dryden Press, 1972.

Gay, Peter and R.K. Webb. *Modern Europe.* New York: Harper & Row, 1973.

Gedye, G.E.R. *Betrayal in Central Europe: Austrian and Czechoslovakia.* New York: Harper and Row, 1939.

Goldstein, Robert. *The Road Between The Wars 1918-1941.* New York: Fawcett Crest, 1978.

Grunwald, Max. *History of Jews in Vienna.* Philadelphia: Jewish Publication Society of America, 1936.

Hale, Oron J. *The Great Illusion: 1900-1914.* New York: Harper & Row, 1971.

Holborn, Hugo. *The Political Collapse of Europe.* New York: Alfred A. Knopf, 1955.

Langsam, Walter C. *The World Since 1914.* New York: The Mac Millan Co., 1936.

Masur, Gerhard. *Prophets of Yesterday.* New York: Harper and Row, 1961.

Seton-Watson, Hugh & Christopher. *The Making of A New Europe.* Seattle: University of Washington Press, 1981.

Sforza, Count Carlo. *Makers of Modern Europe: Portraits and Personal Impressions and Recollections.* Indianapolis: The Bobbs Merrill Co., 1930.

Sontag, Raymond J. *A Broken World: 1919-1939.* New York: Harper & Row, 1971.

Taylor, A.J.P. *The Habsburg Monarchy.* New York: Penguin Books, 1948.

_____. *Europe: Grandeur and Decline.* Penguin Books, First Published in 1950.

_____. *From Sarajevo to Potsdam.* London: Thames and Hudson, 1965.

Taylor, Edmond. *The Fall of Dynasties.* New York: Doubleday & Co., 1963.

Thomas, Hugh. *An Unfinished History of the World.* London: Kamish Hamilton, 1979.

Tuchman, Barbara. *The Proud Tower.* New York: Bantam Books, 1967.

Van Sittart, Peter. *Voices: 1870-1914.* New York: Avon Books, 1984.

II. Austria

Askin, Leon & C. Melvin Davidson. *Quietude and Quest.* Riverside, Calif.: Ariadne Press, 1989.

Asprey, Robert. *The Panther's Feast.* Carroll & Graf Publishers, 1959.

Barea, Ilsa. *Vienna.* New York: Alfred A. Knopf, 1966.

Beller, Steven. *Vienna and The Jews, 1867-1938.* Cambridge: Cambridge University Press, 1989.

Berczeller, Richard. *Time Was: A Memoir.* New York: Viking Press, 1971.

Berkley, George. *Vienna and Its Jews.* Cambridge, Mass.: ABT Books, 1988.

Bettelheim, Bruno. *Freud's Vienna and Other Essays.* New York: Alfred A. Knopf, 1990.

Bourgoing, Jean de., ed. *The Incredible Friendship: The Letters of Emperor Franz Joseph to Katharina Schatt.* New York: State Univ. of N.Y., 1966.

Braunthal, Julius. *Vienna: The Image of a City in Decline.* New York, MacMillian, 1938.

Broch, Hermann. *Hugo von Hofmannsthal and His Time: The European Imagination 1860-1920.* Chicago: Univ. of Chicago Press, 1984.

Bukey, Evan Burr. *Hitler's Hometown: Linz, Austria; 1980-1945.* Bloomington: Indian University Press, 1986.

Busch, Wilhelm, 1832-1908. Reprint of Jubilee Edition. New York: Frederich Ungar Publishing Co., (N.D.).

Busch, Wilhelm. *Max and Moritz* (ed. by Arthur H. Klein). New York: Dover Books, 1962.

Canetti, Elias. *The Play of the Eyes.* New York: Farrar, Straus and Giroux, 1986.

_____. *The Torch in My Ear.* New York: Farrar, Straus and Giroux, 1982.

Cassels, Lavender. *The Archduke and the Assassin.* New York: Dorset Press, 1984.

Christensen, William Langseth. *A Design for Living: Vienna in The Twenties.* New York: Viking Penguin, 1987.

Clare, George. *Last Waltz in Vienna*. New York: Holt, Rinehart and Winston, 1980.

Crankshaw, Edward. *Vienna: The Image of a City in Decline*. New York, Macmillan, 1938.

_____. *The Fall of the House of Habsburg*. New York: The Viking PRess, 1963.

Day, Ingeborg. *Ghost Waltz: A Memoir*. New York: Viking Press, 1980.

Drucker, Peter F. *Adventures of a Bystander*. New York: Harper & Row, 1978.

Edmondson, C. Earl. *The Heimwehr and Austrian Politics: 1918-1936*. Athens, Georgia: The University of Georgia Press, 1978.

Emrich, Wilhelm. *The Literary Revolution and Modern Society and Other Essays*. New York: Frederick Ungar Pub. Co., 1971.

Field, Frank. *The Last Days of Mankind: Karl Kraus*. London: Macmillan, 1967; New York: St. Martins Press, 1967.

Fraenkel, Josef ed. *The Jews of Austria*. London: Valentine Mitchell, 1967.

Freidenreich, Harriet Pass. *Jewish Politics in Vienna, 1918-1938*. Bloomington: University of Indiana Press, 1991.

Fuchs, Martin. *Showdown in Vienna: The Death of Austria*. New York: G.P. Putnam's Sons, 1939.

Gainham, Sarah. *The Habsburg Twilight*. New York: Atheneum Books, 1979.

Gay, Peter and R.K. Webb. *Modern Europe*. New York: Harper & Row, 1973.

_____. *Freud, Jews and Other Germans*. New York: Oxford University Press, 1978.

Gregor, Joseph. *Geschite Des Osterreichischen Theaters*, Vienna, Donauverlag, 1948.

Grunfeld, Frederic V. *Prophets Without Honor*. New York: McGraw-Hill, 1979.

Grunwald, Max. *History of Jews in Vienna*. Philadelphia: Jewish Publication Society of America, 1936.

Gulick, Charles A. *Austria: From Habsburg to Hitler, Vol. I&II*. Berkeley: Univ. of Calif. Press, 1948.

Haboeck, M. *Austria* (Trans. by Thomas H. Nash & Basil W. Tucker). Vienna: Fiba-Verlag, 1937.

Harding, Bertita. *Lost Waltz: A Story of Exile*. New York: Bobbs & Gerill Co., 1944.

Henderson, Sir Neville. *Failure of A Mission: Berlin 1937-1939*. New York: G.P. Putnam's Sons, 1940.

Hickman, Hannah. *Robert Musil and the Culture of Vienna*. La Salle, Illinois: Open Court Publishing Co., 1984.

Hoffman, Paul. *The Viennese: Splendor, Twilight and Exile*. New York: Doubleday, 1988.

Holborn, Hugo. *The Political Collapse of Europe*. New York: Alfred A. Knopf, 1955.

Hurlimann, Martin. *Vienna*. New York: The Viking Press, 1970.

Janetschek, Ottokar. *The Emperor Franz Joseph* (Trans. by H. S. Whitman). London: Werner Laurie, Ltd., 1953.

Janik, Allan and Toulmin, Stephen. *Wittgenstein's Vienna*. New York: Simon and Schuster, A Touchstone Book, 1973.

Jarka, Horst, ed. and trans. *The Legacy of Jura Soyfer, 1912 - 1939*. Montreal: Engendra Press, 1977.

Jaszi, Oscar, *The Dissolution of the Hapsburg Monarchy*. Chicago: University of Chicago Press, 1929.

Jelavich, Barbara. *Modern Austria: Empire and Republic 1800-1986*. Cambridge, England: Cambridge University Press, 1987.

Johnston, William M. *The Austrian Mind.* Berkeley and Los Angeles: The University of Calif. Press, 1972.

Jungk, Peter Stephan. *Franz Werfel,* (trans. Anselm Hollo). New York: Grove Weidenfeld, 1990.

Kann, Robert A. *A History of the Habsburg Empire 1526 - 1918.* Berkeley and Los Angeles: Univ. of Calif. Press, 1977.

Knoch, W.J.G. *Short History of Austria and the Habsburgs.* Vienna: Knoch's Informator Ed., 1960.

Kraus, Karl. *In These Great Times.* Edited by Harry Zohn. Manchester, England: Carcanet Press, 1976.

Lehne, Inge & Lonnie Johnson. *Vienna - The Past in the Present.* Wein: Osterreickischer Bundesverlag, 1985.

Listowel, Judith. *A Habsburg Tragedy: Crown Prince Rudolf.* New York: Dorset Press, 1978.

Luft, David S. *Robert Musil and the Crisis of European Culture 1880-1942.* Berkeley: University of California Press, 1980.

Maass, Walter B. *Assassination in Vienna.* New York: Charles Scribners Sons, 1972.

Macartney, C.A. *The House of Austria: The Later Phase 1790-1918.* Edinburgh: The University Press, 1978.

_____. *The Social Revolution in Austria.* Cambridge: University Press, 1926.

Magris, Claudio. *Danube* (trans. from Italian by Patrick Creagh). New York: Farrar, Strauss, Giroux, 1989.

Marek, George R. *The Eagles Die: Franz Joseph, Elizabeth and Their Austria.* New York: Harper and Row, 1974.

May, Arthur J. *The Habsburg Monarchy: 1867-1914.* New York: Norton, 1951.

McCagg, William O. Jr. *A History of Hapsburg Jews: 1670-1918.* Bloomington: Indiana University Press, 1989.

McGuinness, Brian. Ed. *Wittgenstein and His Times.* Chicago: Univ. of Chicago Press, 1982.

Mehring, Walter. *The Lost Library: The Autobiography of a Culture.* New York: The Bobbs Merril Co., 1951.

Mendelsohn, S. Felix. *The Jew Laughs.* Chicago: L.M. Stein Publisher, 1935.

Monk, Ray. *Ludwig Wittgenstein: The Duty of Genius.* New York: The Free Press, 1990.

Morton, Frederic. *A Nervous Splendor: Vienna 1888-89.* Boston: Little, Brown & Co., 1979.

_____. *Thunder at Twilight: Vienna 1913-14.* New York: Charles Scribner Sons, 1989.

Murad, Anatol. *Franz Joseph I of Austria and His Empire.* New York: Twayne Publishers, 1968.

Pauley, Bruce F. *The Hapsburg Legacy 1867-1939.* Malabar, Florida: Robert E. Krieger Pub. Co., 1981.

Pears, David. *Ludwig Wittgenstein.* New York: Penguin Books, 1970.

Pick, Robert. *The Last Days of Imperial Vienna.* New York: The Dial Press, 1976.

Pulzer, Peter G. J. *The Rise of Political Anti-Semitism in Germany and Austria.* New York: John Wiley & Sons, 1964.

Purtscher-Wydenbruck, Nora. *An Austrian Background.* London: Methuen & Co., 1932.

Rabinbach, Anson. *The Crisis of Austrian Socialism.* Chicago: The University of Chicago Press, 1983.

Rezzori, Gregor von. *The Snows of Yesteryear: Portraits for an Autobiography* (trans. by H. F. Broch de Rotherman). New York: Alfred A. Knopf, 1989.

Rickett, Richard. *A Brief Survey of Austrian History.* (1988 - 9th Edition) Goeorg Prachner Verlag, 1966.

Rozenblit, Marsha L. *The Jews of Vienna: 1867-1914.* Albany: State University of New York Press, 1983.

Seaman, L.C.B. *From Vienna to Versailles.* London: Methewn & Co., 1955.

Schnitzler, Arthur. *My Youth in Vienna* (trans. Catherine Hutter). New York: Holt Rinehart Winston, 1970.

Schuschnigg, Kurt Von. *The Brutal Takeover.* New York: Atheneum, 1971.

_____. *My Austria* (trans by John Segrue). New York: Alfred A. Knopf, 1938.

Schweitzer, Albert. *Goethe: Two Addresses by Albert Schweitzer* (Trans. by Charles R. Joy). Boston: The Beacon Press, 1948.

Schorske, Carl E. *Fin-de-Siecle Vienna.* New York: Random House-Vintage Books, 1981.

Sedgwick, Henry Dwight. *Vienna: The Biography of a Bygone City.* Indianapolis: Bobbs-Merrill, 1939.

Shepherd, Gordon Brook. *The Last Habsburg.* New York: Weybright and Talley, 1968.

_____. *The Austrian Odyssey.* London: Macmillan & Co., 1957.

_____. *The Anschluss.* New York: J. B. Lippincott Co., 1963.

Sked, Alan. *The Decline and Fall of the Hapsburg Empire 1815-1914.* London: Longman, 1989.

Spiel, Hilde. *Vienna's Golden Autumn 1866-1938.* New York: Weidenfeld and Nicolson, 1987.

Steed, Henry Wickham. *The Hapsburg Monarchy* (2nd ed., 1914 reprinted in U.S.). New York: Howard Fertig, 1969.

Sulzberger, C.L. *The Fall of Eagles*. New York: Crown Publishers, 1977.

Szeps, Berta. *My Life and History*. New York: Alfred A. Knopf, 1939.

Tapie, Victor L. *The Rise and Fall of the Hapsburg Monarchy*. New York: Praeger Publishers, 1971.

Taylor, A.J.P. *The Habsburg Monarchy*. New York: Penguin Books, 1948.

Thorne, Christopher. *The Approach of War 1938-19*. New York: St. Martins Press, 1967.

Timms, Edward. *Karl Kraus Apocalyptic Satirist*. New Haven: Yale University Press, 1986.

Waissenberger, Robert. *Vienna 1890-1920*. New York: Tabard Press, 1984.

Wechsberg, Joseph. *The Vienna I Knew: Memories of A European Childhood*. Garden City, New York: Doubleday and Co., 1979.

Weismann, Sigrid, ed. *Gustav Mahler in Vienna*. New York: Rizzoli International Publications, 1976.

Whitman, Sidney. *Austria*. New York: G. P. Putnam's Sons, 1901.

Wistrich, Robert S. *The Jews of Vienna in the Age of Franz Joseph*. New York: Oxford University Press, 1990.

Zanuso, Billa. *The Young Freud*. Oxford: Basil Blackwell, 1986.

Zemen, Zab. *Twilight of the Habsburgs*. New York: American Heritage Press, 1971.

Zohn, Harry, ed. & trans. *Karl Kraus: Half Truths and One-and-a-Half Truths*. Chicago: University of Chicago Press, 1990.

Zweig, Friderike. *Stefan Zweig*. New York: Thomas Y. Crowell, Co., 1946.

Zweig, Stefan. *The World of Yesterday*. New York: The Viking Press, 1943.

III. Holocaust Studies, Austria and World War II

Abzug, Robert H. *Inside the Vicious Heart.* New York/Oxford: Oxford University Press, 1985.

Alexander, Edward. *The Resonance of Dust.* Columbus: Ohio State University Press, 1979.

Arendt, Hannah. *Eichmann in Jerusalem.* New York: Viking Press, 1963.

Bauer, Yehuda & Nathan Rotenstreich, eds. *The Holocaust as Historical Experience.* New York: Holmes & Meier Publishers, 1981.

Berben, Paul. *Dachau: The Official History, 1933-1945.* London: Norfolk Press, 1975. (Originally published in Belgium, 1968.)

Bettelheim, Bruno. *Surviving and Other Essays.* New York: Alfred A. Knopf, 1979.

_____. *The Informed Heart.* Glencoe, Illinois: The Free Press, 1960.

Blatter, Janet & Sybil Milton. *Art of the Holocaust.* New York: The Rutledge Press, 1981.

Buber-Neumann, Margarete. *Milena* (Trans. by Ralph Manheim). New York: Seaver Books, 1988.

Chartock, Roselle & Jack Spencer. *The Holocaust Years: Society on Trial.* New York: Bantam Books, 1978.

Cholawski, Shalom. *Soldiers from the Ghetto.* San Diego: A.S. Barnes & Co., 1980.

Churchill, Winston S. *The Gathering Storm.* Houghton Mifflin Co., 1948.

Dawidowicz, Lucy S. *The War Against the Jews.* New York: Holt, Reinhart and Winston, 1975.

Des Pres, Terrence. *The Survivor.* New York: Oxford University Press, 1976.

Distel, Barbara & Ruth Jakusch, eds. *Concentration Camp Dachau 1933-1945.* Brussels: Museum of Dachau, 1978.

Distel, Barbara & Wolfgang, Benz, Dachau Review. *History of Nazi Concentratoin Camps, Studies, Reports, Documents, Vol.* I. Published by Museum of Dachau.

Edmondson, C. Earl. *The Heimwwehr and Austrian Politics 1918-1936.* Athens: The University of Georgia Press, 1978.

Eliach, Yaffa and Gurewitsch, Brana. *The Liberators.* Brooklyn, New York: Center for Holocaust Studies, 1981.

Elson, Robert T. *Prelude to War.* Alexandria, Virginia: World War II - Time Life Books, 1976-77.

Encyclopedia Judaica, *Holocaust.* Jerusalem: Keter Publishing House Ltd., 1974.

Ezrani, Sidra DeKoven. *By Words Alone: The Holocaust in Literature.* Chicago: Univ. of Chicago Press, 1980.

Evans, Richard J. *In Hitler's Shadow: West German Historians and the Attempt to Escape From the Nazi Past.* New York: Pantheon, 1989.

Feig, Konnilyn G. *Hitler's Death Camps.* New York: Holmes & Meier Publishers, 1979.

Fest, Joachim C. *Hitler.* New York: Harcourt Brace Johanovich, 1974.

Frankl, Viktor. *Man's Search for Meaning.* New York: Washington Square Press, 1963.

Friedlander, Albert H. *Out of the Whirlwind.* New York: Schocken Books, 1976.

Freidlander, Saul. *Reflections of Nazism.* New York: Avon Books, 1982.

Gilbert, Martin. *The Holocaust.* New York: Holt, Rinehart and Winston, 1985.

_____. *Atlas of Jewish History.* New York: Macmillan Pub. Co., 1977.

_____. *The Holocaust: Maps and Photographs.* New York: Farrar, Straus & Giroux, 1978.

_____. *Atlas of the Holocaust.* London: Michael Joseph Limited, 1982. (Reprinted, 1988, Pergamon Press, N.Y.

Grobman, Alex and Landes, Daniel, eds. *Genocide: Critical Issues of the Holocaust.* Los Angeles: The Simon Wisenthal Center, 1983.

Gunther, John. *Procession.* New York: Harper and Row, 1965.

Halperin, Irving. *Messengers From the Dead.* Philadelphia: The Westminster Press, 1970.

Heimler, Eugene. *Concentration Camp.* London: Corgi Books, 1959.

Hirschfeld, Gerhard, ed. *The Policies of Genocide.* London: Allen & Unwin, 1986.

Jenks, William A. *Vienna & the Young Hitler.* New York: Columbia University Press, 1960.

Jones, Sidney J. *Hitler in Vienna 1907-1913.* New York: Stein and Day Publishers, 1982.

Karas, Joza. *Music in Terezin.* New York: Beaufort Books, 1985.

Klein, Dennis B. & Judith Herschlag Muffs, eds. *The Holocaust in Books and Films* (International Center for Holocaust Studies: Anti-Defamation League of B'nai B'rith) New York: Hippocrene Books, 1978.

Kogon, Eugen. *The Theory and Practice of Hell.* New York: Farrar, Straus and Cudahy, 1950.

Krall, Hanna. *Shielding the Flame.* New York: Henry Holt & Co., 1977.

Laks, Szymon. *Music of Another World.* Evanston, Illinois: Northwestern University Press, 1989.

Laqueur, Walter & George L. Mosse, Editors. *International Fascism: 1920-1945.* New York: Harper Torchbooks, 1966.

Lehmann, John. *In My Own Time.* Boston: Little, Brown and Co., 1969.

Leitner, Isabella. *Fragments of Isabella.* New York: Laurel Books, 1978.

Leitner, Isabella with Irving A. Leitner. *Saving the Fragments*. New York: New American Library, 1985.

Lengyel, Olga. *Five Chimneys*. London: Panther Books, 1959.

Lennhoff, Eugene. *The Last Five Hours of Austria*. New York: Frederick A. Stokes Co., 1938.

Levi, Primo. *Survival in Auschwitz*. New York: The Orion Press, 1958.

_____. *The Drowned and the Saved*. New York: Summit Books, 1986.

Levin, Nora. *The Holocaust*. New York: Schoken Books, 1973.

Lewin, Rhoda ed. *Witnesses to the Holocaust: An Oral History*. Boston: Twayne Publishers, 1990.

Marrus, Michael R. *The Holocaust in History*. Hanover: University Press of New England, 1987.

Marx, Otto, Prisoner 346. *Dachau, 1933-1935*. Trans. by Harry J. Marx. New York: Vantage Press, 1987.

Mayer, Arno J. *Why Did the Heavens Not Darken*. New York: Pantheon Books, 1988.

Mermelstein, Mel. *By Bread Alone*. Huntington Beach, CA: Auschwitz Study Foundation Inc., 1979, 1981.

Molden, Fritz. *Exploding Star: A Young Austrian Against Hitler*. New York: William Morrow & Co., 1979.

Neuhausler, Johann Dr. *What Was It Like in the Concentration Camp of Dachau?* Munich: Trustees for the Movement of Atonement in the Concentration Camp at Dachau, 1960.

Payne, Robert. *The Life and Death of Adolf Hitler*. New York: Praeger Publishers, 1973.

_____. *Eyewitness*. New York: Doubleday & Co., 1972.

Poliakov, Leon. *Harvest of Hate*. Philadelphia: The Jewish Publication Society of America, 1954.

Poller, Walter. *Medical Block Buchenwald.* New York: Lyle Stuart, 1961.

Read, Anthony & David Fisher. *Kristallnacht: The Nazi Night of Terror.* New York: Random House, 1989.

Robertson, E.K. *Paul Schneider: The Pastor of Buchenwald.* London: SCM Press Ltd., 1956.

Rost, Nico. *Concentration Camp Dachau.* Brussels: Comite Internationale de Dachau, 7th Edition.

Rothchild, Sylvia, ed. *Voices from the Holocaust.* New York: New American Library, 1981.

Rousset, David. *The Other Kingdom* (Trans. Ramon Guthrie). New York: Reynal & Hitchcock, 1947.

Sable, Martin K. *Holocaust Studies: A Directory and Bibliography of Bibliographies.* Greenwood, Florida: The Penkeville Publishing Co., 1987.

Sattler, Stanislaw. *Prisoner of 68 Months: Buchenwald & Auschwitz.* Melbourne: Kelly Books, 1980.

Schoenberner, Gerhard. *The Yellow Star.* New York: Bantam Books, 1973.

Schuschnigg, Kurt Von. *Austrian Requiem.* (Trans. Franz von Hildebrand). New York: G.P. Putnam's Sons, 1946.

Segev, Tom. *Soldiers of Evil.* New York: McGraw-Hill, 1987.

Selzer, Michael. *Deliverance Day.* New York: J.B. Lippencott Co., 1978.

Shapell, Nathan. *Witness to the Truth.* New York: David McKay Co., 1974.

Shepherd, Godon Brook. *The Anschluss.* New York: J.B. Lippincott & Co., 1963.

_____. *Dollfuss.* London: Macmillan & Co., 1961.

Sheridon, R.K. *Kurt Von Schuschnigg.* London: The English Universities Press Ltd., 1942.

Shirer, William L. *The Nightmare Years: 1930-1940*. New York: Bantam Books, 1984.

Szajkowski. *An Illustrated Sourcebook on the Holocaust*. Vol. I, II, III, New York: Ktav Publishing House, Inc., 1979.

Thalman, Rita & Emmanuel Feinermann. *Crystal Night*. New York: Coward, McCann & Geoghegan, 1974.

Thorne, Christopher. *The Approach of War 1938-39*. New York: St. Martin's Press, 1967.

Toll, Nelly. *Without Surrender: Art of the Holocaust*. Philadelphia, PA: Running Press, 1978.

Unser Lied. London: Verlag Jugend Voran, 1944.

Vrba, Rudolf & Alan Bestic. *44070: The Conspiracy of the Twentieth Century*. Bellingham, Washington: Star and Cross Publishing House, 1989.

Lieder Aus Den Faschistischen Konzentrations-Lagern. Leipzig: Veb Friedrich Hofmeister, 1962. (Includes the Dachau Lied)

Wagner, Dieter & Tomkowitz, Gerhard. *Anschluss: The Week Hitler Siezed Vienna*, (trans. Geoffrey Strachan). New York: St. Martin's Press, 1971.

Weinstock, Eugene. *Beyond The Last Path*. New York: Boni & Gaer, 1947.

Wistrich, Robert. *Hitler's Apocalypse: Jews and The Nazi Legacy*. New York: St. Martins Press, 1985.

IV. Art: Fin De Siecle

Ammann, Gert. *Alfons Walde 1891-1958*. Innsbruck-Wien: Tyrolia Verlag, 1987.

Bisanz, Hans. *Vienna 1900*. Bristol, England: Artlines Editions, 1990.

Chipp, Herschel B. *Jugendstil & Expressionism in German Posters*. Berkeley: University of California, 1965.

Comini, Alessandra. *Egon Schiele*. New York: George Braziller, 1976.

_____. *The Fantastic Art of Vienna*. New York: Alfred A. Knopf, 1978.

Kallir, Jane. *Austria's Expressionism*. New York: Rizzoli, 1981.

_____. *Arnold Schoenberg's Vienna*. New York: Galerie St. Etienne, 1984.

Plaut, James S., Intro. *Oskar Kokoschka: A Retrospective Exhibition*. New York: Chanticleer Press, 1948.

Reinhold, Count Bethusy-Huc. *Homage to Kokoschka*. London: Victoria and Albert Museum, 1976.

Robert Gore Rifkind Foundation. *The Human Image in German Expressionist Art*. Berkeley: University Art Museum, 1981.

Sabarasky, Serge. *Kokoschka: Drawings and Watercolors*. New York: Rizzoli, 1986.

Sarmany-Parson, Ilona. *Gustav Klimt*. New York: Crown Publishers Inc., 1987.

Schiele, Egon. *I, Eternal Child*. New York: Grove Press, 1985.

Varnedoe, Kirk. *Vienna 1900: Art, Architecture and Design*. New York: The Museum of Modern Art, 1986.

Vergo, Peter. *Art in Vienna: 1898-1918*. Ithaca, New York: Cornell University Press, 1975.

Walde, Alfons 1891-1958. Catalog: Avktionhaus-Wolfoie Trigt Hassfurther, Wien, 1988.

Whitford, Frank. *Oskar Kokoschka: A Life*. New York: Atheneum, 1986.

_____. *Egon Schiele*. London: Thames and Hudson Ltd., 1986.

Wien Um 1900. Sezon Museum of Art. Tokyo: Fujisu Ag., 1989.

Willett, John. *Expressionism*. New York: World University Library (McGraw-Hill), 1970.

V. Music of Vienna

Blaukopf, Herta. Ed. (Trans. by Edmund Jeshcott) *Gustave Mahler, Richard Strauss: Correspondence 1888-1911*. Chicago: Univ. of Chicago Press, 1984.

Gal, Hans. *The Golden Age of Vienna*. London: Max Parrish & Co., 1948.

Gartenberg, Egon. *Vienna: Its Musical Heritage*. University Park: The Pennsylvania State University Press, 1968.

Grout, Donald Jay. *A History of Western Music (3rd Ed.)*. New York: W. W. Norton & Co., 1984.

_____. *A Short History of Opera (3rd Ed.)*. New York: Columbia University Press, 1988.

Hexworth, Peter. Ed. *Conversations with Klemperer*. London: Faber and Faber, 1985.

Hanslick, Eduard. *Vienna's Golden Years of Music: 1850-1900*. (Trans. and Edited by Henry Pleasants III). New York: Simon and Schuster, 1950.

Leinsdorf, Erich. *Cadenza: A Musical Career*. Boston: Houghton Mifflin Co., 1976.

Neighbor, Oliver, Paul Griffiths, and George Perle. *The New Second Viennese School*. New York: W. W. Norton & Co., 1980.

Slonimsky, Nicolas, ed. *Baker's Biographical Dictionary of Musicians (7th Ed.)*. New York: Schirmer Books, 1984.

Smith, Joan Allen. *Schoenberg and His Circle*. New York: Schirmer Books, 1986.

Vaughn, Roger. *Herbert von Karajan*. New York: W. W. Norton & Co., 1986.

Walter, Bruno. *Theme and Variations: An Autobiography*. New York: Alfred A. Knopt, 1946.

Wilhelm, Kurt. *Richard Strauss: An Intimate Portrait*. New York: Rizzoli, 1989.

VI. The Pacific

Arthur, Anthony. *Deliverance at Los Banos.* New York: St. Martin's Press, 1985.

Breuer, William B. *Retaking the Philippines.* New York: St. Martins Press, 1986.

Buss, Claude. *The Far East.* New York: Macmillan Co., 1955.

Costello, John. *The Pacific War: 1941-45.* New York: Quill Edition, 1981.

Craig, William. *The Fall of Japan.* New York: Dell Publishing Co., 1968.

Dower, John W. *War Without Mercy.* New York: Pantheon Books, 1986.

Dunn, William J. *Pacific Microphone.* College Station: Texas A&M University Press, 1988.

Falk, Sidney. *Liberation of the Philippines.* New York: Ballantine Books, 1971.

Hamilton, John Maxwell. *Edgar Snow.* Bloomington: Indiana Univ. Press, 1988.

Karnow, Stanley. *In Our Image: America's Empire in the Philippines.* New York: Random House, 1984.

Lucas, Celia. *Prisoners of Santo Thomas.* London: Leo Cooper Ltd., 1975.

Manchester, William. *American Caesar: Douglas MacArthur 1880-1964.* New York: Dell Publishing Co., 1978.

Morison, Samuel Eliot. *The Liberation of the Philippines.* (Volume XIII, History of the United States Naval Operations in World War II). Boston: Little, Brown Co., 1969.

Nash, Grace. *That We Might Live.* Scottsdale, Arizona: Shano Publishers, 1984.

Sharpe, George. *Brothers Beyond Blood.* Austin, Texas: Diamond Books, 1989.

Spector, Ronald H. *Eagle Against the Sun.* New York: The Free Press (MacMillan), 1985.

Steinberg, Rafael. *Return to the Philippines.* New York: Time Life Books, Inc., 1979.

Sulzberger, C.L. *World War II.* Boston: Houghton Mifflin Co., 1966.

Toland, John. *The Rising Sun.* New York: Random House, 1970.

VII. The USA Years

Bassett, Richard. *Waldheim and Austria.* New York: Penguin Books, 1988.

Berry, Faith. *Langston Hughes: Before and Beyond Harlem.* Westport, Connecticut: Lawrence HIll & Co., 1983.

Castro, Josve de. *The Geography of Hunger.* Boston: Little, Brown & Co., 1952.

Cowley, Malcolm. *The View From 80.* New York: Viking Press, 1980.

_____. *Blue Juanita.* New York: Vikingg Penguin Books, 1968.

Cummins, Paul F. *Poems.* Published in *Timeless Shoes* (Alex Steward, Ed.). Chula Vista, CA: The New Horizons Poets, 1989.

Davenport, Marcia. *Too Strong for Fantasy.* New York: Charles Scribner's Sons, 1967.

Des Pres, Terrence. *Writing Into the World: Essays 1973-1987.* New York: Viking Penguin, 1991.

Dubrovic, Milan. *Veruntreute Geschichte* (Embezzled History): *The Viennese Salons and Literary Cafes.* Frankfurt: Fishertaschenbuck Verlag, 1987.

Esterhazy, Christa. *Vienna.* New York: A.S. Barnes and Co., 1966.

Fermi, Laura. *Illustrious Immigrants.* Chicago: The University of Chicago Press, 1971.

Friedrich, Otto. *City of Nets.* New York: Harper and Row, 1986.

Gay, Peter. *Freud: A Life for Our Time.* New York: W. W. Morton & Co., 1988.

Goldman, Eric F. *The Crucial Decade - And After: America, 1945-1960.* New York: Vintage Books, 1961.

Hazzard, Shirley. *Countenance of Truth: The United Nations and The Waldheim Case.* New York: Viking Press, 1989.

Heilbut, Anthony. *Exiled in Paradise.* Boston: Beacon Press, 1983.

Herzstein, Robert Edwin. *Waldheim: The Missing Years.* New York: Paragon House, 1989.

Hughes, Langston. *The Langston Hughes Reader.* New York: George Braziller, Inc., 1958.

Jezic, Diane Peacock. *The Musical Migration and Ernst Toch.* Ames, Iowa: Iowa State University Press, 1989.

Josephson, Matthew. *The Money Lords.* New York: Weybright and Talley, 1972.

Kennedy, Paul. *The Rise and Fall of the Great Powers.* New York: Random House, 1987.

Lewis, Flora, *Europe.* New York: Simon and Schuster Inc., 1987.

Miller, Alice. *For Your Own Good.* New York: Farrar, Straus & Giroux, 1983.

Osborn, Fairfield. *The Limits of the Earth.* Boston: Little, Brown and Co., 1953.

_____. *Our Plundered Planet.* Boston: Little, Brown and Co., 1948.

Peterson, Susan. *The Living Tradition of Maria Martinez.* New York: Harper and Row, 1977.

Polikoff, Barbara. *An Affectionate Chronicle.* The Music Center of the North Shore, Winnetka, Illinois, 1982.

Rampersand, Arnold. *The Life of Langston Hughes, Vol. II: 1941-1967.* New York: Oxford Univ. Press, 1988.

Rockefeller, David Jr., Chair. *Coming to Our Senses: The Significance of the Arts for American Education.* New York: McGraw-Hill Book Co., 1977.

The JDR 3rd Fund. *The JDR 3rd Fund and Asia, 1963-1975.* The JDR 3rd Fund: 50 Rockefeller Plaza, New York, 10020.

Rosenzweig, Luc & Bernard Cohen. *Waldheim.* New York: Adama Books, 1987.

Schwartz, Hilel. *Century's End.* New York: Doubleday, 1990.

Schweitzer, Albert. *Out of My Life and Thought.* New York: Henry Holt & Co., 1949.

Seagrave, Sterling. *The Marcos Dynasty.* New York: Harper & Row, 1988.

Shi, David E. *Matthew Josephson: Bourgeois Bohemian.* New Haven: Yale University Press, 1981.

Smalley, Webster, ed. *Five Plays by Langston Hughes.* Bloomington: University of Indiana Press, 1963.

Spalding, Henry D. *Joys of Jewish Humor.* New York: Jonathan David Publishers, Inc., 1985.

Spaulding, E. Wilder. *The Quiet Invaders: The Story of the Austrian Impact Upon America.* Vienna: Osterreichischer Bundesverlag fur Unterricht, Wissenshaft und Kunst (distributedin U.S. by Frederick Ungar Pub. Co.), 1968.

Taylor, John Russell. *Strangers in Paradise.* New York: Holt, Reinhart and Winston, 1983.

Zipper, Herbert. *Collected Speeches and Projects* (unpublished). Available by request from Herbert Zipper or Paul Cummins, (c/o Crossroads School, 1714-21st Street, Santa Monica, CA 90404).

VIII. China

Binyan, Liu. *Tell The World* (Trans. by Henry L. Epstein). New York: Pantheon Books, 1989.

Clark, James I. *China*. Evanston, Illinois: McDougal, Littell and Co., 1976.

Hsia, C.T. Ed. *Twentieth Century Chinese Stories*. New York: Columbia University Press, 1971.

Hsu, Immanuel C.Y. *The Rise of Modern China*. London: Oxford University Press, 1970.

Leys, Simon. *The Burning Forest: Essays on Chinese Culture and Politics*. New York: Holt, Rinehart and Winston, 1983.

Morton, W. Scott. *China Its History and Culture*. New York: McGraw-Hill, 1980.

Schell, Orville. *To Get Rich Is Glorious: China in the 80's*. New York: New American Library, 1984.

Seagrave, Sterling. *The Soong Dynasty*. New York: Harper & Row, 1985.

Snow, Edgar. *Red Star Over China*. New York: Random House, 1938.

_____. *The Other Side of the River*. New York: Random House, 1961.

_____. *The Long Revolution*. London: Hutchinson, 1973.

Terrill, Ross. *The White-Boned Demon*. New York: William Morrow and Co., 1984.

Tuchman, Barbara. *Stillwell and the American Experience in China, 1911-1945*. New York: Macmillan Co., 1971.

White, Theodore. *China: The Roots of Madness: A Documentary*. New York: William Sloane Associates, Inc., 1946.

_____. *In Search of History*. New York: Warner Books, 1978.

_____ and Annalee Jacoby. *Thunder Out of China*. New York: William Sloane Associates, Inc., 1946.

IX. European Fiction, Poetry, Drama

Appelfeld, Aharon. *Badenheim 1939*. New York: Washington Square Press, 1980.

_____. *For Every Sin*. New York: Vintage International, 1989.

_____. *The Immortal Bartfuss*. New York: Harper and Row, 1988.

Becker, Jurek. *Jacob the Liar*. New York: Harcourt Brace, 1975.

_____. *Sleepless Days*. New York: Harcourt Brace Jovanovich, 1979.

Bettauer, Hugo. *The City Without Jews* (trans. by Salomea Neumark Brainin). New York: Bloch Publishing Co., 1926.

Bor, Josef. *The Terezin Requiem*. New York: Avon Books, 1963.

Deborn, Edith. *The House in Vienna*. New York: Alfred A. Knopf, 1960.

Demetz, Hana. *The House on Prague Street*. New York: St. Martins Press, 1970.

Djilas, Milovan. *The Leper and Other Stories*. New York: Harcourt, Brace & World, 1964.

Duffy, Bruce. *The World As I Found It*. New York: Ticknor & Fields, 1987.

Fenelon, Fania. *Playing for Time*. New York: Berkeley Books, 1977.

Fuchik, Julius. *Notes From The Gallows*. New York: New Century Publishers, 1948.

Goethe, Johann Wolfgang Von. *Faust*. (Many translations.)

_____. *Gotz von Berlichingen*. Trans. by Charles E. Passage. New York: Frederick Ungar Publishing Co., 1976.

Greene, Graham. *The Third Man*. New York: Viking Press, 1950.

Gunther, John. *The Lost City*. New York: Harper and Row, 1964.

Habe, Hans. *The Mission* (trans. by Michael Bullock). New York: Coward-McCann Inc., 1966.

Jelinek, Elfriede. *The Piano Teacher*. New York: Weidenfeld & Nicholson, 1988.

Julitte, Pierre. *Block 26: Sabotage at Buchenwald.* New York: Doubleday & Co., 1971.

Keneally, Thomas. *Schindler's Ark.* Kent: Hodder and Stoughton Ltd., 1982.

Kuznetsev, Anatoly. *Babi Yar.* New York: Dell Publishing Co., 1967.

Lehmann, John. *The Age of The Dragon: Poems 1930-1951.* London: Longmans, Green & Co., 195 .

Levi, Primo. *If Not Now, When.* New York: Penguin Books, 1985.

_____. *Moments of Reprieve.* London: Michael Joseph, 1986.

Lothar, Ernst. *Return to Vienna.* New York: Doubleday & Co., 1949.

Mendelssohn, Peter. *Across the Dark River.* New York: Doubleday, Doran & Co., 1940.

Malraux, Andre. *Days of Wrath.* New York: Random House, 1936.

Mark, Fritzi. *The Endless Peril.* London: Regency Press, N.D.

Miller, Arthur. *Playing For Time* (screenplay based on book by Fania Fenelon). New York: Bantam Books, 1981.

Oberski, Jona. *Childhood.* New York: New American Library, 1978.

Orgel, Doris. *The Devil in Vienna.* New York: The Dial Press, 1978.

Price, Reynods. "Waiting at Dachau" (short story in) *Permanent Errors.* New York: Ballantine Books, 1990.

Rezzori, Gregor von. *The Death of My Brother Abel* (trans. by Joachim Neugroshel). New York: Viking Elizabeth Sifton Books, 1985.

Richter, Hans Peter. *Friedrich.* (Orig. published, 1961) Trans. by Edite Kroll. New York: Holt, Rinehart & Winston, 1970.

Roth, Joseph. *The Radetzky March* (Trans. by Eva Tucker. Originally published in 1932). New York: Penguin Books, 1984.

———. *The Silent Prophet* (originally written 1923). Translated by David Le Vay. Woodstock, New York: The Overlook Press, 1989.

———. *Weights and Measures* (pub. 1937). Translated by David Le Vay. London: Peter Owen, 1982.

———. *Flight Without End* (pub. 1927). Translated by David Le Vay. London: Peter Owen, 1977.

———. *The Spider's Web and Zipper and His Father* (pub. 1923). Translated by John Hoare. Woodstock, NY: The Overlook Press, 1989.

Schnitzler, Arthur. *Vienna 1900*. New York: Penguin Books, 1973. (Four stories originally published in 1914, 1924, 1926 and 1929).

Schwart-Bart, Andre. *The Last of the Just*. New York: Atheneum, 1960.

Scott, Joanna. *Arrogance*. New York: Linden Press, 1990.

Steiner, Jean-Francois. *Treblinka*. New York: Simon Schuster, 1967.

Uhlman, Fred. *Reunion*. New York: Farrar, Strauss and Giroux, 1977.

Werfel, Franz. *Cella: Or The Survivors* (written circa 1939). New York: Henry Holt & Co., 1989.

Wiesel, Elie. *Night*. New York: Avon Books, 1958.

———. *The Gates of the Forest*. New York: Holt, Rinehart and Winston, 1966.

Wiesenthal, Simon. *The Sunflower*. New York: Schoken Books, 1976.

Zweig, Stefan. *The Royal Game*. New York: E.P. Dutton, Inc., 1983. (Originally written in 1922-1942.)

———. *Beware of Pity*. New York: New American Library, 1984. (Originally published in 1939.)

———. *Conflicts*. Trans. by Eden & Cedar Paul. New York: The Viking Press, 1927.

X. The Nature of Biography

Bowen, Catherine Drinker. *Adventures of A Biographer*. Boston: Little Brown and Co., 1946.

―――――. *Biography: The Craft and The Calling*. Boston: Little Brown & Co., 1969.

Brown, Francis, ed. *Highlights of Modern Literature: Essays from The New York Times Book Review*. New York: Mentor Books, 1954.

Edel, Leon, *Writing Lives*. New York: W.W. Norton & Co., 1984.

Ellmann, Richard. *Golden Codgers*. New York & London: Oxford University Press, 1973.

Empson, William. *Using Biography*. Cambridge, MA: Harvard Univ. Press, 1984.

Garraty, John A. *The Nature of the Biography*. New York: Alfred A. Knopf, 1957.

Gittings, Robert. *The Nature of Biography*. Seattle: Univ. of Wash. Press, 1978.

Homberger, Eric & John Charmley, Eds. *The Troubled Face of Biography*, New York: St. Martins Press, 1988.

Honan, Park. *Author's Lives*. New York: St. Martins Press, 1990.

Kendall, Paul Murray. *The Art of Biography*. New York: W.W. Norton & Co., 1985.

Keynes, John Maynard. *Essays and Sketches in Biography*. New York: Meridan Books, 1956.

Lomask, Milton. *The Biographer's Craft*. New York: Harper and Row, 1986.

Shelston, Alan. *Biography*. London: Metheun & Co., 1977.

Strachey, Lytton. *Biographical Essays*. New York: Harcourt Brace Jovanovich, Publishers, 1931-33. Reprint.

Zinsser, William, ed. *Extraordinary Lives.* New York: American Heritage, Inc., 1986.

XI. FILMS (An idiosyncratic and brief list of films relating to Zipper's life and times)

38 Vienna Before the Fall (1987) Produced by Michael von Wolkenstein; Directed by Wolfgang Gluck.

September 1939 (1961) Video Images, Sandy Hook, Ct.

Video of Cabarets (a recreation of 1930's Viennese cabaret, filmed in Vienna, available from Paul Cummins).

Crusade in the Pacific: MacArthur and the War at Sea, Vol. IV (1951) Embassy Home Entertainment, Los Angeles, CA.

XII. Musical Translations and Arrangements by Herbert Zipper (An Incomplete Listing)

In 1965 translated Ernst Toch's opera *The Last Tale* from English into German, but it has never been performed. (Published by Mills Music, Inc.)

Music Edited and Arranged by Herbert Zipper. (Numerous works published by Edward B. Marks Music Corporation, N.Y. and, Broude Brothers, New York.) A partial list includes:

Three tradtional Christmas carols, E.B. Marks Co. #2202, O Thou Joyful Day (O Sanctissima) Marks Co.; Dvorak, songs of Nature, pg. 63, Broude Brothers; Palestrina, Missa Iste Confessor, No. 16, E.B. Marks Co.; Schubert, Song of the Spirits Over the Waters, no. 41, E.B. Marks; Brahms, Three Sacred Choruses, pg. 37, Broude Brothers; Ravel, Pavane Pour Une Infante Defunte (for four-part mixes, chorus with piano), Broude Brothers; Faure, Pavane, Op. 50 (for orchestra and chorus), Broude Brothers; Rossini, "O Salutacis Nostia," Broude Brothers, Toch, *The Last Tale* (an opera translation from English to German by Herbert Zipper), Mills Music, Inc., 1965.

Collected Unpublished Works of Herbert Zipper: Available by writing to Herbert Zipper, Henry Holt, or Paul Cummins. See the following:

A. Musica seria

1. "Dance Music" to the play "The Emporer's new clothes" (1932) (Full orchestral score-last page missing-and piano reduction)

2. Two dances for Trudl Dubsky; piano score (1936); orchestral score missing

3. "Capricio"; piano solo (1926)

4. Comic opera "Bunbury", Libretto by Hans Weigel based on Oscar Wilde's "The Importance of being Ernest." (Three fourths of Act I, piano, vocal score; score in pencil, (particell) (1937).

5. Four fugues, (teenage work.)

B. Music for the "Kleinkunstbühnen" (Literary Cabaret)

1. "Das Lied vom Krieg" (The song of war) Lyrics by Hans Weigel (1936)

2. Music to the play, "Der ewige Danubius" (The eternal Danubius by Rudolph Weys (1934)

3. Pencil sketch of "Der Tag der Musikpflege" (The day of music cultivation) text by Hans Weigel (1935)

4. "The Newspaper Opera" by Rudolph Spitz (only the part for the second piano is extant) (1935)

5. Chansons to Lyrics by Erich Kästner, Lothar Metzel, Hans Weigel, Rudolph Weys. (1933-36)

C. Transcriptions

For orchestra, for two pianos, for piano solo of various classical composers. (1941-45)

D. Ensemble music for young people

1. Short pieces for various combinations of strings and wind instruments (1980-91)

2. Theme and variations, "Homage to my musical Ancestors" for piano-string quartet. (also version for orchestra) (1984)

3. Suite for four clarinets. (four movements) (1989)

4. Suite for violin-cello duo. (five monuments) (1990)

5. Foxtrot 85 for piano, clarinet and strings. (1985)

6. Short pieces for elementary school orchestras (1954-91)

7. Printed editions of choral music and own arrangements published by E. B. Marks, N. Y. and Broude Brothers, N. Y.

Index

Adler, Kurt Herbert 22, 218
Alger, Russell A. 155, 156, 161
Agens, Harriet 116
Altenberg, P. 4
Andersen, Hans Christian 16
Andis, Helli 114
Anschluss 4, 55, 69, 73, 104, 258, 261, 262, 280, 286, 287
Asch, S. 59
Atilon, Ramon 144
Augustin 15, 87, 257

Bach, J. S. 17, 22, 35, 36, 40, 118, 255
Baguio 119, 135, 270
Balsam, Arthur 173
Bahr, H. 4, 42
Bauer, O. 53, 282
Beecham, Sir Thomas 54, 163
Beer-Hofmann, R. 4
Beethoven, L. 11, 14, 17, 24, 32, 40, 47, 68, 147, 148, 149, 163, 164, 199, 211, 229, 243, 247, 255
Beijing 146, 230, 234, 235, 237, 238, 240, 243-248, 255
Beglarian, Grant 7, 215-18, 221, 222
Bennett, Carolyn Dopke 224
Bennett, Roy 123, 124
Bergner, Elizabeth 218
Berkley, G. 5, 6, 265, 275
Bernstein, Leonard 165, 173
Bettauer, H. 43, 295
Bettelheim, Bruno 99, 100, 101, 107, 256, 269, 275, 282
Bettenbauen 79, 236
Blacher, B. 59
Blume, Ebie 167, 168
Blume, Peter 167, 168
Bobby, Count 19, 34, 41, 44
Bodenwieser, Madame 45, 46, 61, 62
Bohlen, Charles 194
Boris Gudonov 200
Bradley, Omar 175

Brahms 35, 39, 40, 55, 229, 236, 255, 260, 299
Bregenz 17, 20
Breisach, Paul 64, 65
Breitner, H. 52
Broch, H. 4, 275, 280
Brooklyn 151, 163, 164, 166, 168, 169, 173, 174, 175, 177, 179, 180, 188, 255, 283
Broz, J. (Tito) 20
Buber, M. 4, 282
Buchenwald 49, 67, 82, 91, 93-96, 98-108, 115, 116, 122, 133, 136, 138, 140, 156, 169, 170, 171, 177, 189, 201, 230, 253, 256, 263, 268, 269, 286, 296
Busch, William 16
Busoni, F. 17, 36
Buss, Claude 120, 121, 123, 141, 254, 270, 289

Cafe Rebhuhn 71
Cafe Schottenthor 45
Campbell, Wallace 146, 147
Canetti, Elias 63, 266, 275
Carl, Archduke 30
Carr, Gary 221
Carmen 206, 207, 271
Carson, Rachel 172
Caruso, E. 23
Casals, Pablo 17
Chang Jie 239
Chang, Kai-shek 168
Chen Yi-Shin 241
Churchill, Winston 66, 121, 157, 282
Clare, George 72, 266, 276
Colburn, Richard D. 177, 180, 181, 182, 189, 220, 222, 224, 225
Collins, Harrison 177, 183
Colloff, David 221
Corpus Christi Procession 14, 16
Corregidor Memorial 194

Cortes, Nancee 221, 222, 224, 225
Cousteau, Jacques 172
Cowley, Malcolm 166, 167, 168, 254, 270, 291
Cowley, Muriel 167, 168
Craig, William 134, 270, 290
Crown, John 215
Cummins, Anna 249
Cummins, Emily 249
Cummins, Mary Ann 221
Cummins, Paul 93, 265, 266, 268, 271, 291, 293, 299

D'Albert, E. 17
Dachau 1, 3, 4, 8, 10, 12, 16, 49, 67, 75-92, 94, 96, 98, 102, 104-107, 113-116, 122, 133, 136, 138, 140, 148, 156, 157, 163, 170, 171, 174, 177, 189, 201, 230, 249, 253, 256, 262-264, 266-268, 282, 283, 285, 286, 296
Dachau Lied 89-91, 114, 260, 262-264, 266-268, 287
Debussy, C. 36-38, 205
Deng Xiao-Ping 231
Des Pres, Terrence 95, 269, 282, 291
Die Fackel 42, 43
Disston, Harry 143
Dollfuss, E. 62, 63, 64, 66, 69, 247, 286
Dornbirn 17, 18, 20
Doubrava (Librarian) 39, 40
Drix, Walter (Herbert Zipper) 1, 4, 6, 7, 11, 12, 13, 14, 16, 20, 21, 22, 25, 26, 29, 31, 47, 53, 61, 67, 68, 69, 74, 75, 77, 78, 81, 82, 84, 88, 89, 91, 96, 97, 104, 107, 113, 114, 117, 118, 120, 128, 132, 137, 138, 140, 147, 230, 233, 236, 239, 248, 253, 255, 256, 260, 262, 263, 265, 266, 268, 269, 270, 271, 273, 293, 299
Dubrovic, Milan 258, 265, 271, 291
Dubsky, Trudl Zipper 45, 46, 47, 54, 62, 66, 115, 118, 127, 225, 300
Dunn, William J. 147, 270, 290
Dushkin, David and Dorothy 180, 181
Dzhugashuili, J. (Stalin) 20, 26, 65, 165

Eastman, Max 163
Ebner, Hugo 78, 88, 98, 105, 266

Egan, Chua 200
Ehlers, Alice 215
Ehrlich, Paul 172
Esterhazy, Count and Family 19, 63, 265, 292
Evans, Jean 182, 190, 191

Fellers, Bonner 142
Feuermann, E. 17
Fine Arts Quartet 190, 191, 201
Fischer, Lehrer 22
Fischer Von Erlach, J. B. 15, 24, 29, 101
Fisher, Howard 181, 182, 189
Forster 102, 215
Fortner, W. 59
Francesscatti, Zino 173
Frank, Anne 264
Frankfurter, Felix 165
Frankl, Viktor 84, 266, 283
Franz Ferdinand, Archduke 14, 29, 86
Franz, Joseph I. 6, 7, 13, 14, 30, 31, 51, 247, 257, 261, 275, 277, 278, 279, 281
Freud, S. 4, 20, 41, 42, 59, 256, 257, 261, 275, 276, 281, 292
Friedell, E. 4
Friedman, I. 17

Gal, Erna 40
Gal, Hans 4, 40, 54, 262, 289
Garcia, Carlos P. 195
Gedye, G. E. R. 73, 101, 269, 273
Gieseking, W. 17
Gifford, Worden 150
Gilbert, Martin 73, 103, 266, 269, 284
Gobineau 26
Goethe 3, 13, 16, 24, 31, 43, 56, 57, 58, 75, 83, 84, 93, 161, 193, 229, 254, 266, 268, 269, 280, 296
Goldmark, K. 4
Gýring 69
Gorky, M. 59
Goebbels 69
Gregor, Joseph 66, 266, 276
Grey, Lord 29
Grimm's Fairy Tales 15, 18, 29
Grynszpan, Zindel 97
Guan Wen-Ning 240

Hancock-Houghton 219, 220
Handel G. F. 54, 58
Hansen, T. 24
Hanslick, E. 4, 289, 290
Hapsburg Empire 3, 20, 30, 51, 107, 253, 257, 281
Hartendorp, A. V. H. 123
Harth, Sidney 192
Haydn, J. 14, 40, 71, 72
Heifetz, J. 23
Heine, H. 16, 59, 197
Heller, Hugo 41, 42
Hesse, Herman 201
Himmler, Heinrich 75, 76, 80
Hindemith, P. 42, 58
Hindenburg, Chancellor 59, 63, 244
Hitler, Adolph 3, 4, 6, 20, 26, 56, 58, 59, 60, 65-70, 74, 77, 84, 91, 97, 119, 125, 147, 157, 165, 169, 244, 246, 247, 258, 262, 264, 269, 273, 275, 277, 283, 284, 286, 288
Hoffman, E. T. A. 16, 18
Hoffenberg, Max 105
Hohenberg, Countess 29, 87
Holt, Hedy (Zipper) 162, 169, 201, 248
Holzel, A. 75
Horner, Harry 218
Horwitz, Fritz (Fred) 70, 107, 162
Huang, Cheng Yung 130, 200
Huang, Dorothy 130
Huang, Felix 235
Hughes, Langston 165, 174, 175, 270, 291-294
Hull, Denison Bingham 181, 182, 190
Hurok, Sol 65
Husserl, E. 4

Idyllwild 216, 217
Istomin, Eugen 199

Jarka, Horst 66, 68, 69, 105, 266, 269, 277
Jaray, Hans 218
Jiang Ding-Xian 241
Joaquin, Nick 207
Johanneson, Grant 173
Johnson, Alvin 170

Joseph II 25
Josephson, Hannah 168
Josephson, Matthew 167, 270, 292, 293

Kafka, F. 27
Kahan, Robert 8
Kanner, Hedwig 164
Karlweiss, Oskar 114
Kasimir, Luigi 260
Kaspar, E. 17
Kaufman, Charles 149. 182
Kephardt, Edward 166
Kiesler, Emil 218
Kiesler, Hedwig (Hedy Lamarr) 218
Kinsky, (Family) 14
Klemperer, Otto 4, 77, 113, 164, 218, 289
Klimt, G. 26, 32, 42, 288
Knappertsbusch, Hans 108, 113, 269
Kodaly, Zoltan 232
Kogon, Eugen 95, 100, 269, 284
Kokoschka, O. 26, 40-42, 265, 288
Korngold, Erich Wolfgang 4, 218
Kortner, Fritz 218
Kraprielian, Zhorab 225
Kraus, Karl 4, 29, 42, 43, 63, 276, 278, 281
Krone, Max and Bernice 216
Kurka, Robert 144

Lass, Stella 210, 211
Laufer, Dr. 20
Legarda, Alejandro 142
Legarda, Benito F. 118, 121, 122, 129, 130, 134, 195
Legarda, Benito Jr. 118
Legarda, Filomena 118
Legarda, Jose 118
Lennhoff, Eugene 74, 285
Leopold, I. 5, 15
Leopoldstadt 5, 6
Lewis, Brenda 173
Liang Qichao 242
Lin Mohan 234
Li Peng, Premier 243-248
Lippay, Alexander 115, 117
Literatur am Nachmarkt 67

Liu Chunhua 238
Lloyd, William 181
Loft, Abe 191, 192
Loos, Adolf 42
Lowman, William 216
Luce, Henry 235
Locsin, Leandro 195, 199

MacArthur, Gen. Douglas 121, 123, 127, 128, 134, 135, 142, 143, 144, 234, 290, 299
Macapagal, Pres. 195, 198
Mahler, Gustav 4, 22, 58, 176, 199, 257, 271, 281, 289
Manchester, William 135, 136, 270, 278, 290
Mandyczewski, E. 39
Manila 59, 66, 115-118, 120-131, 133-136, 138-143, 145, 147-151, 155, 157, 161-163, 166, 171, 173, 177, 179, 180, 181, 186, 192, 193-195, 198-203, 206-208, 225, 230, 234, 244, 246, 249, 253, 255, 256, 263, 270
Manila Cultural Center 195, 198, 208
Marcos, Ferdinand 198
Marcos, Imelda 198, 199
Maremont, Arnold 183, 184, 190
Mark, Charles C. 208
Martin, Ellie 182, 191
Martinez, Maria 216, 217, 271, 292
Marx, Karl 59
Marx, Joseph 35-39, 75, 205
Mayer, Clara W. 186
Mayman, Toby 225
Masur, G. 21, 265, 274
McCray, Porter 202, 209
McCool, Wilma 209
McCullough, Dick 123
Mendelssohn, Felix 58
Merrill, Robert 173
Meyerowitz, Jan 174, 175, 176
Mikos, Count 19
Milhaud, D. 59
Montgomery, Lucy 182, 191
Moussorgsky, M. 200
Mozart, W. A. 17, 38, 40, 68, 118, 119, 121, 164, 229
Museum Cafe 42

Musil, Robert 51, 277, 278
Mussolini, Benito 26, 62, 247

Nash, Grace 126, 127, 177, 179, 180, 270, 290
Nash, Ralph 126, 127, 177
Newark 210, 211, 212, 220
Niemeyer, E. Vic 195, 196
Novak, Kalman 208

Osmeña, Sergio 155, 193
O'Neill, Emmet 193
Orff, Karl 209, 233
Oriol, Ramon 124
Orozco, Jose Clemente 165
Osborn, Fairfield 172, 173, 270, 292
Osias, Judge 81

Painleve, Paul 60
Paunzen, Arthur 35, 40
Pertinax, M. 3
Peterson, Susan 216, 217, 271, 292
Pilzer, E. 17
Piscator, Erwin 166, 177
Polikoff, Barbara 184, 187, 270, 292
Poller, Walter 93, 268, 269, 286
Pontius, Dale 146
Porter, Katherine Anne 133
Preminger, Otto 4, 217
Price, Reynolds 249, 296
Prihodko, Vasili 117

Quezon, Aurora 117

Rachmaninoff, S. 17
Radovani, N. 16
Rahn, Muriel 175
Raimund, Ferdinand 53
Rampersand, Arnold 270, 292
Ravel, M. 37, 38, 39, 75, 299
Reger, Max 55
Reinhardt, Max 218
Remarque, E. M. 59
Resnick, Regina 173

Reti, Richard 156
Reti, Rudolf 156
Ringelnatz, Joachim 197
Ringstrasse 23, 24, 31, 45, 64, 108
Rýdl 96, 97
Rolland, Romain 26, 59
Roller, A. 22
Roller, Prof. 22, 26
Roberg, Ruth 182, 183, 184, 185, 191
Robinson, Jackie 174
Rockefeller, John D. III 202, 204
Rockefeller, Winthrop 209
Roosevelt, Eleanor 165
Roosevelt, Franklin D. 170, 217
Rosenberg, Anna 171, 268
Rosenthal, Felix 35
Rosenthal, Moritz 164
Rothstock, O. 43
Roxas, Manuel (Pres.) 163
R`diger, Josephine, "Fini" (Littlejohn) 68
Rumage, Benjamin 179, 190
Rutherston, Jeannette 54, 66

Saint Saens, C. 37
Saltonstall, Leverett 195
Saltzman, Michael 209
Samford, Horace 144, 145, 146
Santa Cruz Church 147
Sarajevo 27, 29, 87, 274
Sauer, Emil 17
Sayre, Francis B. 120, 121, 123-125, 171, 187
Schenker, H. 35
Schiele, Egon 26, 32, 42, 266, 288
Schiller, F. 11, 16, 23, 253
Schirokauer, Arno 77-79, 89
Schnitzler, A. 4, 59, 280, 297
Schoenberg, Arnold 4, 20, 35, 41, 42, 55, 59, 191, 217, 218, 249, 288, 289
Schorske, C. 24, 265, 280
Schubert, F. 17, 24, 68, 299
Schuschnigg, Kurt von 69-73, 81, 88, 280, 286
Schweitzer, Albert 56-58, 266, 280, 293
Seipel, I. 52
Seitz, Karl 32, 52, 62
Sharpe, George 270, 290
Shey, Dr. 80

Shirer, William 73, 266, 287
Simon, Eric 8, 40, 63-65, 70, 114, 116, 164, 166, 167, 169, 173, 175, 187, 225, 229, 254
Simon, Ruth 166, 167, 169
Sitte, G. 25
Smith, Aura 194
Smith, Perry Dunlap 181
Simons, Hans 165, 187
Snow, Edgar 168, 234, 235, 248, 254, 271, 290, 294
Sopkin, Carol 182
Soriano, Andres 142
Soyfer, Jura 66-68, 78, 87-89, 91, 98, 99, 101, 103-105, 114, 255, 263, 266-269, 277
Spiele, Hilde 257
Spitz, Rudolph 67, 69, 300
Stangl, Franz 96
Starhemberg, Count 14, 52
Steiner, Max 52, 218
Stern, Issac 173
Stevens, Roger 208
Stiedry, Fritz 39, 65
Stokowski, Leopold 173
Stravinsky, I. 58, 59
Strauss, Richard 38, 39, 75, 223, 289
Strauss, O. 4
Szell, George 4, 39
Szenkar, Eugen 65
Szeps, Berta 31, 32, 265, 266, 281

Tandler, J. 52
Tibbett, Lawrence 175
Tienjin 236
Tillinger 87, 102
The Barrier 174-176
The Last Tale 218, 299
Theresa, Maria 5
Thimig, Helene 218
Thomas, Michael Tilson 221
Thompson, Frank 194, 195
Thorn, (Poet) 30, 31, 230
Tiananmen Square 243-246
Toch, Ernst 4, 218, 292, 299
Toland, John 270, 291
Treblinka 82, 96, 297
Trotsky, L. 20

Ulanowsky, Peter 83, 84
Ulanowsky, Paul 83
Uszler, Marianne 221

Valdes, Basilio 122, 126, 141, 143
Valdes, Rosario 118
Vallejo, Ernesto 144
Von Karajan, H. 7, 289
Von Rath, Ernst 97
Von Schleicher, K. 59
Von Sternberg, J. 4
Von Stroheim, E. 4, 217
Vienna 3-8, 11, 13-17, 20, 23, 25, 26, 30-33, 35-38, 40-44, 51-55, 58, 60-75, 83, 87-89, 91, 98, 102-104, 106-108, 113, 114, 123, 137, 147, 162, 163, 166, 177, 187, 201, 204-206, 217, 218, 220, 225, 230. 231, 242, 247, 253, 256-258, 260-263, 265, 266, 269, 271, 273, 275-281, 284, 287-289, 291, 293, 295-297, 299
Vujica, Peter 262
Vukovic, M. 17

Wade, Pamela 232, 233
Wagner 17, 226, 287
Wagner, O. 25, 32
Walde, Alfons 206, 287, 288
Waldheim, Kurt 258, 262, 291-293
Wallace, Henry 168-69
Walter, Bruno 4, 42, 64, 289
Walton, William 59
Werfel, Franz 4, 27, 71, 266, 278, 297
Weigel, Hans 66-68, 114, 300
Weigel, Karl 4
Weill, Kurt 42, 59
Weimar 91, 93, 98, 103, 106
Weinstock, Eugene 95, 287
Weisbach, H. 56-61
Westreich, E. 31
Weys, Rudolf 67, 68, 205, 300

White, Theodore 168, 234, 235, 254, 271, 294
Wiesbachhorn 33, 34
Wiesel, Elie 264, 297
Wilde, Oscar 66, 300
Wilder, B. 5, 217
Williams, Lynn 181, 182
Wittgenstein, L. 4, 261, 277, 279
Wolte, Wolfgang O. T. (Dr.), 258
Wu Zuo Ren 238
Wurlitzer, Rembert 169, 174, 209

Yamashita, Tomoyuki 134, 135, 136
Yeats, W. B. 11, 253
Yu Juang 238

Zador, Eugen 4, 55, 56, 218
Zarubick, Fran 221, 225
Zeisl, Erich 4, 218
Zeman, Z. A. B. 14, 265
Zerkowitz, Fritz Dr. 80, 115
Zicheng, Wang 234
Zinneman, Fred 4
Zipper, Emil 6, 13, 16, 19, 20, 21, 22, 26, 30, 40, 70, 74, 162, 169, 170, 197, 198, 201, 218
Zipper, Otto 7, 13, 70, 74, 113, 162, 198, 229, 231, 255
Zipper, Walter 7, 8, 13, 21, 30, 70, 74, 96, 97, 99, 104, 106, 107, 113, 120, 229, 236, 255
Zipper, Hedy 7, 13, 16, 18, 19, 20, 21, 30, 40, 45, 70, 113, 162, 170, 201, 229, 236
Zipper, Regina - Westreich (Rosie), 13, 14, 17, 35, 39, 40, 70, 169, 201
Zheng Shengtian 238
Zweig, A. 4
Zweig, S. 6, 27, 59, 261, 265, 271, 281, 297

ABOUT THE AUTHOR

Paul Cummins attended Stanford University (B.A., 1959), Harvard University (M.A.T., 1960), and the University of Southern California (Ph.D., 1967). For more than 40 years, Dr. Cummins has devoted his career to creating opportunities for all children to have equitable access to quality education. In 1971, he co-founded Crossroads School and built it into one of the city's most successful independent schools, now well respected nationwide as a progenitor of Engaged Education. In 1995, he founded New Visions Foundation to serve as a catalyst in educational and social innovations for disadvantaged children and youth. As Founder, President, and CEO of New Visions Foundation, Cummins continued to create successful models of Engaged Education, founding New Roads School, another now-renowned independent school based on principles of social justice and diversity, as well as three charter schools and a nonprofit organization, PS Arts, which provides arts classes to children in title I schools. In addition, New Visions has implemented several innovative Engaged Education programs that help at-risk children and youth, including foster youth, those in the juvenile justice system, and economically disadvantaged children and youth. Also a prolific author, Cummins has written several books on education, two volumes of poetry, a collection of essays, a biography of Herbert Zipper, an autobiography, and three children's books. He lives in Santa Monica with his wife Mary Ann. They have four daughters and three grandchildren.

www.ingramcontent.com/pod-product-compliance
Lightning Source LLC
Chambersburg PA
CBHW052044220426
43663CB00012B/2436